AUSTRALIA
LBC Information Services—Sydney

CANADA and USA
Carswell—Toronto

NEW ZEALAND
Brooker's—Auckland

SINGAPORE and MALAYSIA
Thomson Information (S.E. Asia)—Singapore

Personal Insolv
A Practical Gu

Personal Insolvency: A Practical Guide

IAN S. GRIER, LL.M. (LONDON)

Solicitor and licensed insolvency practitioner
Partner, Sprecher Grier, London WC1

RICHARD E. FLOYD, F.C.A., F.I.P.A., F.S.P.I.

Chartered accountant and licensed insolvency practitioner
Consultant, Baker Tilly, Guildford

THIRD EDITION

London
Sweet & Maxwell
1998

First edition 1987
Second edition 1993
Third edition 1998

Published in 1998 by
Sweet & Maxwell Limited of
100 Avenue Road, Swiss Cottage,
London NW3 3PF
Typeset by MFK Information Services Ltd
of Hitchin, Hertfordshire
Printed and bound in Great Britain by
Butler and Tanner Ltd, Frome and London

No natural forests were destroyed to make this product;
only farmed timber was used and replanted

A CIP catalogue record for this book is available from the British Library

ISBN 0 421 59100 5

PREFACE

Since publication of the second edition of this work, the procedures laid down in the Insolvency Act 1986 have been further polished by the development of good practice, guidance notes issued by professional bodies and the judgments of the courts. These factors have enabled us to expand and clarify the subject matter of this book.

The Insolvent Partnerships Order 1994 introduced a new framework for dealing with insolvent partnerships and a separate chapter has been devoted to this topic.

The decision in *Re Landau* has caused trustees in bankruptcy to revise their approach to the debtor's pension rights and we have added a section on this aspect.

As in the previous work, the first 12 Chapters deal primarily with the law as it applies to England and Wales. Differences relating to Scotland and Ireland are explained in the final chapters by specialists from the countries concerned, to whom we are most grateful.

We should also like to thank various partners and members of staff of Sprecher Grier and Baker Tilly who have contributed to the research, or who have checked the proofs and made useful suggestions and amendments. We also acknowledge the advice and encouragement received from the publishers, although naturally we accept responsibility for the contents.

The law is stated as at June 30, 1997.

I. S. Grier
R. E. Floyd

November, 1997

ACKNOWLEDGMENTS

Acknowledgment of permission to reproduce copyright material is due to the following:

Forms Q, II, JJ and KK in Appendix I are reproduced by kind permission of the Solicitors Law Stationery Society plc.

Appendix III is extracted from *County Court Practice 1992* (Butterworth Law Publishers Limited).

Appendices VII and IX are reproduced by kind permission of the Administration of the Royal Courts of Justice.

Appendix VIII is reproduced by kind permission of the Insolvency Service in Northern Ireland.

CONTENTS

TABLE OF CASES

[*All references to paragraph numbers*]

TABLE OF STATUTES

[*All references are to paragraph numbers*]

Republic of Ireland Statutes

TABLE OF STATUTORY INSTRUMENTS

[*All references are to paragraph numbers*]

Republic of Ireland Statutory Instruments

ABBREVIATIONS

A.I.E.D.P.O.	Administration of Insolvent Estates of Deceased Persons Order 1986
B.A. 1914	Bankruptcy Act 1914
C.A.	Companies Act
C.A.U.	Central Accounting Unit (a part of the Insolvency Service)
C.J.A. 1988	Criminal Justice Act 1988
C.T.T.A. 1984	Capital Transfer Taxes Act 1984
D.P.P.	Director of Public Prosecutions
D.T.I.	Department of Trade and Industry
F.A. 1985	Finance Act 1985
F.S.A.	Financial Services Act 1986
I.A.	Insolvency Act 1986
I.H.T.A. 1984	Inheritance Tax Act 1984
I.P.O.	The Insolvency Partnerships Order 1994
I.R.	Insolvency Rules 1986 (as amended)
I. Reg	Insolvency Regulations 1986
I.S.	The Insolvency Service (an Executive Agency within the Department of Trade and Industry)
I.V.A.	Individual Voluntary Arrangement
L.P.A. 1925	Law of Property Act 1925
O.R.	Official Receiver
P.A. 1890	Partnership Act 1980
P.A.O.	Partnership Administration Order
R.S.C.	Rules of the Supreme Court
T.C.G.A. 1992	Taxation of Chargeable Gains Act 1992

Notes

Where there is a reference merely to a "section" or to the "Act", this is intended, unless otherwise stated, to refer to the Insolvency Act 1986. However, in Chapter 13 only, the "Act" refers to the Bankruptcy (Scotland) Act 1985 and, in Chapter 15 only, the "Act" refers to the Republic of Ireland statute, known as the Bankruptcy Act 1988.

Where there is a reference merely to a "rule" or to the "Rules", this is intended, unless otherwise stated, to refer to the Insolvency Rules 1986 (as amended).

Chapter 1
TYPES OF PERSONAL INSOLVENCY

Let all things be done decently and in order—1 Corinthians xiv, 40.

1.01 The reform of insolvency law in 1985 and 1986, culminating in the passing of the Insolvency Act 1986 and the bringing in of the Insolvency Rules of that year, substantially changed the previously complex rules relating to bankruptcy law and procedure. In particular the old concept of an "act of bankruptcy" was abolished and new and simplified procedures were adopted. One major reform was the introduction of statutory demands for debts in excess of £750.

1.02 In essence, so far as possible, the law and procedures were brought in line with that relating to limited companies and this feature will be seen throughout this book.

1.03 The majority of bankruptcy petitions are presented by creditors either on the basis of a statutory demand or where there is an unsatisfied judgment. The procedures for a creditor's petition are dealt with in paragraphs 1.08–1.80 below.

1.04 A debtor may, however, present his own petition in cases where he is unable to satisfy his debts. This is dealt with in paragraphs 1.80–1.104 below.

1.05 A petition can also be presented where a voluntary arrangement entered into under Part VIII of the Act fails, where the petition is presented in most cases by the supervisor, but it can be presented by any person other than the debtor bound by a voluntary scheme or composition. Voluntary arrangements are dealt with in Chapter 5. The procedures for criminal bankruptcy will not be dealt with as these have been abolished by the provisions of CJA 1988.

1.06 There are of course those cases where formal bankruptcy procedures are neither suitable nor wanted by either the debtor or his creditors. In such cases, the voluntary arrangement procedure is appropriate. Individual voluntary arrangements (IVAs) are in the authors' view one of the major success stories of the 1986 reforms.

1.07 In a majority of cases it will be possible for practitioners to avoid reference to B.A. 1914. There are increasingly fewer "old" bankruptcies around but in cases of bankruptcies in existence on December 29, 1986, B.A. 1914 still applies save for the exceptions set out in the transitional provisions (I.R. 1986, Sched. 11). It is not proposed in this work to deal with the transitional provisions in detail or to make reference, save where necessary, to B.A. 1914.

1. Creditor's Petition

(a) Petitioner: I.A. 1986, s.264

1.08 The persons who may issue a bankruptcy petition are set out in I.A. 1986, s.264 and are:

(i) a creditor or creditors jointly;

(ii) the supervisor of a voluntary arrangement made under the provisions of the I.A.;
(iii) any person (other than the debtor) who is for the time being bound by a voluntary arrangement made under the Act;
(iv) the debtor himself.

(b) Domicile: I.A. 1986, s.265

1.09 The provisions as to domicile are set out in I.A. 1986, s.265. A bankruptcy petition may not be presented to the court unless the debtor:

(i) is domiciled in England and Wales;
(ii) is personally present in England and Wales on the day on which the petition is presented; or
(iii) at any time in the period of three years following the day on which the petition is presented;
  (a) has been ordinarily resident, or has had a place of residence, in England and Wales; or
  (b) has carried on business in England and Wales.

Jurisdiction

1.10 "Carrying on business" includes the carrying on of business by an individual as a partner in a firm or business.

1.11 In the case of *Theophile v. Solicitor General* [1950] A.C. 186 (applied by Hoffmann J. in *Re A Debtor* (No. 784 of 1991) [1992] Ch. 554) the House of Lords decided, on similar provisions under B.A. 1914, that a person who at one time carried on business in England and Wales did not cease to do so unless he had discharged all trading debts and liabilities, including taxes, relating to his business. Accordingly, even if trade had apparently ceased more than three years before, a debtor might still be brought within the ambit of the bankruptcy provisions.

1.12 "Ordinarily resident" could apply to a person who carries on business, say, in London, but lives in hotels during an extended period—even if that person has a home abroad (*Re Brauch* [1978] Ch. 316; *Re Charles Bright* (1903) 19 T.L.R. 203).

(c) Venue

1.13 The Act makes provision for both the High Court and certain County Courts to have bankruptcy jurisdiction. This jurisdiction is not, however, granted to every County Court and a list of those courts which have bankruptcy jurisdiction is set out in Appendix III together with relevant addresses and telephone numbers. Provisions as to venue are set out in I.R. 6.9.

1.14 A petition will be presented in the High Court:

(i) if the debtor has resided or carried on business within the London insolvency district for the greater part of the six months immediately preceding presentation of the petition, or for a longer period in those six months than in any other insolvency district;
(ii) if the debtor is not resident in England and Wales; or
(iii) if the petitioner is unable to ascertain the residence of the debtor or his place of business.

1.15 In any other case the petition must be presented to the County Court for the insolvency district in which the debtor has resided or carried on business for the longest period during those six months.

If the debtor has for the greater part of those six months carried on business in one insolvency district and resided in another, the petition must be presented to the court for the insolvency district in which he has carried on business and if he has carried on business in more than one insolvency district then it is the court for the district in which for the longest period in those six months he has had his principal place of business. **1.16**

Notwithstanding any other provisions of I.R. 6.9, where there is in force for the debtor a voluntary arrangement under Part VIII of the Act (see Chap. 5) the petition shall be presented to the court to which the nominee's report under section 256 was submitted (I.R. 6.9(4A)). **1.17**

(d) Grounds for petition

The grounds on which a creditor's petition may be presented are set out in I.A. 1986, ss.267 and 268. **1.18**

Inability of the debtor to pay the debt

The pre-1986 legislation, B.A. 1914, had as a prominent feature the concept of "acts of bankruptcy". These were swept away in 1986 to be replaced by a single concept: that of the inability of the debtor to pay the debt on which the petition is based or, in cases where the debt is not immediately payable, of the debtor appearing to have no reasonable prospect of being able to pay. The statutory demand procedure was introduced whereby if the debtor fails to comply with the terms of the demand, subject to any rights he may have to set the same aside, he is deemed to be unable to pay his debts. This brings individual insolvency more in line with the corresponding provisions in relation to limited companies. There is also under I.A. 1986, s.268(1)(b) an alternative provision whereby a petition can be presented based upon an unsatisfied judgment. **1.19**

Conditions to be satisfied

Certain conditions must be satisfied before a creditor's petition may be presented to the court (I.A. 1986, s.267(2)): **1.20**

(i) the amount of the debt, or the aggregate amount of the debt, must equal or exceed the bankruptcy level. At the moment the bankruptcy level is £750 but it may be raised by Statutory Instrument. A debt at this level must exist *at the time the petition is presented* (*Re Patel* [1986] 1 W.L.R. 221). The level has remained at £750 since the inception of the Act but may be increased by a statutory instrument at some time in the future. A debt for these purposes may be a sum due in a foreign currency (*Re A Debtor 51/SD/1991* [1992] 1 W.L.R. 1294) but if the petition is based upon a foreign judgment then there may be some scope for dispute unless the judgment is recognised under the Civil Jurisdiction and Judgments Act 1982;

(ii) the debt must be for a liquidated sum payable to the petitioning creditor, or one or more of the petitioning creditors, either immediately or at some certain future time and must be unsecured (subject to the exception in s.269—see below);

(iii) the debt is one which the debtor appears to be either unable to pay or have no reasonable prospect of being able to pay; and

(iv) there is no outstanding application to set aside a statutory demand served under section 268 in respect of the debt.

(e) Inability to pay

The statutory demand

1.21 Section 267 of the Act requires proof that the debtor is either unable to pay the debt or of there being no reasonable prospect of the debtor being able to pay. Inability to pay is further defined in section 268 which introduces the provision of the statutory demand.

1.22 A distinction is made between debts which are payable immediately and those which are not payable immediately.

1.23 In the case of a debt payable immediately, the debtor appears to be unable to pay the debt if either:

(i) the petitioning creditor has served a statutory demand in the prescribed form (see below) requiring payment of the debt and three weeks have elapsed and the demand has neither been complied with nor set aside; or
(ii) execution or some other process in respect of a *judgment debt* has been issued by the creditor and has been returned by the court unsatisfied wholly or in part.

1.24 In the case of a debt not payable immediately, the debtor is deemed to have no reasonable prospect of paying if:

(i) the petitioning creditor has served a statutory demand requiring the debtor to establish to his satisfaction that there is a reasonable prospect of his being able to pay the debt when it falls due;
(ii) at least three weeks have elapsed since the demand was served; and
(iii) the demand has been neither complied with nor set aside.

1.25 Creditors are not expected to have unlimited patience: in a case where a debtor made a number of offers which would take more than three years to discharge and offered security, but took no steps to advance this, it was held that the debtor had no reasonable prospects of being able to pay his debts and the petitioners had not unreasonably refused an offer. A bankruptcy order was made (*Re Gilmartin (A Bankrupt)* [1989] 1 W.L.R. 513). It has been held in *Re A Debtor (No. 2389 of 1989)* [1991] Ch. 326 that the proposal for a voluntary arrangement by the debtor is not to be regarded as an offer within the meaning of section 271(3) for the purpose of deciding whether the petitioning creditor has unreasonably refused to accept it; the proposed voluntary arrangement is an offer to creditors as a class, and is not to be regarded as an offer open to acceptance or rejection by individual creditors, including the petitioning creditor. In *Re a Debtor (No. 6349 of 1994)* [1996] B.P.I.R. 271, it was held that the Inland Revenue were not unreasonable in refusing an offer by the debtor to secure the petition debt. The Revenue was the best judge of whether it was reasonable to accept such an offer.

1.26 The three-week period which must elapse after service of a statutory demand may in one case be shortened and an expedited petition issued. This is where the creditor alleges in the petition that there is a serious possibility that the debtor's property or the value of any of his property would be significantly diminished during the period of the statutory notice (I.A. 1986, s.270). This may happen even where there is an outstanding application by the debtor to set aside a statutory demand *Re A Debtor (No. 22 of 1993)* [1994] 1 W.L.R. 46, also reported as (*Focus Insurance Co Limited v. the Debtor*).

Requirements of statutory demand

1.27 The rules contain detailed provisions relating to the form, content and service of the statutory demand and the information which has to be given therein and further provisions relating to the setting aside of such a demand. There are prescribed forms depending upon whether the debt is payable immediately or at a future date or whether the debt is a judgment debt and specimens of these forms will be found at Appendix I, Forms A and B:

(i) the demand must be dated and signed either by the creditor himself (if an individual) or by a person stating himself to be authorised to make the demand on the creditor's behalf (I.R. 6.1);

(ii) it must be served on the debtor (see below) although the rules do recognise a procedure akin to substituted service whereby the creditor may be able to show that the demand must have come to the debtor's attention;

(iii) it must specify whether it is made in respect of a debt payable immediately (s.268(1)) or in respect of a debt not so payable (s.268(2)), and the consideration for it or, if there is no consideration, how it arose;

(iv) it must state the amount of the debt and, if it is founded on a judgment or court order, details of that judgment or order must be given. It should be noted that the statutory demand will not have to be served in a case where execution or other process had been issued and has been returned by the court unsatisfied wholly or in part (s.268(1)(b)) but a statutory demand will be needed where the creditor has not tried to issue execution. If the statutory demand contains errors as to the amount owed, this will not necessarily invalidate it. This is clear from the ruling of the Court of Appeal in *Re A Debtor (No. 1 of 1987)* [1989] 1 W.L.R. 271. The Court took there what has been described as a "relaxed view" of a statutory demand (Sealy and Milman, *Annotated Guide to the 1986 Insolvency Legislation* (4th ed.)). The Court refused to set aside the demand on the grounds that no injustice had been done to the debtor. This decision was followed by Hoffmann J. in *Re A Debtor (No. 490 of 1991)* [1992] 1 W.L.R. 507 where the debtor alleged that the demand had overstated the debt by £5,000, a credit to which he was allegedly entitled. He indicated that a debtor was able to avoid the presumption of inability to pay the debt by complying with the demand as to the part which was admitted. The debtor could then apply to have the demand set aside on the basis that the rest was disputed. Even a "grossly overstated" statutory demand would not automatically be set aside. Where the statutory demand is based on a judgment, the court cannot go behind the judgment or inquire as to the validity of the debt. A statutory demand may stand even where an application to set aside the judgment is pending (*Re A Debtor (No. 657 SD of 1991)* [1992] S.T.C. 751) or where only part of the debt is disputed;

(v) if it is served in respect of a debt not payable immediately it must state the grounds on which it is alleged that the debtor appears to have no reasonable prospect of paying the debt;

(vi) claims in the nature of interest or other charges must be separately identified and the grounds for payment of such interest or other charges stated;

(vii) if the creditor holds any security for his debt, the full amount of the debt must be specified but the demand must state the nature of the security and the value put upon it as at the date of the demand. The demand shall be for the full amount of the debt less the amount specified as the value of the security. The phrase "any security in respect of the debt" (I.R. 6.1(5)) means security over any property of the debtor and not the security held over any third party's property (*Re A Debtor (No. 310 of 1988)* [1989] 1 W.L.R. 452). If, however, the demand fails to refer to security, the court may allow it to stand if the debtor has suffered no prejudice by reason of the defect (*Re A Debtor (No. 106 of 1992), The Independent*, April 20, 1992).

(viii) the demand must include the following information for the debtor:
- (a) the purpose of the demand and the consequences which may ensue if it is not complied with;
- (b) the time within which the demand must be complied with if those consequences are to be avoided;
- (c) the methods of compliance which are open to the debtor;
- (d) his right to apply to the court for the demand to be set aside;

(ix) the debtor must be told how he may enter into communication with a named individual with a view to the securing or compounding of the debt to the creditor's satisfaction or establishing that there is a reasonable prospect that the debt may be paid when it falls due. That individual might of course be the creditor himself or a solicitor or accountant serving the demand (I.R. 6.2).

(f) Service of the statutory demand

1.28 On the hearing of a petition (see below) the court must be satisfied by affidavit evidence of the service of the statutory demand (I.R. 6.11).

1.29 Service may be proved by:

(i) personal service;

(ii) any other method if the debtor, or some other person expressly authorised to accept service, has acknowledged service in writing; or

(iii) if neither of those two methods apply, the creditor is required to give evidence by a person having direct personal knowledge of the means adopted for service of demand and must give particulars of the steps taken to serve the demand, the means whereby, those steps having been ineffective, it was sought to bring the demand to the debtor's attention, and must specify the date by which the demand must have come to that debtor's attention (I.R. 6.11). This last procedure is similar to that relating to substituted service and indeed I.R. 6.11 provides that the particulars given must be such as would be requisite under the rules for obtaining an order for substituted service of a petition. Certain Practice Directions were issued at the end of 1986 with regard to substituted service of statutory demands and petitions and proof of service of statutory demands and these (Nos. 4/86 and 5/86) are reproduced in Appendix VII.

1.30 Needless to say it is recommended that statutory demands are served personally in order to avoid the considerable costs to the creditor if non-service is alleged.

(g) Setting aside a statutory demand

Conditions for grant of application

1.31 Within 18 days of service upon him of a demand, the debtor may apply to the court for an order setting it aside (I.R. 6.4). Such an application has the effect of suspending the running of time of the demand. The application must be supported by an affidavit specifying the date on which the demand came to his notice and stating the grounds on which he claims it should be set aside.

The form of application to set aside a statutory demand is prescribed—see Appendix I, Form C.

1.32 The court may grant the application if:

(i) the debtor appears to have a counterclaim, set-off or cross-demand which equals or exceeds the amount of the debt;
(ii) the debt is disputed on substantial grounds;
(iii) it appears that the creditor holds some security and either the rules relating to security (see below) have not been complied with or the court is satisfied that the value of the security equals or exceeds the amount of the debt; or
(iv) the court is satisfied on other grounds that the demand ought to be set aside.

1.33 On receipt of an application to set aside a statutory demand, the court may, if satisfied that no sufficient cause be shown for it, dismiss the application without notice to the creditor. If it does so time for compliance with the demand will begin to run again (I.R. 6.5). An application is therefore initially in the manner of an *ex parte* application by the debtor.

1.34 If the court does not dismiss the application "out of hand" it must then fix a time and place for hearing the application and give not less than seven days' notice of this to the debtor (or his solicitor if he makes the application) and to whoever is named in the demand as the person with whom the debtor may enter into communication with reference to it.

1.35 On dismissal of an application made by a debtor, the court must make an order authorising the creditor to present a bankruptcy petition either forthwith or on or after a date specified in the order.

1.36 Further guidance is given by the court in Practice Note No. 1/87, "Application to Set Aside Statutory Demand", which is reproduced in Appendix VII.

1.37 At the hearing to set aside a statutory demand the court will consider the evidence which will be in affidavit form, and may either dismiss the application then or grant it or adjourn and give further directions. The most frequent reason why applications are issued to set aside statutory demands is that the debt is disputed on "substantial grounds". This often involves a conflict of evidence. Provided the evidence given by the debtor is not obviously spurious, the bankruptcy court is not the proper venue for adjudicating disputed debts. The court in such a case would normally set aside the statutory demand and oblige the creditor to pursue its claim through the action in the High Court or County Court (*Re A Debtor (No. 1157 of 1987) (Portsmouth)*, an unreported case referred to at paragraph F 2.12 of *Totty and Moss: Insolvency*). In this respect the practice is similar to that used in the companies court when there is a winding-up petition based on a disputed debt.

1.38 Apart from disputed debts, I.R. 6.5(4)(d) allows the court to set aside the demand if it is satisfied "on other grounds" that the demand ought to be set aside. This, according to the authors of *Totty and Moss: Insolvency*, allows the court to set aside a statutory demand if there are:

> "... circumstances which would make it unjust for the statutory demand to give rise to those consequences [*i.e.* a bankruptcy petition] in the particular case. The court's intervention is called for to prevent that injustice" (para. F 2.12).

1.39 That seems to contain an admirable summary of the law. In the main the court's attention has been drawn to technical defects or other mistakes in the statutory demand. It must be remembered that until the demand has been set aside it is regarded as valid (*Re A Debtor (No. 1 of 1987)* [1989] 1 W.L.R. 271).

1.40 The Court of Appeal has certainly indicated (see *Re A Debtor (No. 1 of 1987)* referred to above) that it will be alert to see whether or not the debtor is prejudiced by formal or other defects, *e.g.* stating the wrong amount in the claim (*Re A Debtor (No. 490 of 1991)*). If not, then the demand will be allowed to stand. The courts have particularly emphasised the need to avoid the sort of technicalities which bedevilled the pre-1986 legislation (see also *per* Vinelott J. in *Re A Debtor (No. 190 of 1987)*, *The Times*, May 21, 1988). The hearing of an application to set aside a statutory demand is not, however, permitted to be used as a test of the reasonableness, (or otherwise) of a debtor's offer or to deal with questions over disputed security. The first point was established in *Re A Debtor (No. 415/SD/93)* [1994] 1 W.L.R. 917; the second point by a decision of the Court of Appeal in *Platts v. Western Trust & Savings Limited* [1996] BPIR 339. The view taken by the courts in these matters is that the debtor is afforded protection in that he can argue these issues on the substantive hearing of the petition rather than on the application to set aside the statutory demand.

(h) Secured debts

1.41 Although secured debts are specifically excluded from the ambit of the bankruptcy provisions (I.A. 1986, s.267(2)(b)), an exception is made by section 269. This states that a debt need not be unsecured if either:

(i) the petition contains a statement by the person having the right to enforce the security that he is willing, in the event of a bankruptcy order being made, to give up his security for the benefit of all the bankrupt's creditors; or

(ii) the petition is expressed not to be made in respect of the secured part of the debt and contains a statement by that person of the estimated value, at the date of the petition, of the security for the secured part of the debt.

(i) The petition

1.42 The petition must contain certain prescribed information which is set out in the Insolvency Rules. The Rules also prescribe the procedure for presentation, filing, verification and service of the petition. There are various prescribed forms of petition which will be found at Appendix I, Forms E and F. Reference should also be made to Practice Note 3/86—see Appendix VII.

Limitation

1.43 It has been held in *Re A Debtor (No. 50A-SD-1995)* [1997] 2 W.L.R. 57 that bankruptcy proceedings based on a judgment debt obtained more than six years earlier were "an action" within the meaning of section 24 of the Limitation Act 1980 and were statute-barred as a result.

Prescribed information

1.44 **Identification of debtor**—The petition must state the following matters with respect to the debtor, so far as they are within the knowledge of the petitioning creditor (I.R. 6.7):

(i) his name, place of residence and occupation (if any);

(ii) the name or names in which he carries on business, if other than his true name, and whether in the case of any business of a specified nature he carries it on alone or with others;

(iii) the nature of the business and its address;
(iv) any name, other than his true name, in which he has carried on business at or after the time the debt was incurred and whether he has done so alone or with others;
(v) any address or addresses at which he has resided or carried on business at or after that date, and the nature of that business.

Identification of debt—The petition must state (I.R. 6.8): 1.45

(i) the amount of the debt, the consideration for it and the fact that it is owed to the petitioner;
(ii) when it was incurred;
(iii) details of any charge by way of interest (or other charge) not previously debited and notified to the debtor and the grounds on which it is claimed to form part of the debt, provided that such amount or rate must, in the case of a petition based on a statutory demand, be limited to that claimed in the demand. This aspect must be separately identified;
(iv) either:
  (1) that the debt is for a liquidated sum payable immediately and that the debtor appears to be unable to pay it;
  (2) that the debt is for a liquidated sum payable at some certain, future time (the date must be specified) and that the debtor appears to have no reasonable prospect of being able to pay it; or
  (3) that the debt is unsecured—but this is of course subject to the exception (see above) in I.A. 1986, s.269;
(v) where a statutory demand has been served the petition must state:
  (1) the date and manner of service of the demand; and
  (2) that the demand has been neither complied with nor set aside in accordance with the Rules and that no application to set it aside is outstanding;
(vi) in a case where the petition is based on a judgment debt, where execution on the judgment debt has not been satisfied (I.A. 1986, s.268(1)(b)), the court from which the execution or other process issued must be specified, and particulars must be given with regard to the return.

Procedure

Presentation and filing 1.46

(i) The petition must be verified by affidavit (I.R. 6.10)—see below—and delivered to the court.
(ii) Two extra copies will be required, one of which is for service on the debtor and the other to be exhibited to the affidavit of service.
(iii) The court will fix the date and time for hearing the petition when it is filed.

Verification 1.47

(i) The petition must be verified by an affidavit that the statements in it are true to the best of the deponent's knowledge, information and belief. The affidavit must exhibit the petition (I.R. 6.12) (see at App. I, Form G).
(ii) The affidavit is made by the petitioner or some person such as a director, company secretary or solicitor, who has been concerned in the matters giving rise to the presentation of the petition, or by some

responsible person who is authorised to make the affidavit and has the requisite knowledge of those matters.

(iii) Where the maker of the affidavit is not the petitioner or one of a number of joint petitioners, he must state in the affidavit the capacity in which, and the authority by which, he makes it and the means of his knowledge of the matters deposed to.

(iv) If the petition is based on a statutory demand and more than four months have elapsed between service of the demand and presentation of the petition, the affidavit must state the reasons for the delay (I.R. 6.12(7)).

1.48 **Deposit**—The petitioner is required to pay a deposit to cover the O.R.'s fees. The amount of this deposit may be increased from time to time but is at present £300.

1.49 **Notice to the Chief Land Registrar**—When the petition is filed, the court sends notice to the Chief Land Registrar of the petition together with a request that it may be registered in the register of pending actions (I.R. 6.13).

1.50 **Security for costs**—I.R. 6.17 contains provisions for security for costs to be given by the petitioning creditor following an application by the debtor in cases where I.A. 1986, s.268(2) applies—that is where the petition is for a liquidated sum payable at some *future* time and the creditor alleges that the debtor appears to have no reasonable prospect of being able to pay the debt.

1.51 In such a case the debtor may apply to the court for an order that the creditor gives security for the debtor's costs, the nature and amount of which are in the court's discretion. If an order for security is made, the petition will not be heard until the whole amount of the security has been paid.

1.52 **Service of petition**—Service is effected either by an officer of the court or the petitioner or his solicitor or by some other authorised person on his behalf who must deliver a sealed copy to the debtor (I.R. 6.14).

1.53 If the court is satisfied, by the filing of appropriate evidence, that the debtor is deliberately avoiding service then substituted service may be ordered in such manner as the court thinks fit.

1.54 If a debtor dies before service is effected the court may order service on the personal representatives or such other persons as it thinks fit.

1.55 If to the petitioner's knowledge there is in force a voluntary arrangement under Part VIII of the Act, and the petitioner is not himself the supervisor of the arrangement, a copy of the petition must be served on the petitioner.

1.56 The affidavit of service exhibiting the sealed copy petition must be delivered to the court for filing immediately after service.

1.57 **Opposition by debtor**—Whether or not the debtor opposes the petition the court has a discretion whether or not to make a bankruptcy order (I.A. 1986, s.271). However, where the debtor intends to oppose the petition, I.R. 6.21 provides that he shall not later than seven days before the day fixed for the hearing:

(i) file in the court a notice (see App. I, Form H) specifying the grounds on which he will object to the making of a bankruptcy order; and

(ii) send a copy of the notice to the petitioning creditor or to his solicitor.

1.58 **The hearing**—Normally at least 14 days must elapse between service of the petition and the hearing (I.R. 6.18). However, if the debtor has absconded or if he consents or if it appears to the court that for some other reason there should be an expedited hearing, that time may be abridged.

Attendance at hearing

1.59 The hearing may be attended by the debtor, the petitioning creditor and any other creditor who has given notice of intention to appear under I.R. 6.23. A prescribed form of notice will be found at Appendix I, Form I. This rule provides a procedure for other creditors to give formal notice to the petitioning creditor of their intention to appear at the hearing and I.R. 6.24 requires the petitioning creditor to prepare for the court a list of the names and addresses of those creditors who have given such notice. A creditor who has not given notice may appear only with the leave of the court. It is virtually obligatory for the petitioning creditor to appear since I.R. 6.26 provides that if the petitioning creditor fails to appear on the hearing, no subsequent petition against the same debtor, either alone or jointly with any other person, shall be presented in respect of the same debt without the leave of the court to which the previous petition was presented.

Hearing

1.60 The position of would-be supporting creditors is somewhat odd. In contrast to compulsory winding up of companies, there is no provision in the Act or the Rules for a bankruptcy petition to be advertised, either in the *Gazette* or in a newspaper. Accordingly a would-be supporting creditor or someone who wishes to be substituted as petitioner (see below) may only find out about the petition by chance—if he tries to present his own petition.

Powers of the court

1.61 The court has a general power, if it appears to it appropriate to do so on the grounds that there has been a contravention of the Rules or for any other reason, to dismiss a bankruptcy petition or to stay proceedings on it. Where the court stays proceedings, it may do so on such terms as it thinks fit (I.A. 1986, s.266(3)).

The bankruptcy order

1.62 I.A. 1986, s.271 requires the court to satisfy itself before the making of a bankruptcy order that either:

(i) the debt is one which, having been payable at the date of the petition or having since become payable, has neither been paid nor secured nor compounded for; or
(ii) it is a debt which the debtor has no reasonable prospect of being able to pay when it falls due.

In order to satisfy the court on these points, Practice Note 1/86, "Proof of Continuing Debt on the Hearing of Bankruptcy Petition", which will be found in Appendix VII, requires the petitioning creditor to lodge with the court a certificate of continuing debt. The form of certificate which is found in the Practice Note will be regarded as satisfactory.

1.63 Section 271(4) defines "a reasonable prospect" with reference to the time when the creditor allowed the debtor to incur the liability. The creditor must show that, in respect of a debt payable at a future time, circumstances have altered and, at the time the debt was incurred, there was a reasonable prospect that the debtor would be able to pay the debt on time. This, according to one commentator on the Act (Ian Fletcher, *The Insolvency Act 1986* (Sweet & Maxwell)):

> "...prevents a creditor from taking a calculated risk concerning the debtor's continuing solvency, in the anticipation that it will be possible for him to resort to bankruptcy proceedings ahead of the repayment date if that assumption proves ill-founded..."

Dismissal of the petition

1.64 Pursuant to section 271(3) the court may dismiss the petition if it is satisfied that the debtor is able to pay all his debts or is satisfied:

(i) that the debtor has made an offer to secure or compound for a debt in respect of which the petition is presented;
(ii) that the acceptance of that offer would have required the dismissal of the petition; and
(iii) that the offer has been unreasonably refused.

1.65 In determining whether the debtor is able to pay all his debts the court must take into account his contingent and prospective liabilities.

1.66 The court must be satisfied not only that a debtor is unable to pay his debts before he is made bankrupt but also that a creditor has not been unreasonable in refusing a debtor's offer to secure or compound for the debt. Presumably the onus is upon the debtor to show that he has made such an offer which has been unreasonably refused. There is nothing in either I.A. 1986 or the Rules indicating on what basis a court should come to such a decision as to whether a creditor is behaving unreasonably in refusing the debtor's offer and therefore this will be left to the discretion of the individual registrar hearing the case.

1.67 The somewhat unsatisfactory nature of this provision has been subject to comment. Presumably the court has to compare what the debtor is offering to the petitioning creditor out of such assets as can be made available with what might be offered to the petitioning creditor along with all the other creditors out of the assets as a whole should a bankruptcy order be made. In such a calculation the preferential debts would also figure quite largely. As one distinguished commentator (Mr Muir Hunter Q.C. in an article in *Insolvency Law & Practice* (1985) Vol. 1, No. 2) puts it:

> "This creates a difficult situation for the court; for what is it that is to be compared with the offer (presumably of cash on the nail) which the creditor is alleged to have unreasonably refused?"

1.68 It might be added that not only is the situation difficult for the court, but it must be even more difficult for the petitioning creditor who is faced with such an offer or compromise. In effect, he can be compelled to accept this if he believes that his petition is likely to fail because of the exercise of the court's discretion. It will certainly require some careful judgment by the petitioning creditor.

1.69 In *Re Gilmartin (A Bankrupt)* [1989] 1 W.L.R. 513, which is referred to at paragraph 1.25 above, Harman J. held that the registrar had been correct in deciding that the debtor's offer had not been unreasonably refused by the petitioner and the supporting creditors. A further interesting problem was thrown up in *Re A Debtor (No. 2389 of 1989)* [1991] 2 W.L.R. 578. Here the court had to deal with a case where the debtor had proposed a voluntary arrangement which had been rejected by the creditor. Could the creditor then be treated as having unreasonably refused the debtor's offer of composition? Vinelott J. held that there had not in effect been an offer to the individual creditor. A voluntary arrangement was an offer to creditors as a class and an individual creditor could not therefore have been said to have unreasonably refused the debtor's offer. However, the learned judge suggested, albeit *obiter*, that an offer could presumably be put to each creditor individually, acceptance to be conditional upon acceptance by all the creditors. If the individual creditor then refused there could presumably be at least the grounds of an argument that there had been unreasonable refusal by the creditor. That point has never formally been argued. Reference should also be made to *Re a Debtor (No. 6349 of 1994)* [1995] B.P.I.R. 271, referred to at paragraph 1.25, above.

1.70 If the petition is brought in respect of a judgment debt or a sum due under a court order, the court may stay or dismiss the petition on the ground that an appeal is pending from the judgment or order, or that there has been a stay of execution on the judgment (I.R. 6.25) (but see *Re A Debtor (No. 657 SD of 1991)* referred to at para. 1.27(iv) above).

1.71 If the court for any reason adjourns the hearing (*e.g.* because the debtor has for some reason not been served) the petitioning creditor must, unless the court orders otherwise, send the debtor a notice of the adjournment stating the new time and date and the venue for the hearing.

1.72 If the court dismisses the petition or it is withdrawn with leave, an order must be made at the same time permitting vacation of the registration of the petition as a pending action and the court will send a sealed copy of the order to the debtor.

1.73 The procedures following the making of a bankruptcy order, if one is made, and the consequences thereof are dealt with in Chapter 2.

Substitution of petitioner

1.74 I.R. 6.30 and 6.31 allow the court, if it thinks fit, to substitute a new petitioner, or to change the carriage of the petition in favour of a suitably "qualified" creditor.

1.75 Substitution is permissible where the creditor who petitions is subsequently found not entitled to do so, or where the petitioning creditor consents to withdraw the petition or allows it to be dismissed, or consents to an adjournment, or fails to appear in support of it or where he appears but does not ask for an order in the terms of his petition.

1.76 A creditor wishing to be substituted must show:

(i) that he has given notice of intention to appear under I.R. 6.23;
(ii) that he wishes to prosecute the petition;
(iii) that he satisfies the basic requirements of section 267(2), in respect of his debt, which are set out at paragraph 1.22 above and which would have enabled him to have issued his own petition.

1.77 On the hearing of the petition a person claiming to be a creditor who has given notice of intention to appear under I.R. 6.23 may apply to be given carriage of the petition.

1.78 Before it makes a change of carriage order, the court must be satisfied that:

(i) the applicant is an unpaid and unsecured creditor; and
(ii) the petitioning creditor either:
  (a) intends by any means to secure the postponement, adjournment or withdrawal of the petition; or
  (b) does not intend to prosecute the petition either diligently or at all.

1.79 The court must *not* make a change of carriage order if it is satisfied that the petitioning creditor's debt has been paid, secured or compounded for by means of a disposition of property by a third party or one by the debtor with the court's approval.

1.80 It may be appropriate to summarise the main powers available to the court on the hearing of a bankruptcy petition:

(i) power to adjourn the petition;
(ii) power to dismiss the petition, or stay proceedings on such terms as the court thinks fit;
(iii) power to dismiss the petition;
(iv) power to substitute any creditor in place of the original petitioning creditor;

(v) power to grant leave for the petition to be withdrawn.

2. DEBTOR'S PETITION

1.81 Bankruptcy legislation has always allowed a debtor to present his own petition provided he could show inability to pay his debts. This power was retained in I.A. 1986, s.272, which states that a debtor's petition may be presented to the court only on the grounds that the debtor is unable to pay his debts.

1.82 The debtor must, together with the petition, provide to the court on presentation a statement of affairs verified by affidavit.

1.83 The petition will be presented either to the High Court or to a local County Court having bankruptcy jurisdiction (see App. III), the rules for venue being the same as those in respect of which a creditor's petition is presented (see above).

1.84 The Rules lay down prescribed information which must be contained in the petition which also relate to the presentation and filing thereof. In particular the petition must be accompanied by a statement of affairs verified by affidavit containing certain prescribed information (see below). A form of petition is at Appendix I, Form J.

(a) Identification of debtor

1.85 The petition must state the following information with respect to the debtor (I.R. 6.38):

Prescribed information

(i) his name, residence and occupation (if any);
(ii) the name or names in which he carries on business, if other than his true name, and whether, in the case of any business of a specified nature, he carries it on alone or with others;
(iii) the nature of his business, and the address or addresses at which he carries it on;
(iv) any name or names, other than his true name, in which he has carried on business in the period in which any of his bankruptcy debts were incurred; and
(v) any address or addresses at which he has resided or carried on business during that period, and the nature of that business.

(b) Admission of insolvency

1.86 The petition must contain a statement that the petitioner is unable to pay his debts, and a request that a bankruptcy order be made against him (I.R. 6.39).

1.87 If within the period of five years ending with the date of the petition the petitioner has been adjudged bankrupt, or has made a composition with creditors or a scheme of arrangement, or has entered into any voluntary arrangement, or has been subject to a County Court administration order (see paras 1.122–1.130 below), particulars of these matters must be given in the petition.

1.88 If there is, at the date of the petition, a voluntary arrangement under Part VIII of the Act in force for the debtor, the particulars required must contain a statement to that effect and the name and address of the supervisor of the arrangement.

(c) The statement of affairs

1.89 The petition must be accompanied by a statement of affairs verified by affidavit. I.R. 6.67–6.72 apply to the statement of affairs which must contain the following information:

(i) details of all his assets;
(ii) an itemised list of debts, with particulars in respect of each one showing to whom it is owed, when and in what circumstances it was incurred, and whether it is secured and, if so, in what manner;
(iii) a summary of assets and liabilities, showing the difference between them;
(iv) the amount of any regular income and the sources of such income;
(v) the amount of any regular expenditure and the manner in which it is incurred;
(vi) the number and identity of any dependants; and
(vii) the amount of any surplus income which is or may become available to creditors.

1.90 The statement should also show details of the following matters:

(i) any distress which has been levied against the bankrupt by or on behalf of any creditor;
(ii) any execution or other process issued against him by any court in England and Wales and outstanding at the date of presentation of the petition; and
(iii) any attachment of earnings order enforced against him at that date.

The debtor must also in the statement declare whether he expects to be in a position to introduce a voluntary arrangement with his creditors under Part VIII of the Act. Voluntary arrangements are dealt with in detail in Chapter 5.

(d) Presentation and filing

Procedure

1.91 The petition and the statement of affairs are delivered to the court together with three copies of the petition and two of the statement of affairs. The court will then fix a date and time for the hearing (I.R. 6.42).

1.92 Of the three copies of the petition, one is sent to the petitioner endorsed with the time and date of hearing, one is sent to the O.R. and one is retained by the court to be sent to an insolvency practitioner if one is appointed under I.A., s.273(2) (see below). Similarly with the statement of affairs; one is sent to the O.R. and the other one retained for the insolvency practitioner, if appointed.

1.93 As with creditor's petitions, a debtor will be required to deposit a prescribed sum on presentation of the petition to cover the O.R.'s fees. This sum will also be used, if required, to pay some of the fees of an insolvency practitioner appointed under section 273(2).

(e) Notice to the Chief Land Registrar

1.94 When the petition is filed the court must forthwith send the Chief Land Registrar notice of the petition, for registration in the Register of Pending Actions.

(f) The hearing: bankruptcy order

1.95 On the hearing of a debtor's petition, the court must not make a bankruptcy order if it appears to the court (s.273(1)):

(i) that if such an order were made, the aggregate amount of the bankruptcy debts, so far as unsecured, would be less than £20,000*;
(ii) that if an order were made, the value of the bankrupt's estate would be equal to or more than £2,000*;
(iii) that within a period of five years ending with the presentation of the petition, the debtor has neither been adjudged bankrupt nor made a composition or scheme of arrangement with his creditors; and
(iv) that it would be appropriate to appoint an insolvency practitioner to make a report under section 274.

1.96 This provides a means for the court to obtain a report on the debtor's affairs before coming to a decision as to whether or not to make a bankruptcy order (section 273(1)).

Appointment of an insolvency practitioner

1.97 Where on the hearing of the petition the above facts are present, the court may appoint a qualified insolvency practitioner to prepare a report on the debtor and to act in relation to any voluntary arrangement to which the report relates either as a trustee or otherwise for the purpose of supervising its implementation (s.273(2)).

1.98 The insolvency practitioner's report is prepared in accordance with section 274. The practitioner appointed makes inquiries into the debtor's affairs within such period as the court may direct and submits a report to the court stating whether the debtor is willing, for the purposes of Part VIII of the Act, to make a proposal for a voluntary arrangement.

1.99 Where the report states that the debtor is willing to make such a proposal, it must also state whether, in the opinion of the insolvency practitioner making the report, a meeting of creditors should be summoned to consider the proposal and must recommend the date, time and place of such a meeting.

1.100 The court will then appoint a date for considering the insolvency practitioner's report and a debtor, who is entitled to receive a copy, may also attend the hearing. Indeed, the court may in some cases compel him to do so.

1.101 On considering an insolvency practitioner's report under section 274 the court may:

(i) make an interim order under section 252. This has the effect of bringing in a moratorium for the debtor in that during the period of the interim order no bankruptcy petition may be presented or proceeded with and no other proceedings or execution may be commenced or continued without the leave of the court. This interim order may cease to have effect if the bankruptcy order is made;
(ii) if it thinks it inappropriate to make an interim order, make a bankruptcy order forthwith (s.274(3)).

1.102 If an interim order is made it ceases to have effect at the end of such period as the court may specify for the purpose of enabling the proposal by the debtor to be considered by creditors in accordance with the provisions of I.A. 1986, Pt. VIII which deal with voluntary arrangements.

1.103 In the majority of cases referred to practitioners under section 273, it is not possible to recommend that a voluntary arrangement be implemented as

* These are the limits under the Insolvency Proceedings (Monetary Limits) Order 1986 at the time of writing and may change.

there are usually insufficient assets available for a distribution to creditors whether under the auspices of a voluntary arrangement or a bankruptcy. Accordingly the practitioner can only recommend that the bankruptcy proceed. This is because the court only has power to make such referrals in small cases. In the opinion of the authors, it is unfortunate that the court does not have a wider discretion to refer debtors to insolvency practitioners as in many of the larger cases, where bankruptcy orders are made without such a referral, a voluntary arrangement would provide a more commercial recovery from the bankrupt's resources for the benefit of creditors.

(g) Summary administration

1.104 Where on the hearing of a debtor's petition a court makes a bankruptcy order and the circumstances exist as set out in section 275, the court may issue a certificate for summary administration of the bankrupt's estate. This would apply *inter alia* where the criteria for ordering an insolvency practitioner's report were met, but the court did not wish to have such a report or in a case where a report had been made and an interim order was not thought appropriate.

(h) Remuneration of insolvency practitioner

1.105 The remuneration of the insolvency practitioner for work done up to the time of the court's consideration of his report is paid by the O.R. on a prescribed scale from the deposit paid by the debtor. This seems a potentially unsatisfactory state of affairs. The deposit is relatively small and does not cover the charge-out rates of practitioners called upon to prepare such a report. (The question of a trustee's remuneration is considered at Chap. 4, paras 4.114–4.144.)

3. PETITION ON DEFAULT IN CONNECTION WITH A VOLUNTARY ARRANGEMENT

1.106 A petition may be presented by the supervisor of, or any person (other than the debtor) who is for the time being bound by, a voluntary arrangement made under Part VIII of the Act (I.A. 1986, s.264(1)(c)).

1.107 The circumstances in which an order may be made are governed by section 276. Before making the order the court must be satisfied:

(i) that the debtor has failed to comply with his obligations under the voluntary arrangement; or
(ii) that information which was false or misleading in any material particular or which contained any material omissions was contained in any document supplied by the debtor or in any statement of affairs or was made available by the debtor to any meeting of his creditors called to consider the voluntary arrangement; or
(iii) that the debtor has failed to do all such things as may have been reasonably required by the supervisor of the voluntary arrangement to enable the arrangement to succeed.

1.108 Where a bankruptcy order is made in these circumstances, any expenses properly incurred as expenses of the administration of the voluntary arrangement are a first charge on the bankrupt's estate. This effectively makes the expenses of the supervisor of a voluntary arrangement which is superseded by a bankruptcy adjudication a pre-preferential debt.

1.109 When a voluntary arrangement has failed to meet its objectives, a supervisor will frequently issue a "certificate of non-compliance", which indicates that the arrangement is at an end. Thereafter the supervisor may present a bankruptcy petition himself or this may be done by a creditor. Care should be taken when drafting a proposal to clarify the debtor's obligations particularly as to time and amounts of contributions so that there is no dispute as to whether he has failed to comply.

1.110 The voluntary arrangement should be drafted so as to ensure that the supervisor is either permitted or mandated to petition for the debtor's bankruptcy in the event of the arrangement failing and that monies are retained within the arrangement to pay the costs of such petition. It has recently become the practice of some District Judges and Registrars to refuse Interim Orders unless assured that sufficient monies are available to petition in the event of an arrangement failing.

4. WITHDRAWAL OF PETITION

1.111 A bankruptcy petition, whether creditor's or debtor's (see below), may not be withdrawn without the leave of the court (I.A. 1986, s.266(2)).

1.112 This provision, formerly contained in B.A. 1914, s.5(7), is designed to prevent abuse of the bankruptcy procedure by creditors. In other words it should not be used simply as a means of debt collection (*cf.* the view taken by the Companies Court with regard to winding-up petitions). Once a petition has been presented, other creditors may have an interest in the proceedings and they have a right (see I.R. 6.23) to appear on the hearing and in certain circumstances (I.R. 6.30) to be substituted as petitioner. Unlike winding-up petitions, bankruptcy petitions are not advertised and a would-be supporting creditor might only find out about one by chance.

1.113 Even if the petitioning creditor has been paid in full, or has been offered payment in full, he may not be able to prevent further proceedings being taken on the petition. However, it has been held in cases under B.A. 1914, s.5(7) that where a petitioning creditor has been paid in full leave to withdraw should not be refused unless there is another creditor willing to be substituted (*Re Bebro* [1900] 2 Q.B. 316; *Re Mann* [1958] 1 W.L.R. 1272).

1.114 Where a petitioner applies to the court for the petition to be dismissed or for leave to withdraw it, he must, unless the court otherwise orders, file an affidavit specifying the grounds of the application and the circumstances in which it is made (I.R. 6.32). The same rule states that if, since the petition was filed, any payment has been made to the petitioner by way of settlement (in whole or in part) of the debt or debts in respect of which the petition was brought, or the debt has been secured or compounded for, then full details of any such dispositions of property (whether by the bankrupt or any third party) must be given in the affidavit. Leave to withdraw cannot be given before the petition is heard (I.R. 6.32(3)).

1.115 If the court dismisses the petition or it is withdrawn with leave, an order must be made at the same time permitting vacation of the registration of the petition as a pending action, and the court will send a sealed copy of the order to the debtor.

5. OTHER PROCEDURES

1.116 There are many alternatives to a formal bankruptcy and that favoured by the majority of the population is, quite simply, to avoid getting into a state of insolvency. Small comfort for the unsuccessful businessman, who is summoned before the O.R., but it is nevertheless true that a high proportion of new businesses fail to survive for even five years. Preparation and research are more important than a quick start and anyone setting up business for the first time, even if technically competent in the chosen activity, should seek advice on the general business and commercial aspects from such sources as other businesses, a bank manager, solicitor or accountant. The omission of these preliminaries can be an expensive economy.

1.117 Constant "health checks" are essential. The new businessman, including the director of a small company, should seek advice as to the financial records to be maintained and the information which should be produced regularly to enable him to monitor progress, spot the warning signs and take corrective action when difficulties arise. In generations past, many businesses suffered from a lack of adequate financial records so that proprietors were unaware of the true financial position until it was too late to alter course. Nowadays, computers can produce data quickly and relatively cheaply so that there is little excuse for the businessman not to keep himself appraised of his financial state.

1.118 If, despite these precautions, disaster strikes, there are procedures which may be put to creditors that will be less traumatic than a formal bankruptcy.

(a) Informal arrangements

1.119 Outside the scope of consumer credit legislation, the law places few obstacles in the way of consenting debtors and creditors to prevent them from making what arrangements they will. There is therefore infinite scope for informal arrangements between debtor and creditor. Indeed every day solvent traders make such arrangements to assist them with their cash flow.

1.120 The purchaser may arrange for his period of credit to be extended, perhaps until receipt of cash from a subsequent purchaser of the goods. Often extra credit is taken without consultation with the supplier and, if it goes unchecked, the purchaser will make continuing use of this procedure.

1.121 Sometimes a trader with cash flow problems may have to come to special terms with a number of his major creditors. If the creditors are few in number, even if individual amounts are substantial, the debtor may be met with a sympathetic response. He will have built up a relationship with his suppliers, who have a vested interest in seeing him survive in business. If creditors are more numerous, it may be necessary to call an informal meeting and put proposals in the form of a well-documented presentation with the assistance of professional advisers. An informal moratorium may be arranged in this way, thereby avoiding the costs of a more formal scheme and enhancing the prospects for creditors. However, informal schemes depend upon the consent of every creditor involved and it is therefore frequently necessary to pursue a more formal arrangement whereby the small dissenting creditor is unable to frustrate the wishes of the majority.

(b) County Court administration orders

1.122 This procedure is designed to assist individuals with few, if any, assets, but who have an income from which small debts can be repaid over a period.

1.123 The procedure should not be confused with the administration order under Part II of I.A. 1986 which applies to corporate bodies. County Court administration orders relating to individuals are made under the County Courts Act 1984, ss.112–117 and the procedures are governed by Order 39 of the County Court Rules 1981.

1.124 Under section 112 of the County Courts Act 1984, an administration order may be made where a debtor is unable to pay the amount of the judgment made against him and where he alleges that the whole indebtedness amounts to a sum not exceeding the County Court limit (currently £5,000) inclusive of the debt for which the judgment was obtained.

1.125 If an administration order is made then it may provide for the payment of debts by instalments or otherwise. So long as an administration order is in force a creditor, whose name is included in the schedules to the order, cannot without leave (subject to some exceptions) present a bankruptcy petition. Moreover, where the order is made, and until it is revoked, a creditor will not obtain leave to issue execution since the object of an order is to secure equal division of the debtor's property amongst all his creditors (*Re R.A. Frank* [1894] 1 Q.B. 9).

Procedure

1.126 The procedures may be initiated by the debtor who files a request for an order in the County Court for the district in which he resides or carries on business (Ord. 39, r.2). Alternatively where a debtor, who is subject to an oral examination, furnishes to the court a list of creditors and particulars of his means, the court may proceed as if the debtor had filed a request for an administration order (Ord. 39, r.2). The debtor is required to verify the statements he makes on oath.

1.127 Once the request for an order is made, the court must notify each of the creditors on the list provided by the debtor and each creditor has a right to prove for his debt and to object to any other debt included in the list. The court will appoint a day on which the application for the administration order is to be heard and the creditors are then entitled to attend and present their views. Prior to the hearing, the court may stay proceedings against the debtor.

1.128 If a person becomes a creditor after the date of the order, he may apply to be scheduled as a creditor but will only rank for a dividend after original creditors have been paid. There is no provision in an administration order for preferential creditors.

Conduct of the order

1.129 The conduct of the order is in the hands of the court through its chief clerk, or other proper officer, who is required to take all proper steps to enforce the order, or to bring to the attention of the court any matter which may make it desirable to review the order. The court is empowered to suspend the order or vary it if there has been a material change in circumstances, or revoke it if it feels that the debtor has failed to comply with any conditions specified by the court or to make an attachment of earnings order (Ord. 39, r.14). The debtor is also empowered to apply to the court for a review—presumably this would happen if he were unable to keep up the scheduled payments.

1.130 The order will be finally discharged on payment of the whole amount but this would not release the debtor from obligations to creditors who were not scheduled.

1.131 The administration order is a useful procedure but appropriate only in the smaller cases where the costs of a bankruptcy would not be justified. It will usually be initiated by the debtor in situations where he wishes to pay off creditors over a period of time and creditors are threatening, say, execution of a judgment or immediate attachment of earnings. It is certainly a cheaper and less cumbersome procedure for the debtor than filing his own petition of bankruptcy—and without the consequent disabilities.

(c) Deeds of arrangement

1.132 Without any involvement of the court, a debtor may execute a deed of arrangement placing his property in the hands of a trustee for the benefit of his creditors. The deed and the creditors' assents thereto must be registered with the D.T.I. in accordance with D.A.A. 1914. The procedure is nowadays rarely used since the voluntary arrangement (see para. 1.133 below and Chap. 5) has proved a more effective means to the same end. The subject of deeds was fully explained in the first edition of this book. The I.S. has issued a concise guide to practitioners on this subject.

(d) Voluntary arrangements

1.133 The voluntary arrangement provides a useful half-way procedure between the County Court administration order (see paras 1.122–1.131 above) and the full rigours of bankruptcy.

1.134 I.A. 1986, ss.252–263 sets out procedures for voluntary arrangements between an insolvent debtor and his creditors, similar to those applicable to companies (ss.1–7), which can be implemented whether or not the debtor is bankrupt. These procedures are discussed in Chapter 5.

Chapter 2
THE BANKRUPTCY ORDER

My deeds upon my head! I crave the law—William Shakespeare, *Merchant of Venice.*

Commencement

2.01 The bankruptcy of an individual commences on the day on which the bankruptcy order is made (I.A. 1986, s.278).

1. The Order

2.02 The order is settled by the court whether the petition is one brought by a creditor or by the debtor himself (I.R. 6.33).

2.03 The order must state the date of presentation of the petition on which the order is made and the date and time of the making of the order. It will contain a notice requiring the bankrupt forthwith after service upon him to attend on the O.R. at the place stated in the order.

2.04 Subject to I.A. 1986, s.346 (Enforcement Procedures—see Chap. 9), the order may include a provision staying any action or proceeding against the bankrupt (I.R. 6.33).

2. Proceedings and Remedies

Restrictions

2.05 I.A. 1986, s.285 allows the court to prevent creditors (other than secured creditors seeking to enforce their security) from proceeding against the person or property of the debtor or bankrupt at any time after the presentation of a petition or after a debtor has been adjudged bankrupt. In effect a court-imposed moratorium may be brought in from the time the petition is presented. Section 285(1) provides that at any time when proceedings on a bankruptcy petition are pending, or where an individual has been adjudged bankrupt, the court may stay any action, execution, or other legal process against property or person of the debtor or, as the case may be, of the bankrupt.

2.06 Any court in which proceedings are pending against any individual may, on proof that a bankruptcy petition has been presented in respect of that individual or that he is an undischarged bankrupt, either stay the proceedings or allow them to continue on such terms as it thinks fit (s.285(2)). In *Polly Peck International plc v. Nadir* [1993] B.C.L.C. 187, the court refused to stay proceedings alleging fraudulent breaches of duty against Mr Nadir although the latter had been adjudicated bankrupt. The court held that the power to stay proceedings in section 285(2) was put there for the protection of the bankrupt's estate for the benefit of all creditors. Since it was possible for a claim based on fraud to survive the debtor's discharge from bankruptcy, the court exercised its discretion not to stay the proceedings.

2.07 After the making of a bankruptcy order no person who is a creditor of the bankrupt in respect of a debt provable in the bankruptcy shall have any remedy against the property or person of the bankrupt in respect of that debt or, before the discharge of the bankrupt, commence any action or other legal proceedings against him except with the leave of the court (s.285(3)). The House of Lords has held in *Re Smith (A Bankrupt), ex p. Braintree District Council* [1990] 2 A.C. 215 that section 285 enabled the Court to stay proceedings against the debtor for committal for non-payment of rates (which would also include its replacements) as this is included within the definition of "other legal process" in section 285(1). This last provision is, however, subject to sections 346 and 347 which deal respectively with enforcement procedures and a landlord's limited right of distress, dealt with in greater detail in Chapter 9.

2.08 Where any goods of an undischarged bankrupt are held by any person by way of pledge, pawn or other security, the O.R. may, after giving notice in writing of his intention to do so, inspect the goods. Where such notice has been given to any person, that person is not entitled, without the leave of the court, to realise his security unless he has given the trustee a reasonable opportunity of inspecting the goods and of exercising the bankrupt's right of redemption (s.285(5)).

2.09 It should be stressed that section 285 does not in any way operate a general or automatic stay of proceedings (or execution) simply on the presentation of a petition or even adjudication. As the court had held, considering B.A. 1914, s.9, an order is required on an application to stay proceedings (*Realisations, etc. v. Loescher* [1957] 1 W.L.R. 1026). Although the court may stay proceedings, it may give leave for such proceedings to be continued. In general if a trial is pending against an individual and it comes to the notice of the court that a bankruptcy petition has been presented, the court will stay the proceedings until either the result of the bankruptcy proceedings is known or the bankruptcy court itself gives leave for the other proceedings to continue. In the case of *Re Hutton* [1969] 2 Ch. 201 the Court said that in these cases the bankruptcy court should leave decisions to the ordinary courts where no point of bankruptcy law was involved, unless the court's own authority or the protection of its officers was in issue.

3. RESTRICTIONS ON DISPOSITION OF PROPERTY

2.10 I.A. 1986 contains provisions restricting dispositions of the bankrupt's property (including cash) between the time the petition is presented and the time the estate vests in the trustee under Part IX, Chap. IV of the Act. The effect of these provisions is to render void a disposition of the property made by the bankrupt after presentation of the petition unless made with the consent of the court either given at the time or by subsequent ratification. This will, however, be given subject to certain protections to persons receiving property in good faith and without notice of the bankruptcy order.

2.11 When a person is adjudged bankrupt, any disposition of property (including payments in cash or otherwise) made by that person between the time of presentation of the petition and the vesting of his estate in his trustee is void except to the extent that it is or was made with the consent of the court, or was subsequently ratified by the court (I.A. 1986, s.284(1)–(3)). A transfer of property by court order on matrimonial proceedings, the order being made between the date of presentation of the petition and the bankruptcy order, is also void under section 284 and may not be set aside (*Re Flint (A Bankrupt)* [1993] 2 W.L.R. 537).

2.12 Where a payment is void by virtue of section 284(1), the person paid will hold the sum as part of the bankrupt's estate.

Property or payment received in good faith

2.13 Although the foregoing provisions render any disposition or payment void once made after presentation of the petition, protection is given by section 284(4) to persons receiving property or payment in good faith before the date of the bankruptcy order and without notice that a petition had been presented. Similarly, a person deriving an interest or title in the property from someone whose interest is already protected will himself be protected against claims made by the trustee.

2.14 In the case of bankers and others a further protection is given by section 284(5) in certain cases where the bankrupt incurs a debt after the commencement of his bankruptcy (bankruptcy commences on the date the order is made: section 278). Where, after the bankruptcy order, a bankrupt has incurred a debt to a banker or other person by reason of a payment which would otherwise be void under section 284, the debt is deemed to have been incurred before the bankruptcy order unless:

(a) the banker or other person had notice of the bankruptcy before the debt was incurred; or
(b) it is reasonably practicable for the amount of the payment to be recovered from the persons to whom it is made.

2.15 An example of this might be where the bank, after adjudication, honours a cheque drawn by the bankrupt before adjudication, this cheque being a payment otherwise void under section 284(2)—provided the bank did not have notice of the bankruptcy before the debt was incurred and provided it is not reasonably practicable to recover it from the eventual payee. Then the payment by the bank is deemed to have been made before the commencement of the bankruptcy and will be a provable debt in the bankruptcy.

4. ACTION FOLLOWING A BANKRUPTCY ORDER

(a) Procedure

2.16 The Rules provide for the procedures following the making of a bankruptcy order:

(i) at least two sealed copies of the order must be sent by the court to the O.R., who must forthwith send one of them to the bankrupt (I.R. 6.34);
(ii) the O.R. must:
 (a) send notice of the making of the order to the Chief Land Registrar for registration in the Register of Writs and orders affecting land;

(b) cause the order to be advertised in such local paper as the O.R. thinks fit; and
(c) cause the order to be gazetted (I.R. 6.34).

2.17 The court may, however, on the application of the bankrupt or of a creditor, order the O.R. to suspend action under I.R. 6.34 pending a further order of the court, but the O.R. must be informed of any such application to the court by the bankrupt or by a creditor.

(b) Debtor's petition

2.18 The above rules with regard to applications following the making of a petition apply also in the case of a debtor's petition.

2.19 On the making of the bankruptcy order the bankrupt immediately becomes subject to the disabilities outlined in Chapter 10.

Chapter 3
THE OFFICIAL RECEIVER

The official world, the corridors of power—C.P. Snow.

1. Duties and Status

3.01 O.R.s are appointed by, and are employees of, the D.T.I. but are also officers of the court to which they are attached.

3.02 Their duties extend to compulsory liquidations and bankruptcies and relate to both the conduct of the debtor and the administration of the estate. Frequently a trustee, other than the O.R., is appointed to administer the estate (Chap. 4) but in the absence of such appointment the O.R. acts as trustee. In all cases the O.R. retains his responsibility concerning the conduct of the debtor.

2. Interim Receivership

(a) The power to appoint

Protection of the bankrupt's estate

3.03 Bankruptcy commences with the making of the bankruptcy order (I.A. 1986, s.278(a)) but section 286 provides some protection for the bankrupt's estate before the making of the order.

3.04 By section 286(1) the court may, if it is shown to be necessary for the protection of the debtor's property, at any time after the presentation of a bankruptcy petition and before making a bankruptcy order, appoint the O.R. to be interim receiver of the debtor's property. That could arise either on a creditor's or a debtor's petition. However, where on a debtor's petition the court has appointed an insolvency practitioner to report under section 273 and there exists a danger to the debtor's property, the court may, without making a bankruptcy order, appoint that practitioner instead of the O.R. to be interim receiver of the debtor's property (s.286(2)).

(b) Procedure for appointment

3.05 An application to the court for the appointment of an interim receiver under section 286 may be made *ex parte* by a creditor or by the debtor or (in the case of a debtor's petition) by the insolvency practitioner appointed to report under section 273.

3.06 The application may be made at any time after presentation of the petition and must be supported by an affidavit stating the grounds on which it is proposed that the interim receiver should be appointed (I.R. 6.51).

3.07 The order appointing the interim receiver should state the nature and a short description of the property of which he is to take possession and the duties to be performed by him in relation to the debtor's affairs (I.R. 6.52).

Before an order appointing the O.R. as interim receiver is made, the applicant must pay a deposit in such sum as the court directs to cover his fees and expenses and a further deposit may be required if this is insufficient (I.R. 6.53). **3.08**

Appointment of an insolvency practitioner

In the case of an appointment of an insolvency practitioner as interim receiver his appointment will not take effect until proper security is given by way of a bond. The cost of providing security is paid by the person appointed to be interim receiver but, if a bankruptcy order is not made, the court may order that the person so appointed be reimbursed out of the debtor's property. If the order is made, and the creditors or their committee so resolve, the interim receiver is reimbursed out of the estate in the prescribed order of priority (I.R. 6.54). **3.09**

The debtor has a positive duty to co-operate and must give the interim receiver such inventory of his property and other information, and shall attend on him at such times, as he may reasonably require for the purpose of carrying out his functions. The order of appointment may include directions as to the transfer or delivery up of any property of the debtor to which the order relates (s.286(5) and I.R. 6.52). **3.10**

(c) Termination of appointment

The appointment of an interim receiver will cease if the bankruptcy petition relating to the debtor is dismissed, if a bankruptcy order is made on the petition, or if the court by order otherwise terminates the appointment (s.286 (7)). **3.11**

The appointment may be terminated by the court on the interim receiver's own application, or on that of the O.R. (in cases where an insolvency practitioner is interim receiver) or on the application of the debtor or any creditor (I.R. 6.57). **3.12**

If the appointment terminates, in consequence of the dismissal of the petition or otherwise, the court may give such directions as it thinks fit with respect to any matters arising from the termination. **3.13**

3. RECEIVERSHIP PENDING APPOINTMENT OF TRUSTEE

There is in most cases a lapse of time between the making of the bankruptcy order and the appointment of the trustee, in whom the estate of the bankrupt will vest automatically under I.A. 1986, s.306 (see Chap. 4, para. 4.35). There is an exception in respect of the "special cases" under section 297, where the O.R. is immediately constituted as trustee of the bankrupt's estate. **3.14**

Protection of the bankrupt's estate

To safeguard the bankrupt's property during this interval, section 287(1) provides that the O.R. is to be the receiver and manager of the bankrupt's estate. The function of the O.R. while acting as such receiver or manager is stated to be "to protect the estate" (s.287(2)); and for this purpose: **3.15**

(i) he has the same powers as if he were a receiver or manager appointed by the High Court; and
(ii) he is entitled to sell or otherwise dispose of any perishable goods comprised in the estate and any other goods so comprised, the value of which is likely to diminish (s.287(2)).

3.16 While acting as receiver or manager of the estate, the O.R. must take all such steps as he thinks fit for protecting any property which may be claimed for the estate by the trustee but he is not, except as directed by the D.T.I., required to do anything which involves him incurring expenditure (s.287(3)). He may (if he thinks fit), and shall if so directed by the court, at any time summon a general meeting of the bankrupt's creditors (s.287(3)(c)). Meetings of creditors are considered in Chapter 4, para. 4.47.

3.17 In his capacity as receiver or manager pending the appointment of a trustee, the O.R. is given immunity in respect of any property seized or disposed of by him which is not part of the estate so long as he has a bona fide belief on reasonable grounds that he is entitled so to act. In such a case he is not liable for any loss or damage unless caused by his negligence. He also has a lien on the property or the proceeds of sale for such of the expenses of the bankruptcy as were incurred in connection with the seizure or disposal (s.287(4)).

3.18 It should be noted, however, that section 287 does not apply where by virtue of section 297 (the "special cases") the bankrupt's estate vests in a trustee immediately on the making of the bankruptcy order.

4. INVESTIGATION OF THE BANKRUPT'S AFFAIRS

(a) The duty to investigate

3.19 In all cases, save where a certificate of summary administration of the estate is in force, the O.R. is charged with the duty to investigate the conduct and affairs of every bankrupt and to make such report (if any) to the court as he thinks fit (I.A. 1986, s.289(1)).

3.20 He is also charged under section 289(2) to make a report to the court in respect of certain prescribed matters where the bankrupt applies for his discharge under section 280. (See Chap. 10.)

3.21 The investigation may be far-reaching. It will include the bankrupt's conduct and affairs before the making of the bankruptcy order by which he was adjudged bankrupt. It will also be prima facie evidence of the facts stated in the report in any proceedings (s.289(3) and (4)).

3.22 Where an order for summary administration is in force, the O.R. will only carry out an investigation if he thinks fit.

(b) The statement of affairs

3.23 Except in the case of a debtor's petition, where the statement of affairs is submitted with the petition (section 272), the bankrupt must submit a statement of his affairs to the O.R. within 21 days of the bankruptcy order (I.A. 1986, s.288(1)).

3.24 The statement of affairs must be in the form prescribed by the Rules (I.R. 6.59 and form 6.33 (see App. I, form K)) and must contain all the particulars required by that form.

The statement of affairs must be verified by affidavit and delivered to the O.R., who will file it with the court. It is the duty of the O.R. to furnish the bankrupt with instructions for the preparation of the statement of affairs and forms required for that purpose (I.R. 6.60). **3.25**

Provisions exist for the release of the bankrupt from the duty to file a statement of affairs and for an extension of time to be granted. **3.26**

Preparation of the statement of affairs

The O.R. may, if he thinks fit, either release the bankrupt from his duty to submit a statement of affairs or extend the time for its submission, and where the O.R. has refused to grant a release or extend time, the court may exercise that power (s.288(3) and I.R. 6.62). This power may be exercised of the O.R.'s own motion or at the bankrupt's request. If the bankrupt without reasonable excuse either fails to comply with his obligations as to the statement of affairs or submits one which does not comply with the requirements in the Rules, he will be guilty of a contempt of court and liable to be punished accordingly (in addition to any other punishment to which he may be subject) (s.288(4)). **3.27**

If the bankrupt cannot himself prepare a proper statement of affairs, the O.R. may, at the expense of the estate, employ someone to assist him in its preparation. Alternatively, he may, at the request of the bankrupt, make an allowance to the bankrupt to enable him to employ someone to assist in its preparation (I.R. 6.63). The O.R. is given a wide discretion by the Rules as to who shall be employed for this purpose and at what cost, but an estimate must be given in advance if the bankrupt wishes to employ his own assistance. Notwithstanding these provisions, the Rules do make it clear that the primary duty as to the preparation of the statement of affairs and its submission remains with the bankrupt and he must also provide any information reasonably required by the O.R. in his investigations or inquiries. **3.28**

The O.R. may also at any time request the bankrupt to submit in writing further information amplifying, modifying or explaining any matter contained in his statement of affairs or accounts and such information must be verified by affidavit if the O.R. so requests (I.R. 6.66). **3.29**

Creditors are given a right on payment of a prescribed fee to inspect a copy of the statement of affairs which is filed at the court and to take a copy of or extract from it (I.R. 7.28, 7.61), which appear to give rights to non-creditors too to inspect all documents filed subject to the court's discretion to refuse inspection. **3.30**

The O.R. may also require the bankrupt to submit trading or other accounts in respect of any period commencing with a date not earlier than three years before the date of presentation of the petition. Indeed if an application is made to the court the O.R. may go back earlier than the three-year time limit and he may also require those accounts to be verified by affidavit (I.R. 6.64–6.65). The rule as to employment of assistance (I.R. 6.63) also applies in respect of the preparation of accounts for this purpose. **3.31**

(c) Duties of the bankrupt in relation to the O.R.

Under section 291, duties are imposed on debtors to co-operate with their creditors and with the O.R. and to deliver up property, etc. These duties even extend until after discharge of the bankrupt. **3.32**

Where a bankruptcy order has been made, the bankrupt is under a duty: **3.33**

(i) to deliver possession of his estate to the O.R.; and
(ii) to deliver up to the O.R. all books, papers and other records of which he has possession or control and which relate to his estate and affairs

(including any which would be privileged from disclosure from any proceedings, *e.g.* those which might otherwise be covered by legal professional privilege).

Extent of duty

3.34 The extent of the bankrupt's duty was illustrated in a case under the similar provisions of B.A. 1914, s.22(3) which required the bankrupt "to aid, to the utmost of his power, in the realisation of his property and the distribution of the proceeds". In *Fryer v. Brook* (1984) 81 L.S.Gaz. 2856, the bankrupt, who was an occupier of premises, applied for an adjournment of possession proceedings in order to enter a defence against his trustee. His application was refused on appeal as the Court of Appeal held that his duty under section 22(3) precluded him from claiming any personal right of occupation against his trustee in bankruptcy which would in any way stop the trustee from realising that interest in the property for the benefit of the bankrupt's creditors. The Court also found that there appeared in any event to be no triable defence and therefore dismissed the bankrupt's appeal.

3.35 In the case of any part of the estate which consists of things, possession of which cannot be delivered to the O.R., or in the case of any property which may be claimed for the estate by the trustee, it is the bankrupt's duty to do all such things as may reasonably be required by the O.R. for the protection of those things or that property (s.291(2)).

3.36 It should be noted that the above provisions do not apply where the estate vests immediately in the trustee on the making of a bankruptcy order by virtue of section 297 of the Act, the so-called "special cases".

3.37 The bankrupt must give the O.R. such inventory of his estate and such other information and shall attend on the O.R. at such times as the O.R. may reasonably require. This will apply even after the bankrupt's discharge (s.291(4) and (5)).

3.38 If the bankrupt, without reasonable excuse, fails to comply with any obligation imposed by section 291 he will be guilty of a contempt of court and liable to be punished accordingly (in addition to any other punishment to which he may be subject (s.291(6))).

5. THE PUBLIC EXAMINATION

(a) The application

3.39 The O.R. has a discretion under I.A. 1986, s.290(1) to apply to the court for the public examination of the bankrupt. He may apply at any time before the discharge of the bankruptcy. On an application made by the O.R. the court must accede to the request (s.290(3)). This power is, however, rarely exercised.

3.40 Section 290(2) gives an additional power—this time to the creditors. If a creditor applies to the O.R. for a public examination of a bankrupt to be held and that request is supported by at least one-half in value of the creditors (including the creditor making the application) the O.R. is obliged to apply to the court under section 290(1). There is, however, in this case a discretion vested in the court which does not exist if the O.R. applies of his own volition and the court may refuse the application.

3.41 If the O.R. applies to the court for an order under s.290(1) a copy of the order must be sent to the bankrupt (I.R. 6.172). At least 14 days' notice of the hearing must then be given to any special manager, to the trustee if appointed or nominated, and subject to any contrary direction of the court to every known creditor (I.R. 6.172). The O.R. is also empowered to advertise the public examination.

Creditor requests public examination

3.42 If a creditor requests a public examination under section 290(2) he must make this request in writing to the O.R. and include a list of creditors supporting the request with a list of their claims (I.R. 6.173). Unless the requisitioning creditor's debt is of itself sufficient, he must also supply written confirmation from every supporting creditor and the reasons why an examination is requested. Before an application to the court is made on the request, the O.R. may demand a deposit lodged with him as security for costs of a public examination if one is ordered (I.R. 6.173).

3.43 If the O.R. is of the opinion that a creditor's request for a public examination is unreasonable in the circumstances, he may apply to the court for an order releasing him from the obligation to apply for the examination under section 290(2) but in the absence of any such release he must within 28 days of receiving the request make an application (I.R. 6.173).

3.44 The Court of Appeal in *Re Seagull Manufacturing Co Limited* [1993] B.C.C. 241 held, in proceedings under section 133 (which relates to liquidations) that the court was empowered to order a person who was resident outside the jurisdiction to attend before it. In contrast, in *Re Tucker (a Bankrupt)* [1988] 2 W.L.R. 748, where the person to be examined resided outside the jurisdiction but was a British subject, the court could not order service to be effected outside the jurisdiction. This was a case under what was B.A. 1914, s.25 (now I.A. 1986, s.366), which applies to *private* examination by the trustee. However, the position may be different in cases where section 426 (co-operation between courts exercising jurisdiction in relation to insolvency) applies.

(b) The hearing

3.45 The public examination may be attended by the O.R., the trustee in bankruptcy, any special manager who has been appointed, or by any creditor who has tendered a proof. It should be noted, however, that it is not obligatory for the O.R. to appear on the examination although he will normally be represented.

3.46 Procedure at the hearing is governed by I.R. 6.175. The bankrupt is examined on oath and is required to answer all such questions as the court may put, or allow to be put, to him.

3.47 Any of the persons who are allowed to appear (see above) may appear in person or by a solicitor or counsel or may authorise another person to question the bankrupt on his behalf.

3.48 The bankrupt too may employ a solicitor or counsel who may put to him any such questions as the court may allow for the purpose of explaining or qualifying his answers and the legal adviser may also make representations on the bankrupt's behalf.

Criminal proceedings

3.49 A record of the public examination may be taken at the court's discretion and these notes will then be read over by or to the bankrupt and signed by the latter and verified by affidavit. The record may be used in evidence against the bankrupt in any proceedings whether under the Act or not (I.R. 6.175). If criminal proceedings have been instituted against the bankrupt and the court is of the opinion that continuing the public examination would prejudice a fair trial, the court may adjourn the hearing (I.R. 6.175). In any event the court is empowered to adjourn the public examination from time to time, either to a fixed date or generally (I.R. 6.176). Where the examination has been adjourned generally the O.R. may, there and then, make an application under s.279(3) for suspension of the automatic discharge provisions (see Chap. 10), although where there is a general adjournment either the O.R. or the bankrupt may apply for it to be resumed (I.R. 6.176).

3.50 The power to adjourn in these circumstances may therefore be of considerable importance in that a general adjournment of the public examination may lead to a postponement of the automatic discharge of the bankrupt under section 279 until the bankrupt obtains an order restoring and concluding the examination.

3.51 The scope of the public examination is wide. Even questions which may tend to incriminate the bankrupt may be put. As recent cases with regard to private examinations show (see Chap. 9 below) the so-called privilege against self-incrimination is now generally disregarded by the courts. The object of an examination is essentially to protect the public and, if appropriate, to expose wrongdoing by the bankrupt or his associates.

(c) Non-attendance of bankrupt

3.52 Failure by the bankrupt to attend his public examination may be wilful or through some disability. Wilful failure to attend renders the bankrupt liable to punishment. By section 290(5) if the bankrupt, without reasonable excuse, fails at any time to attend his public examination he is guilty of a contempt of court and liable to be punished accordingly (in addition to any other punishment to which he may be subject).

Mental or physical disability

3.53 The rules do, however, allow for non-attendance where the bankrupt is suffering from some mental or physical disability rendering him unfit to undergo or attend his public examination (I.R. 6.174). An application may be made on behalf of the bankrupt in such cases and the court may either stay the order for public examination or direct that it be conducted in such manner or at such place as the court thinks fit. An application under this rule may be made either by a person appointed by a United Kingdom court to manage the bankrupt's affairs or to represent him, or by a relative or friend whom the court considers a proper person to make the application, or by the O.R. Unless the application is made by the O.R., medical evidence on affidavit must be produced and at least seven days' notice of the application is to be given to the O.R. or to the trustee.

3.54 The powers of the O.R. or the trustee to conduct a private examination of the bankrupt, his spouse or former spouse or other persons believed to have property comprised in the estate or to be able to give information concerning the bankrupt are dealt with in Chapter 9.

6. REPORTS TO CREDITORS

3.55 In accordance with I.R. 6.73 the O.R. must, at least once after the making of the bankruptcy order, send a report to creditors with respect to the bankruptcy proceedings and the state of the bankrupt's affairs. This will apply only for those creditors known to the O.R. or who are identified by the bankrupt on his statement of affairs.

3.56 Where a statement of affairs has been lodged with the court the O.R. must send out to creditors a report summarising the statement with such observations (if any) as he thinks fit. This will not, however, be required if the O.R. has previously reported to creditors with respect to the bankrupt's affairs and if he is of the opinion that there are no further matters to be brought to their attention (I.R. 6.75).

3.57 Where the bankrupt has been released from the duty to submit a statement of affairs the O.R. must still send to creditors a report containing a summary of the bankrupt's affairs so far as within his knowledge and his observations, if any, on it—unless he has already reported to creditors and he is of the opinion that there are no additional matters on which to report (I.R. 6.76). The court is generally empowered to release the O.R. from his reporting duties under the Rules (I.R. 6.77).

3.58 The involvement of the O.R., in calling the first meeting of creditors to appoint the trustee, is considered in Chapter 4.

Chapter 4
THE TRUSTEE

He was a gentleman on whom I built an absolute trust—William Shakespeare, *Macbeth*.

4.01 If no trustee is appointed to administer a bankrupt's estate, then the O.R. acts as trustee. However, where there are assets to be realised for the benefit of creditors, a trustee is likely to be appointed as described in paragraphs 4.14–4.34 below. The speed with which the assets can be converted into money in the hands of creditors will materially depend upon the assiduity of the trustee. His principal tasks include the realisation of the assets and agreement of creditors' claims, leaving to the O.R. the task of investigating the bankrupt's affairs and reporting to the court.

4.02 The Act and Rules define the duties of the trustee and the powers available to him to perform this task effectively.

4.03 Whilst this Chapter is principally concerned with the trustee in bankruptcy, many similar considerations apply to the trustee under a deed of arrangement and to the supervisor of a voluntary arrangement as described in Chapter 5.

1. Qualifications And Monitoring

4.04 Before 1986 there was no requirement for any professional or other qualification to act as a trustee in bankruptcy; nor was there any means of ensuring competence to hold that office.

4.05 One of the objectives of the reform of insolvency law in 1986 was, in the words of the 1984 White Paper which preceded it, "to ensure that those who act in cases of insolvency are competent to do so and conduct themselves in a proper manner".

4.06 The Act seeks to do this by ensuring that no one who takes appointment as trustee in bankruptcy, interim receiver, trustee under a deed of arrangement, supervisor of a voluntary arrangement or administrator of an insolvent estate of a deceased person shall hold such office unless suitably licensed, qualified and bonded. This mirrors the provisions which apply in respect of corporate insolvency.

4.07 The Act provides that an insolvency practitioner must be an individual (s.390(1)) although two or more individuals may act jointly.

4.08 A person who acts as a trustee or in any of the above-mentioned capacities while not qualified to do so commits an offence and is liable to a fine or imprisonment or to both for so doing (s.389(1)).

(a) Principal requirements

4.09 The Act lays down three principal requirements:

(i) authorisation by a "recognised professional body" or "a competent authority" (s.390(2));
(ii) a prescribed security, *i.e.* bonding or insurance (s.390(3));

(iii) that he is not disqualified by virtue of s.390(4), *e.g.* if he has himself been adjudicated bankrupt (see below).

(b) Recognised professional body

With respect to the first requirement, authorisation to act is given in two ways: **4.10**

(i) By membership of a "recognised professional body" provided that the individual is authorised to act as an insolvency practitioner under the rules of that body (s.390(2)). Under the Insolvency Practitioners (Recognised Professional Bodies) Order 1986 (S.I. 1986 No. 1764) the following are recognised professional bodies:

The Chartered Association of Certified Accountants
The Insolvency Practitioners Association
The Institute of Chartered Accountants in England and Wales
The Institute of Chartered Accountants in Ireland
The Institute of Chartered Accountants of Scotland
The Law Society
The Law Society of Scotland

This means that the licensing of practitioners is delegated to those professional bodies and it is up to them to ensure that their members who apply to be insolvency practitioners comply with both the statutory requirements and the rules of the body concerned. This is by far the most common method by which any individual gains the right to practise as an insolvency practitioner. It means that not every person having a practising certificate from one of the recognised bodies is able to obtain a licence—indeed those bodies require completion of a minimum specified period of practical work on insolvency matters. Since 1989 all new applicants for licences have been required, at least by their professional bodies, to have taken specialist examinations.

In 1990 a separate organisation was set up to which members of various disciplines (*e.g.* lawyers and accountants) holding licences may belong. This is the Society of Practitioners of Insolvency (S.P.I.). Although not a recognised licensing body, it does have an important parallel function in the training field and publishes a journal which provides a good deal of technical information and other guidance for practitioners.

In particular the S.P.I. has over the past few years been assiduous in producing technical information for insolvency practitioners as well as a number of Statements of Insolvency Practice (S.I.P.s) which seek to clarify what is regarded as best practice in the profession. Although these have no statutory force they may well be regarded as highly persuasive, particularly when such matters as disciplinary proceedings against practitioners are under consideration by the relevant licensing bodies.

(ii) If a person is not a member of a recognised professional body then he may practise if he holds authorisation from the "competent authority" set up by the D.T.I. For this purpose licensing is in the hands of the body set up by the Department. There is a right of appeal against refusal or withdrawal of a licence to the Insolvency Practitioners Tribunal (s.396).

It is not intended in this book to detail the mechanisms by which qualification is gained or the process of appeal against refusal and reference should therefore be made to the relevant regulations. **4.11**

The licensing arrangements provide some protection for those persons affected by the actions of insolvency practitioners both by ensuring that only qualified persons act in that capacity and by providing a complaints procedure. Practitioners are subject to regular visits, normally every three years, by inspectors from monitoring units set up by the regulatory bodies. Two of the RPBs, the Institute of Chartered Accountants in England and Wales and the Insolvency Practitioners Association, participate in a joint insolvency monitoring unit (JIMU). The Chartered Association of Certified Accountants (ACCA) has its own separate monitoring unit as does the D.T.I. in respect of the small number of practitioners licensed by it. These inspectors examine the competence of practitioners, and compliance with regulations. Initially the inspectors tended to concentrate on the minutiae of detailed compliance but the process continues to evolve and inspectors are now being encouraged to take a broader view of the quality of work. Detailed reports are sent to the regulatory bodies, and defects may result in investigation leading to disciplinary action and, in the worst cases, the loss of a practitioner's licence. In addition to these random visits, the inspectors may make special visits in response to a particular complaint. The regulatory bodies each have their own complaints procedure, supported by investigation and disciplinary committees, to provide the machinery to investigate complaints and in appropriate cases discipline the errant practitioner.

Licences are also subject to review at the time of renewal. Those licences issued by the D.T.I. are renewable after three years, whereas those issued by the regulatory bodies are renewed annually. At the time of renewal, the practitioner must answer a detailed questionnaire to establish, *inter alia*, continuing relevant professional experience and adequate continuing professional education. As a consequence, professional training courses and conferences continue to be well supported.

The stated aim of the monitoring units, which has largely been achieved, was to make visits to practitioners at least once every three years. However, where there are specific complaints by members of the public, creditors or others, a targeted visit may be made to the practitioner. The effect of all these changes is largely to have turned matters full circle. From a previously largely unregulated profession, insolvency is now highly regulated—indeed some practitioners have complained that it is over-regulated. However, on balance, additional regulation is regarded as beneficial by most of the profession.

Practitioners should notify any change of circumstances, including their address and telephone numbers not only to the authorising body but also to the Insolvency Practitioners Control Unit (IPCU) in Birmingham. Practitioners in multi-office practices are also required to advise IPCU in writing when the conduct of specific cases is moved for administrative reasons to another address. In bankruptcy cases, the relevant O.R. should also be notified.

(c) Requirements as to security or bonding

4.12 The second requirement, as to security or bonding, is provided by section 390(3) which states that a person is not qualified to act as an insolvency practitioner at any time unless there is in force at that time sufficient security for the proper performance of his functions.

(d) Disqualifications

4.13 A person is not qualified to practise as an insolvency practitioner if at that time:

(i) he has been adjudged bankrupt or there has been a sequestration of his estate and (in either case) this has not been discharged;
(ii) he is subject to a disqualification order under the Company Directors' Disqualification Act 1986; or
(iii) he is a patient within the meaning of the Mental Health Act 1983 or the Mental Health (Scotland) Act 1984.

2. APPOINTMENT

4.14 The processes by which a trustee in bankruptcy may be appointed are complex, there being three different ways in which the trustee may attain his appointment. I.A. 1986, s.292 vests the power to appoint a trustee, whether the first trustee or one appointed to fill any vacancy, either:

(a) in a general meeting of the bankrupt's creditors (except at a time when a certificate for summary administration of the estate is in force);
(b) under sections 295(2), 296(2) or 300(6) of the Act in the D.T.I. These provisions are considered below except for the appointments under section 300(6) which relate to the filling of vacancies, which will be considered in detail in paragraphs 4.138–4.164 of this Chapter; or
(c) in the court where section 297 (the "special cases") applies.

4.15 All of these methods of appointment allow for joint trustees to be appointed but joint appointments must make provision as to the circumstances in which the trustees must act together and the circumstances in which one or more of them may act for the others (s.292(3)). In practice, although joint appointments are common in the case of corporate insolvency, they are extremely rare in bankruptcy.

4.16 An appointment of a trustee takes effect only if the appointment is accepted in accordance with the Rules. Subject to this, the appointment takes effect at the time specified in his certificate of appointment (s.292(4)).

(a) Appointment by the first meeting of creditors

4.17 Unless there is in force a certificate of summary administration, or the bankruptcy order has been made as a consequence of a criminal bankruptcy order, the O.R. must decide within 12 weeks of the making of the bankruptcy order whether to call a meeting of creditors for the purpose of appointing a trustee (s.293(1)).

4.18 If the O.R. decides to call a meeting, notice must be given to the court, to the D.T.I. for gazetting and to every creditor who is known to the O.R. or identified in the bankrupt's statement of affairs (I.R. 6.79). Notice must also be given by public advertisement.

4.19 If the O.R. decides not to summon a meeting, he is required before the end of the 12-week period to give notice of his decision to the court and to every creditor so identified as above (s.293(2)). Once the O.R. gives such a notice to the court, he will become the trustee of the bankrupt's estate, although another trustee may subsequently be appointed as described below.

4.20 The Act also allows any creditor of the bankrupt to requisition a meeting on notice to the O.R. Provided not less than one-quarter in value of the creditors support such request (including the creditor making the request) the O.R. is duty bound to call a meeting for not more than three months from receipt of the request (s.294(2) and I.R. 6.79).

4.21 The first meeting (if convened) will be chaired by the O.R. or a person nominated by him (normally his assistant) and its business, *inter alia*, is to appoint a named insolvency practitioner as trustee (I.R. 6.80). The meeting is also empowered to establish a creditors' committee. Further details with regard to the creditors' committee and its function will be found in paragraphs 4.172–4.195 below.

4.22 In summary, pursuant to I.R. 6.80(1), the business of the first meeting of creditors is limited to the following functions:

(i) appointing a named insolvency practitioner to be trustee in bankruptcy or two or more named practitioners as joint trustees;
(ii) establishing a creditors' committee;
(iii) unless it has been resolved to establish such a committee, passing a resolution specifying the terms on which the trustee is to be remunerated, or to defer consideration of that matter;
(iv) if two or more persons are appointed to act jointly, to pass a resolution specifying whether acts are to be done by both or all of them, or by only one;
(v) where the meeting has been requisitioned by a creditor under section 294, passing the resolution authorising payment out of the estate, as an expense of the bankruptcy, of the cost of summoning and holding the meeting;
(vi) passing a resolution to adjourn the meeting for not more than 3 weeks and
(vii) passing any other resolution which the chairman thinks it right to allow for special reasons.

Certification of appointment

4.23 I.R. 6.120 provides that the chairman of the meeting shall certify the appointment but not unless and until the person appointed has provided him with a written statement to the effect that he is a duly qualified insolvency practitioner.

4.24 Unless the O.R. is the chairman of the meeting, the certificate relating to the appointment must be sent to him but in any event the O.R. must file it with the court. The trustee's appointment is effective from such time and date as the certificate is filed with the court.

4.25 As soon as possible after the certificate of appointment has been filed with the court, the trustee must give notice of his appointment in such newspaper as he thinks most appropriate for ensuring that it comes to the notice of the creditors. He is entitled to be reimbursed out of the estate for the cost of the advertisement (I.R. 6.124).

(b) Appointment by the D.T.I.

Discretion of the D.T.I.

4.26 The general meeting of creditors, whether called by the O.R. on his own volition under section 293 or summoned by creditors under section 294, may fail to appoint a trustee. In that case section 295 provides that it is the duty of the O.R. to decide whether or not to refer the matter to the D.T.I. The D.T.I. have a discretion: they may or may not appoint a named insolvency practitioner as trustee. If the O.R. decides not to refer the matter to the D.T.I.

or the D.T.I. decline to make an appointment, notice must be given by the O.R. to the court and, as from the date of giving such notice, the O.R. becomes trustee (s.295(4)).

4.27 Section 296 contains further provisions allowing the D.T.I. to appoint a trustee. At any time where the O.R. is the trustee, he may apply to the D.T.I. for the appointment of another person as trustee. Such an application may be made notwithstanding that a previous application has been made under section 295 or 300(4). On an application under section 296 the D.T.I. must either make an appointment as trustee or decline to make one (s.296(2)). In practice the O.R. initiates the appointment, as agent of the D.T.I., approaching a potential trustee from a "rota" of insolvency practitioners. The majority of appointments of trustees are made in this way rather than at meetings of creditors.

4.28 Where the trustee has been appointed by the D.T.I., whether under section 296 or otherwise, he must notify the creditors of his appointment or, if the court so allows, he may advertise his appointment as directed by the court. The notice or advertisement must:

(i) state whether the trustee proposes to call a general meeting of creditors for the purpose of establishing a creditors' committee under section 301; and
(ii) if he does not propose to summon such a meeting, set out the power of the creditors under the Act to require him to summon one (s.296(5)).

4.29 Where the O.R. applies under section 296 for the appointment of a trustee, the application must be accompanied by a statement in writing by the proposed appointee to the effect that he is a duly qualified insolvency practitioner. If the D.T.I. makes the appointment it must be advertised in accordance with I.R. 6.124.

(c) Appointment by the court

Special cases

4.30 In certain "special cases" section 297 of the Act provides that the power to appoint a trustee is vested in the court.

4.31 Where the court issues a certificate for the summary administration of the bankrupt's estate, unless the court appoints a person (*i.e.* a qualified insolvency practitioner) other than the O.R. to act, the O.R. shall be trustee (s.297(2), (3)).

4.32 Where a bankruptcy order is made, in a case in which an insolvency practitioner's report has been submitted to the court under section 274 (debtor's petition—see Chap. 1, paras 1.81–1.105) but no certificate of summary administration of the estate is issued, the court may, on making the order, appoint that insolvency practitioner to be trustee (s.297(4)).

4.33 Where a bankruptcy order is made at a time when there is a supervisor of an approved composition or scheme under Part VIII of the Act, the court may, on making the order, appoint the supervisor as trustee (s.297(5)).

4.34 Where the petition contains a request for the appointment of the former supervisor as trustee, the supervisor must, not less than two days before the day appointed for the hearing of the petition, file in court a report including particulars of:

(i) the date on which he gave written notification to creditors bound by the arrangement of his intention to seek appointment as trustee, such date must be at least 10 days before the day on which the report is filed, and

(ii) details of any response from creditors to that notice, including any objections to his appointment (I.R. 6.10(6)).

4.35 Where the trustee has been appointed by the court, he must give notice to the creditors of his appointment or, if the court so allows, he may advertise his appointment in accordance with the court's directions and in that notice or advertisement he must:

(i) state whether he proposes to summon a general meeting of the creditors for the purpose of establishing a committee of creditors under section 301; and
(ii) if he does not propose to summon such a meeting, set out the power of the creditors under the Act to require him to summon one (s.297(8)).

4.36 Where the court appoints a trustee under section 297(3), (4) or (5) the order cannot be issued until the person appointed has delivered to the court a statement to the effect that he is a duly qualified insolvency practitioner. Upon issue the court will send copies of the order to the O.R. and to the D.T.I. for gazetting.

3. VESTING OF PROPERTY

4.37 The bankrupt's estate vests in the trustee immediately upon his appointment taking effect or, in the case of the O.R., on his becoming trustee (I.A. 1986, s.306(1)) and it so vests without any conveyance, assignment or transfer (s.306(2)). The question of what constitutes the estate of the bankrupt will be further considered in Chapter 7 below.

4. DUTIES OF THE TRUSTEE

4.38 Various duties are imposed on the trustee both in relation to the O.R. and generally by the provisions of I.A. 1986.

4.39 The function of the trustee is stated to be to get in, realise and distribute the bankrupt's estate in accordance with the provisions of the Act, and in carrying out those functions and in the management of the bankrupt's estate he is entitled, subject to following the statutory provisions and the Rules, to use his own discretion (I.A. 1986, s.305).

4.40 It is important to appreciate that although some onerous duties are imposed upon practitioners who take office as trustee, they are nevertheless allowed a great deal of discretion. The courts are usually most unwilling to interfere with the trustee's discretion provided it is exercised reasonably and in good faith. This is illustrated by the case of *Leon v. York-O-Matic Limited* [1966] 1 W.L.R. 1450, a case of corporate insolvency, but where the same principles apply.

(a) Duties in relation to the O.R.

4.41 It is the duty of the trustee, if he is not the O.R.:

(i) to furnish the O.R. with such information;
(ii) to produce to the O.R. and permit inspection by him of such books, papers and other records; and
(iii) to give the O.R. such other assistance

that the O.R. may reasonably require for the purpose of enabling him to carry out his functions in relation to the bankruptcy (s.305(3)).

4.42 The court, may, on the application of the O.R., make such orders as it thinks necessary for enforcement of the trustee's duties under section 305(3) and in these circumstances the court's order may provide that all costs, which are incidental to the O.R.'s application, shall be borne by the trustee (I.R. 6.149). Although technically the trustee is subject to the control both of the O.R.'s department and ultimately the court, in practice O.R.s rarely interfere with a trustee's administration and, as stated above, a trustee is in any event allowed a very wide degree of discretion.

(b) General duties

4.43 (i) The trustee must take possession of all books, papers and other records which relate to the bankrupt's estate or affairs and which belong to him or are in his possession or under his control (including any documents which would be privileged from disclosure in any proceedings) (s.311(1)). The entitlement of a trustee to obtain such privileged documents may be of great importance, particularly in cases where the trustee is seeking to enforce an order, with regard to the matrimonial home, against a spouse or former spouse (see *Re Konigsberg (a Bankrupt)* [1989] 1 W.L.R. 1257 where the evidence of a solicitor who had acted for a bankrupt husband and also for the non-bankrupt wife jointly for the purpose of transferring property could not be excluded from the trial because privilege was enjoyed by two parties jointly and therefore the husband's privilege devolved upon his trustee).

4.44 (ii) He must notify the creditors' committee (see below, paras 4.172–4.195) if he employs a solicitor or if he disposes of any property to an "associate" of the bankrupt (s.314(6)). This provision does not apply if the O.R. is the trustee.

4.45 The requirement that there be notification of any disposal of property to an associate of the bankrupt is designed to prevent abuse of his position by the trustee. This requirement allows the creditors' committee or any member thereof to apply to the court under section 303(1), when the court will review the trustee's conduct and take such action as may be necessary, which may include an order under section 304 requiring the trustee to recompense the estate. The question of control by the court and the possible liability of the trustee is considered in paragraphs 4.105–4.113 below.

4.46 (iii) The trustee has duties with regard to the distribution of dividends (s.324) which are considered in further detail in Chapter 8.

4.47 (iv) He must summon a general meeting of the bankrupt's creditors if required to do so by a creditor with the concurrence of not less than one-tenth, in value, of the creditors (including the creditor making the request). Any request by a creditor for such a meeting must be accompanied by a list of the creditors concurring with the request and the amount of their respective claims in the bankruptcy (I.R. 6.83). If the trustee considers the request is properly made he must fix a time and place for the meeting, not more than 35 days from the receipt of the request, and notice of the meeting should be given to every creditor. The trustee may also call a meeting of creditors of his own volition at any time (s.314(7)).

4.48 (v) He, provided he is not the O.R., must also convene a final meeting of creditors in the circumstances set out in section 331. This applies where it appears to him that the administration of the estate is for all practical purposes complete. The final meeting will receive the trustee's report of his administration of the estate and will determine whether the trustee should have his release under section 299 of the Act. It is the trustee's duty to retain sufficient sums from the estate to cover the expenses of summoning and holding the final meeting (s.331(4)).

4.49 There are special provisions under section 332 where the trustee has been unable to realise the bankrupt's home or his former home occupied by his spouse (or former spouse) which have the effect of delaying the final meeting. These provisions will be considered in detail in Chapter 7.

4.50 (vi) The trustee must report to the creditors' committee all such matters as appear to him to be, or as they have indicated to him as being, of concern to the committee with respect to the bankruptcy (I.R. 6.152).

4.51 He need not comply with the request for information if it appears to him that the request is frivolous or unreasonable, or where it would be excessively costly or the estate is without funds sufficient to enable him to reply.

4.52 Where the committee has come into being more than 28 days after the trustee's appointment he must report to them, in summary form, what actions he has taken since his appointment and he must answer such questions as they may put to him regarding his conduct of the bankruptcy (*ibid.*). As and when directed by the committee he must send a written report to every member setting out the position generally as regards the progress of the bankruptcy and matters arising in connection with it to which he (the trustee) considers the committee's attention should be drawn. However, even in the absence of such directions, he must send a report to committee members not less than once every six months (I.R. 6.163).

4.53 (vii) The trustee must make available to any member of the committee records of the bankruptcy and any committee member may demand an explanation of any matter within the committee's responsibility.

4.54 (viii) He must keep accounts as described in paragraphs 4.129–4.139 below.

4.55 (ix) He also has certain duties to account before he obtains his release (see Chap. 12).

5. POWERS OF THE TRUSTEE

4.56 Wide powers are vested in the trustee in bankruptcy by the provisions of I.A. 1986 although the Act also states that some of these powers may only be exercised with the permission of the creditors' committee or of the court. In exercising any of these powers the trustee must be aware of his overriding function and duty set out in section 305 which is to get in, realise and distribute the bankrupt's estate in accordance with the provisions of the Act and the Rules. It will be recalled that in the exercise of that function the trustee is entitled to use his own discretion.

4.57 The trustee's powers are considered below under three separate headings: those powers which may be exercised by the trustee without sanction either of the court or the creditors' committee; those powers which may be exercised with the sanction of either the court or the committee; and finally those powers which may only be exercised with the sanction of the court.

(a) Powers exercisable without sanction

(i) The trustee may apply to the court for directions in relation to any particular matter arising under the bankruptcy (s.303(2)). It has been held that applications for directions are equivalent to actions at law and a trustee who makes an unsuccessful application may be ordered to pay costs. Such costs are usually recoupable out of the estate but the trustee must ensure that the estate is sufficient and the action is bona fide. (See *ex p. Angerstein* (1874) L.R. 9 Ch. 479; *Pitts v. La Fontaine* (1880) 6 App.Cas. 482.) **4.58**

Prescribed forms of application will be found in I.R., forms 7.1 and 7.2: see Appendix I, Forms L and M. **4.59**

(ii) The trustee may sell any part of the bankrupt's property or estate, including the goodwill and book debts of any business (s.314 and Sched. 5). If he sells to an associate of the bankrupt he must notify the committee of this (s.314(6)). **4.60**

(iii) He may give receipts for money received by him effective to discharge the paying party (Sched. 5). **4.61**

(iv) He may prove, rank, claim and draw a dividend in respect of debts due to the bankrupt (Sched. 5). **4.62**

(v) He may exercise powers in relation to any property vested in him (Sched. 5). **4.63**

(vi) He may deal with entailed property as the bankrupt might himself have dealt (Sched. 5). **4.64**

(vii) He has all the powers of a receiver appointed by the High Court in relation to and for the purpose of acquiring or retaining the bankrupt's estate (s.311(2)). **4.65**

(viii) He may transfer any part of the bankrupt's estate consisting of stocks or shares in a company as a bankrupt might have done (s.311(3)). **4.66**

(ix) Where goods forming part of the estate have been pledged, pawned or otherwise made subject to a security, he may serve a notice, unless the O.R. has already served one, under section 285(5) giving him the same rights as the O.R. to inspect goods and to exercise the bankrupt's right of redemption (s.311(5) and also see Chap. 2). **4.67**

(x) He may demand delivery up by the bankrupt, the O.R., any former trustee or a supervisor of a voluntary arrangement of any books, papers or records of the bankrupt (s.312). Failure to deliver up such books, etc., to the trustee without reasonable cause may render the holder liable in contempt of court. **4.68**

(xi) He may demand of the holder any books, papers or other records of a bankrupt and, to this end, liens will be unenforceable unless the lien is over a document of title which is held as such (s.349). **4.69**

(xii) He may inspect the Land Registry records. **4.70**

(xiii) He may require of certain public utilities (electricity, gas, water and telephone) that they continue to supply him with the service without having to meet arrears as a precondition, although he may be required to guarantee future supplies personally (s.372). This section assists trustees who wish to continue running the bankrupt's business. **4.71**

(xiv) He may take part in the bankrupt's public examination (see Chap. 3, paras 3.39–3.54). **4.72**

(xv) He may repay any fees paid by an apprentice or articled clerk of the bankrupt where the period of apprenticeship, etc., has not expired **4.73** and he may also transfer the apprenticeship, etc., to a third party (s.348).

4.74 (xvi) He may at any time summon a general meeting of creditors (s.314(7) and I.R. 6.81).

4.75 (xvii) He may determine when and where meetings of the creditors' committee are held (I.R. 6.153).

4.76 (xviii) For the purpose of the exercise of his other powers he is empowered by section 314 and Schedule 5, Pt III to hold property of every description, make contracts, sue and be sued, enter into engagements binding on himself and in respect of the estate on his successors in office, employ agents and execute any power of attorney, deed or other instrument and generally to do any other act which is necessary or expedient for the purpose of or in connection with the exercise of his powers.

4.77 (xix) He may disclaim onerous property (s.315); this power is dealt with in detail in Chapter 7.

4.78 (xx) He may employ a solicitor subject only to informing the creditors' committee (s.314(6)).

(b) Powers exercisable with sanction either of the court or the creditors' committee

4.79 (i) He may carry on any business of the bankrupt provided it is necessary for the beneficial winding up and that it does not contravene any requirement imposed by or under any enactment (s.314 and Sched. 5, Pt I).

4.80 If the trustee does decide to carry on the bankrupt's business, he must take care to keep detailed accounts and, of crucial importance, not to become personally responsible in respect of any employees' contracts or for other debts. Generally speaking, where a contract of employment continues, the further liabilities thereunder will not fall personally on the trustee even where he carries on the bankrupt's business. However, a trustee may be liable if he enters into a *new* contract of employment or adopts an existing one. In view of the difficulties which were revealed in corporate insolvencies by the *Paramount* decision (*Re Paramount Airways Limited (No 3), Powdrill v. Watson* [1994] B.C.C. 172), this is an area in which trustees must exercise special care. If the trustee carries on the bankrupt's business, then he may with the approval of the committee or of the court, appoint the bankrupt himself to do this (s.314(2)).

4.81 By I.R. 6.147 if the trustee enters into any transaction with an associate, the court may, on the application of any interested person, set the transaction aside and order the trustee to compensate the estate for any loss suffered as a consequence. However, this does not apply if the transaction was entered into with the prior consent of the court or it is shown to the court's satisfaction that the transaction was for value, and that it was entered into by the trustee without knowing, or having any reason to suppose, that the person concerned was an associate.

Legal proceedings relating to property comprised in the bankrupt's estate

4.82 (ii) He may bring, institute or defend any action or legal proceedings relating to property comprised in the bankrupt's estate (Sched. 5, Pt I). It will be recalled that the trustee does not need the permission of the creditors' committee to employ a solicitor provided he informs the committee of this. However, the requirement that sanction is needed to bring, institute or defend any action in Schedule 5, Pt I seems to contradict Schedule 5, Pt III headed "Ancillary Powers" which allows the trustee to sue or be sued in his official name as an ancillary power to any of his other powers. It must be presumed, therefore, that the power to bring or defend proceedings needs sanction unless that power is in some way ancillary to the exercise of another power granted to the trustee under the Act and itself exercisable without sanction. Reference should also be made to guidance notes published by the D.T.I.

These notes were published in the form of one of the D.T.I.'s "Dear I.P." letters in 1991. This made it clear that the granting of a sanction to commence proceedings was not a "rubber-stamping" process and, amongst other things, the D.T.I. would look at how proceedings were funded. At the time, and this was pointed out, contingent fee arrangements were unlawful and unenforceable (see below). The note went on to state specifically:

> ". . . therefore when the Official Receiver or the Secretary of State is asked to sanction proceedings where payment from the relevant insolvency estate would depend on a successful outcome, it will be necessary to demonstrate that the funding arrangements also provide for some certain responsibility for the payment of the retained solicitors costs in the event of the case being lost."

Matters have, however changed in this respect because trustees in bankruptcy may now be able to take advantage of conditional fee arrangements which came into force on July 4, 1995 pursuant to the Court & Legal Services Act 1990, s.58 and two statutory instruments, the Conditional Fee Agreements Order 1995 (S.I. 1995 No. 1674) and the Conditional Fee Agreements Regulations 1995 (S.I. 1995 No. 1675).

These orders allow for contingency fee agreements to be made in respect of litigation conducted by certain insolvency practitioners including trustees. In effect, although they do not provide for a solicitor to take any percentage of the proceeds of litigation, they do provide for "no win, no fee" arrangements. However, a trustee will still be responsible, unless there are some special arrangements, for the payment of disbursements such as counsel's fees or those of experts. Moreover a trustee will have to concern himself with the possibility that he may lose the case. In that event there may be an order for costs against him (see para. 4.83) and he will need to think very carefully about putting at risk the assets in the estate and, more significantly, his own assets. The trustee may therefore need to consider whether to insure himself against the possibility of losing and some brokers specialising in the insolvency field have arranged such policies with underwriters. Ultimately it means that trustees will have to be selective as regards litigation embarked upon and should not deal with those cases which are purely speculative in the hope that some assets may be recovered for the estate.

The trustee may, as an alternative, try to seek a fighting fund from major creditors which, if possible, should be sufficient to cover the trustee in the event of his being unsuccessful.

4.83 It appears that a trustee who litigates unsuccessfully may be personally liable (*Re London Metallurgical Co.* [1895] 1 Ch. 758) although he may be authorised to recover those costs out of the estate. The trustee who retains a solicitor without sanction may be personally liable to pay that solicitor's costs but sanction can be granted to the trustee retrospectively if the interests of justice demand this (*Re A Debtor (No. 26A of 1975)* [1985] 1 W.L.R. 6).

4.84 In a High Court action, if the sole plaintiff becomes bankrupt and the right of action is one which passes to the trustee, the action does not abate (R.S.C., Ord. 15, r. 7) but the right of action may pass to the trustee only and only he may decide whether or not to continue—presumably with the sanction of the committee or the court. The question of whether a right of action will continue is complex but, in general, causes of action do vest in the trustee except matters relating to, say, personal injuries or actions of a strictly personal nature. Further reference may be made if necessary to the notes to R.S.C., Ord. 15 (set out in Volume 1 to the *Supreme Court Practice (The White Book)*).

4.85 In the County Court the position is governed by section 49 of the County Courts Act 1984 which states that the bankruptcy of the plaintiff in any action which the trustee might maintain for the benefit of the creditors shall not cause the action to abate if, within such reasonable time as the court orders, the trustee elects to continue the action and to give security for the costs. By section 49(2) the hearing may be adjourned until such an election is made. Where the trustee does not elect to continue the action and to give the appropriate security within the time limited by the order, the defendant may avail himself of the bankruptcy as a defence to the action (*ibid.* s.49(3)).

4.86 If the sole defendant becomes bankrupt, the plaintiff cannot force the trustee to become a party. Indeed the action will probably be stayed under section 285, but a stay is not automatic (*Realisations Industrielles v. Loesher* [1957] 1 W.L.R. 1026). The proper course is for the plaintiff to prove in the bankruptcy (*Barter v. Dubeux* (1881) 7 Q.B.D. 413) but if there is a co-defendant who is solvent, the plaintiff can proceed against that co-defendant without joining the trustee provided there is a joint and several claim against them (*Lloyd v. Dimmack* (1877) 7 Ch.D. 398), and the court may impose conditions on a plaintiff who is granted leave to proceed against a bankrupt (*Polly Peck International plc v. Nadir* [1992] B.C.L.C. 746).

4.87 A trustee may be faced with a demand for security for costs. In the County Court the position is governed by section 49 above, which refers to a trustee *continuing* a pending action. Normally, however, security for costs cannot be demanded either in the High Court or the County Court merely because the plaintiff is the trustee, so that a trustee who brings an action for the benefit of the estate would not normally be ordered to give security (see R.S.C., Ord. 23 and the notes thereunder). In this there is a difference between the position of a trustee and the position of a liquidator since the fact that a company is in liquidation is prima facie evidence that it is unable to pay the costs within section 726 of C.A. 1985.

4.88 (iii) He may accept as consideration for the sale of property a sum payable at a future time, but subject to such stipulations as the court or committee think fit (Sched. 5).

4.89 (iv) He may mortgage or pledge any part of the estate to raise money for the payment of debts (Sched. 5).

4.90 (v) He may make payments or incur liabilities to secure any rights, options or powers which belonged to the bankrupt provided it is for the benefit of the creditors (Sched. 5).

(vi) He may refer to arbitration or compromise, on such terms as may be agreed, any debts, claims or liabilities subsisting or supposed to subsist between the bankrupt and any possible debtor of the bankrupt (Sched. 5). **4.91**

(vii) He may compromise claims with the creditors or those persons claiming to be creditors in respect of bankruptcy debts (Sched. 5). **4.92**

(viii) He may compromise or make such arrangements that seem expedient to deal with any claim which might be made by or against the trustee (Sched. 5). **4.93**

(ix) He may appoint the bankrupt to superintend the management of his estate or any part of it, to carry on his business (if any) for the benefit of his creditors, or in any other respect to assist in the administering of the estate in such manner and on such terms as the trustee may direct (s.314(2)). **4.94**

Permission

Any permission given for the above purposes must not be a general permission, but must relate to a particular proposed exercise of the power in question. However, a person dealing with the trustee in good faith and for value is not to be concerned to inquire whether any permission required has been given (s.314(3)). **4.95**

Where the trustee has done anything without the required permission, the court or the creditors' committee may, for the purpose of enabling him to meet his expenses out of the estate, ratify his acts, but the committee must not do so unless it is satisfied that he has acted in the case of urgency and has sought ratification without delay (s.314(4)). **4.96**

There is a further power which is specified to be exercised only with the permission of the committee. By section 326(1) the trustee may with its permission divide in its existing form among the bankrupt's creditors, according to its estimated value, any property which cannot be readily or advantageously sold. **4.97**

(c) Powers exercisable with the sanction of the court

(i) The trustee has wide powers to apply to the court to examine the bankrupt, his spouse or other persons on oath as part of his inquiries into the bankrupt's dealings and property (ss.366, 367). This is considered in detail in Chapter 9. **4.98**

(ii) He may apply to the court to seize property, books or records relating to the bankrupt's affairs (s.365). This is considered in greater detail in Chapters 7 and 10. **4.99**

(iii) For the purpose of a public examination or proceedings under section 366 above, the trustee may apply to the court for an order that an Inland Revenue official produce to the court any returns or accounts submitted by the bankrupt (whether before or after the commencement of the bankruptcy) and also assessments and correspondence (s.369). An order by the court will only be made to the Inland Revenue official who is dealing or has dealt with the bankrupt's affairs. **4.100**

(iv) He may apply to the court to appoint any person to be a special manager of the bankrupt's estate or the business of an undischarged bankrupt. The court will fix the extent of any special manager's powers and he may also be required to give security (s.370). **4.101**

(v) The trustee may ask the court to redirect mail addressed to the bankrupt (s.371). **4.102**

4.103 It should be mentioned that the above powers will also apply where the O.R. is a trustee and that the powers relating to inquiry into the bankrupt's dealings and property (s.366) apply where an interim receiver has been appointed.

4.104 (vi) He may apply to the court for an income payments order under section 310. This is considered in further detail in Chapter 7.

(d) Control by the court

4.105 The Act makes it clear that every bankruptcy shall be under the general control of the court, which shall have full power to decide questions of priorities and all other questions, whether of law or fact, arising in any bankruptcy (s.363(1)). The powers of the court to control the trustee are extremely wide, including the power to fix the trustee's remuneration as happened in *Re Colgate* (1986) 2 W.L.R. 137 where, in default of the creditors' meeting fixing the remuneration, the court took on this function.

4.106 Section 363 further states that an undischarged bankrupt or a discharged bankrupt whose estate is still being administered by a trustee shall do all such things as he may be directed to do by the court for the purpose of his bankruptcy or, as the case may be, the administration of his estate (s.363(2)). Either the trustee or the O.R. is at any time empowered to apply to the court for a direction against the bankrupt under section 363(2) and it is a contempt of court for any person without reasonable excuse to fail to comply with any obligation imposed on him.

Control over the trustee

4.107 The question of control over the trustee is more complex. Sections 301–304 are headed "Control of trustee" and deal with control of the trustee either by the court or the creditors' committee. The creditors' committee will be dealt with below, but ultimately control resides with the court.

4.108 By section 303(1), if a bankrupt or any of his creditors or any other person is dissatisfied by any act, omission or decision of a trustee of the bankrupt's estate, he may apply to the court; and on such an application the court may confirm, reverse or modify any act or decision of the trustee, may give him directions or may make such other order as it thinks fit. It will also be recalled that the trustee may himself apply to the court for directions. This aspect of control by the court over the trustee's actions restates what was formerly contained in B.A. 1914, s.80 but there is a change. Section 80 referred to the bankrupt or any of his creditors being "aggrieved" and it was extremely difficult in practice for the trustee's actions to be impeached unless he was shown to be acting entirely unreasonably (*ex p. Lloyd* [1882] 47 L.T. 64). It was not surprising that the courts were extremely reluctant to interfere with the exercise of the trustee's discretion—particularly at the behest of the bankrupt (see, *e.g. Re A Debtor (No. 400 of 1940)* [1949] Ch. 236). The situation is analogous to the reluctance of the courts to interfere with the exercise by liquidators of their wide powers under I.A. 1986 (*cf. Leon v. York-O-Matic Ltd.* [1966] 1 W.L.R. 1450).

4.109 The reason for the court's reluctance to interfere with the trustee's discretion had been stated by Harman J. in *Re A Debtor* [1949] Ch. 236 as follows:

> ". . . they cannot I think (in the absence of fraud) justify interference in the day to day administration of the estate, nor entitle the bankrupt to question the exercise by the Trustee in good faith of his discretion, not to hold him accountable for an error of judgment. Administration in bankruptcy would be impossible if the Trustee must answer at every step to the bankrupt for the exercise of his powers and discretion in the

management of a realisation of the property." (At 241, and quoted with approval in *Re Hans Place Limited* [1992] B.C.C. 737).

It is possible that the court may, of course, have a somewhat more sympathetic approach to an application by a creditor but the limits of control are stated and the court will not interfere with what is essentially the trustee's discretion unless he has been shown to be unreasonable, fraudulent or perhaps, grossly negligent.

4.110 The trustee is also bound by what is commonly referred to as "the rule in *ex parte James*" (*Re Condon, ex p. James* (1874) L.R. 9 Ch.App. 609) which requires the trustee, as an officer of the court, to act with equity and the utmost fairness.

Professor Gregory in his book, *Bankruptcy of Individuals* (2nd ed.), put it in this way:

> ". . . the trustee must keep within his powers, and must not abuse them, must act carefully and must not put himself in a position where interest and duty conflict without appropriate consent (which consent he should, as an officer of the court, obtain from the court)". (At para. 6.01.)

The rule in *ex parte James* has generally required the trustee to act with equity and utmost fairness and in many cases not to stand upon his strict legal rights. It is not intended to discuss the full circumstances in which the rule may apply, but it covers circumstances where there has been some form of unjust enrichment of the estate (see *Re Clark (a Bankrupt)* [1975] 1 W.L.R. 559). The modern statement of the rule is as stated by Mr Justice Walton in *Re Clark* where he sets out four conditions which have to be satisfied in order to make the rule in *ex parte James* available against a trustee:

(i) ". . . there must be some form of enrichment of the assets of the bankrupt by the person seeking to have the rule applied;
(ii) . . . except in the most unusual cases the claimant must not be in a position to submit an ordinary proof of debt;
(iii) . . . if in all the circumstances of the case, an honest man who will be personally affected by the result would nevertheless be bound to admit: "It's not fair that I should keep the money; my claim has no merits", then the rule applies so as to nullify the claim which he would otherwise have;
(iv) . . . the rule . . . applies only to the extent necessary to nullify the enrichment of the estate; it by no means necessarily restores the claimant to the status *quo ante*".

One interesting, modern example, although it must be admitted that this has not yet been tested, might be the situation with regard to the bankrupt's pension. This is dealt with in some detail in Chapter 7 below. Broadly speaking since the case of *Re Ivan Landau (a Bankrupt)* [1997] B.P.I.R. 229 it has been established that the trustee is entitled to take *the entirety* of the bankrupt's pension including any annuity. This could leave a bankrupt pensioner in a much worse position than, a bankrupt who is still receiving a salary because the latter would only be subject to an income payments order which would leave him sufficient for his normal domestic needs. Although *Re Landau* is of relatively new application, the writers know of some trustees who have already decided to voluntarily apply the rule in *ex parte James* so as not to take the entirety of the pension.

(e) Misfeasance, etc., by trustee

4.111 By section 304, where the court is satisfied:

(i) that the trustee of the estate has misapplied or retained, or become accountable for, any money or other property comprised in the estate; or

(ii) that the estate has suffered any loss in consequence of any misfeasance or breach of fiduciary or other duty by a trustee in the carrying out of his functions,

the court may order the trustee, for the benefit of the estate, to repay, restore or account for any money or other property (together with interest) or to pay such sum by way of compensation in respect of the misfeasance or breach of fiduciary or other duty as the court thinks just.

4.112 An application under section 304 may be made by the O.R., the D.T.I., a creditor (whether or not there is likely to be a surplus) or the bankrupt himself, but the leave of the court is required for the making of an application if it is to be made by the bankrupt or if it is to be made after the trustee has had his release under section 299 (s.304(2)).

Statutory immunity

4.113 A trustee is given statutory immunity by section 304(3) where he seizes or disposes of any property which is not comprised in the bankrupt's estate and, at the time of the seizure or disposal, he believed on reasonable grounds that he was entitled (whether in pursuance of a court order or otherwise) to seize or dispose of that property. He will not be liable to any person in respect of loss or damage resulting from the seizure or disposal except in so far as that loss or damage is caused by his negligence and he has a lien on the property or the proceeds of its sale for such of the expenses of the bankruptcy as were incurred in connection with the seizure or disposal (*cf.* the similar immunity given to the O.R.: see Chap. 3).

6. REMUNERATION AND ACCOUNTS

(a) Trustee's remuneration

4.114 As it is the hope of reward that sweetens labour, this subject must be dear to every insolvency practitioner's heart.

4.115 The trustee is entitled to no remuneration until it is fixed by one of the following methods:

(i) by resolution of the creditors' committee;
(ii) by resolution of the creditors;
(iii) by reference to the O.R.'s scale;
(iv) by the court.

Fixing of remuneration

4.116 The requirements are clearly set out in I.R. 6.138–6.142. The trustee shall apply to the committee, if there is one, to fix his remuneration which shall be fixed as a percentage of the value of the assets realised or distributed or a combination of the two or, in the alternative, by reference to the time properly given by the trustee and his staff in attending to matters arising in the bankruptcy.

4.117 In fixing the remuneration, the committee shall take into account the complexity of the case, any exceptional responsibility connected with the administration, the effectiveness with which the trustee has carried out his duties and the value of the assets with which the trustee has had to deal.

4.118 If there is no creditors' committee, the remuneration shall be fixed by a meeting of the creditors applying the same criteria.

General regulations

4.119 If not fixed as above, the remuneration shall be on the scale laid down for the O.R. by general regulations. The scale is set out in I.Reg. 33 and Schedule 2, Table 1 as follows:

On realisations:
20 per cent. of first £5,000
15 per cent. of next £5,000
10 per cent. of next £90,000
5 per cent. of any sums exceeding £100,000
On distributions to creditors: one-half of the above scale.

4.120 If the trustee is dissatisfied with the rate of remuneration approved by the creditors' committee, he may request that it be increased by a resolution of the creditors.

Application to the court

4.121 The trustee may apply to the court to fix his remuneration if he is dissatisfied with the amount approved by the creditors' committee or by resolution of creditors. He should give at least 14 days' notice of his application to the members of the committee, who may nominate a representative to be heard on the application. If there is no creditors' committee, the trustee's notice shall be sent to such one or more of the bankrupt's creditors as the court may direct. Those creditors may nominate one or more of their number to appear or be represented. The court has discretion to order the costs of the application, including the costs of any committee member or creditor appearing on it, to be paid out of the estate.

4.122 A creditor who feels that the rate of remuneration is excessive may, with the concurrence of at least 25 per cent in value of the creditors (including himself), apply to the court for an order that the remuneration be reduced, on the grounds that it is, in all the circumstances, excessive. The court may, if it thinks that no sufficient cause is shown for the application, dismiss it; but it shall not do so unless the applicant has had an opportunity to attend the court for an *ex parte* hearing, of which he has been given at least seven days' notice.

4.123 If the application is not so dismissed, the court shall fix a venue for it to be heard. The applicant, at least 14 days before the hearing, shall send to the trustee a notice stating the venue, accompanied by a copy of the application and any evidence he intends to produce in support. If the court considers the application to be well founded, it shall make an order fixing the remuneration at a reduced amount or rate.

4.124 Unless the court orders otherwise, the costs of the application shall be paid by the applicant and do not fall on the estate.

4.125 Where the trustee sells assets on behalf of a secured creditor, he is entitled to take remuneration out of the proceeds at a sum equivalent to that chargeable in corresponding circumstances by the O.R. under general regulations.

Joint trustees

4.126 Although joint trustees are seldom appointed, the Rules provide that in such circumstances they shall agree between themselves how the remuneration shall be apportioned, but any dispute between them may be referred to the court for settlement by order, or to the creditors' committee, or a meeting of creditors for settlement by resolution.

4.127 If the trustee is himself a solicitor, and he employs his own firm or a partner therein to act on behalf of the estate, no profit costs shall be paid except with the authority of the committee, the creditors or the court.

4.128 Two important principles were established in *Re A Debtor (No. 29 of 1986)* (unreported). The creditors passed a resolution under which the trustee's remuneration was to be calculated on the O.R.'s scale which amounted to a fee of £3,086.99. The debtor eventually had her bankruptcy annulled on the grounds that all debts and expenses had been paid following the sale of her house by one of the mortgagees at a higher price than the charges thereon, giving a surplus sufficient for the trustee to pay all unsecured creditors in full. She argued that the surplus from the sale of the house was not a realisation and that the trustee had done nothing but receive the surplus from the mortgagee. The Court of Appeal, reversing the decision of the judge at first instance, ruled that the word "realised" meant "got in or reduced into cash" and the trustee was entitled to remuneration calculated on the money he had received from the mortgagee. The Court commented that "the trustee must take the rough with the smooth". He might get a large fee for doing little and on other occasions a very small fee for doing a great deal.

(b) Accounts

4.129 I.A. 1986, Sched. 9, para. 21 indicates that the Rules may provide for the manner in which the trustee handles moneys and fees, etc. Section 403 gives general details as to the insolvency services account and full particulars are contained in I.Reg.

Insolvency services account

4.130 A trustee in bankruptcy is not usually authorised to operate a normal bank account and must pay all moneys received, within 14 days, or forthwith if more than £5,000, into the insolvency services account which is operated at the Bank of England by the Central Accounting Unit (C.A.U.), a part of the Insolvency Service (I.Reg. 5). When the trustee wishes to have a cheque drawn for any outgoings or disbursements he must submit a requisition to the C.A.U. As the trustee then has to wait for the cheque to be issued, the operation of such a bank account is a somewhat outmoded procedure and it is unfortunate that it has survived insolvency law reform. Furthermore a charge is made by the C.A.U. in respect of lodgments and drawings and the trustee (unlike a liquidator under I.Reg. 9) is not entitled to invest surplus moneys or receive any interest on moneys retained in the account. This seems to be a little harsh on creditors if there is some necessary delay in making a distribution or on the debtor himself if there is an eventual surplus. The principle is enshrined in I.A. 1986, s.403 that surplus moneys in the insolvency services account may be utilised by the Treasury. The original justification for this iniquitous system, when it was introduced a century ago, was that the income thereby flowing to the Treasury would compensate for the costs of the O.R.'s service. It is unfortunate that, in the course of law reform, the opportunity has not been taken for devising a simpler system of financing the O.R.'s service and at the same time removing a rather cumbersome administrative procedure that directly deprives creditors and bankrupts of interest on their own moneys.

4.131 A practitioner's guide to the C.A.U. was issued by I.S. in January 1996 detailing, *inter alia*, the table of fees applicable to bankruptcy accounts.

Account of receipts and payments

4.132 Quite properly the trustee is required to keep a detailed account of his receipts and payments. I.Reg. 24 provides that a trustee shall keep separate financial records in respect of each bankrupt and such other financial records as are required to explain the receipts and payments entered in the records.

Any creditor or the bankrupt may, in accordance with I.Reg. 25, request from the trustee a statement of his receipts and payments. Within fourteen days the trustee must then submit a receipts and payments account for the period of one year ending on the most recent anniversary of his becoming trustee which preceded the request.

The Secretary of State has power under I.Reg. 28 to require a trustee to send to the Secretary of State an account of his receipts and payments as trustee of the bankrupt covering such period as the Secretary of State may direct and such account shall, if so required, be certified by the trustee. The account should be accompanied by a summary of the statement of affairs, if one has been submitted, showing the amounts of assets realised and explaining the reasons for any non-realisation. Where no statement of affairs has been submitted, the account should be accompanied by a summary of all known assets and their estimated values, showing the amounts actually realised and explaining any non-realisations.

Prior to October 24, 1994, trustees were in all cases required to send an annual account to the Secretary of State, in accordance with Insolvency Regulations 1986 which have been repealed. The logic behind the repeal of this requirement seems to be that the Secretary of State in any event has access to the records of the trustee through the C.A.U.

4.133 The Secretary of State has power to require that the account be audited and to demand from the trustee any vouchers, bank statements or information relating to the account (I.Reg. 28(6)). The Secretary of State may, in accordance with I.Reg. 29, inspect any accounts, books and other records kept by the trustee who if required must produce records for inspection at his own premises and the Secretary of State should be allowed to remove or take copies of any accounts, books or other records kept by the practitioner whether or not they are kept on his premises.

4.134 I.Reg. 25 requires that the trustee shall, on request from the bankrupt or any creditor, send to that person an account of his receipts and payments during the period of one year ending on the most recent anniversary of his becoming trustee, which preceded the request. Such account shall be sent free of charge within 14 days of receipt of the request.

4.135 Within 14 days of vacating office, an account shall be submitted up to that date from the date of the last account.

Local bank account

4.136 In the exceptional circumstance that the trustee continues the business of the bankrupt, he may apply to the D.T.I. for authorisation to open a local bank account, when authority may be given for the use of a specified bank, subject to a limit, instead of the insolvency services account, if there is an administrative advantage to be derived from having such an account (I.Reg. 20). Most practitioners would consider that the use of a local bank account for every bankruptcy would give a tremendous administrative advantage but it is unlikely that such an argument would impress the Secretary of State.

4.137 **4.138** Any surplus over the authorised amount must be paid into the insolvency services account, as must any balance in hand, upon the trustee ceasing to carry on business or vacating office.

4.139 Where the trustee carries on the debtor's business, he should, in accordance with I.Reg. 26, keep a separate and distinct account of all trading including appropriate particulars of local bank account transactions and incorporate into his financial records the total weekly amounts of receipts and payments.

Submission of records to the creditors' committee

4.140 The creditors' committee (see paras 4.165–4.187 below) has authority under I.Reg. 24(3) to require the trustee to submit to it the financial records and, if not satisfied with the contents, may so inform the Secretary of State giving reasons for its dissatisfaction and the Secretary of State may take such action as he thinks fit (I.Reg 24(4)). In any event the Secretary of State may decide to exercise his powers under I.Reg. 28 (see para. 4.132 above).

4.141 The C.A.U. will send to the trustee a statement when a new estate account is opened and at six monthly intervals. They will also issue trustees with additional statements within five days of a request so to do. Practitioners are recommended to reconcile these statements regularly.

4.142 The accounting procedure for paying dividends is explained in Chapter 8 and the final account is considered in Chapter 12.

4.143 The accounting requirements for a supervisor under a voluntary arrangement are set out in I.R. 5.26–5.27 and are explained in Chapter 5.

4.144 Those financial records which the trustee is required by I.Reg. to maintain must, in accordance with I.Reg. 27, be retained for a period of six years after vacation of office unless delivered to another responsible insolvency practitioner who succeeds him. If the successor is the O.R., the records should only be delivered up if requested.

7. RESIGNATION AND REMOVAL

(a) Resignation

Meeting of creditors

4.145 A trustee is allowed to resign his office by giving notice of his resignation to the court (I.A. 1986, s.298(7)). Before doing so he must call a meeting of creditors for the purpose of receiving his resignation, giving notice of this meeting to the O.R. (I.R. 6.126).

4.146 The general rule is that the trustee may only proceed with his resignation on the grounds of ill-health or because he intends ceasing to be in practice as an insolvency practitioner or because there is some conflict of interest or change of personal circumstances which precludes or makes it impracticable for him to discharge further his duties as trustee (I.R. 6.126(3)(b)).

4.147 If, however, there are two or more persons acting as trustees jointly, any one of them may resign on the grounds that in his opinion and that of the others it is no longer expedient that there should continue to be the present number of joint trustees (I.R. 6.126).

4.148 At the creditors' meeting called to receive the trustee's resignation, the creditors may agree to accept the resignation and may also move resolutions, *inter alia*, refusing the trustee his release or appointing a new trustee in his place (I.R. 6.127).

4.149 If his resignation is accepted notice must be given forthwith to the court and to the O.R. The question of release of the trustee is dealt with in Chapter 12.

4.150 If the creditors refuse to accept the trustee's resignation the court may, on the trustee's application, give him leave to resign and may at the same time give him his release (I.R. 6.128). See Appendix I, Form O.

(b) Removal of trustee

4.151 The power to remove a trustee depends to a great extent on who was responsible for his appointment. It will be recalled that appointments of trustees may be made by the creditors, by the court or by the D.T.I.

General rule

4.152 The general rule, expressed in I.A. 1986, s.298(1), is that a trustee in bankruptcy may only be removed by an order of the court or by a general meeting of creditors summoned specially for that purpose (unless there is a certificate of summary administration in force).

4.153 There are, however, restrictions on the removal of a trustee contained within section 298. If the trustee is the O.R. he cannot be removed from office where a certificate of summary administration is in force. Further, where the O.R. is trustee by virtue of section 293 (this occurs where he decides not to summon a meeting of creditors to appoint a trustee) or by virtue of section 295(4) (where the meeting of creditors has failed to appoint a trustee), or where a trustee is appointed by the D.T.I. or by the court, a general meeting of creditors for removal shall only be called if the trustee thinks fit, or the court so directs, or the meeting is requested by not less than one-quarter in value of the creditors, including the creditor who has made the request (s.298(4)).

4.154 **Meeting of creditors to remove the trustee**—The conduct of these meetings is governed by I.R. 6.129.

4.155 The notice convening the meeting must indicate that the purpose, or one of the purposes, of the meeting is the removal of the trustee and a copy of the notice must be sent to the O.R.

4.156 If it has been resolved to remove the trustee, the chairman of the meeting must send the O.R. a certificate to that effect and he must also send the O.R. a certificate of the appointment of any new trustee. The certificate of removal will be filed at court (I.R. 6.131).

4.157 The court has general power under I.R. 6.130 to regulate any meeting called for the purpose of removing a trustee and it may on the application of any creditor give directions regarding the summoning and holding of such meeting.

4.158 **Removal by the court**—If an application is made to the court for removal of the trustee (a form of order is included at App. I, Form O) the court may, if it thinks that no sufficient cause is shown for the application, dismiss it; but it should not do so unless the applicant has had the opportunity of attending court for an *ex parte* hearing, of which he has been given at least seven days' notice. If the application is not then dismissed the court must fix a venue for the hearing (I.R. 6.132). The applicant must notify the trustee and the O.R. of the venue and they must receive a copy of the application and of any evidence filed.

The High Court has recently had to consider the issue of removal of office holders (including trustees in bankruptcy and supervisors of voluntary arrangements) in a number of cases. In *Re Sankey Furniture Limited, ex p. Harding v. Calorifique Limited, ex p. Betts* [1995] 2 B.C.L.C. 594, Chadwick J. ruled on the court's powers of removal and replacement of office holders who held appointments as liquidators, trustees and supervisors. Mr Betts held a number of appointments of different types and had retired from his practice on grounds of ill-health. He wished Mr Harding (who had become a partner in his former firm, moving from another firm) to take over his appointments. Mr Betts was retiring from his firm on grounds of ill-health. For his part Mr Harding wished his own former partners to take over the appointments which he held at the firm he was leaving.

Chadwick J. found that the court's powers of removal were in principle unrestricted and that there had to be a "cause" for removal—not necessarily an "adverse cause". Removal could be justified even if there was no criticism to be made of the practitioner whose removal was sought, as in this case, on his own application.

The learned judge also accepted that it would be most inconvenient and also very expensive for Mr Betts and Mr Harding to call numerous creditors' meetings to obtain consent for the proposed transfers and that it would be in the interests of the creditors to carry on the work in each case with minimum inconvenience and to preserve continuity of administration. However, in the case of Mr Harding, whose health was not impaired (and nor was there any other cause for his resignation), where he was merely moving to another firm, the judge thought that the creditors could decline to accept his resignation (save in two cases where he was liquidator in a members voluntary liquidation) his request to resign was refused—a creditors' meeting would have to be held. As the headnote to the case puts it:

> "In such a situation, it could not be assumed that if the creditors refused to accept his resignation the court would nevertheless give him leave to resign. This was a situation where the creditors ought to be consulted. To hold otherwise would be to accept that the identity of the person who had been appointed as an office holder was a matter of no importance to them and that only the firm was of importance."

An application may also be made by creditors if they have lost confidence in the trustee or if it is alleged that he has failed to discharge his duties in a proper manner (see, *e.g.*, *Re Keypak Homecare Limited* [1987] B.C.L.C. 409) which sets out some general principles relating to the removal of office-holders.

4.159 It is provided that, subject to any contrary order, the costs of an application to remove a trustee will not fall on the estate (I.R. 6.132).

4.160 **Removal by the D.T.I.**—By I.A. 1986, s.298(5) a trustee who has been appointed by the D.T.I. may always be removed by order of the D.T.I.

4.161 Before the D.T.I. decides to remove the trustee, however, it must notify the trustee and the O.R. of the decision and the grounds for it and the trustee may within a specified period make representations against his removal. Notice of the decision of the D.T.I. must be given to the O.R. and filed at court (I.R. 6.133).

(c) Vacation of office

4.162 The trustee (not being the O.R.) must vacate office if he ceases to be a qualified insolvency practitioner (s.298(6)).

4.163 The trustee vacating office must give notice to the O.R. and the latter will in turn file a copy with the court. The rule as to release (I.R. 6.135—see below) applies in this case as it would in respect of a trustee removed by the court (I.R. 6.144).

4.164 The trustee must vacate office on giving notice to the court that a final meeting has been held under section 331 and of the decision (if any) of that meeting (s.298(8)). Release after a final meeting is considered in Chapter 12.

4.165 The trustee must vacate office if the bankruptcy order is annulled under section 282 (see s.298(9) and Chap. 10).

4.166 Where the trustee intends to vacate office, whether by resignation or otherwise, and there remain in the estate any unrealised assets, he must give notice of his intention to the O.R., informing him of the nature, value and whereabouts of those assets (I.R. 6.145).

4.167 On vacating office a trustee has certain duties: he must forthwith deliver up to his successor the assets of the estate (after deducting any expenses properly incurred and distributions made) and he must also deliver up all records of the bankruptcy, proofs and the bankrupt's own books and records and other papers (I.R. 6.146).

(d) Vacancy

Application of I.A. 1986, s.300

4.168 It is clear from the above provisions that there will be circumstances in which a vacancy occurs in the office of trustee. Where there is such a vacancy, for whatever reason, section 300 applies and until the vacancy is filled the O.R. shall be the trustee. The O.R. may summon a general meeting of the creditors for the purpose of filling the vacancy and he must summon such a meeting if required to do so by a creditor with the concurrence of not less than one-tenth in value of the creditors, including the creditor making the request (s.300(3) and 314(7)).

4.169 Within 28 days of becoming aware of the vacancy, the O.R., if he has not convened such a meeting of creditors, must refer matters to the D.T.I. to see whether they wish to fill the vacancy, but it is not obligatory for them to do so. Unless a meeting is requisitioned by a creditor, it is possible that the vacancy will not be filled and in that case the O.R. will continue in office.

4.170 Where a certificate of a summary administration is in force, the O.R. may refer the need to fill any vacancy to the court (s.300(5)). However, such cases are normally left with the O.R.

4.171 Release of the trustee is dealt with in Chapter 12.

8. CREDITORS' COMMITTEE

4.172 Insolvency administration being a democratic process, the creditors have the power under I.A. 1986, s.301 to appoint a committee either at the first meeting convened pursuant to section 293 or at a subsequent meeting convened by the trustee.

4.173 The establishment of a committee assists the trustee not only in obtaining the formal sanctions required by Schedule 5 to the Act (see paras 4.79–4.97 above) but also as a means of ascertaining creditors' wishes and frequently obtaining information as to the bankrupt's affairs, which may not have been previously disclosed.

4.174 A committee may only be appointed if a trustee other than the O.R. is appointed to act.

(a) Powers exercisable by the trustee with the sanction of the committee

4.175 In accordance with Schedule 5 to the Act, the following powers are exercisable by the trustee only with the sanction of the committee or, if there is no committee, the D.T.I.:

- (i) power to carry on the business of the bankrupt for its beneficial winding-up;
- (ii) power to bring, institute or defend legal actions;
- (iii) power to sell assets for a future consideration;
- (iv) power to mortgage or pledge property;
- (v) power to incur liabilities with a view to obtaining, for the benefit of creditors, any property which is subject to a right, option or power;
- (vi) power to refer to arbitration, or compromise, debts, claims or liabilities.

(b) Formation and conduct

4.176 Detailed regulations for the formation and conduct of the committee are set out in I.R. 6.150–6.166.

4.177 The committee shall consist of between three and five creditors, who have lodged proofs of debt, which have not been disallowed for voting or dividend purposes. A body corporate may be a member of the committee and act by an authorised representative.

4.178 Before the committee can be effective, a certificate of its constitution must be issued by the chairman of the meeting at which it was appointed. The chairman shall not issue such a certificate before at least three of the persons elected to be members have agreed to act. As and when any others agree to act, the trustee shall issue an amended certificate. The certificate and any amendment shall be filed with the court, to whom the trustee shall also report any change in membership. If the chairman is not the trustee (perhaps the O.R.), he shall send a copy of the certificate to the trustee and inform him of the names and addresses of the persons elected.

4.179 It is the duty of the trustee to report to the committee such matters as appear to him to be, or the committee has indicated as being, of concern to committee members with respect to the bankruptcy. The trustee need not, however, comply with a request that is frivolous or unreasonable, or if the cost of complying would be excessive, having regard to the relative importance of the information, or if the estate is without sufficient funds to enable him to comply.

4.180 If the committee was appointed more than 28 days after the appointment of the trustee, then the trustee shall report to the committee in summary form as to actions taken since his appointment. Committee members are entitled to have access to the trustee's cash book and records, and to seek explanations of any matters within the committee's responsibility.

(c) Meetings

4.181 The trustee must call the first meeting within three months of the committee's or his own appointment, whichever is the later, and thereafter meetings shall be held on such dates as may be resolved by the committee, or within 21 days of a request from a committee member, or as determined by the trustee. Seven days' notice in writing of the date and place of any meeting shall be given to every committee member, although waiver may be signified at or before the meeting.

4.182 Meetings shall be chaired by the trustee, or a person appointed in writing by him to act as his deputy. In practice such deputy is likely to be a senior member of the trustee's staff, having the conduct of the administration. He must be either a qualified insolvency practitioner or an experienced employee of the trustee.

4.183 A meeting is duly constituted if due notice has been given to all committee members and at least two are present or represented. The committee acts by a majority of its members present or represented, each person having one vote.

4.184 A committee member may be represented by an authorised person. Such representative must hold written authority, which he must produce to the chairman of the meeting if so called upon. A representative may not be a body corporate or a person who has been adjudged bankrupt or compounded with his creditors and no person may represent more than one committee member. In signing any document, the representative must indicate the name of the committee member for whom he acts.

4.185 If a committee member becomes bankrupt, his trustee in bankruptcy replaces him as a committee member.

4.186 A committee member may resign by notice in writing delivered to the trustee. His membership of the committee will automatically cease if he becomes bankrupt or compounds or arranges with his creditors, is absent at three consecutive committee meetings (unless the third meeting resolves not to apply this rule) or he ceases to be, or is found never to have been, a creditor.

4.187 A committee member may also be removed by a resolution at a meeting of creditors of which at least 14 days' notice is given.

Vacancies on the committee may be filled by appointment by the trustee with the consent of the majority of the other committee members, or at a meeting of creditors of which 14 days' notice is given. As mentioned above, such changes must be notified to the court. The vacancy need not be filled provided that the trustee and a majority of the remaining members agree, and the number does not fall below three. **4.188**

(d) Records

At any meeting of the committee, each member (whether present himself or by his representative) has one vote; and a resolution is passed when a majority of the members present or represented have voted in favour of it. Every resolution passed shall be recorded in writing, either separately or as part of the minutes of the meeting. The record shall be signed by the chairman and kept with the records of the bankruptcy (I.R. 6.161). **4.189**

A trustee may seek postal resolutions from the committee by sending to each member or representative a copy of the proposed resolution, set out in such a way that agreement with or dissent from each separate resolution may be indicated by the recipient on the copy so sent. Concurrence in writing is required by a majority of committee members. Any member of the committee may, within seven business days of the date of the trustee sending out a resolution, require that a meeting be summoned to consider the matters raised. In the absence of such a request the resolution is deemed passed upon receipt of the necessary signed concurrences. A copy of every postal resolution, and a note of the concurrence, shall be kept with the bankruptcy records. (I.R. 6.162). **4.190**

Without prejudice to his general duty to report matters of concern to the committee, a trustee shall issue written reports to the creditors' committee as and when the committee shall direct (but not more than once in two months) or, in the absence of such directions, not less than once in every period of six months (I.R. 6.163). **4.191**

Enthusiasm at committee meetings varies considerably from one administration to another, depending upon such factors as the extent of liabilities and the prospects of a distribution. In many instances committee members will not wish to be burdened with a six-monthly report and may well resolve that such reports be issued as and when required or as may be requested by the committee. **4.192**

(e) Expenses

The trustee may defray, out of the estate, reasonable expenses incurred by members of the committee or their representatives in attending meetings or otherwise on committee business (I.R. 6.164). Committee members may not, however, make a profit out of the estate, either directly or through their employees or agents, or purchase assets of the estate without leave of the court (I.R. 6.165). Similar restrictions apply to associates of committee members. **4.193**

Where there is no committee appointed then the functions of the committee shall be vested in the D.T.I. (I.R. 6.166). No committee shall function at any time that the O.R. acts as trustee (I.A. 1986, s.302). **4.194**

(f) Fiduciary duty

Committee members have been held to occupy a fiduciary position *vis-à-vis* the estate of the bankrupt so that they cannot be involved in any dealings where there may be a conflict of interest: *Re Bulmer* [1937] Ch. 499. **4.195**

9. Registration under Financial Services Act

4.196 Most insolvency practitioners are members of firms authorised to conduct investment business under F.S.A. It is not, however, necessary for them to be so authorised in respect of most of the business which they conduct.

4.197 Normally a trustee selling the business and assets of a bankrupt is entitled to advertise such items for sale without authorisation as he is treated as a quasi-principal in the shoes of the bankrupt. This will normally apply even if he is selling shares in companies controlled by the bankrupt. However, if a practitioner wishes to advertise for sale existing shares in an unlisted company, F.S.A., s.57 will apply and no person other than an authorised person may issue such advertisement unless the contents of the advertisement have been approved by an authorised person. There is an exemption for an advertisement made, or information given, on behalf of a company with a view to the acquisition or disposal of shares having at least 75 per cent. of the voting power. Accordingly most advertisements placed by insolvency practitioners are exempt from F.S.A. regulation.

4.198 If a practitioner becomes trustee in respect of an authorised person, separate personal authorisation will not be required as the practitioner is an exempted person under F.S.A., s.45(2) but he will be subject to certain sections of F.S.A. mainly concerning conduct of business rules and to the rules of the appropriate regulatory body. If a trustee continues the investment business of a bankrupt who did not have proper authorisation, then the trustee will have to obtain it. In practice the majority of authorised persons are corporate bodies so that the problem seldom has to be faced by a trustee in bankruptcy.

4.199 In addition to accepting formal appointment, insolvency practitioners frequently give advice to businesses in trouble. If in the process the practitioner is giving investment advice, he may require authorisation for such work.

Chapter 5
VOLUNTARY ARRANGEMENTS

Where nothing is, a little does ease—Anon.

5.01 Such are the costs and complexities of the formal bankruptcy procedure that it is frequently desirable that the debtor and his creditors should consider whether some alternative approach is likely to have a happier outcome for all concerned.

5.02 Debtors have been making informal arrangements with creditors ever since the invention of credit. In small cases it is possible to obtain an administration order through the County Court (see Chap. 1).

5.03 Without any involvement of the court, a debtor may execute a deed of arrangement, placing his property in the hands of a trustee for the benefit of his creditors. The deed and the creditors' assents thereto must be registered with the D.T.I. in accordance with D.A.A. 1914. The procedure was originally codified in D.A.A. 1887 although informally deeds were executed well before that time. Such deeds were commonplace in the early part of the 20th century as they provided a relatively flexible and often more commercially sensible alternative to bankruptcy for resolving the affairs of insolvent traders. The number of deeds has declined dramatically in recent years partly because most small businesses take the form of limited companies so that voluntary liquidations have, to some extent, taken their place. The procedure has almost reached extinction since the passing of I.A. 1986 which introduced the voluntary arrangement as a more convenient procedure. The number of deeds registered has fallen from 62 in 1986 to only two in 1995. Voluntary arrangements, on the other hand, have gained in popularity reaching a peak of 5,679 during 1993 although the number has subsequently declined a little with the ending of recessionary conditions.

5.04 As the deed has almost disappeared as an insolvency procedure, it will not be discussed here in detail. The reader may refer to the first edition of this work at Chapter 5, the contents of which are still valid, and to D.A.A. 1914 and the Deeds of Arrangement Rules 1925. A specimen deed appears at Appendix I, Form P. Many variations of this specimen are permissible allowing for considerable flexibility. Deeds vary in their scope, as does the degree of responsibility placed upon the trustee. The possibility of inviting a debtor to execute a deed for the benefit of creditors, as offering a better return than bankruptcy, should not be overlooked particularly in cases where it may not be possible to obtain the requisite majority in excess of three-quarters in value to approve a voluntary arrangement. A deed requires the assent of a majority in number and value of all creditors.

5.05 The more popular individual voluntary arrangements are governed by Part VIII of I.A. 1986, ss.252–263 and I.R. 5.1–5.30.

5.06 I.R. 5.1 refers to two types of debtor: an undischarged bankrupt (Case 1) or one who is not an undischarged bankrupt (Case 2). As the general procedure is similar, Case 2 arrangements will first be discussed and then (in paras 5.126–5.135) the variations in the procedure where Case 1 applies.

5.07 In many respects the procedure mirrors the corporate voluntary arrangements outlined in Part I of I.A. 1986.

5.08 The term "voluntary" is a little misleading as the arrangements require the consent of the debtor, his creditors (by a majority in excess of three-quarters in value present or represented at the creditors' meeting) and the court. A novel feature is the establishment of "snakes and ladders" between bankruptcy and voluntary arrangements. An undischarged bankrupt may put forward a proposal for a voluntary arrangement. On the hearing of a debtor's bankruptcy petition, the court may in appropriate circumstances refer the debtor to an insolvency practitioner in accordance with I.A. 1985, s.273 to prepare a report as to a voluntary arrangement. On the other hand a supervisor of a voluntary arrangement, who finds that the debtor is unco-operative, has the option, not normally available to a trustee under a deed, of presenting a bankruptcy petition (I.A. 1986, s.264(1)(c)).

5.09 A useful feature of the voluntary arrangement is that at an early stage, and before the scheme is put to creditors, the insolvent debtor may seek an interim order under I.A. 1986, s.252 which will have the effect of staying proceedings against him, including any bankruptcy petition. Such stay relieves the debtor of immediate creditor pressure and enables him, in consultation with an insolvency practitioner, to prepare for the meeting of creditors. This feature may be regarded as an improvement upon the corporate voluntary arrangement since in the case of companies the equivalent of an interim order can only be obtained by entering into the more complex and costly administration procedure.

1. DIAGNOSIS AND DECISION

5.10 Every candidate for a voluntary arrangement must be, or be about to become, insolvent but able to put forward a proposal the outcome of which will place creditors in a better position than would result from bankruptcy. At his first interview with the debtor, the practitioner will consider whether these circumstances apply. An approximate statement of affairs and an assessment of the costs that would arise in bankruptcy will suggest a minimum target. Funds for distribution to creditors are likely to come from one or more of the following sources:

(a) the debtor's own assets, possibly to be sold on a more commercial basis than could be achieved in bankruptcy;
(b) income from the debtor's business or employment, so that the potential may be enhanced by the absence of bankruptcy; or
(c) contributions from a third party.

5.11 The practitioner should at an early stage obtain authority from the debtor to contact principal creditors and other relevant parties. It is sometimes possible to save the costs of abortive time by an informal approach to major creditors at the outset in order to ascertain whether a proposal is likely to receive sympathetic consideration, and to discuss the type of proposal that is likely to be acceptable. If an impasse is reached at the that stage, it may be possible to advise the debtor to embrace the bankruptcy process thereby avoiding unnecessary costs. Unfortunately, however, Government Departments and some leading clearing banks, who are frequently major creditors, seem reluctant to give even a preliminary opinion until they have the full proposal before them.

If the conditions are right, the practitioner will take instructions to assist the debtor in preparing a proposal for a voluntary arrangement and to act as the nominee therein. In addition to considering whether a proposed scheme is financially feasible, the practitioner should consider the background to the insolvency and the reliability of the debtor. A voluntary arrangement implies a degree of co-operation between the debtor and his creditors, so that if the practitioner considers that the debtor is not making full disclosure of all his assets then he may wish to decline to act. The circumstances in which the debtor became insolvent should be fully discussed as they will give a clue as to the debtor's character and willingness to co-operate with the practitioner and the creditors. An arrangement should not be regarded as a soft option but one that will demand a greater effort on the part of the debtor if he is to avoid the stigma of bankruptcy. **5.12**

If these criteria appear present, the practitioner can put the debtor's good intentions to an early test, before drafting the proposal, by requiring that the fee for the initial work be secured. **5.13**

2. THE PROPOSAL

The proposal is the key document in any voluntary arrangement. In it the debtor sets out the precise manner in which he will pay, or compromise with, his creditors. **5.14**

Taken literally, the Act suggests that the debtor, who has created such sad disorder in his own affairs, is blessed with the competence to produce of his own volition a viable proposal and present the same to an insolvency practitioner, known as the nominee, for comment. In practice, whilst the debtor must provide the facts, the practitioner will normally aid the debtor in drafting the proposal. **5.15**

The document must provide a short explanation as to why, in the debtor's opinion, a voluntary arrangement is desirable and give reasons why the creditors may be expected to concur therewith. **5.16**

The document will contain three basic elements: **5.17**

(a) matters required to be disclosed by I.R. 5.3(2);
(b) clauses which the practitioner, as a matter of good practice, has chosen to adopt as standard clauses, to the extent relevant; and
(c) clauses peculiar to the individual's circumstances.

These three elements may overlap. For example, the Rules require the proposal to state the manner in which liabilities are to be dealt with but the detailed explanation will depend upon the debtor's circumstances.

The following are the matters required to be included by virtue of I.R. 5.3(2): **5.18**

(a) so far as within the debtor's immediate knowledge—
 (i) his assets, with an estimate of their respective values;
 (ii) the extent (if any) to which the assets are charged in favour of creditors;
 (iii) the extent (if any) to which particular assets are to be excluded from the voluntary arrangement;
(b) particulars of any property, other than assets of the debtor himself, which is proposed to be included in the arrangement, the source of such property and the terms on which it is to be made available for inclusion;

(c) the nature and amount of the debtor's liabilities (so far as within his immediate knowledge), the manner in which they are proposed to be met, modified, postponed or otherwise dealt with by means of the arrangement and (in particular)—
   (i) how it is proposed to deal with preferential claims (defined in s.258(7)) and creditors who are, or claim to be, secured;
   (ii) how associates of the debtor (being creditors of his) are proposed to be treated under the arrangement; and
   (iii) in Case 1 (where the debtor is an undischarged bankrupt) whether, to the debtor's knowledge, claims have been made under section 339 (transactions at an undervalue), section 340 (preferences) or section 343 (extortionate credit transactions), or (Case 2) there are circumstances which would give rise to the possibility of such claims in the event that he should be adjudged bankrupt (see Chapter 9);

   and, where any such circumstances are present, whether, and if so how, it is proposed under the voluntary arrangement to make provision for wholly or partly indemnifying the insolvent estate in respect of such claims;

(d) whether any, and if so what, guarantees have been given of the debtor's debts by other persons, specifying which (if any) of the guarantors are associates of his;

(e) the proposed duration of the voluntary arrangement;

(f) the proposed dates of distributions to creditors, with estimates of their amounts;

(g) the amount proposed to be paid to the nominee (as such) by way of remuneration and expenses;

(h) the manner in which it is proposed that the supervisor of the arrangement should be remunerated, and his expenses defrayed;

(j) whether, for the purposes of the arrangement, any guarantees are to be offered by any persons other than the debtor, and whether (if so) any security is to be given or sought;

(k) the manner in which funds held for the purposes of the arrangement are to be banked, invested or otherwise dealt with pending distribution to creditors;

(l) the manner in which funds held for the purpose of payment to creditors, and not so paid on the termination of the arrangement, are to be dealt with;

(m) if the debtor has any business, the manner in which it is proposed to be conducted during the course of the arrangement;

(n) details of any further credit facilities which it is intended to arrange for the debtor, and how the debts so arising are to be paid;

(o) the functions which are to be undertaken by the supervisor of the arrangement;

(p) the name, address and qualification of the person proposed as supervisor of the voluntary arrangement, and confirmation that he is (so far as the debtor is aware) qualified to act as an insolvency practitioner in relation to him (see Chap. 4).

(Note that above paras (a) to (p) are numbered as per I.R. 5.3(2), thus omitting (i).)

5.19 In the specimen proposal at Appendix II, Form H, the above requirements are dealt with in the corresponding clauses marked (a) to (p) whilst other clauses follow with the roman numerals. Requirements of particular major creditors may be included at this stage if they are acceptable to the debtor and the nominee. This will save unnecessary debate over modifications at the time of the meeting. For example, clauses (vi) and (vii) in the specimen require that taxation and V.A.T. matters be kept up to date, because, if such clauses are not included, they are likely to be introduced as modifications from the authorities concerned. In addition to the clauses set out in the specimen, practitioners may like to add further standard conditions to plug any remaining gaps on such matters as interpretation, procedure, obligations of the debtor, powers of the supervisor and application of bankruptcy provisions.

5.20 Clause (i) in the specimen proposal states that the supervisor may petition for bankruptcy should the scheme fail. This serves to make the situation clearer to all concerned although the supervisor in any event has power to petition for bankruptcy under section 264.

5.21 Where the scheme depends upon the debtor contributing from income as an alternative to selling his property, then the scheme may well provide that the supervisor shall sell the assets if the predicted income is not forthcoming. In such circumstances it may be necessary to protect the supervisor and the creditors under the scheme from the possible dissipation of such assets, particularly against the eventuality that the debtor may later become bankrupt in respect of post-arrangement debts. It may therefore be advisable for the supervisor to register a charge over freehold property and for the scheme to create a trust in favour of the creditors under the scheme.

5.22 Whether such a trust would survive a subsequent bankruptcy is unclear. In *Re Essengin Hussain (Davis v. Martin-Sklan)* [1996] B.P.I.R. 160 it was held that where a bankruptcy order had been made against the debtor on a petition by a supervisor under section 264(1)(c) in respect of a failed voluntary arrangement, the trusts in the voluntary arrangement were brought to an end thus allowing all monies held by the supervisor to be used for the benefit of creditors generally (not just those bound by the voluntary arrangement) and such monies were to be handed over to the trustee subject to a deduction in respect of the supervisor's reasonable costs and disbursements. It is not, however, clear that this would apply in cases where the voluntary arrangement was brought to an end on a petition by a post-voluntary arrangement creditor (see *Re Bradley-Hole (a Bankrupt)* [1995] B.C.C. 418).

5.23 A clause may also be included to the effect that creditors inadvertently omitted from the scheme may be included in distributions. Such a clause will not bind those creditors to the scheme but will overcome objections from the original creditors to the dilution of their dividend.

5.24 Once the drafting is complete and the wording approved by the debtor and the nominee, both these parties must carefully consider whether the scheme is one that should be recommended to creditors in that it makes full disclosure, is the best that can be achieved on the creditors' behalf in the circumstances, and produces an outcome no worse than that achievable in bankruptcy, but does not put so great a burden on the debtor as to be incapable of fulfilment.

5.25 In theory, as the Act was originally drafted, a debtor could perhaps have applied for an interim order under section 253(1) before preparing the proposal, on the basis that he intended to make a proposal. However, as a result of I.R. 5.5(2), the debtor must exhibit the proposal to the affidavit supporting his application for an interim order. This ensures that time and costs are not wasted on applications for interim orders where the debtor has no serious proposal. As indicated below the nominee does have a duty to satisfy himself that the proposal is a serious and feasible one which should be put before the creditors. It has placed the proposal at the forefront of the procedure, but means that, where creditors are pressing, the proposal will have to be prepared in haste.

3. THE NOMINEE

5.26 The proposal must provide for some person (known as the nominee) to act in relation to the voluntary arrangement as trustee or otherwise for the purpose of supervising its implementation (s.253(2)). The nominee is accordingly the person named in the proposal as the proposed supervisor. As mentioned in paragraph 5.18(p) above, it is provided in I.R. 5.3(2)(*p*) that there shall be stated the nominee's name, his address and qualification, and confirmation, so far as the debtor is aware, that the person concerned is qualified to act as an insolvency practitioner in relation to him. Like a trustee in bankruptcy, the nominee must be a qualified insolvency practitioner (see Chap. 4), have no conflict of interest with regard to the debtor's affairs, and have the resources to carry out the proposed task.

5.27 The nominee's principal tasks are to prepare the report (paras 5.41–5.55 below), chair the meeting of creditors (paras 5.55–5.64) and file his report with the court. Thereafter his task as nominee has ended, although in the majority of cases he continues to act in the role of supervisor.

5.28 In some cases, the nominee will confine himself to the functions specified under the Act and Rules, particularly if the debtor is guided through the preliminary stages by a separate professional adviser. However, in the majority of cases the nominee will also advise the debtor, particularly if he has no other professional advice, in the necessary formalities including the preparation of the proposal and application to court for an interim order. The practitioner should however make it clear that, whilst being fair to the debtor's position, he is not acting solely in the personal interests of the debtor but with due regard to the interests of all concerned, particularly of the creditors.

5.29 The amount proposed to be paid to the nominee, as such, by way of remuneration and expenses must be disclosed in the proposal (I.R. 5.3(2) (*g*)). In practice a prudent nominee will take steps to secure his fees and expenses before commencing work on the debtor's affairs, or at least before filing the nominee's report with the court.

4. INTERIM ORDER

5.30 At an early stage in the procedure, the debtor should seek an interim order from the court under section 252, the effect of which is that no bankruptcy petition relating to the debtor may be presented or proceeded with, and no other proceedings, and no execution or other legal process, may be commenced or continued against the debtor or his property except with the leave of the court.

5.31 Such an order gives to an individual debtor a moratorium early in the proceedings, an advantage not available to a limited company seeking a voluntary arrangement under Part I of the Act.

5.32 Whilst the interim order provides some protection to the debtor's estate until creditors have an opportunity to consider the proposal, this protection has some limitation. The order prevents completion of the execution process on behalf of judgment creditors *Re Peake* [1987] C.L.Y. 215 (Blackburn County Court). It will not, however, debar a landlord from enforcing his right of distress for non-payment of rent *McMullen and Sons v. Cerrone* [1994] B.C.C. 25. This favoured position of the landlord was again upheld in *Re A Debtor No. 13A10 of 1994; Re a Debtor No. 14A10 of 1994; The Debtors v. Joyner* [1996] B.C.C. 57 when it was held that the landlord did not require leave of the court under section 252(2)(b) to re-enter premises for breach of covenant. It has also been held that an interim order does not affect the rights of a receiver in respect of assets covered by a restraint order under the Drug Trafficking Offences Act 1986 *Re M* [1991] T.L.R. 192.

5.33 Application to the court for an interim order may, according to section 253(1), be made where the debtor intends to make a proposal to his creditors for a composition in satisfaction of his debts or a scheme of arrangement of his affairs, *i.e.* a voluntary arrangement. In practice, as explained in paragraph 5.24 above, the proposal will by this stage have been prepared as it must accompany the application.

5.34 In any case the debtor, whether or not an undischarged bankrupt, may make such an application. However, if the debtor is an undischarged bankrupt, the application may in the alternative be made by the trustee of his estate or by the O.R. (s.253(3)).

5.35 An application for an interim order must, in accordance with I.R. 5.5, be accompanied by the debtor's affidavit on the following matters:

(a) the reasons for making the application;
(b) particulars of any execution or other legal process which, to the debtor's knowledge, has been commenced against him;
(c) that he is an undischarged bankrupt or (as the case may be) that he is able to petition for his own bankruptcy;
(d) that no previous application for an interim order has been made by or in respect of the debtor in the period of 12 months ending with the date of the affidavit; and
(e) that the nominee under the proposal (naming him) is a person who is qualified to act as an insolvency practitioner in relation to the debtor, and is willing to act in relation to the proposal.

5.36 A specimen application appears at Appendix II, Form D. It shall be accompanied (I.R. 5.5(2), as amended) by exhibits containing a copy of the notice to the intended nominee, with his consent to act endorsed thereon, and the debtor's proposal. The granting of an interim order is at the court's discretion. The court may decline to grant an interim order where it does not consider that the proposal is serious and viable, notwithstanding evidence of potential support from creditors (*Cooper v. Fearnley; Re A Debtor (No. 103 of 1994)* [1997] B.P.I.R. 20). Debtors and practitioners should not assume that the court will automatically grant an interim order whenever the requisite application is made.

5.37 Except in the case of a bankrupt, the application must in accordance with I.R. 5.5A be made to the court under which the debtor would be entitled to present his own bankruptcy petition (see Chap. 1). In cases of doubt, the debtor or his adviser may telephone the nearest court with bankruptcy jurisdiction (see App. III) to check that the court concerned is the one with appropriate jurisdiction.

5.38 The debtor must give two days' notice of the hearing to any creditor who to the debtor's knowledge has presented a bankruptcy petition. It is not strictly necessary to give notice to other creditors who may have commenced legal proceedings, notwithstanding that they will be affected by the order. Notice shall also be given to the nominee. In hearing the application the court shall take into account any representations made by those persons entitled to notice of the application. In practice the High Court, and some County Courts, are prepared to streamline the procedure in that, once the documents are delivered, they will be put before the registrar or district judge without the presence of the debtor, nominee, or petitioning creditor and without serving notice on the interested parties. In some cases the order can be available immediately and may be a "concertina order" described in paragraph 5.50

below, extended to a date after that of the proposed creditors' meeting. In other County Courts the procedure can be slower with a hearing for the interim order fixed some 14 days after the papers are delivered and with a subsequent date fixed for the hearing of the nominee's report.

5.39 Initially the order is made for 14 days (s.255(6)) although the court has power to extend that period. If the court makes an interim order it shall, in accordance with I.R. 5.6(3), fix a venue for consideration of the nominee's report at the date of, or prior to, the cessation of the interim order.

5.40 The court will normally extend the interim order, if an extension of time has been granted for filing the nominee's report. At least two sealed copies of the order shall be sent by the court to the person who applied for it and that person shall serve one of the copies on the nominee and also give notice to any persons who were given notice of the hearing but were not present or represented (I.R. 5.7).

5. THE NOMINEE'S REPORT

5.41 Where an interim order has been made, the nominee is required in accordance with section 256 to submit a report to the court stating whether in his opinion a meeting of the debtor's creditors should be summoned to consider the debtor's proposals and, in that event, the date, time and a place at which he proposes the meeting be held. A specimen proposal appears at Appendix II, Form H. Whilst section 256 appears to envisage that a report may be prepared after the interim order has been obtained, in practice, as the proposal has to be prepared prior to the interim order and the nominee must at that stage indicate that he is willing to act, the nominee's report is invariably prepared prior to the order, and filed at the same time as the application for the interim order.

5.42 The nominee will have received from the debtor, in accordance with section 256, a copy of the proposal and statement of affairs. The nominee has wide powers under I.R. 5.9 to obtain from the debtor such further information as is necessary for the preparation of his report.

5.43 The nominee may call upon the debtor to provide him with:

(a) further and better particulars as to the circumstances in which, and the reasons why, he is insolvent or (as the case may be) threatened with insolvency;
(b) particulars of any previous proposals which have been made by him under Part VIII of the Act;
(c) any further information with respect to his affairs which the nominee thinks necessary for the purposes of his report (I.R. 5.9(1)).

5.44 The nominee may also call upon the debtor to inform him whether and in what circumstances he has at any time been concerned in the affairs of a company which has become insolvent or has himself been adjudged bankrupt or entered into any arrangement with creditors (I.R. 5.9(2)). The nominee is entitled, for the purpose of considering the debtor's proposal, to have access to the debtor's accounts and records (I.R. 5.9(3)).

5.45 The nominee must, in accordance with I.R. 5.10, deliver his report to the court not less than two days before the interim order ceases to have effect, although in practice his report will normally be available at the time that the application for an interim order is heard. With the report shall be delivered the debtor's proposal and any amendments agreed by both debtor and nominee and a copy of the statement of affairs. Assuming that the nominee is in favour of putting the proposals to creditors, his report must have annexed to it his comments on the debtor's proposal (I.R.5.10(3)). It will be noted that the specimen report is very brief because the nominee will normally have discussed the proposal in detail with the debtor so that if the nominee had reservations they will have been taken into account by agreed amendments to the proposal before it reaches final form. In so doing the nominee should not be partial to the debtor's narrow interests but ensure that the proposal is, as far as possible, fair to both the debtor and his creditors. However, if the nominee's advice is not heeded in this respect but nevertheless he feels that creditors should have the opportunity of considering the proposal, his comments may be more detailed.

5.46 In *Re A Debtor (No. 140/10 of 1995)* [1996] 2 B.C.L.C. 429 the court issued guidance to nominees when dealing with debtors, who are economical with the truth, as follows:

"(1) The nominee is initially heavily reliant upon information provided by the debtor and there is therefore a need for complete candour by the debtor. Where doubts reasonably arise as to the accuracy and reliability of the information provided by the debtor, the nominee must satisfy himself as to the amount and quality of such information so that he may arrive at what is a fair prima facie or provisional view as to whether a particular claimant should be admitted or rejected in respect of his claim for voting purposes and also as to at what figure, if any, an agreement should be reached in order to attribute a minimum value for voting purposes to any unliquidated or unascertained debt;

(2) It is not to be expected that in every case the nominee must personally verify every figure and test every part of the proposal. Financial resources may be limited or the figures might be plain and undoubted. But, within the scheme of I.A. 1986, where the fullness or candour of the debtor's information has come into question, the nominee must take such steps as are in all the circumstances reasonable to satisfy himself on the following:

(i) that the debtor's true position as to assets and liabilities does not appear to the nominee in any material respect to be different substantially from that to be represented to the creditors;

(ii) that it appears that the debtor's proposals as put to the creditors' meeting have a real prospect of being implemented. A measure of modification to the proposal was possible under section 258, such that this question can be approached broadly;

(iii) that the information provided a basis for determining that there was no manifest yet unavoidable prospective unfairness to any class of creditors.

(3) As to (i)–(iii) above, reasonable steps will vary in each particular case according to such matters as the quality of the debtor's answers or the ease or difficulty with which independent enquiry might be made. If the nominee's enquiries in questionable cases have been so restricted or unsatisfactory that the nominee is not able to assure creditors that he has satisfied himself that those three minima above have been met, he should not unequivocally report, under section 256(1)(a), that in his opinion a meeting of creditors should be summoned. Creditors should vote upon a proposal which had survived the scrutiny of the nominee, and not the debtor's own raw material.

(4) The Court's role under section 256(5) was not merely to rubber stamp the nominee's report. The Court had to be satisfied that a meeting of creditors should be held." (At 429, 430.)

Whilst nominees will be expected to make reasonable enquiries in line with the above guidance, in cases where there is significant doubt as to the accuracy of the facts or reliability of the debtor, a nominee will carefully consider whether to act at all. In such cases where the nominee agrees to act, he should express his reservations to the debtor and point out that to proceed on the basis of a heavily qualified nominee's report may mean that creditors will reject the scheme and the money that has been spent on the nominee's fee will be wasted.

5.47 The rule (I.R. 510(3)) also states that the nominee shall give reasons for his opinion if he considers that the proposal is not worthy of consideration by the creditors. In practice a debtor will not normally put forward a proposal unless he has found a nominee who will give it at least qualified approval, and he would be ill-advised so to do.

5.48 The court shall cause, in accordance with I.R. 5.10(4), the nominee's report to be endorsed with the date it is filed. It is open to inspection, on the court file, by any creditor. A copy of the report, together with the proposal and statement of affairs, must be sent to any creditor who has presented a bankruptcy petition.

5.49 The nominee must send to any person, who has presented a bankruptcy petition, a copy of the debtor's proposal, a copy of the nominee's report and any accompanying comments and a copy of the summary of the debtor's statement of affairs. If the debtor is an undischarged bankrupt, the same documents shall also be sent to the O.R. and any trustee (I.R. 5.10(5)).

5.50 Since in practice the nominee's report is normally filed with the court at the same time as the debtor's application for an interim order, many courts will consider the nominee's report immediately after making the interim order. Indeed the High Court has indicated in a Practice Direction (Appendix VII) that in certain circumstances it will make a "concertina" order combining the interim order and the order made on considering the nominee's report. Furthermore, in suitable cases it will be prepared to make such orders without the attendance of the parties. Such procedure is designed to save time and costs but is not intended to discourage attendance.

5.51 Whilst a similar flexibility is adopted by some County Courts, others prefer, upon making the interim order, to set a further date for the consideration of the nominee's report. In either event the court will consider the nominee's report and, in accordance with section 256(5), if satisfied that a meeting of the debtor's creditors should be summoned to consider the proposal, shall direct that the period for which the interim order has effect should be extended for such further period as it may specify in the direction, for the purposes of enabling the debtor's proposal to be considered by his creditors. The various County Courts vary in their practice as to the period for which interim orders are extended which tends to vary from four to as long as 49 days after the date of the creditors' meeting. In the High Court, the period is normally 21 days.

5.52 Alternatively the court may discharge the interim order in the rare circumstance that the debtor has failed to supply the appropriate information to the nominee to enable him to prepare his report, or if for any other reason it would be inappropriate for a meeting of the creditors to be summoned (s.256(6)).

5.53 At the hearing by the court to consider the nominee's report, a creditor who has petitioned for bankruptcy may appear or be represented (I.R. 5.12).

6. PROCEDURE

5.54 The documents which are to be filed with the court are as follows:

(a) Originating application (Rule 7.2, Official Form 7.1) for an interim order under I.A. 1986, s.252. (Form D, App. II).
(b) An affidavit to accompany such application (Rule 5.5(1)). (Form E, App. II).
(c) The debtor's sworn proposal for an individual voluntary arrangement (Rule 5.3). (Form H, App. II).
(d) The debtor's sworn approximate statement of affairs (Rule 5.8). (Form I, App. II).
(e) A notice to intended nominee (Rule 5.4) and confirmation of willingness to act as nominee. (Form F, App. II).
(f) The nominee's report to court pursuant to section 256 (Rule 5.10.) (Form G, App. II).

A specimen covering letter to the court, which accompanies the above documents, is shown in Appendix II, Form C. The package is taken to the bankruptcy clerk, who will allocate a case number and place the papers before the district judge or registrar who will normally make the interim order *ex parte*. If it is decided to call a hearing prior to making the order, then four days' notice is usually given to interested parties. A fee of £30 is currently payable in county courts, whilst this figure escalates to £120 in the High Court.

Within a few days, the court will send the nominee two copies of the interim order made under Rule 5.7; one for service on the debtor, one to be retained by the nominee for his records. In the rare event of a creditor commencing or continuing with bankruptcy proceedings between the notification and holding of the creditors' meeting, a copy of the interim order should be despatched immediately, together with a covering letter pointing out that such action constitutes a contempt of court.

The High Court has issued a reminder note concerning the preparation of affidavits and exhibits which appears at Appendix VII.

7. THE MEETING OF CREDITORS

5.55 As soon as the nominee's report has been considered by the court, and assuming that there is no court direction to the contrary, the nominee should immediately circulate all the creditors with the following documents:

(a) an explanatory letter (App. II, Form B);
(b) the proposal (App. II, Form H);
(c) the statement of affairs (App. II, Form I) and list of creditors;
(d) notice to the nominee and the nominee's consent to act (App. II, Form F);
(e) notice of meeting of creditors together with an explanation of creditors' voting rights and the requisite majorities that will be required at the meeting (App. II, Forms K and L);
(f) form of proxy (App. II, Form O);
(g) copy of the interim order and extension thereof;
(h) claim form (App. II, Form N);

(i) such other information as the nominee considers necessary to enable creditors to make an informed decision on the proposal. For example, if continuation of the debtor's business is envisaged, copies of recent accounts together with a budget may be included at this stage, if not already attached to the proposal itself.
Whilst further information may be made available to the meeting, the outcome may depend upon proxy votes so that the result may become apparent before the meeting commences. Accordingly full information should be circulated.

The nominee is required to give notice of the meeting to all the creditors specified in the debtor's statement of affairs, and any other creditors of whom the nominee is otherwise aware (I.R. 5.13(2)). He cannot, therefore, merely exclude a difficult creditor at the request of the debtor. Notice should also be given to secured creditors, even if it is thought that they may be fully secured.

5.56 The date on which the meeting is held shall be not less than 14 days from that on which the nominee's report is filed with the court and not more than 28 days from that on which that report is considered by the court (I.R. 5.13). In practice certain courts are, as mentioned in paragraphs 5.39–5.40 above, extending interim orders for up to 49 days and permitting meetings to be held at any time within the period notwithstanding the 28-day rule. In common with other insolvency procedures, the creditors' meeting must be convened at a venue convenient to creditors and the meeting shall be summoned for commencement between 10 a.m. and 4 p.m. on a business day.

5.57 Rule 5.13(2) provides: "Notices calling the meeting shall be sent by the nominee, at least 14 days before the day fixed for it to be held, to all the creditors specified in the debtor's statement of affairs, and any other creditors of whom the nominee is otherwise aware." This means that notices must be sent to creditors at least 14 clear days before the date of the meeting, so the nominee should ensure that notices are posted at least 16 days beforehand. Where a creditor has been inadvertently omitted, attempts have been made in the past to resolve the problem by arranging an adjournment of the creditors' meeting so that a creditor previously omitted could receive the requisite 14 days' notice. This procedure has been shown to be ineffective because in *Mytre Investments v. Reynolds (No. 2) (Re Bielecki)* [1996] B.P.I.R. 464 Blackburne J. ruled that creditors must have the requisite notice of the original meeting, of which the adjournment is deemed to be a mere continuation. The problem of creditors who have not had the requisite notice is considered further at 5.108 below.

5.58 The problem thrown up by the decision in *Mytre Investments Limited v. Reynolds (No. 2)* cannot easily be resolved. In effect it means that a "late" creditor who does not emerge (or is not notified to the nominee) until after the first meeting has been called may be outside the voluntary arrangement altogether—thus potentially defeating its object. If such a creditor is not willing to be bound (his permission should of course be sought) this may only be resolved by a further application to the court for leave to abandon the meeting (rather than adjourn it) and to re-convene a new meeting given the requisite notice required by the rules. This problem is discussed further in a useful article by Steven Heffer which appears in *Insolvency Intelligence*, Vol. 9, No. 1, at pp. 5–7.

5.59 The meeting must be chaired by the nominee or his deputy, being either a qualified insolvency practitioner or an employee of the nominee who is experienced in insolvency matters.

5.60 The chairman cannot utilise any proxy held by him to increase or reduce the amount of the remuneration or expenses of the trustee or supervisor unless the proxy specifically directs him to vote in that way.

5.61 Creditors' voting rights and requisite majorities are set out in I.R. 5.17 and 5.18. Votes are calculated, in the case of a bankrupt, according to the amounts of claims at the date of the bankruptcy order and in other cases as at the date of the meeting. Creditors cannot vote in respect of unliquidated claims except at an estimated minimum value accepted by the chairman (I.R. 5.17(3)). The chairman has power to admit or reject creditors' claims for voting in whole or in part but his decision is subject to appeal to the court by any creditor or by the debtor. If in doubt as to whether a claim shall be admitted, the chairman shall mark it as "objected to" and allow the creditor to vote subject to his vote being subsequently declared invalid if the objection is sustained. Guidance as to how the chairman of the meeting should deal with a disputed debt was given by Harman J. in *Re A Debtor (No. 222 of 1990), ex p. Bank of Ireland* [1992] B.C.L.C. 137. The chairman is not obliged to go into a lengthy discussion or debate as to the exact status of a debt. He has the power to admit or reject and if he is in doubt he must mark the vote as "objected to" under rule 5.17 but allow the creditor to vote. As the learned judge put it:

> "... if it is plain or obvious that if it is good he admits it, if it is plain or obvious that it is bad he rejects it, and if there is a question, a doubt, he should admit it but mark it as objected to."

5.62 In these circumstances it seems that it would only be on rare occasions that the chairman would be allowed to reject a vote; say, if a debt was obviously statute-barred. In all other cases the chairman should exercise his discretion in favour of allowing the creditor to vote but mark the vote as "objected to".

5.63 The treatment of unliquidated claims has been influenced by the decision in *Re Cranley Mansions Ltd; Saigol v. Goldstein* [1994] B.C.C. 576. Although this case involved a company voluntary arrangement, similar principles arise and the equivalent rule for companies at 1.17 is almost identical to I.R. 5.17. A creditor had submitted an unliquidated claim against the company for an estimated £900,000 together with legal costs. The chairman purported to exercise his right under I.R. 1.17(3) and placed a nominal minimum value of £1 on her claim for voting purposes. The creditor applied for an order under section 6 (the corporate equivalent of s.262) revoking or suspending the arrangement or for such relief by way of an appeal under I.R. 1.17(5). Ferris J. dispelled any notion that the chairman's agreement of an estimated minimum value for the purpose of voting in accordance with I.R. 1.17(3) (similar to I.R. 5.17(3)) can be a unilateral act on his part. If the two parties cannot agree then the creditor is not entitled to vote but is not bound by the arrangement and can pursue the claim against the company. This decision presented a number of problems for chairmen of meetings and could potentially have led to an abuse of the voting procedure if creditors insisted upon voting for large unliquidated sums or, on the other hand, if a nominee or director encouraged such claims from friendly parties to achieve a desired outcome.

Unless challenged, the decision in *Re Cranley Mansions Ltd* could have presented great problems where a creditor sought to vote for a large unliquidated claim. Effectively, that creditor might have been able to "scupper" the voluntary arrangement simply by failing or refusing to agree with the chairman the amount for which he is entitled to vote. The chairman would then have been unable to impose a value unilaterally and that creditor could have been left outside the arrangement altogether and therefore free to proceed with a winding up action. This is indeed what happened in *Re Cranley Mansions Ltd* with the result that the creditor applied to the court to revoke the approval which had previously been given at the creditors' meeting.

Fortunately, this unsatisfactory decision was not followed in *Re A Debtor (No. 162 of 1993) (Doorbar v. Alltime Securities Ltd)* [1994] B.C.C. 994; [1995] B.C.C. 728, involving an individual voluntary arrangement. In this case, the landlord sought to vote at the creditors' meeting, not only in respect of arrears of rent but also with regard to future rent, up to the date of expiry of the lease. The nominee proposed to admit the landlord for voting purposes in respect of the arrears and offered to admit an amount equivalent to one further year for future rent on the basis that the landlord had a duty to mitigate his claim and could not be admitted to vote for the whole sum. The parties could not agree and the resolution was passed. Knox J. ruled that it was sufficient that the chairman had offered to agree an amount for voting purposes for the landlord to be bound by the arrangement in respect of future rent.

The *Doorbar* decision was upheld by the Court of Appeal on November 30, 1995 ([1995] B.C.C. 1149), confirming that the provisions of I.R. 5.17(3) did not require the chairman to agree an estimated minimum value with the creditor concerned. It was sufficient for the chairman to put an estimated value on the debt. The estimate of one year's rent placed by the chairman on the landlord's claim, did not constitute a material irregularity. A further point was resolved by the Court of Appeal. The landlord had argued that the arrangement was unfairly prejudicial as the lease contained a clause obliging the debtor and his wife to take a new lease in the event of the debtor's bankruptcy. As the landlord was bound in respect of future rent, he could not petition for bankruptcy and therefore could not activate the clause concerned. Knox J. had held that the landlord had not been unfairly prejudiced as he retained his right of re-entry, and this view was upheld.

In the following cases there is to be left out of account a creditor's vote in respect of any claim or part of a claim where:

(a) written notice of the claim was not given, either at the meeting or before it, to the chairman or convenor of the meeting;
(b) the claim or part is secured; the correct interpretation of this rule is that where part of a claim is secured, then only that part is discounted for voting purposes (*Calor Gas v. Piercy and others* [1994] B.C.C. 69). However, the creditors' right to *enforce* his security cannot be removed without his express consent (I.A. 1986, s.258(4)). In *Re A Debtor (No. 10 of 1992), Peck v. Craighead* [1995] B.C.C. 525 it was held that an execution creditor where the sheriff had taken walking possession under a writ of *fi.fa.* was a secured creditor for the purpose of section 258;
(c) the claim is in respect of a debt wholly or partly on or secured by a current bill of exchange or promissory note, save after deducting the amount of an antecedent liability (I.R. 5.18(3)).

5.64 The court may order another meeting to be summoned if the chairman's decision is reversed or varied or a creditor's vote is declared invalid. Any application to court, to vary the chairman's decision, shall be made within 28 days of the nominee's report to the court on the outcome of the meeting. Normally the chairman is not personally liable for any costs incurred by any person who appeals against his decision. Despite the apparent prohibition on ordering costs, in the above-mentioned case the conduct of the chairman was regarded by the court as being so unsatisfactory that a cost order was made against him. It must be added, however, that the reasons for that cost order were largely connected with the "material irregularity" since the appeal was also under section 262 (see below) where there is an unlimited discretion to the court. Unfortunately, that part of the judgment was not reported.

Modifications

5.65 Section 258 provides that creditors may propose modifications to the voluntary arrangement, but such modifications will only be effective if the debtor consents thereto. The Act states "they shall not include any modification by virtue of which the proposal ceases to be a proposal such as is mentioned in section 253".

5.66 The meaning of this section is uncertain, but presumably modifications must not be so fundamental as to be effectively a completely new proposal. It is for this reason that, as recommended earlier, consultation should take place at an early stage with major creditors so that their wishes can, as far as possible, be reflected in the proposal itself. Modifications shall not vary the rights of secured or preferential creditors without the concurrence of the creditors concerned.

5.67 Practitioners will be accustomed to the modifications normally put forward by banks and government departments, who are regular creditors, and include their normal requirements as standard conditions. For example, where a proposal depends upon regular contributions from the debtor's income falling short of eventual payment in full, many banks will normally require that contributions continue for a minimum of five years, notwithstanding that a debtor would be unlikely to expect to have to make contributions for more than three years in bankruptcy. Standard modifications put forward by the Inland Revenue appear at Appendix IX. It is the practice of the Inland Revenue to review proposals critically and exercise their right to vote, normally by proxy. Where the Inland Revenue vote in favour of a proposal, such acceptance is normally subject to adoption of such of those modifications that are not already in the proposal. At one time, Customs & Excise were also active in perusing proposals but, since devolving the work to local offices in 1994, have become more passive participators.

5.68 The chairman will have to use some discretion in dealing with proxy votes where a creditor submits a proxy for the chairman to vote in favour of any proposal but is silent as to modifications. If modifications, as is frequently the case, are aimed to give creditors better terms than in the original proposal, the chairman will normally feel able to exercise such votes in favour of the modified proposal. Alternatively, the creditor may authorise the chairman or other proxy-holder to vote in favour of the proposal together with such modifications as are approved by the creditors at the meeting. As a last resort, the creditor has the right as explained above to appeal to the court against the chairman's decision.

5.69 Major creditors may wish to exercise their right to nominate the supervisor. This they can do by way of a modification replacing the nominee with another insolvency practitioner acceptable to the creditors. If it is intended to appoint some person other than the nominee to be the supervisor and that person is not present, then his written consent must be produced. In any event a proposed supervisor must produce his written confirmation that he is so qualified to act. An impasse may arise where there are different nominations, none of which alone can obtain the requisite majority. Such impasse is normally settled by compromise, usually in favour of the proposed supervisor or nominee with the greatest support. It is seldom economic to appoint joint supervisors from separate firms.

5.70 The proposal, or any modification, must be passed by a majority in excess of three-quarters in value of creditors in person or by proxy and voting. Votes of "associates" (see App. V) may be included by the chairman, who should carefully distinguish them from other creditors as a second test has to be applied to the result in order to conform with I.R. 5.18(4). The effect of this rule is that if more than half of the votes from those who are not associates are against any resolution then that resolution will fail notwithstanding that more than 75 per cent. in value of the total votes are in favour.

5.71 If the requisite majority for the approval of the voluntary arrangement (with or without modifications) has not been obtained, the chairman may, and shall if it is so resolved, adjourn the meeting for not more than 14 days.

There may be more than one adjournment but the final adjournment shall not be later than a day 14 days after that on which the meeting was originally held (I.R. 5.19). In practice the court has been known to accede to a nominee's application, made at the behest of creditors, to permit an adjourned meeting to take place at a later date.

5.72 At the conclusion of the meeting, if the proposal is approved, with or without modifications, it can be implemented immediately and the supervisor can commence his new duties. If the nominee mentioned in the proposal is confirmed as supervisor he is transmogrified into his new role. There is, however, one duty left to the chairman of the meeting, whether or not he is the supervisor or a representative thereof, namely, to file the chairman's report with the court setting out the result of the meeting, whether this be for the acceptance or the rejection of the arrangement. That report must, in accordance with I.R. 5.22:

(a) state whether the proposal for a voluntary arrangement was approved or rejected and, if approved, with what (if any) modifications;
(b) set out the resolutions which were taken at the meeting, and the decision on each one;
(c) list the creditors (with their respective values) who were present or represented at the meeting, and how they voted on each resolution; and
(d) include such further information (if any) as the chairman thinks it appropriate to make known to the court.

5.73 The original of the report to court of the chairman of the creditors' meeting must be filed in court within four days of the meeting and the court must cause it to be endorsed with the date of filing. A copy of the report will be sealed by the court, stamped with the date of filing and returned to the supervisor. All those who were sent notice of the meeting, including the creditors, must then also be served with a copy of the chairman's report. Such service must take place immediately after filing at court. Upon hearing of the chairman's report, the district judge or registrar will discharge the interim order, and a copy of the "order discharging interim order" will be sent to the supervisor by the court. If the creditors have declined the debtor's proposals outright, or it has not been possible to agree on modifications, the creditors are free, should they so wish, to petition for the bankruptcy of the debtor, who no longer has the protection of the court. In other cases the approved arrangement will take effect and be binding on all those creditors who had notice of, and were entitled to vote at, the meeting whether or not they were present or represented.

5.74 The meeting's decision may be challenged by application to the court by the debtor, a creditor, the nominee or any trustee in bankruptcy or the O.R. if the arrangement unfairly prejudices the interests of a creditor or the debtor or there has been some material irregularity in relation to the meeting. Details will be found in I.A. 1986, s.262 and I.R. 5.25.

5.75 An application under this section shall not be made after the end of a period of 28 days beginning with the day on which the report of the creditors' meeting is made to the court under section 259 (s.262(3)). In *Tager v. Westpac Bank Corporation and Others, The Times*, December 24, 1996 the court considered the possible conflict between this time limit and the court's discretion under section 376 to extend the time. The High Court decided that it has jurisdiction to extend the period of 28 days notwithstanding that such an extension may not be available in respect of a company voluntary arrangement.

In *Re A Debtor (No. 87 of 1993) (No. 2)* [1996] B.P.I.R. 64, the material irregularity relied on by the applicants, who were creditors of the debtor, was that the debtor's statement of affairs allegedly failed accurately to disclose the debtor's assets and liabilities. The debtor and the supervisor claimed that "material irregularity" referred only to some irregularity in the convening or conduct of the meeting. Rimer J. rejected this argument and had no hesitation in making an order under section 262(4) revoking the approval of the arrangement.

5.76 Immediately after filing his report with the court, the chairman must also, in accordance with I.R. 5.24, send a report to the Secretary of State giving details as follows:

(a) the name and address of the debtor;
(b) the date on which the arrangement was approved by the creditors;
(c) the name and address of the supervisor; and
(d) the court in which the chairman's report has been filed.

The report shall be accompanied by a cheque payable to the D.T.I. in accordance with fee No. 1 of Part II of the Schedule to the Insolvency Fees Order 1986, which is currently £35.

Reform

5.77 In October 1993 the Insolvency Service issued a consultative document (Company Voluntary Arrangements and Administration Orders) and following submissions thereon a further consultative document in April 1995. These documents considered in particular the rights of secured creditors, and also the lack of a moratorium pending a company voluntary arrangement, in contrast to individual voluntary arrangements where an interim order is available. Whilst the consultative documents are concerned with corporate matters and many of the issues, for example directors' conduct, do not have a parallel in individual insolvency, there are some areas in which similar considerations might apply.

There is a suggestion that whilst the 75 per cent requirement should remain, secured creditors can vote for the full amount of their claim. In the authors' view such an amendment would be inappropriate with regard to creditors, who intend to rely on their security.

The question of creditors inadvertently omitted from the proposal is also discussed. It is suggested that a voluntary arrangement be binding upon these creditors, provided their existence has not been deliberately concealed, but that a further meeting of creditors must be called to reconsider a proposal where the effect of unknown claims would be to reduce the payment to creditors by 10 per cent or more. In the authors' view, such an amendment would be helpful in cases where a creditor has been inadvertently excluded but it could be difficult in practice to establish whether concealment had been deliberate. At present, proposals in practice usually provide for the inclusion of creditors whose claims subsequently come to light. Such a clause cannot, however, bind subsequent creditors without their agreement.

Despite two consultative documents and discussion as to the amendment of insolvency law, particularly to make corporate recovery procedures more effective, such reforms appear to have faded from the priorities for parliamentary time.

8. THE SUPERVISOR

(a) Appointment

5.78 As mentioned in paragraph 5.65 above, the supervisor's appointment takes effect upon conclusion of the meeting of creditors. He must give written notice of his appointment to the Secretary of State (I.R. 5.24(2)). In common with other insolvency appointments, the supervisor will attend to a number of compliance matters. He must take out a specific bond relating to the appointment (see Chap. 4), he must conform to the requirements of the Insolvency Practitioners Regulations 1990 and retain the records required by regulation 17 thereof. It is advisable that the supervisor should take over responsibility for insuring the assets dealt with in the arrangement, or at least seek the advice of his own insurance brokers that adequate arrangements are in place.

5.79 The practical tasks required of the supervisor in implementing the arrangement will depend upon the wording of the proposal and its modifications. The supervisor will have to study these carefully before accepting the appointment to see that he is willing to carry out these tasks. The practitioner should avoid accepting such an appointment where the scheme places onerous duties upon the supervisor such as the day-to-day management of the debtor's business. A voluntary arrangement normally implies a degree of co-operation and trust between the debtor and his creditors, leaving the supervisor with a monitoring role and the task of agreeing claims of the creditors and handling the distributions when moneys become available for that purpose. The supervisor should also have the task of declaring non-compliance when such is the case (see paras 5.88–5.101 below) and bringing the arrangement to an end. If the creditors cannot place sufficient trust in the debtor to operate his own day-to-day business affairs, it would normally be unsatisfactory and uneconomic to put such responsibilities upon the supervisor and it would normally be more appropriate for bankruptcy to intervene. Accordingly any ongoing business is likely to be operated under the debtor's day-to-day control, including the conduct of the business bank account. The supervisor should operate a separate bank account receiving only such moneys as are available for creditors and the costs of the arrangement, by way of third party contributions, sale of assets, available profits from a business, or contributions from the debtor's income.

5.80 The court has power under section 263(5) to make an order appointing a person who is so qualified to act as supervisor either in substitution for the existing supervisor or to fill a vacancy. This power has been exercised in a number of instances where the supervisor has ceased to be qualified. In such a case it may be expedient to make an application to the High Court for the appointment of a substituted supervisor in respect of a number of voluntary arrangements previously in the hands of a disqualified practitioner, perhaps originating in a number of different county courts. The High Court has jurisdiction to appoint a new supervisor even if the original proceedings under which the arrangement came into being were commenced in the County Court (*Re Stella Metals Ltd* [1997] B.P.I.R. 293; *Re a Licence-Holder* [1997] B.C.C. 666).

(b) Accounts

5.81 The supervisor is required to keep an account and records of his acts and dealings and every 12 months to prepare an abstract of receipts and payments and send copies, together with comments as to progress and efficacy of the arrangement, to the court, the debtor, and all those creditors bound by the arrangement (I.R. 5.26). Alternatively he shall distribute a statement of no receipts and payments. Such abstracts must be circulated within two months of the end of the period to which they relate.

5.82 If, under the terms of the arrangement, the supervisor is not authorised to carry on the debtor's business, realise assets or otherwise administer funds (and he will normally be authorised to do at least one of these things), he shall each year circulate a report on the progress and efficacy of the arrangement.

5.83 The D.T.I. has power to audit the accounts and call for the production of records of accounts at the supervisor's premises or elsewhere and for such information and assistance as may be needed for the purposes of the audit (I.R. 5.27).

5.84 Upon completion of the arrangement, the supervisor will have to complete a further account as outlined in paragraph 5.137 below.

5.85 If the debtor, any of the creditors, or any other person, is dissatisfied by any act, omission or decision of the supervisor, he may apply to the court under section 263 and the court has power to confirm, reverse or modify any such decision, give directions to the supervisor or make such other order as it thinks fit. The supervisor himself has power to apply to the court for directions in relation to any particular matter arising under the voluntary arrangement (s.263(4)). The court does not, however, have the general control over the arrangement that it exercises in bankruptcy (Chap. 4).

5.86 Any application by a supervisor for directions will be somewhat similar to that by a liquidator under section 112. The right is one which a supervisor will use sparingly in view of the costs of the application but it is most commonly applied when the supervisor approaches decisions that are likely to be controversial. In such cases the supervisor will normally set out the decision that he is minded to make, and seek the court's approbation.

5.87 The court has power under section 263(5) to make an order appointing a supervisor either in substitution for the existing incumbent or to fill a vacancy. Such power is to be utilised where it is expedient to appoint a supervisor but inexpedient to do so without the assistance of the court. This section has been utilised to deal with situations where the supervisor retires, say on grounds of ill health or loss of his insolvency licence (see *Re Stella Metals Ltd* [1997] B.P.I.R. 293).

9. NON-COMPLIANCE

5.88 As every scheme must have an end, a supervisor before accepting appointment should make sure that the proposal sets out how this is to be achieved. In most cases this will be by the happy fulfilment of the proposal's objects, which may be the eventual payment of creditors or their compromise by a distribution from available funds. The proposal should also set out a time scale for its achievement.

5.89 Unfortunately some arrangements will fail. Frequently, after the debtor has paid instalments from income for a year or two, his circumstances will change through redundancy or other unforeseen problems and it is necessary for the supervisor to petition for the debtor's bankruptcy.

5.90 In order to avoid uncertainty, a proposal may set out specified circumstances in which the proposal will be deemed to have failed: for example, if a given sum of money is not recovered by the supervisor by a stated date. It may be desirable to allow the supervisor some discretion to permit the scheme to continue if there is a minor setback, but it should also give him authority to issue a certificate of non-compliance when it becomes apparent to him that the scheme has manifestly failed. In appropriate circumstances a debtor may put forward a proposal for a second IVA provided that 12 months have elapsed from the date of the first application for an interim order (s.255 (1)(c)).

5.91 Once there is non-compliance, bankruptcy is the usual, but not inevitable, consequence. A scheme based upon contributions from income may permit an alternative strategy, should the expected receipts fail to materialise, by giving the supervisor power to realise the debtor's assets as in bankruptcy. In such cases it may still be possible to achieve for creditors a better result than could be obtained in bankruptcy.

5.92 The supervisor has inherent power under section 264 to petition for the debtor's bankruptcy but it may be desirable to spell out in the proposal the circumstances in which the supervisor is likely to exercise that right and also to provide that, during the continuance of the scheme, the supervisor shall retain sufficient moneys to pay the cost of such petition should the need arise. This power may also be exercised by a creditor or the debtor himself.

5.93 If the supervisor is not in funds, he may prefer merely to circulate creditors to the effect that the scheme has failed. This will leave the creditors with the option of presenting a petition should they so desire. In any event the final reports shall be made as set out in paragraph 5.137 below.

5.94 Before commencing bankruptcy proceedings or taking other steps to declare non-compliance, the supervisor should establish that there is no realistic prospect of the debtor complying with the spirit of the arrangement. If, for example, there has been a minor set-back and the debtor is able to resume contributions, it may be possible to negotiate with creditors an extension of time. If such endeavours to recover the situation fail, the supervisor will ensure that the debtor appreciates the consequence of failure and the supervisor's duty to petition for his bankruptcy.

5.95 Any moneys that are in the estate should be paid to the creditors after drawing the supervisor's fee, together with disbursements and VAT and allowing sufficient to defray the costs of the bankruptcy and the time costs which will be involved.

5.96 The debtor, creditors, district judge and I.S. should all be advised of the default and a copy of the supervisor's receipts and payments account for the period of the arrangement appended to the notice. The supervisor then has to swear an affidavit of truth of statements in bankruptcy petition (I.R. 6.12) (App. I, Form G) and this is prepared by the supervisor together with the "bankruptcy petition for default in connection with voluntary arrangement" (I.R. 6.6). The form of petition is similar to that which appears at Appendix I, Form F save that item 2 of the petition will read:

> "2. On .... day of .... 19 .... a voluntary arrangement proposed by the debtor was approved by his creditors and I am the supervisor of the said voluntary arrangement."

5.97 Notwithstanding any other provisions of the rules, the petition must be presented to the court to which the nominee's report under section 256 was submitted (I.R. 6.9(4A)), unless the debtor has changed address in the meantime, in which case the County Court with bankruptcy jurisdiction over the new address should be used. The supervisor, after swearing the affidavit should take the forms to the relevant court with three additional copies. A court fee of £80, together with a deposit of £300 must be paid. Cheques are to be made payable to HMPG-LCD. The bankruptcy clerk will then seal the documents, retaining the original for the court files and returning the three copies to the supervisor, having completed the endorsement showing full details of the bankruptcy hearing. One copy is for personal service on the debtor and one is retained on the supervisor's records. The third copy is attached to Form 6.17 which is the "affidavit of personal service of bankruptcy petition" (I.R. 6.15). This affidavit is sworn by the individual who served the documents and states that the bankruptcy petition has indeed been served personally on the debtor. The sealed copy of the petition is attached as an exhibit marked "A".

5.98 District judges will only make bankruptcy orders if the correct procedure has been meticulously followed. It is prudent to get the debtor to sign a letter stating that he acknowledges the service of the petition and that furthermore he will liaise with the supervisor in order to expedite the matter in hand. It is helpful to attach the letter as a further exhibit together with a copy of the original proposal which, although it should be on the court file and laid before the registrar or district judge at the time of the hearing, is frequently not available.

5.99 The affidavit and exhibits are then taken to the court and filed. It is important to note that I.R. 6.15(2) states that the affidavit and exhibit should be filed in court immediately after service. It is imperative to comply with that requirement, and the supervisor must either file the affidavit on the day of service or the day following to avoid any criticism.

5.100 Service on the debtor should be made as soon as possible, in any case it must be within 14 days of the hearing and, in theory, the debtor has seven days before the date fixed for the hearing to give notice that he intends to oppose the petition. At the hearing the registrar or district judge will automatically grant the petition assuming that all details have been correctly filled in and the procedure scrupulously complied with. Any deviation from the approved methods will result in an adjournment. The O.R. will be notified by the court's bankruptcy clerk of the details of the bankruptcy, and the debtor will be required to attend on the O.R. for an oral examination, normally within two weeks.

5.101 After three months or so have elapsed, the O.R. will probably request from the supervisor a list of creditors and their addresses and it saves time if, as a courtesy, the supervisor sends details to the O.R. as soon as the bankruptcy order has been made. In addition, it is good practice to circulate creditors, informing them of the date of the bankruptcy order, the court name and reference number and the address of the appropriate O.R. This has the effect of stemming any flow of correspondence from creditors, who must now take up any problem with the O.R. and not the former supervisor. The question of funds remaining upon the failure of an IVA was considered in *Re Essengin Hussein (Davis v. Martin-Sklan)* [1996] B.P.I.R. 160, where the supervisor petitioned under section 264(1)(c) and sought directions concerning funds still in his hands as supervisor. The Registrar had held that on the making of the bankruptcy order the IVA was not terminated and the supervisor should distribute the money amongst those creditors who were party to the IVA. On appeal, the court held that as the arrangement had not been honoured by the debtor, the IVA was at an end and the supervisor should hand over the funds to the trustee for distribution to all the creditors of the bankrupt. Notwithstanding this decision, and subject to the terms of the proposal, it might be possible in such a case for the supervisor to distribute funds before he exercises his right to petition for bankruptcy but he cannot do so thereafter.

10. JOINT ESTATES

5.102 The Act sets out no formal procedure for partnership or other joint estates, and itself contains no provision for a "partnership voluntary arrangement". However, new procedures are now available by way of partnership voluntary arrangements and partnership administration orders, pursuant to the Insolvent Partnerships Order 1994 (S.I. 1994 No. 2421) and these are dealt with in Chapter 6 below. Moreover, partners also enter into interlocked or linked individual voluntary arrangements and these too are dealt with in Chapter 6.

11. MISCELLANEOUS

(a) Claims

5.103 For the purpose of the meeting of creditors, the chairman of the meeting shall consider the amount at which creditors' claims should rank for voting purposes. Subsequently, as in other insolvency procedures, the supervisor should examine all claims and settle the list for purposes of distribution.

5.104 For voting purposes, votes are calculated in accordance with I.R. 5.17, at the date of the bankruptcy order if there is one, otherwise as at the date of the meeting. In respect of an unliquidated amount, or any debt whose value is not ascertained, the creditor shall not vote except if the chairman agrees to put upon the debt an estimated minimum value for voting purposes. The chairman may admit or reject a creditor's claim for voting purposes in whole or in part. The chairman's decision on entitlement to vote is subject to the right of a creditor or the debtor to appeal to the court. If the chairman is in doubt whether a claim should be admitted or rejected, he shall mark it as "objected to" but allow the creditor to vote, subject to his vote being subsequently declared invalid if the objection to the claim is sustained (I.R. 5.17(6)). Such procedure may mean that the outcome of the meeting is not clear until after an appeal to the court and wherever possible the chairman should make a decision on the matter. He will have as a starting point the list of creditors supplied by the debtor and although he may be unable to scrutinise all the facts prior to the meeting, he will normally be able to make an assessment sufficient to fix a sum for voting purposes. If on an appeal the chairman's decision is reversed or varied, or a creditor's vote is declared invalid, the court may order another meeting to be summoned, or make such other order as it thinks just. This power is only exercisable by the court if it considers that the matter gives rise to unfair prejudice or material irregularity. Such applications to the court must be made within 28 days of the meeting. I.R. 5.17(9) states that the chairman is not personally liable for any costs incurred by any person in respect of an appeal under that rule. However, if the creditor can bring himself within section 262 (material irregularity) and can show that the nominee/chairman was at fault, then he may be able to recover costs (*Re A Debtor (No. 222 of 1990) (No. 2)* [1993] B.C.L.C. 233).

5.105 For all practical purposes, secured and preferential creditors will have the same class rights as in other insolvency proceedings unless they voluntarily waive these rights.

5.106 A meeting of creditors shall not approve any proposal or modification which affects the right of a secured creditor of the debtor to enforce his security, except with the concurrence of the creditor concerned (s.258(4)). Such concurrence might be available where the secured creditor is a connected party or where the value of the security on a forced sale basis is negligible and the creditor concerned may obtain some better recompense under the proposal. Failure to respect the rights of secured creditors may lead to the decision of the meeting being overturned for material irregularity, as happened in *Re A Debtor (No. 20 of 1992), Peck v. Craighead* [1995] B.C.C. 525. Likewise section 259(5) provides that preferential creditors shall be given their usual priority and shall rank *pari passu* unless they agree to the contrary.

5.107 The Rules are silent as to the voting rights of preferential creditors and it is presumed that they are entitled to vote for the full amount.

5.108 The arrangement, if approved, binds every person who had notice of the meeting and was entitled to vote thereat whether or not he was present or represented (s.260(2)(b)). It is therefore important that the debtor is encouraged from inception to produce a list of creditors that is as complete as possible and check with his records that there are no omissions. If any creditor is not given notice of the meeting he will not be bound by the scheme and may continue some other process against the debtor notwithstanding that he might have been outvoted had he been included. For good measure the list of creditors annexed to the statement of affairs and filed with the court should also be complete.

5.109 It follows that creditors who are not given notice, even if the omission is inadvertent, are not bound by the arrangement and are thus entitled to serve a statutory demand on the debtor with a view to, if the same is not complied with, the presentation of a bankruptcy petition. This requirement has been strictly interpreted by the courts. In *Re A Debtor (No. 64 of 1992)* [1994] B.C.C. 55, notice was sent on May 18, 1992 to Bradford & Bingley Building Society, a creditor, of a meeting of creditors pursuant to section 257 to be held on June 8, 1992 which would have been adequate notice had it not been addressed to premises that did not become the head office of the creditor until June 1, 1992. It is reported that the creditor was therefore ignorant of the meeting and did not attend. It is not reported whether anybody opened the post between June 1 and 8. The court held, allowing an appeal against an order of the District Judge made at Hertford County Court, that the creditor was not bound by the arrangement. It is advisable for practitioners to telephone, a few days before the meeting, those major creditors from whom no proxy has been received thereby creating a dialogue which may well lead to the production of an appropriate proxy form. Such action of itself cannot rectify lack of proper notice, but may lead to a mutual agreement to ignore the irregularity. This particular case may seem a little harsh on the debtor and suggest that a change in statute to enable the inclusion of creditors inadvertently omitted might in some circumstances be appropriate. Nevertheless it may be assumed in this case that, had the creditor in question found the proposal acceptable, it would have agreed to be bound, and, conversely would have voted against the proposals if present at the meeting. However, a creditor who does not receive notice but learns about the meeting independently, say by search of the court file, can validly vote at the meeting (*Re Debtors (Nos. 400 and 401 of 1996)* [1997] B.P.I.R. 431). Such creditor would appear also to have the option of claiming that as he had not received adequate notice he was not bound by the arrangement.

A person who is jointly liable with the debtor to a particular creditor, *e.g.* a co-surety in respect of a lease, will not in the absence of any express provision to that effect be released from his joint liability by reason of the debtor's voluntary arrangement (*Johnson and Another v. Davies and Another* [1997] B.P.I.R. 221).

5.110 Prior to distributing moneys to creditors, the prudent supervisor will examine all claims submitted by creditors and admit amounts for distribution purposes. This will involve normal commercial criteria but, as a last resort, the aggrieved creditor may apply to the court if dissatisfied with the supervisor's decision in this respect.

5.111 If the supervisor becomes aware of a creditor whose claim was omitted from the scheme at inception, whether inadvertently or otherwise, and if that creditor is willing nevertheless to participate in the scheme *pari passu* with other creditors, the simplest outcome is to include the creditor for the purposes of distribution. However, it is advisable that the proposal should empower the supervisor to permit the inclusion of late claims, otherwise the original creditors may be aggrieved that their expected dividend has been diluted. Such a clause will not, however, oblige the late claimant to participate in the scheme.

(b) Applications to court and challenges to the meeting of creditors

5.112 The decision of the creditors' meeting may be challenged on application to the court in accordance with section 262 where the voluntary arrangement unfairly prejudices the interests of a creditor or a debtor or there has been some material irregularity at, or in relation to, the meeting. Application may be made by the debtor, any person entitled to vote at the creditors' meeting, the nominee or his replacement or, where the debtor is an undischarged bankrupt, the trustee or O.R. Such application must be made within 28 days of the date on which the report of the meeting is filed with the court.

5.113 If the court is satisfied that the application is justified, it may revoke or suspend any approval given by the meeting or give a direction for the summoning of a further meeting of creditors to consider a revised proposal or to reconsider the original proposal.

5.114 In a case of alleged material irregularity, the court may, if it considers that the nominee has been at fault, make an order for costs against him (*Re A Debtor (No. 222 of 1990) (No. 2)* [1993] B.C.L.C. 233). This may be contrasted with the position in respect of appeals under I.R. 5.17 which relate to voting at the creditors' meeting, where the chairman is not personally liable for costs (I.R. 5.17(9)).

5.115 Where the court gives a direction for the summoning of a meeting to consider a revised proposal, and becomes satisfied that the debtor does not intend to submit to such proposal, the court shall revoke the direction and may revoke or suspend any approval given at the previous creditors' meeting. It may also where appropriate extend any interim order and give supplemental directions as it thinks fit.

5.116 Where no application is made to the court, any approval given to a proposal by creditors is not invalidated solely by any irregularity in relation to the meeting.

5.117 As mentioned in paragraph 5.104 above, an appeal may be made against the chairman's decision as regards voting (I.R. 5.17).

5.118 Whilst the court does not exercise the general control over the proceedings that apply in bankruptcy, it is open to the debtor or any creditor, during the conduct of the scheme, if dissatisfied with any act, omission or decision of the supervisor, to apply to the court (s.263(3)). In such a case the court may confirm, reverse or modify any act or decision of the supervisor, give directions or make such order as it thinks fit.

5.119 Moreover, the supervisor may himself apply to the court for directions in relation to any particular matter arising under the voluntary arrangement (s.263(4)). Whilst this is a general power for a supervisor to seek directions on any particular matter, it is a power to be used sparingly and should not in practice be adopted where a matter may be resolved by other means, for example, by seeking the views of creditors or exercising such powers as are open to him by statute or under the terms of the proposal. Such an application is therefore most frequently applied where a decision is likely to be controversial. In such cases the supervisor should not merely ask the court to make decisions but he should make a preliminary decision himself and invite the court to ratify the same or give such other directions as appear appropriate. This is similar to an application by a trustee in bankruptcy described in Chapter 4.

5.120 The court may upon application make an order appointing a qualified insolvency practitioner to act as supervisor either to fill a vacancy or in substitution of the existing supervisor but will make such appointment only when it is expedient to do so and at the same time inexpedient, difficult or impracticable for the appointment to be made without the assistance of the court.

(c) Taxation

The establishment of a voluntary arrangement and the appointment of a supervisor does not relieve the debtor of his ongoing taxation responsibilities. He will be required to complete his tax returns and account for tax on income and capital gains. The supervisor has no responsibility in this regard. **5.121**

The supervisor must, however, ensure that the tax liabilities of the debtor attributable to the period covered by the arrangement are identified so that amounts which are a claim against the estate are included and dealt with correctly under the arrangement. **5.122**

The Inland Revenue will, in many cases, be a substantial creditor and support for an arrangement from them will be required. There is no general policy on the part of the Inland Revenue as to the acceptance or rejection of arrangements and each proposal will be considered on merit. There is an underlying responsibility on the part of the Inland Revenue to be seen to treat all taxpayers equally and to ensure that all taxpayers meet their obligations. It is inevitable that one of the requirements to gain Inland Revenue support will be that all outstanding and overdue compliance matters will be brought up to date and continue to be kept in good order. Certain taxes constitute a preferential debt and will need to be dealt with accordingly. The taxes concerned are set out in Chapter 8. **5.123**

Where the debtor continues to carry on a trade there are potential problems of a fiscal nature. A creditor who forgoes part of a trade debt as part of the arrangement should be able to claim relief from tax. However, as far as the debtor is concerned the Inland Revenue are likely to consider that the amount waived by the creditor is a taxable receipt of the debtor's business. Where funds are to come from a third party as part of the composition, an assignment of the debt may be appropriate so that the total amount outstanding remains without reduction. **5.124**

Customs and Excise are also likely to be a creditor for unpaid VAT. As with the Inland Revenue each case will be considered on merit. An element of the unpaid VAT will constitute a preferential claim as set out in Chapter 8 and the supervisor will need to take this into account. Trade creditors should be able to claim bad debt relief if they have not already done so under normal VAT regulations. Customs and Excise will require all outstanding compliance failures to be addressed. Customs and Excise may also require the provision of security for future VAT payments. The amount of such security is normally an amount equal to six months estimated VAT liability (four months if monthly returns are made). Failure to provide the security will effectively stop the trading activities as it is an offence to make taxable supplies where a security deposit is requested but not provided. **5.125**

12. THE UNDISCHARGED BANKRUPT (CASE 1)

Previous sections in this Chapter have dealt mainly with the situation where the debtor is not an undischarged bankrupt and accordingly has put forward his proposal with a view to avoiding bankruptcy proceedings. This is referred to as Case 2 in I.R. 5.1. As mentioned in the introduction, a debtor who is an undischarged bankrupt may nevertheless put forward a proposal for a voluntary arrangement (known as Case 1) but may not do so if he has previously submitted a proposal, during the past 12 months, which has been rejected. In most respects the procedures are the same and, except as indicated in this section, the procedures described in respect of Case 2 arrangements also apply to Case 1. **5.126**

5.127 Where a debtor is already bankrupt, he should carefully consider whether there really are advantages for also proposing a voluntary arrangement, bearing in mind that a procedure for resolving his affairs is already in progress. Indeed a voluntary arrangement is not an easy option but is likely to require some extra commitment on his part. Whilst certain bankruptcy costs will already have been incurred, others may be saved if an arrangement is introduced. If adopted, the arrangement will lead to the annulment of the bankruptcy order, an objective which may assist the debtor's income prospects.

5.128 The debtor should find a third party willing to advance the nominee's fee since this cannot be paid from the estate as the debtor's own funds vest in the trustee.

5.129 The rules relating to the contents of the proposal described in paragraphs 5.14–5.25 above are unchanged. The nominee may be the trustee himself or some other insolvency practitioner who is qualified to act. The nominee or other practitioner advising the debtor, or the debtor himself, should at an early stage speak to the O.R. and ascertain whether there is likely to be any objection to the arrangement. In most cases the O.R. will co-operate with the debtor and nominee so far as is practical and will not take steps that are likely to undermine the arrangement and, save in respect of perishable goods, is likely to leave the assets to be dealt with under the proposal, if adopted. It is not unknown for a practitioner, when approaching the O.R. in these circumstances, to be appointed, by the D.T.I., as trustee in bankruptcy pending the voluntary arrangement.

5.130 The application for the interim order under section 253(3) may, as explained in paragraphs 5.30–5.40 above, be made by the debtor, the trustee in bankruptcy or the O.R. It would, however, be unusual for the O.R. to make such an application himself and he is more likely to secure the appointment of a trustee and suggest that such trustee look into the possibility of an arrangement.

5.131 The applicant for the interim order must give at least two days' notice of the hearing to the bankrupt debtor, the O.R. and the trustee, whichever of those three is not himself the applicant (I.R. 5.5(4)). The same parties must also be served with notice of the making of the order once this is achieved (I.R. 5.7(2)). The application shall be made to the court having the conduct of the bankruptcy and filed with those bankruptcy proceedings (I.R. 5.5A(3)).

5.132 The nominee must, in accordance with I.R. 5.10(5), send to the O.R. and the trustee a copy of the debtor's proposal, the nominee's report and a statement of affairs or summary thereof. At the hearing of the nominee's report, the O.R. or trustee may appear or be represented (I.R. 5.12).

5.133 Where the creditors' meeting approves the proposed voluntary arrangement, with or without modifications, the court may in accordance with section 261 do one or both of the following, namely:

(a) annul the bankruptcy order; and/or
(b) give such directions with respect to the conduct of the bankruptcy and the administration of the bankrupt's estate as it thinks appropriate for facilitating the implementation of the approved voluntary arrangement.

5.134 The court shall not annul a bankruptcy order for at least 28 days from the day on which the report of the creditors' meeting is made to the court (s.261) or at any time when an application is pending under section 262 to challenge the decision of the meeting. In practice, in the absence of a challenge, the annulment is normally granted 28 days from the date the court hears the chairman's report, irrespective of the date of filing. A challenge under section 262, as described in paragraph 5.74 above, may be made by the trustee or the O.R.

5.135 In practice, once time has passed for any successful challenge to be made to the decision of the meeting of creditors, the court is likely to annul the bankruptcy order and the arrangement will be implemented in the normal way. The supervisor, however, retains the right to petition for bankruptcy should there be non-compliance with the arrangement.

13. CLOSING THE ARRANGEMENT

5.136 A minority of arrangements end in failure, usually because the debtor or a third party does not produce the funds anticipated in the proposal. In these cases, the supervisor will issue a certificate of non-compliance and bring the scheme to an end as described above.

5.137 Happily the majority of arrangements are successfully completed with distributions to creditors in line with the proposal. Once the arrangement is completed, the supervisor shall within 28 days send notice to all creditors and to the debtor to that effect, together with a summary of his receipts and payments and explaining any difference between the actual implementation and the proposal approved at the creditors' meeting. Copies of the notice shall be sent to the D.T.I. and the court.

5.138 The process is then complete but the Rules contain one final warning. If the arrangement was approved as a result of false representation, or other fraud, then the person guilty of such offence shall be liable to imprisonment or a fine or both (I.R. 5.30).

Chapter 6
INSOLVENT PARTNERSHIPS

I never promised you a rose garden—Hannah Green.

6.01 In this chapter, in contrast to the rest of the book, references to "the Act" are to the Partnership Act 1890 (P.A. 1890) and *not* to the Insolvency Act which will be referred to as I.A. 1986. References to "the Order" are to the Insolvent Partnerships Order 1994, (S.I. 1994 No. 2421) (I.P.O. 1994). The Order also allows for the company voluntary arrangement procedure and the company administration procedure to be adapted for insolvent partnership. Although there is no specific legal term, for ease of reference (and because these terms are commonly in use) we shall refer to such procedures as partnership voluntary arrangements (P.V.A.) and partnership administration orders (P.A.O.).

6.02 Dealing with the affairs of insolvent partnerships, whether in terms of their winding-up and dissolution or, hopefully, putting into place rescue procedures, creates particular difficulties for insolvency practitioners. A number of reasons might be adduced for this.

6.03 First, partnership law is itself a subject of some complexity. The same might also be said about company law and yet practitioners generally have little difficulty with procedures involving limited companies, where there is the question of familiarity. Insolvency practitioners are used to dealing with the winding-up of limited companies and have become familiar with company voluntary arrangements and administration orders. They are also, in general, knowledgeable about procedures involving individuals, whether bankruptcies or Individual Voluntary Arrangements (I.V.A.s). Cases where partnerships are involved, however, are much less common. The legal aspects of the partnership are difficult and some knowledge of partnership law, even at a basic level, may be required. The Partnership Act 1890 provides only a framework and as the Act itself makes clear (s.19), partners are entirely free to vary their mutual rights and duties. The Act has been described, in our opinion accurately, as: "By modern standards . . . relatively short, and *deceptively* clear" (our emphasis) (*Insolvent Partnerships* (Jordans) at para. 1.3).

6.04 Second, partnerships vary enormously, not only in size, but in the legal structures used to set up and regulate them. A partnership may consist of simply a husband and wife running a corner shop, or it may comprise a multi-national conglomerate with hundreds of partners, as with the large firms of accountants. Within those larger partnerships there may be sub-partnerships in particular locations or for particular areas of work. Partnerships, whether large or small, may be governed by minimal documentation, or, at the other extreme, by a substantial partnership agreement running into hundreds of pages to which each partner will subscribe. It does not necessarily follow incidentally that just because a partnership is large it will be regulated by an agreement—it is not unknown for large and medium size firms of accountants and solicitors to have no such documents.

6.05 All of the above, imports a certain hybrid quality into partnerships, particularly when dealing with insolvency problems. Small partnerships may be regarded simply as individuals who happen to be trading together. The larger partnerships have a much more corporate structure but they are still partnerships. The insolvency practitioner faced with the problems of an insolvent partnership has, as will be seen, an array of options which may involve features of both corporate and individual insolvency.

6.06 Before discussing the specific provisions of I.P.O. 1994, it is necessary to look briefly at some general features of partnership. An understanding of these may be necessary, for the reasons set out above, as a preliminary to considering specific solutions to financial problems.

1. THE NATURE OF PARTNERSHIP

6.07 The definition of the relationship which gives rise to what is legally described as a partnership is contained in section 1(1) of P.A. 1890: "Partnership is the relation which subsists between persons carrying on a business in common with a view of profit."

6.08 Partnership is regarded primarily as a contractual relationship between the partners but one which, curiously, does not require any formal document for it to exist. As we have seen (para. 6.1 above) it is often the case that there is no partnership deed but there may be other documents, *e.g.* correspondence, memoranda, or heads of agreement, which evidence more clearly the relationship between the partners. However, a partnership can subsist "at will" simply by the fact that the partners are in business together and behaving as partners. The classic "corner shop" fits well within this scenario.

6.09 It is not necessary for the "persons" described in section 1(1) to be natural persons. A partnership can subsist between an individual or individuals and a company, or between two companies, or even between two partnerships. For the purposes of this Chapter, however, it is assumed that the subject is a partnership of individuals.

6.10 The two essentials of partnership from the above definition, are:

(a) ". . . carrying on a business in common . . ."; and
(b) ". . . with a view of profit."

What is meant by "business" is not precisely defined in the Act but it includes a trade, occupation or profession (s.45). However, the mere fact that parties may enter into joint ownership of property does not of itself connote a partnership (s.2(1)) because there has to be some element of commercial activity. Accordingly, individuals who happen to own property jointly in which they live or use, *e.g.* to accommodate an elderly relative, are not legally in partnership. If, however, they purchase a property jointly with a view to developing it or letting it, then they may be.

6.11 The second element is the requirement that the business is carried on with a view to making a profit. This excludes organisations which are set up to be non-profit making, *e.g.* charities, clubs, and other social groups or associations, *e.g.* a railway preservation society (*Goddard v. Mills* (1929), *The Times*, 16 February, 1929).

2. PARTNERS RIGHTS AND DUTIES BETWEEN THEMSELVES

6.12 At the simplest level, the P.A. 1890 assumes equality between the partners on the following principles:

(a) every partner is entitled to share equally in capital, profits and losses (s.24(1));
(b) every partner may take part in the management of the business (s.24 (5));
(c) the consent of all existing partners is required for any change in the nature of the partnership business, or before a new partner is admitted, although decisions on "ordinary" matters connected with the partnership business may be decided by a majority of partners (s.24).

6.13 The Act, however, does make it clear that the above provisions are subject to any agreement, express or implied, between the partners so that in many cases the partnership deed or heads of agreement becomes the governing constitution of the partnership.

6.14 Between themselves partners have certain rights of indemnity so that a partner who pays more than his share of the partnership debt is entitled to a contribution from his co-partners (*Halsbury's Laws of England,* Vol. 35, para. 68). However, partners are not, as regards partnership dealings, considered as debtor and creditor between themselves until the concern is wound up or until there is a binding settlement of the accounts, although a person who has left the partnership by retirement or expulsion, may have the relationship of debtor/creditor to his former partners, as the case may be (*ibid., para. 147*).

6.15 The partners also have between themselves a fiduciary relationship, that is one of utmost good faith towards the other partners, so that a partner cannot make a secret profit out of any transaction and, needless to say, must not compete with his fellow partners without their express consent.

3. RELATIONS WITH THIRD PARTIES

6.16 The significance of the relationship between the partnership and third parties is that this may be of crucial importance in establishing the identity of creditors and the amount for which they are likely to vote or prove. There may be a question of determining whether one or more of the partners has authority (as defined below) to bind the partnership in respect of a particular transaction.

6.17 Relations between the partnership and third parties, "the world outside the partnership" as (Davis, Steiner Cohen: *Insolvent Partnerships: (Jordans) para. 2.5*) is likely to be dominated by two features:

(a) the principles of agency;
(b) the concept of joint and several liability.

(a) Agency

6.18 Section 5 of the Act defines the role of partners in agency terms:

> "Every partner is an agent of the firm and his other partners for the purpose of the partnership; and the acts of every partner who does any act for carrying on in the usual way business of the kind carried on by the firm of which he is a member bind the firm and his partners, unless the partner so acting has in fact no authority to act for the firm in the particular matter, and the person with whom he is dealing either knows that he has no authority, or does not know or believe him to be a partner."

The partners may have *actual* authority on behalf of the firm; or *implied* or *usual* authority, or ostensible (apparent) authority. Actual authority, of course means that the person concerned is genuinely invested with certain authority by the partners and it will be a question of fact. **6.19**

This applies even in the case of non-partners. If the firm's personnel officer, a non-partner, acts within his authority in hiring a secretary, then the partners are bound by that contract of employment. **6.20**

In the absence of actual authority resort may be had to what is described as usual or implied authority and in the event of a dispute, the court will have to consider evidence as to what is usual in a particular trade or profession (see, *e.g. United Bank of Kuwait v. Hammond and Others* [1988] 1 W.L.R. 1051, where the court had to consider usual authority of solicitors). **6.21**

If the third party has notice of any lack of authority vested in a particular partner then of course that third party cannot seek to enforce against the other partners any agreement which is made in breach of such restriction, *e.g.* a contract for more than a certain value where he has notice that the partner's authority is limited. **6.22**

A more difficult problem arises with regard to ostensible or apparent authority. This should be briefly explained. Ostensible authority is a concept of the law of agency whereby it is held that the principal by words or by conduct, *represents* that the agent has certain authority. If the third party then relies upon that representation and makes an agreement with the agent, the principal will be bound. It must be remembered that ostensible authority is not only vested in other partners; there may be employees or other agents of the firm who have ostensible authority to make contracts which are binding on the principles. In each case it will be a question of fact and to examine the relevant circumstances to show whether such authority exists. **6.23**

(b) Joint liability

Partners have joint liability in respect of the debts and other obligations of the partnership: **6.24**

> "Every partner in a firm is jointly liable with the other partners for all debts and obligations of the firm incurred while he is a partner." (s.9)

Being a joint liability, a settlement against one partner will extinguish the claim. However, there must be a settlement and the court will be reluctant to construe one save where there is express agreement on the point. In *Artman v. Artman; Re a Bankrupt (No. 622 of 1995)* [1996] B.P.I.R. 511 Walker J. felt that it was open to a petitioning creditor to proceed with a petition for bankruptcy while coming to terms with the bankrupt's partner in respect of the same debt, so long as the terms agreed with the partner did not amount to payment in full, or the compounding of the bankrupt's debt. **6.25**

The concept of joint liability applies in respect of those persons who were partners when the liability arose; a person who has come in as a partner cannot be sued on a cause of action which arose before he joined the partnership unless he has agreed with the creditor that he accept liability. **6.26**

Although there is joint liability, the creditor has a choice: he may sue one partner, say the solvent one, or he may sue the firm. He is certainly not obliged to sue all of the partners—in effect he can "cherry pick" and enforce judgment against a solvent partner leaving that partner to pursue remedies for an indemnity against his co-partners (see s.3 of the Civil Liability (Contribution) Act 1978). **6.27**

The above governs the position in respect of contracts but special rules apply in other cases. In respect of torts (*e.g.* negligence), provided that the partner is acting in the ordinary course of the business of the firm, or with the authority of his co-partners, the liability is joint and several. A similar rule **6.28** applies where there has been a misapplication of money or property which has been misapplied by one or more of the partners (P.A. 1890, ss.10–12).

4. DISSOLUTION

6.29 Dissolution may occur for a multitude of reasons, *e.g.* the partners agree to dissolve the partnership but, in the absence of any specific agreement between the partners, every partnership is dissolved as regards all the partners by the death or bankruptcy of any partner (s.33(1)) and it is therefore of considerable importance for partners to provide in the agreement, if they have one, for such an event. However, automatic dissolution under section 33 does require a bankruptcy order to be made so that the fact that an individual partner has become insolvent, and has entered into an I.V.A., would not of *itself* mean a dissolution unless the partnership agreement so provides. It is not uncommon, however, for a partnership deed to give other partners the right to expel a partner who has become insolvent or made a composition with his creditors, very often providing also that such expulsion would not dissolve the partnership as regards the other partners.

6.30 The deed may also specify other cases where dissolution will occur but in the main, because of tax and other implications, partners are often at pains, if they go to the trouble of preparing a partnership deed, to ensure that there is no dissolution of the existing partnership simply because one partner becomes insolvent or commits an act which leads to his or her expulsion.

6.31 Apart from such cases of automatic dissolution, a partnership may also be dissolved on an application to the court by one or more of the existing partners (s.35) and the circumstances in which dissolution may be ordered are set out in that section.

5. DEFINING THE PARTNERSHIP: EQUITY AND SALARIED PARTNERS

6.32 Defining who is a partner is of major significance when considering the affairs of an insolvent partnership.

6.33 In preparing for a P.V.A. or a P.A.O. the practitioner will need to satisfy himself as to the identity, status, and financial position of each partner in the light of the possibility that some who are apparently partners do not in law enjoy that status.

6.34 The first point of reference in determining partnership status will be a partnership agreement, failing that the headed notepaper may be a useful guide or a list of partners kept at the principal place of business. In some cases, unfortunately, the position may be sufficiently confused for the practitioner himself to be required to take some independent legal advice as to whether an individual is truly a partner.

6.35 Both the Act and I.P.O. 1994 are of some limited assistance. Specifically
6.36 section 14 of the Act imports the concept of liability by "holding out":

> "every one who by words spoken or written or by conduct represents himself, or knowingly suffers himself to be represented, as a partner in a particular firm, is liable as a partner to any one who has on the faith of any such representation given credit to the firm, whether the representation has or has not been made or communicated to the person so giving credit

by or with the knowledge of the apparent partner making the representation or suffering it to be made."

6.37 What this section does not do is to make such persons partners. It makes them liable by way of sharing the joint liability of partners in certain circumstances, in other words such an individual may be liable by "holding out" to a particular creditor but would not share responsibility for the other debts of the partnership.

6.38 I.P.O. 1994 recognises the concept of "holding out" by defining a "member" of a partnership in the following terms: "[It] . . . means a member of a partnership and any person who is liable as a partner within the meaning of section 14 of the Partnership Act 1890" (I.P.O. 1994, art. 2(1)).

6.39 This concept may bring into the net junior and salaried partners and it is quite clear that such persons, even if their share is much smaller than those of other partners, may still be caught in terms of joint liability. The fact that a salaried partner may be given an indemnity from other partners will be of little comfort to him or her if that indemnity proves to be worthless particularly since such an indemnity ranks behind the claims of third-party creditors.

6.40 This places salaried partners in a potentially vulnerable position; they may not have an equal say in management, they may have not been enjoying the lavish lifestyles of some of the senior partners, and yet they may be liable jointly and severally for all of the debts.

6.41 One word of caution needs to be advanced: not every salaried partner is truly a partner with the rights and obligations which go with that status. A person who has been put on the notepaper but is basically a salaried employee with no real say in the management of the business may be able to argue that he is not a true partner.

6. THE OPTIONS AVAILABLE—THE INSOLVENT PARTNERSHIPS ORDER 1994

6.42 Broadly speaking, I.P.O. 1994 modifies and extends the Insolvency Act 1986 to provide a number of different remedies and solutions to insolvency, both to the creditors and to the members of the partnership.

6.43 There are no less than eight different procedures, of which the first three may fall under the heading of rescue procedures:

(a) Partnership Voluntary Arrangement (P.V.A.) (arts 4 and 5 and Sched. 1 to the Order);
(b) Interlocking I.V.A.s (under Pt VIII of I.A. 1986);
(c) Administration Order (art. 6 and Sched. 2);
(d) winding up of the insolvent partnership only on a creditor's petition (art. 7 and Sched. 3);
(e) winding up of the insolvent partnership on a creditor's petition with concurrent petitions against the members for bankruptcy (art. 8 and Sched. 4);
(f) winding up of the insolvent partnership on a member's petition with no concurrent petition by that member against another member (art. 8 and Sched. 3, Pt 1 and Sched. 5);
(g) winding up the partnership on a member's petition with concurrent petitions for bankruptcy against all members (art. 10 and Sched. 6, Pt of Sched. 4 and Sched. 7);
(h) joint bankruptcy petition by individual members without winding up the insolvent partnership (art. 11 and Sched. 7).

7. LIQUIDATION OF THE PARTNERSHIP: CREDITORS' PETITIONS

6.44 An insolvent partnership may be wound up as an unregistered company under Part V of I.A. 1986, ss.220–229 as modified by I.P.O. 1994.

6.45 A petition may be against the partnership only, without a concurrent petition against any of the members, pursuant to Article 7 of I.P.O., or against both the partnership and one or more of the members under Article 8.

6.46 Since it is beyond the scope of this book to deal with what is in effect compulsory winding up procedure it is not proposed by the authors to give more than a summary of the law and procedure, with regard to such petitions.

6.47 (a) *Who may present a petition:* Article 7 provides that a petition may be presented by a creditor, or a responsible insolvency practitioner, the Secretary of State, or any other person other than the member.

There is an express provision that an insolvent partnership cannot be wound up voluntarily (I.A. 1986, s.221(4) (as modified)) which should not be confused with "winding up" following dissolution—not a true insolvency procedure.

6.48 (b) *The circumstances in which the partnership may be wound up:* section 221, as modified, applies and an insolvent partnership may be wound up as an unregistered company if:

(i) the partnership is dissolved, or ceases to carry on business, or is carrying on business only for the purpose of winding up its affairs;
(ii) if the partnership is unable to pay its debts;
(iii) if the court is of the opinion that it is just and equitable for the winding up of an insolvent partnership under Part V of I.A. 1986.

6.49 All of the usual provisions apply as regards the winding up of companies, in a modified form, *e.g.* for the appointment of a provisional liquidator and there is imported a statutory demand procedure so that in respect of any debt exceeding £750 (the present limit, which may be raised) a statutory demand may be served by the creditor on an officer of the partnership and if left unpaid for more than 21 days this may be on itself found a petition.

For the purposes of I.P.O. 1994 an "officer" of a partnership is widely defined as either:

(a) a member; or
(b) a person who has management or control of the partnership business.

6.50 In the case of insolvent partnerships, there is also a provision (which applies in the case of unregistered companies) by way of a modification of I.A. 1986, s.221 to the effect that a partnership is deemed unable to pay its debts if an action or other proceeding has been instituted against a member for any debt or demand due, or claimed to be due, from the partnership, or from him in his character of member and (a) notice in writing of the institute of the action or proceeding has been served on the partnership in a specified manner; and (b) the partnership has not within three weeks after service of the notice paid, secured or compounded for the debt or demand or procured the action or proceedings to be stayed or sisted or, indemnified the defendant or defender to his reasonable satisfaction against the action or proceeding and against all costs, damages and expenses to be incurred by him because of it.

6.51 Once an insolvent partnership has been wound up as an unregistered company, then the powers of the liquidator are those which are set out in Schedule 4 to the I.A. 1986.

6.52 The second form of procedure which is envisaged by the I.P.O. 1994 involves the presentation of a winding up petition against the partnership as an unregistered company together with concurrent petitions against corporate or individual members or former members.

6.53 There are prescribed forms of petition which are set out in Schedule 9 to the Order together with a prescribed form of statutory demand by a creditor.

6.54 The procedure requires, except as the court otherwise directs, simultaneous presentation of the petitions but the hearing of the petition against the partnership fixed by the court must be in advance of the hearing of any petition against the insolvent member (I.A. 1986, s.124 (as amended)). Generally speaking, the options available to the court in respect of the partnership, whether with regard to concurrent petitions or otherwise, are those which are set out in the procedures relating to registered limited companies.

6.55 As indicated above, we do not intend to deal with those aspects in detail. It would, however, be appropriate to consider what the court may do in respect of petitions against individual members.

6.56 If a winding up order has been made against the partnership, the court may make bankruptcy orders against the individual members. If the court has dismissed the winding up petition against the partnership, it may dismiss the bankruptcy petition against the individual members. If an insolvency order is, however, made against the member, that is without the partnership being wound up—then that bankruptcy will proceed as if it were a "normal" bankruptcy, without reference to I.P.O. 1994.

6.57 Even where a winding up order has been made against the partnership, the court may dismiss the petition against an insolvent member, if it believes it is just to do so because of a change in circumstances since the making of the winding up order (I.A. 1986, s.125A(6)). This in effect reverses the decision in *Re Marr (a Bankrupt)* [1990] Ch. 773.

6.58 If an individual member is a limited partner then the court may dismiss the petition against him if he lodges in court for the benefit of the partnership creditors sufficient money or security, to the court's satisfaction, to meet his liabilities for his debts and obligations of the partnership, or if he satisfies the court that he is no longer under any liability in respect of the partnership obligations or debts (I.A. 1986, s.125A(7)).

6.59 Once a bankruptcy order has been made then the provisions of the I.A. 1986, with modifications, will apply in respect of such matters as the role and functions of the O.R., the appointment of what is described as "a responsible insolvency practitioner", the statements of affairs and public examination, and private examinations by the trustee.

8. PRIORITY OF EXPENSES AND DEBTS

6.60 This is a subject of some complexity. Substantial modifications have been made to sections 175 and 328 of the Insolvency Act 1986, pursuant to Schedule 4 to the I.P.O. 1994.

6.61 The modified section 175 is reproduced in its entirety in Appendix X to this book. It deals with priority of expenses, priority of debts in the joint and separate estates and some general provisions relating to distribution. The rules as to distribution may, however, be modified on an application to the court by the responsible insolvency practitioner.

6.62 A primary effect of the modified section 175 is that where the winding-up of the partnership takes place together with the concurrent petitions against one or more members (under art. 8), the debt of a partnership creditor which is not satisfied out of the partnership estate will rank as a debt having equality with the debts of the member as regards the separate estate. That debt is, however, not provable by the creditor, but by the responsible insolvency practitioner. If there is not a concurrence of orders—the possibility of separate petitions exist—it would appear that that rule does not apply although the court has power to adjust priorities on an application by the liquidator on the insolvent partnership.

6.63 There are a few points of general importance with regard to distribution which should be noted. First, no *member* of the partnership may prove for a joint or separate debt in competition with joint creditors, unless the debt has arisen:

(a) as a result of fraud; or
(b) in the ordinary course of business carried on separately from the partnership business.

6.64 This may prejudice the position, not only of a current member of the partnership—because it reflects the fact that the partners may not compete with the creditors—but a retired member too. It is possible that such a retired member may become liable for obligations incurred while he was a partner if persons leaving the firm have not been given notice of the change (a notice in the *London Gazette* would usually suffice in respect of future creditors (P.A. 1890, p. 36)). Such a retired partner may find that his indemnity from those partners who remain behind may be valueless if it is likely to be subordinated to the claims of third party creditors.

6.65 Although the effect of the modified section 175 may be to involve the transfer of surpluses (if any) from a joint estate to separate estates, it is specifically provided that the O.R. or responsible insolvency practitioner may not claim remuneration for fees in relation to the transfer of such surpluses.

9. LIQUIDATION ON MEMBER'S PETITION

6.66 This is dealt with by articles 9 and 10. **Article 9:** winding-up of insolvent partnership as unregistered company on member's petition where no concurrent petition is presented against the member; and **article 10:** winding-up of insolvent partnership as unregistered company on member's petition where concurrent petition is presented against all members.

6.67 Such a petition is presented under the modified I.A. 1986, s.221A(1) (I.P.O., Sched. 5). It may only be presented if the partnership consists of not less than eight members. Such a partnership cannot be wound up voluntarily.

6.68 A petition may also be presented by a member of the partnership with the leave of the court, where there are seven or fewer members, if the court is satisfied that:

(a) the member has served on the partnership a written demand in respect of a joint debt or debts exceeding £750 then due from the partnership but paid by the member, other than out of partnership property;
(b) the partnership has for three weeks after service of the demand neglected to pay the sum or to secure or compound for it to the member's satisfaction and

(c) the member has obtained judgment or an order of the court against the partnership for reimbursement to him of the amount of the joint debt or debts so paid and has taken all reasonable steps (other than insolvency proceedings).

6.69 Procedures and other matters concerning the winding-up of the partnership are dealt with in I.A. 1986, ss.117 and 221, as modified by the Order.

10. WINDING-UP OF INSOLVENT PARTNERSHIP AS UNREGISTERED COMPANY ON MEMBER'S PETITION WHERE CONCURRENT PETITIONS ARE PRESENTED AGAINST ALL THE MEMBERS

6.70 This is article 10 of the Order and the petitions must be in the prescribed forms set out in Schedule 9 to the Order. A petition for the winding-up of the partnership may only be presented by a member of the partnership on the grounds that the partnership is unable to pay its debts, and:

(a) the petitions must at the same time be presented by that member for insolvency orders against every other member of the partnership including himself, and
(b) each member is willing for an insolvency order to be made against him or it and the petition against him or it contains a statement to that effect (I.A. 1986, s.124(2) (as modified)). These petitions should all be presented to the same court, and, unless the court otherwise permits, on the same day and, apart from the petitions against individual members, it should be advertised.

6.71 The hearing of the petition against the partnership fixed by the court must take place before the hearing of the petitions against the insolvent members. An insolvent member is entitled to be heard by the court on any petition relating to the winding-up of the partnership.

6.72 Leave to withdraw the petition may only be granted if at the same time the petitioner withdraws every other petition which was presented under the relevant section as modified and the court must be given at least three days notice before the hearing of the petitioners intention to withdraw.

11. JOINT BANKRUPTCY PETITIONS

6.73 Article 11 allows the presentation of a joint bankruptcy petition, that is for individual members without the winding-up of the partnership as an unregistered company.

6.74 Although presentation should normally be by all the members, on the application of any member of an insolvent partnership, if the court is satisfied that a petition presented by all of the members would be impracticable, it may direct for the petition to be presented by such a member or members as are specified by the court. This may apply if one of the members is untraceable or has gone abroad but it is not clear whether this would permit the presentation of a petition by one or more members if another member simply refused to agree to its presentation even where the partnership was clearly insolvent.

6.75 A joint bankruptcy petition cannot be withdrawn without the court's leave.

12. GROUNDS FOR A JOINT BANKRUPTCY PETITION

6.76 A petition can only be presented on the grounds that the partnership is unable to pay its debts (I.A. 1986, s.272 (as modified)).

6.77 The petition must be presented together with a statement of each member's affairs in the prescribed form containing particulars of creditors, debts and other liabilities and assets.

6.78 Other provisions concerning meetings of creditors, the power to appoint a trustee, restrictions on disposition of property (I.A. 1986, s.284), definition of a members estate, and summary administration, in general follow procedure as regards the bankruptcy of individuals.

13. PRIORITY OF EXPENSES AND DEBTS

(a) Priority of expenses

6.79 Where a partnership is being wound up under article 11 of the Order, a modification is made in respect of I.A. 1986, s.328 dealing with the priority of expenses incurred by the responsible insolvency practitioner of an insolvent partnership and of any insolvent member of that partnership against whom an insolvency order has been made. The modified section 328 is reproduced in Appendix X.

6.80 The effect of these provisions is to ensure, so far as possible, that where there is a deficiency, the expenses incurred in the joint estate and in the separate estates rank pari passu so that any deficiency is made up from the other estate or estates.

6.81 Notwithstanding the provisions of section 328 (as modified), the responsible insolvency practitioner may, with the sanction of the liquidation committee (if any) or the court:

(a) pay out of the joint estate as part of the expenses to be paid out of that estate any expenses incurred for any separate estate of an insolvent member; or
(b) pay out of any separate estate of an insolvent member any part of the expenses incurred for the joint estate which affects that separate estate.

(b) Priority of debts in joint estate

6.82 The provisions concerning priority of debts in the joint estate which have been introduced are contained in the modified section 328A of the Insolvency Act 1986 and mirror those provisions concerning the modified section 175 in respect of petitions under article 8 of the Order.

6.83 After payment of expenses, the joint debts of the partnership are paid out of the joint estate in the following order of priority:

(a) preferential debts;
(b) debts which are neither preferential nor postponed;
(c) interest under section 328(4) on the joint debts (other than postponed debts);
(d) postponed debts;
(e) interest under section 328(4) on the postponed debts.

For ease of reference, the modified section 328 is produced in Appendix X.

6.84 The effect of the modification is that the debt of a creditor of the partnership which cannot be satisfied out of the partnership estate, ranks equally with the debts of the member as regards the separate estate. However, such a debt is provable by the responsible insolvency practitioner and not by the creditor (s.328A(5)(a)).

(c) Priority of debts in the separate estate

6.85 They are dealt with by the provisions of the new section 328B which again mirror those modifications made to I.A. 1986, s.175 (see App. X).

6.86 The separate estate of each member of the partnership shall be applicable, after payment of expenses, in the following order of priority:

(a) preferential debts;
(b) debts which are neither preferential debts nor postponed debts (including debts referred to in s.328A(5)(a));
(c) interest under section 328D on the separate debts under section 328A(6);
(d) the postponed debts of the member;
(e) interest under section 328D on the postponed debts of the member.

14. GENERAL PROVISIONS IN RESPECT OF DISTRIBUTION OF JOINT AND SEPARATE ESTATES

6.87 These general provisions were introduced by the new section 328C (see App. X).

6.88 Distinct accounts should be kept for the joint estate of the partnership and the separate estates of each member. Specifically no member of the partnership may prove for a joint or separate debt in competition with the joint creditors, unless the debt has arisen:

(a) as a result of fraud; or
(b) in the ordinary course of business carried out separately from the partnership business.

6.89 There is a special provision so as to stop the O.R., Secretary of State, and/or a responsible insolvency practitioner from claiming remuneration or fees in relation to the transfer of surpluses between estates or in relation to the distribution of the separate estates. In effect there should be no double counting.

15. RESCUE PROCEDURES

6.90 Three possible rescue procedures are available for partners who might otherwise face bankruptcy or the liquidation of the partnership under the procedures referred to above:

(a) individual voluntary arrangements for each partner under Part VIII of I.A. 1986;
(b) partnership voluntary arrangement (P.V.A.);

(c) partnership administration order (P.A.O.);

The last two procedures are new: they were introduced by I.P.O. 1994.

6.91 In cases where there is a corporate partner, that corporate partner can propose its own company voluntary arrangement (C.V.A.) or administration order but since that matter will be more appropriate to another text it is not proposed to deal with it in detail. However the authors refer readers to their earlier work: *Corporate Recovery: Administrations and Voluntary Arrangements* (F.T. Law & Tax).

16. INDIVIDUAL VOLUNTARY ARRANGEMENTS FOR PARTNERS

6.92 Individual voluntary arrangements have always been available for partners, whether acting alone or in conjunction with the other partners. Indeed if a partnership is insolvent, it is open to one partner alone to propose an I.V.A. even if the other partners should decide not to do so. However, it will be assumed for the purposes of this chapter that the partners act together. In that case there are likely to be a number of individual I.V.A.s which are linked together, commonly referred to as "interlocking I.V.A.s" all of which contain similar terms.

6.93 The nominees must ensure that each partner's separate assets and liabilities are dealt with because there may well be separate obligations outside the partnership.

6.94 The procedures for individual voluntary arrangements have been amply covered in Chapter 5 and it is not proposed to repeat them here but deal only with special features relating to partnerships.

(a) P.V.A. or separate I.V.A.s?

6.95 This question should always be raised at the first meeting between the I.P. and the partners, and a partner should be made aware of the choice of procedures available.

6.96 Cost will be a factor. For small partnerships, of two or three partners, interlocking I.V.A.s will generally be the cheapest route. However, once a partnership is over a certain "critical mass"—perhaps six or more partners—a P.V.A. will often be the cheapest procedure.

6.97 There is, unfortunately, one pitfall: a P.V.A. will protect an individual partner's estate from the claims of partnership creditors. It will not protect his estate from any creditor who is outside the partnership and therefore if a partner has "outside" creditors, then he will need to think also in terms of an I.V.A. If a partner has borrowed money in order to buy into a partnership, that debt to the bank will not be a partnership debt unless the partnership as a whole has separately guaranteed the bank: it will be a debt of the individual partner and a P.V.A. would not protect him.

6.98 It has also been suggested, although the point is as yet untested in court, that a partnership administration order may not protect the individual partners from litigation and bankruptcy petitions by joint estate creditors. If so, it would appear to render the entire partnership administration procedure rather meaningless (see *Insolvent Partnerships (op. cit.)* at paras 6.2 and 8.19.5). It is accordingly suggested that some partners might be forced to propose I.V.A.s thus affording the protection given by an interim order to ensure that the individual creditors are bound by the arrangement.

(b) Interlocking I.V.A.s

6.99 The nominee should examine all partnership documents carefully and in particular deal with the position of any salaried partners and retired partners, if they still have liability and they wish to consult him.

6.100 He will also need to ensure that there is no conflict between the partners—at least nothing that would stop him acting as nominee for all the partners. If there is a conflict then some partners should be prepared to consult a different insolvency practitioner. The nominee will also need to concentrate on the distinction between the joint and the separate estates and to deal with those assets and liabilities which may fall entirely outside the partnership.

6.101 Claims between partners should be dealt with on the basis that a partner is not allowed to compete with joint creditors and therefore, unless such claims have arisen because of fraud or are entirely outside the partnership business, such debts should always be deferred (see also I.P.O. art. 8).

6.102 It is not proposed to deal here at length with the detailed procedures as regards notification to creditors, the meeting, etc., because these are all fully dealt with in Chapter 5 but the nominee should note that not only is it necessary to serve notice of the meeting on every creditor of the *partnership* but also to the separate estate creditors.

6.103 As regards the creditors' meetings, each I.V.A. is technically separate and even if from a practical standpoint the nominee decides to hold all the meetings together, it will still be necessary, under the rules, to have separate votes and a proper account of the votes given at *each* meeting—failure to do so would be a material irregularity potentially allowing any dissatisfied creditor to apply to set aside the arrangement under I.A. 1986, s.262.

(c) Partnership Voluntary Arrangements

6.104 The P.V.A. is, as indicated above, essentially a corporate procedure adapted by I.P.O. 1994 for use with partnerships. It unfortunately suffers from two particular defects:

(i) There is no interim order available. Accordingly the assets of the partnership may be at risk until such time as the creditors' meeting has been held and the arrangement has been passed by the requisite majority (see below). This means that partners may be forced in addition to propose I.V.A.s simply to obtain the protection afforded by an interim order which makes the entire procedure extremely cumbersome and expensive.

(ii) A P.V.A. may not be appropriate for dealing with claims against the separate estates of each member arising out of the affairs of the partnership.

6.105 A P.V.A. may be proposed for any partnership which has carried on business in England and Wales within the previous three years, and which either has, or at any time has had, a principal place of business in England and Wales.

(d) Presenting a P.V.A. proposal

6.106 The provisions mirror those with regard to other C.V.A.s. An insolvency practitioner will act as nominee in relation to the voluntary arrangement which may be proposed by the following persons:

(i) the members of the partnership;

(ii) the administrator of the partnership, where a partnership administration order is in force (see below);
(iii) the liquidator of the partnership (where it has been wound up as an unregistered company);
(iv) the trustee of the partnership, where there is a joint bankruptcy petition under article 11 of I.P.O. 1994.

6.107 The most common situation would be for the proposal to be presented by the members of the partnership. The nominee will need to satisfy himself that the partners have authority to make the proposal. This may depend upon the partnership deed or on ensuring that there is unanimity. Since P.A. 1890, s.24(8) requires all the partners to agree to a change in the nature of the partnership business, it is likely that a resolution of all partners would be required for the P.V.A. to be proposed. This raises a potential difficulty with regard to salaried partners since it will be recalled that definition of a "member" of a partnership includes anyone who is liable as a partner within P.A. 1890, s.14.

6.108 Needless to say in any partnership with more than a couple of members, the practitioner should be wary of accepting instructions, even from the senior partners because they may not have authority to bind the partnership to a P.V.A.

(e) The proposal

6.109 The proposal will follow the usual C.V.A. form and reference should be made to I.R. 1.3, which contains a list of the matters which must be dealt with in any proposal. The partners must also deliver to the nominee a statement of their affairs giving, *inter alia*, details of assets and liabilities and they must make their accounts available to the nominee.

(f) Reports to the court

6.110 Once the proposal has been made, the nominee has 28 days or such longer period as the court may allow, within which to submit a report to the court, stating whether in his opinion the meetings of the members of the partnership and its creditors should be held to consider the proposal.

6.111 The nominee will then suggest a date, time and venue for the meeting. It should be emphasised that the court has no formal role at this stage. As with other C.V.A.s, there is no interim order and the court will merely endorse the proposal with a special number for reference purposes.

6.112 As with I.V.A.s, the nominee cannot simply act as a mouthpiece for the debtors. He is required to give the proposal proper consideration to see if it *merits* being placed before the creditors (see *Re A Debtor (No. IO 140 of 1995)* [1997] B.P.I.R. 24).

6.113 If the nominee feels that the proposal merits consideration then two meetings will be held, one for the members of a partnership, which might include salaried partners or even retired partners if they have been held out as being members (in other circumstances a retired partner would not be a member) and one for creditors.

6.114 The creditors are defined as those who are creditors of a partnership and a creditor of the separate estate only should not be invited to attend. However, subject to that all creditors, whether actual or contingent or secured should be invited to attend.

6.115 The creditors' meeting must be held not less than 14 and not more than 28 days from the day when the nominee's report is filed in court. The remaining rules as to meetings follow those with regard to other C.V.A.s.

(g) Voting at meetings

6.116 The rules for voting are the same as those which have been adopted with regard to other voluntary arrangements. Since there has been a full discussion in Chapter 5, it is not proposed to repeat them in detail. However, the partnership agreement may allocate more votes to particular partners by reason of their seniority or larger equity share, and this will have to be reflected in considering the requisite majority.

6.117 There may be an issue as regards the entitlement of a salaried partner to vote at the members' meeting because voting is according to the members' voting rights in the partnership and this may be regulated by an agreement or deed but failing that P.A. 1890 gives equal rights to all partners (s.24(1)).

6.118 The requisite majority to be achieved, as with other voluntary arrangements, is 75 per cent of the creditors present in person or by proxy and voting on the resolution (I.R. 1.19(1)). The usual rules apply as regards secured creditors' votes (*Calor Gas v. Piercy* (1994) B.C.C. 69 (para. 5.63, above)) and unascertained or unliquidated claims (*Doorbar v. Alltime Securities Ltd* [1995] B.C.C. 728 (para. 5.63, above)). Needless to say creditors cannot vote if they have not given written notice of the claim to the chairman of the meeting (I.R. 1.19(3)(a)).

6.119 As regards members' meetings, the requisite majority is 50 per cent.

(h) Challenging the vote

6.120 The decision at a meeting may be challenged within 28 days of the date of the chairman's report to the court on the grounds that either:

(a) the voluntary arrangement unfairly prejudices a creditor of the debtor; or
(b) there has been some material irregularity at or in relation to either of the meetings.

6.121 The court's powers on a challenge being mounted are wide and include revoking or suspending the approvals given by the meetings, or directing further meetings to take place.

(i) The Supervisor

6.122 The person who is charged with ensuring that the arrangement is successfully concluded is the supervisor who, in a majority of cases, will be the same person as the nominee—although it is possible for the creditors to nominate a different supervisor or joint supervisor. He will have the power to go to the court for directions on any matter concerning the arrangement and if any creditor or anyone else is dissatisfied with his acts, omissions or decisions, that person may apply to the court, which can confirm, reverse, or modify any act or decision (I.A. 1986, s.7(3)).

(j) Trading and finance

6.123 Many P.V.A.s will involve a continuation of trading. In contrast, many I.V.A.s are based upon a one-off payment to creditors. P.V.A.s for professional partnerships will often require ongoing trading although there may be changes in the composition of the partnerships. Therefore matters such as securing future finance, whether by bank lending or otherwise, need to be addressed at the outset.

6.124 It is likely that the partnership's bank would have to be brought in at a very early stage. Consideration might also be given to factoring or otherwise charging the book debts.

6.125 The supervisor is unlikely to become involved in day to day management. However, he will need to ensure that a management team is in place which is able and willing to achieve the objectives of the P.V.A. Consideration may have to be given to cutting down or modifying the powers of the previous senior partners or management committee if there is one. All these matters should be provided for in detail in the proposal to avoid misunderstandings.

(k) Failure

6.126 The P.V.A. may fail. Consideration will have to be given to the powers available to the supervisor. In particular, he will have the ability to wind-up the partnership, or it may be that powers are built in to effect variations. There is nothing in principle to stop a second P.V.A. being proposed within one year because the restrictions with regard to interim orders only apply in the case of I.V.A.s.

(l) Completion of the arrangement

6.127 A P.V.A. will normally last for a fixed time and the rules specify that not more than 28 days after its final completion, the supervisor must send to all creditors, and to all members, and to the court, a notice that the P.V.A. has been fully implemented. This must be sent together with a summary of receipts and payments (I.R. 1.29).

(m) Partnership administration orders

6.128 This too has been introduced by I.P.O. 1994 and is closely modelled on company administration orders as provided for in Part II of the I.A. 1986.

6.129 As this is truly corporate procedure, it is not proposed to deal with this subject apart from the briefest mention. Those readers who are particularly interested in this procedure should refer to other specialist texts on the subject. In particular, the matter is dealt with in depth in the authors work: *Corporate Recovery: Administrations and Voluntary Arrangements* (F.T. Law & Tax).

Chapter 7
REALISATION OF ASSETS

Completed labours are pleasant—Cicero.

(a) Task of the trustee

7.01 At its simplest, the task of the trustee in bankruptcy is to gather in the assets of the insolvent debtor and distribute the net proceeds to the creditors. The various powers and duties devolving upon the trustee must be seen as ancillary to this role. The task of realising the assets lies at the very heart of every bankruptcy administration.

7.02 The task calls for commercial wisdom and common sense. The prudent trustee will assess the available assets and engage the services of the appropriate experts to advise as to their value and best means of realisation. Such experts may include an estate agent and chattel auctioneer in the case of the debtor's home and possessions, a motor dealer in respect of vehicles and specialists such as antique dealers for more unusual items.

(b) Duty of the bankrupt

7.03 The bankrupt has a duty to disclose his assets in the statement of affairs (see Chap. 3) and to co-operate with the trustee in handing over the assets so that they can be sold. Unfortunately there have always been some bankrupts who have failed to co-operate to the full in this respect. It is reported that in November 1761 a bankrupt was hanged at Smithfield for concealing part of his effects. Although such Draconian remedies are no longer available, the modern trustee has considerable powers to investigate the affairs of the bankrupt and obtain possession of the assets. In this respect the trustee may make use of the many powers set out in Chapter 4 and he is supported by the powers of the court, which exercises general control over every bankruptcy.

7.04 The bankrupt's estate is defined by section 283 as "all property belonging to or vested in the bankrupt at the commencement of the bankruptcy". There is a definition of "property" at section 436 as including "money, goods, things in action, land and every description of property wherever situated and also obligations and every description of interest, whether present or future or vested or contingent, arising out of, or incidental to, property". Subject to further provisions of the Act, the definition is a wide one including most items of value that belonged to the bankrupt. All the bankrupt's estate shall vest in the trustee immediately upon his appointment taking effect, without the need for any conveyance, assignment or transfer (I.A. 1986, s.306). Apart from certain excepted items, the bankrupt therefore loses the power to deal with the assets. The bankrupt moreover has a positive duty, when called upon, to assist the trustee or O.R., who may apply to the court for an order that the bankrupt shall do all such things as he may be directed to do by the court for the purposes of the bankruptcy (s.363).

7.05 In cases of difficulty, the trustee may apply to the court under section 365 for a warrant authorising the seizure of the bankrupt's property. The bankrupt is guilty of an offence if, with intent to defraud or conceal the state of his affairs, he fails to disclose all the property comprised in his estate or to deliver up such part of his property as is in his possession which he is required by law to deliver up (ss.353 and 354).

(c) Powers of trustee and court

7.06 The trustee will wish to make inquiries if he suspects that any property has not been disclosed. To this end he may also seek a warrant under section 365 for the seizure of any books, papers or records relating to the bankrupt's affairs. He may also put questions to the debtor at his public examination (if one is held) or apply to the courts under section 366 for the private examination of the bankrupt, the bankrupt's spouse or any person known or believed to have any property comprised in the bankrupt's estate in his possession or to be indebted to the bankrupt or able to give information concerning the bankrupt or the bankrupt's dealings, affairs or property (see Chap. 9). The court has power to cause a warrant to be issued for the arrest of such person and the seizure of any books, papers, records, money or goods in that person's possession. If it appears to the court that there are reasonable grounds for believing that the debtor has absconded or is about to abscond or remove his goods with a view to preventing possession by the trustee or is about to conceal or destroy his goods or any books, papers or records in connection with his estate, the court may cause a warrant to be issued for the arrest of the debtor. A trustee may also be assisted in his investigation by applying to the court under section 369 for an order that an Inland Revenue official produce to the court any return or accounts submitted by the bankrupt, assessments or correspondence. The procedure is set out in I.R. 6.194–6.196.

7.07 Liens on books, papers or other records of the bankrupt are unenforceable against the O.R. or trustee (s.349) other than liens on documents which give title to property.

7.08 It should be further noted that, under section 312, the bankrupt is required to deliver up to his trustee the property, papers or other records he has in his possession to which the trustee is entitled, as is the O.R., any former trustee, or supervisor of a voluntary arrangement. The bankrupt, or any person who holds property on the bankrupt's account, shall pay or deliver to the trustee all property in his possession which forms part of the estate. Any person who without reasonable excuse fails to comply with such obligation is guilty of contempt of court.

7.09 It must be acknowledged that the majority of bankrupts, many of whom have presented their own petitions, recognise their obligation to surrender their property as well as their books and records to the trustee notwithstanding that the shadow of the hangman's noose has disappeared. Recourse to the courts in order to investigate the bankrupt's affairs and recover his property can be time-consuming and costly, giving scope for a minority of bankrupts who either conceal or abscond with their assets, giving the trustee a good run for his money.

7.10 The trustee will need to examine events prior to the bankruptcy order with a view to tracing the assets of the bankrupt and even the proceeds of such assets if they have been profitably invested. In *Trustee of the Property of F. C. Jones and Sons (a Firm) v. Jones*, [1996] B.P.I.R. 644, involving a partnership bankruptcy, the wife of one of the partners had opened an account, before adjudication, under the I.A. 1986 procedure, with a commodity broker where dealings in potato futures had proved highly profitable so that the wife had received cheques totalling £50,760. The Court of Appeal held that the trustee in bankruptcy was entitled to recover not only the original £11,700 but also the profits made from the use of such money.

1. BUSINESS ASSETS

7.11 If the bankrupt has been in business, either as a sole trader or a partner, then his business assets or share thereof are as much a part of his estate as his personal effects and the business or its assets should be realised for the benefit of creditors. In the early part of this century, it was common for trustees in bankruptcy and trustees under deeds of arrangement to find themselves with trading operations on their hands. Nowadays the majority of even small businesses are operated through limited companies so that trustees are usually concerned only with personal assets even when the bankruptcy arises from guarantees given by a debtor in respect of a company's operation. The trustee may find himself with shares in a private company but frequently that company will itself be in insolvent liquidation and the shares valueless.

7.12 Whilst some businesses, such as retail shops, may find their way into a trustee's hands, it is more frequently the professional practice, which traditionally could not ethically or legally be operated by a limited company, which is liable to be part of the bankrupt's estate. It is likely that such a business or practice will have been carried on by a partnership and the various procedures relating to joint estates outlined at Chapter 6 should be noted.

7.13 Immediate steps have to be taken to preserve the business, if it is thought to be viable and can be sold as a going concern. The O.R. or trustee may apply to the court for the appointment of a special manager (I.A. 1986, s.370 and I.R. 6.167–6.171).

7.14 The trustee may continue the bankrupt's business with a view to achieving a beneficial realisation but will require the sanction of the court or the creditors' committee (see Chap. 4). He should not, however, be so enthusiastic as to seek to continue the business indefinitely, merely with a view to improving its goodwill or earning profits, as it is not for a trustee to expose creditors to the risk of losses.

Sale of the business

7.15 The sale of the business will follow very much the pattern adopted by a liquidator or receiver. The advice of a specialist agent may be sought and the business advertised in the appropriate trade press and by approaches to competitors.

7.16 If the bankrupt operated a one-man business, *e.g.* as plumber, carpenter or handyman, there may in reality be no business that can effectively be sold but it may be expedient for the bankrupt himself to continue in business subject to the restrictions imposed upon him by bankruptcy and making use of the tools of his trade as exempt assets (see paras 7.48–7.55 below). The trustee will then be empowered to call for accounts of the business at least every six months and for a contribution to the estate from the income (see paras 7.81–7.84 below).

7.17 Whilst a global sale of the business assets as a going concern will usually offer the maximum net realisation, the trustee will have to consider a piecemeal sale of assets, possibly with the assistance of selling agents or auctioneers, if a global realisation cannot be obtained. The trustee should be resourceful in seeking out all realisable assets incidental to the bankrupt's business which may well include intangible property or intellectual rights. For example, in *Re Rae (a Bankrupt)* [1995] B.C.C. 102 the trustee argued successfully that an entitlement, although not legally enforceable, to be considered for the grant of fishing licences was as much an asset vesting in him as the fishing vessels concerned. This decision may have implications in relation to intangible assets including benefits which might have been considered personal to the bankrupt.

7.18 The trading stock used by a bankrupt, may well have been supplied by a creditor under retention of title conditions and in such circumstances the supplier will normally have the right to repossess his stock which will thus not be available to the trustee. This problem arises more frequently in corporate insolvency, and the reader may wish to refer to a work on that subject for a detailed discussion. See for example the authors' work entitled *Voluntary Liquidation and Receivership: A Practical Guide* (3rd ed., 1991, F.T. Law & Tax) at Chapter 8.

7.19 Where the bankrupt has sold goods subject to a retention of title clause, to a sub-purchaser under similar conditions and such sub-purchaser has not paid the price of the goods, the original seller is likely to be able to reclaim the goods in the hands of the sub-purchaser (in *re Highway Foods International Limited (In Administrative Receivership), The Times*, November 1, 1994).

2. THE MATRIMONIAL HOME AND OTHER JOINT ASSETS

7.20 In the majority of contemporary bankruptcies, the matrimonial home is the principal asset. Its disposal is a sensitive issue, affecting the rights of the bankrupt's spouse and family. Bankruptcy often gives rise to considerable hardship and this is compounded where an innocent wife and children are involved, and their interest in preserving the family home may conflict with that of the trustee in seeking to realise the estate for the benefit of creditors. This conflict has in the past given rise to difficult policy decisions both for the courts and the legislators. The Act attempts to find a balance which treats the bankrupt and his family with fairness while at the same time giving due weight to the interests of creditors.

(a) Situations which may arise

7.21 Three situations may arise:

(i) the house may be owned solely by the bankrupt's spouse;
(ii) the house may be jointly owned;
(iii) the house may be owned solely by the bankrupt.

Before considering these three situations it should be noted that where any property consisting of an interest in a dwelling-house occupied by the bankrupt or his spouse (or former spouse) is comprised in the estate and the trustee is, for any reason, unable for the time being to realise that property, he may apply to the court for an order imposing a charge on the property for the benefit of the estate (I.A. 1986, s.313(1)). Further, by section 332(2), where an order has been made or has been applied for under section 313, the trustee may still summon a final meeting of creditors under section 331 despite the fact that he has been unable to realise part of the property in the estate. This section must obviously be read in conjunction with sections 336 and 337 (see below) which deal with the rights of occupation of the bankrupt and the bankrupt's spouse. The learned editors of *Muir Hunter on Personal Insolvency* suggest that an application under this section may be made where either the trustee has not the funds to litigate with the spouse or former spouse a contested application for possession and sale of the matrimonial home or alternatively such an application is made and fails, because the circumstances of the case are "exceptional" (ss.336(5) and 337(6)) (see *Muir Hunter on Personal Insolvency*, para. 3–225).

7.22 Creditors' contingent rights in a property to which the bankrupt has legal title will also be protected, depending on whether the land is registered or unregistered, either by a caution or an entry in the Land Charges Register.

7.23 Where an application is made by the trustee under section 313, I.R. 6.237 states that the bankrupt's spouse or former spouse shall be made respondent to the application and the court may, if it thinks fit, direct other persons to be made respondents also, in respect of any interest which they may have in the property.

(b) Property owned solely by spouse or former spouse

7.24 Prima facie, the trustee or O.R. has no interest in such property for the estate. However, circumstances may exist enabling the trustee to "attack" the spouse's interests. If, say, a transfer from the bankrupt to the spouse had taken place in suspicious circumstances it may give rise to a claim on behalf of the trustee under section 339 (transactions at an undervalue) or as a transaction intended to defraud creditors under section 423. These provisions are dealt with in Chapter 9.

(c) Property in joint names

7.25 This is likely to be the most common situation between a bankrupt and his spouse or former spouse. A joint interest gives rise to a trust for sale and, under L.P.A. 1925, s.30, the trustee must obtain an order from the court before he can realise the bankrupt's interest in the property. A form of application will be found at Appendix I, Form S.

7.26 In such cases the court is directed by I.A. 1986, s.336(4) to make such order as it thinks just and reasonable having regard to the following factors:

(i) the interests of the bankrupt's creditors;
(ii) the conduct of the spouse or former spouse, so far as contributing to the bankruptcy;
(iii) the needs and financial resources of the spouse or former spouse;
(iv) the needs of any children; and
(v) all the circumstances of the case other than the needs of the bankrupt.

No mention is made of other dependants and the needs of the bankrupt are specifically excluded. Subject to what is said below, no factor is given special weight.

7.27 There is no reference in I.A. 1986, nor in the Matrimonial Homes Act 1983, (this is specifically referred to in I.A. 1986, s.336), to the interest of persons other than a spouse even if such persons are co-habitees of the bankrupt. Nor do these provisions specifically apply to persons who are not "cohabiting" but nevertheless share a property (see, *e.g. Bernard v. Josephs* [1982] Ch. 391 and *Re Sharpe* [1980] 1 W.L.R. 219). Accordingly, no special factors apply in such cases which would prevent the trustee from proceeding under L.P.A. 1925, s.30.

7.28 Under section 336(5) special provisions apply where an application is made by the trustee after the end of the period of one year beginning with the vesting of the bankrupt's estate in the trustee. Here the court must assume, unless the circumstances of the case are exceptional, that the interests of the bankrupt's creditors outweigh all other considerations. In general terms, therefore, if the trustee chooses to wait for the one year after vesting of the property in him (pursuant to s.306) the bankrupt's spouse and children will find it difficult to resist his application for possession under section 336.

7.29 Any application made by the trustee under L.P.A. 1925, s.30 must be made to the court having jurisdiction in respect of the bankruptcy. The right of trustees to "break" the trust for sale and effectively force the sale of a jointly-owned matrimonial home has been examined in a large number of cases both before and after the passing of I.A. 1986. In general the courts in recent years had not been overly sympathetic to the rights of the bankrupt's spouse and family, choosing rather to uphold the interest of the trustee on behalf of the creditors save in exceptional circumstances.

7.30 A more sympathetic approach had been taken in *Re Holliday* [1981] 2 W.L.R. 996 where the property was jointly owned by the husband and wife. The wife applied for a property adjustment order on divorce. The husband then issued his own petition in bankruptcy, which the wife claimed was merely to prevent her from obtaining such an order. The Court of Appeal held that the interests of the children and the wife and wife's obligations to look after them were matters it had to consider in exercising its discretion whether or not to order a sale, and the sale was postponed until after the two eldest children had attained the age of 17. However, in *Re Lowrie* [1981] 3 All E.R. 353, the trustee's application for an immediate sale was granted. The court considered that there had to be exceptional circumstances justifying the postponement of the trustee's rights. The court did not think that the mere fact that there were young children living in the house was an exceptional circumstance justifying such a postponement. These were circumstances generally present in all such cases and the court distinguished *Re Holliday*. In particular, the court was concerned as to the hardship to creditors which might be caused by such a postponement.

7.31 The approach of the court as demonstrated in *Re Lowrie*, in contrast to *Re Holliday*, has been demonstrated in a recent post-1986 decision: *Re Citro* [1990] 3 All E.R. 952, a decision of the Court of Appeal. It was a case where two brothers, Domenico and Carmine Citro, had been made bankrupt. The only assets in each bankruptcy were their half-shares in their matrimonial homes. In both cases the wives and children lived in the house although one brother was separated from his wife. At first instance Hoffmann J. granted the trustees an order for sale of the houses but postponed the sales until the youngest children of the bankrupts attained the age of 16 years, which would not take place until 1994 and 1995. He applied the principles laid down in *Re Holliday*. The Court of Appeal, Sir George Waller dissenting, allowed the trustee's appeal. The Court declared that the voice of the creditors would usually prevail over that of the spouse and the sale would be ordered within a short period unless there were "exceptional circumstances". It was not an "exceptional circumstance" for the wife and children to face eviction even if they were unable to buy a comparable home in the local area. The natural sympathy of the Court would not overrule the principle that the creditors' interests should prevail. In the circumstances the order for sale was postponed for only six months. A more sympathetic approach was also in evidence in *Re Mott* [1987] C.L.Y. 212 which was described by Hoffmann J. as one of "extreme hardship". The court allowed the sale to be postponed until after the death of the bankrupt's elderly and sick mother but such cases are rare, the trustee will usually obtain an order for sale if application is made after one year.

(d) Property owned solely by bankrupt

7.32 Property owned by the bankrupt alone is of course part of the estate but two particular problems may arise. First, the property may be occupied by a spouse who has rights of occupation under the Matrimonial Homes Act 1983 which gives rights of occupation to a spouse having no legal or beneficial interest in the property. Secondly, it may be occupied by the bankrupt himself either alone or with children of whom he has custody. Sections 336 and 337 of the Act deal with these situations.

Spouse's rights of occupation

7.33 Where the spouse has rights of occupation under the 1983 Act which are a charge on the interest of the bankrupt, that charge continues notwithstanding the bankruptcy. Any application under section 1 of the 1983 Act must be made to the court having jurisdiction in respect of the bankruptcy and in making an order the court is expressly directed to take into account those factors under section 336(4) which are mentioned above in respect of jointly-owned property. Again, if the application is made more than one year after the property has vested in the trustee, the courts must assume, unless the circumstances of the case are exceptional, that the interests of the creditors outweigh all other considerations.

7.34 There is an express provision (s.336(1)) that nothing occurring in the initial period (that is, between the date of presentation of the petition and the date of vesting of the estate in the trustee) is to be taken as having given rise to any rights of occupation under the 1983 Act in relation to a dwelling-house comprised in the estate.

Interest of the bankrupt in the house

7.35 Where the bankrupt has an interest in the house and it is occupied by children under 18, whether or not a spouse has any rights of occupation under the 1983 Act, the bankrupt has the following rights against the trustee granted by section 337:

(i) if in occupation, the right not to be evicted or excluded from the house or any part of it, except with the leave of the court;
(ii) if not in occupation, a right with the leave of the court to enter into and occupy the house, and by section 337(2)(b) these rights granted to the bankrupt are a charge on so much of his estate or interest in the house as is vested in the trustee.

The rights conferred on the bankrupt by section 337 are regarded as rights of occupation under the Matrimonial Homes Act 1983 and therefore the trustee must apply to the court having jurisdiction in respect of the bankruptcy for leave to evict or exclude the bankrupt. By section 337(5), on such an application the court is directed to make such order as it thinks just and reasonable having regard to the interests of the creditors, to the bankrupt's financial resources, to the needs of the children and to all the circumstances of the case other than the needs of the bankrupt. Again, where an application is made after the end of the one-year period from the vesting of the estate in the trustee, the court shall assume, unless the circumstances of the case are exceptional, that the interests of the bankrupt's creditors outweigh all other considerations (s.337(6)). As to what might be determined as "exceptional circumstances" reference should be made to the discussion above.

7.36 Where any premises comprised in the estate are occupied by the bankrupt (whether by virtue of section 337 or otherwise) on condition that he makes payments towards satisfying any liability arising under a mortgage or otherwise towards the outgoings of the premises, section 338 states that he does not, by virtue of those payments, acquire any interest in the premises.

(e) The equity of exoneration

7.37 The wife's so-called equity or right of exoneration applies in a situation where the matrimonial home is in joint names but the wife's beneficial interest has been mortgaged to support the husband's business activities or for other reasons solely connected with the husband from which she may not have benefited. In such cases there is a presumption that the wife is entitled to be exonerated, or to throw the burden of the debt solely on to the husband's estate—clearly a matter which may be of importance in bankruptcy law.

7.38 The principle, which is of some antiquity, is well stated in *Halsbury's Laws of England*, Vol. 22, para. 1071:

> "If the property of a married woman is mortgaged or charged in order to raise money for the payment of her husband's debts, or otherwise for his benefit, it is presumed, in the absence of evidence showing an intention to the contrary, that she meant to charge her property merely by way of security, and in such case she is in the position of surety, and is entitled to be indemnified by the husband and to throw the debt primarily on his estate to the exoneration of her own."

7.39 The application of this principle in modern-day bankruptcy law is shown by the decision of Scott J. in *Re Pittoriou* [1985] 1 All E.R. 285. This was a case where the husband ran a restaurant business as a sole trader. The matrimonial home was in joint names and husband and wife executed a second charge in favour of the bank to secure the borrowings on his bank account. The husband was made bankrupt. The question arose as to the extent to which moneys paid from the bank account, which was secured, should fall against the husband's beneficial interest in the property (owned by his trustee) or should be shared between husband and wife.

7.40 Scott J. found that there were three separate categories of payment:

(i) mortgage instalments and other payments made for the purpose of upholding the property and living expenses of the family. These were payments for the joint benefit of the household;
(ii) debts of the restaurant business in the husband's sole name;
(iii) debts incurred by the husband who set up a separate home with another woman.

7.41 The learned judge felt that the last two categories of payment should fall first against the bankrupt's share of the property; the wife's share was exonerated. It should also be noted that this was a case where the court postponed the sale of the property by the trustee until an inquiry as to how the payment should be apportioned into each category was made and to allow the wife a chance to make a fully informed offer to the trustee to purchase the bankrupt's interest in the property.

7.42 *Re Pittoriou* is an important case but must obviously be treated with caution. The wife's equity of exoneration is a matter of intention. As *Halsbury* states ". . . in the absence of any evidence showing an intention to the contrary . . .". There may be cases where the wife has been fully informed and has made a gift to the husband or otherwise agreed that her share of the assets should be used to support the husband's business. The position of secured creditors against spouses of a bankrupt debtor may well be affected by the decision of the House of Lords in *Barclays Bank Plc v. O'Brien* [1994] 1 A.C. 180. The question which arose for decision in that case was whether a bank was entitled to enforce against a wife an obligation to secure a debt owed by her husband to the bank where the wife had been induced to stand surety by the undue influence or misrepresentation of the husband.

7.43 The matrimonial home had been held in the joint names of Mr and Mrs O'Brien. He agreed to guarantee the debts of his company to the bank in order to obtain an increase in the overdraft. His liability under the guarantee was secured by a second charge on the matrimonial home. He misrepresented to his wife the amount which was secured and Barclays did not take steps to explain the documentation to her or to suggest that she should take independent legal advice.

7.44 The House of Lords held that a creditor is put on inquiry where a wife offers to stand surety for the debts of her husband by the combination of two factors:

(i) that the transaction is not on the face of it to the financial advantage of the wife; and
(ii) that there is a substantial risk in transactions of this kind that, in procuring the wife to stand surety, the husband has committed a legal or equitable wrong that entitles the wife to set aside the transaction.

7.45 A creditor who is put on inquiry must take reasonable steps to satisfy himself that the wife's agreement to stand surety has not been induced by her husband's undue influence of misrepresentation, otherwise the creditor will be fixed with the knowledge of such misrepresentation or undue influence.

7.46 It should be noted that this decision is equally applicable to other personal relationships as well as that of husband and wife and of course there is no reason to suppose that a husband could not rely upon undue influence in circumstances where it was his wife's business.

7.47 As a result of this case banks are obliged to take steps to explain to another contracting party standing guarantor the effect of the documentation which is signed and that the wife should be urged both verbally and in writing to seek independent legal advice.

3. EXEMPT ASSETS

Definition of estate

7.48 The bankrupt's estate shall not include such tools, books, vehicles and other items of equipment as are necessary to the bankrupt for use personally by him in his employment, business or vocation and such clothing, bedding, furniture, household equipment and provisions as are necessary for satisfying the basic domestic needs of the bankrupt and his family (I.A. 1986, s.283(2)).

7.49 Realistically the Act sets no maximum value for these exempt items. Senior practitioners may recall with nostalgic affection the limit of £20 set by B.A. 1914, which strictly speaking remained the limit until it was increased to £250 by I.A. 1976. In practice neither the £20 nor the £250 were strictly adhered to. A practical view was taken that bankrupts should retain personal effects, that were not extravagant, or were necessary to continue their employment and domestic existence. The expression "tools of trade" is intended to mean those required by a workman in order to continue his employment. They were formerly clarified in *Re Sherman* [1916] W.N.26; (1915) 32 T.L.R. 231 but the definition must nowadays be applied more liberally and will include general items of business equipment. The exemption will still not be extended to substantial business assets such as a workshop full of expensive equipment to be operated by a team of employees. It does not include documents even if used by the bankrupt in his business.

7.50 In place of the monetary limit, the trustee is given power by sections 308 and 308A to give notice in writing to the bankrupt that any property which would otherwise be exempt shall vest in him as trustee if it appears that the realisable value exceeds the cost of a reasonable replacement. Upon service of such notice, the property vests in the trustee and such notice relates back to the commencement of the bankruptcy except against a purchaser in good faith, for value and without notice of the bankruptcy. The trustee must apply the funds of the estate, in priority to any distribution, to the purchase of a reasonable replacement of property meeting the reasonably adequate needs of the bankrupt. The trustee must give notice within 42 days of becoming aware of such property unless the court gives leave for notice to be served at a later date. Accordingly, if the bankrupt possesses, for example, an antique dining table and gold-plated cutlery, the trustee would serve notice claiming such items. Whilst the trustee will purchase modest replacements, the bankrupt has no right to expect that the replacement will be delivered immediately. Under I.R. 6.187 the trustee has no obligation to purchase a replacement unless and until he has sufficient funds in the estate for that purpose. The trustee therefore need not be deterred from giving notice by the lack of ready funds to purchase the replacement. Neither need he value the property before giving notice. If the bankrupt wishes to retain the property concerned, he should find a friendly third party to make a proposal to the trustee since I.R. 6.188 provides that where a third party proposes to the trustee to provide the estate with a sum of money enabling the bankrupt to be left in possession of the property then the trustee may accept that proposal if satisfied that the estate will benefit to the extent of the value of the property less the cost of a reasonable replacement.

7.51 Whilst the point may be academic in most bankruptcies, there is also excluded from the estate, by section 283(3), property held by the bankrupt on trust for any other person, or the right of nomination to a vacant ecclesiastical benefice. Certain rights of action may by common law be regarded as exempt.

7.52 The scope of section 283 has been extended by the Housing Act 1988, s.117(1) to exclude also from the estate:

(a) a tenancy which is an assured tenancy or an assured agricultural occupancy, within the meaning of Part I of the Housing Act 1988, and the terms of which inhibit an assignment as mentioned in section 127(5) of the Rent Act 1977;
(b) a protected tenancy, within the meaning of the Rent Act 1977, in respect of which, by virtue of any provision of Part IX of that Act, no premium can lawfully be required as a condition of assignment;
(c) a tenancy of a dwelling-house by virtue of which the bankrupt is, within the meaning of the Rent (Agriculture) Act 1976, a protected occupier of the dwelling-house, and the terms of which inhibit an assignment as mentioned in section 127(5) of the Rent Act 1977; or
(d) a secure tenancy, within the meaning of Part IV of the Housing Act 1985, which is not capable of being assigned, except in the cases mentioned in section 91(3) of that Act. The trustee may, however, give notice in writing pursuant to section 308A that such tenancy is to vest in the trustee as described at 7.50 above.

7.53 The bankrupt is also entitled to retain such part of his salary or other personal earnings as may be necessary for the maintenance of himself or dependants but, in the event of such income being surplus to reasonable requirements, the trustee may seek contributions to the estate (see paras 7.81–7.89 below). Onerous property may be disclaimed by the trustee under section 315 of the Act (See Chap. 9).

7.54 In general, all the assets of the bankrupt including those acquired after his bankruptcy and prior to his discharge and subject to the above exemptions may be claimed by the trustee for the benefit of creditors.

7.55 Book debts and other moneys due to the debtor at the commencement of the bankruptcy vest in the trustee regardless of the date of collection. In the authors' view, these include receivables in respect of work in progress, or work completed but not billed and fees due to a bankrupt barrister notwithstanding the inhibition on pursuing the same.

4. PROPERTY SUBJECT TO CHARGES

(a) General

7.56 In general a secured creditor retains his rights in respect of any property subject to a valid charge which he has before commencement of the bankruptcy. For example, the mortgagee of a property may foreclose if payments are not made in accordance with the agreement.

7.57 When submitting a proof of debt for voting or dividend purposes, a creditor should be careful to deduct the full value of the secured property or he may find that his rights are diminished. If he claims for the full amount of his debt without valuing the security, he may be deemed to have surrendered the property to the trustee and will be debarred from enforcing his security. The secured creditor will normally have the following options:

(b) Options of a secured creditor

7.58
- (i) to surrender the security and prove for the full amount of his claim;
- (ii) to value his security and prove for the balance. This will give the trustee the right, but not the obligation, to redeem the security for the amount of the valuation;
- (iii) to sell his security and claim for the balance, such right being subject to other conditions in the agreement between the parties. Initially he may decline to lodge a proof of debt and rely upon his security. He will be able to lodge a proof of debt for any shortfall after realisation.

The rights of secured creditors and the trustee are set out in I.R. 6.115–6.119.

(c) Revaluation of security

7.59 A secured creditor may, with the agreement of the trustee or the leave of the court, at any time alter the value which he has put upon his security in his proof of debt. However, if he voted in respect of the unsecured balance, he will need the leave of the court to revalue his security. Likewise the court's leave will be required if he was the petitioner and he put a value on his security in the petition. Secured creditors might therefore be wise not to petition or to vote except in respect of an unsecured balance after their security has been redeemed. Whilst, as stated above, the creditor who omits to value his security in his proof of debt will be deemed to have surrendered the same, the court may relieve him from the effect of this rule if the omission was inadvertent or the result of an honest mistake.

7.60 The trustee may at any time give notice, under I.R. 6.117, to a creditor whose debt is secured that he proposes, at the expiration of 28 days from the date of the notice, to redeem the security at the value put upon it in the creditor's proof. The creditor will then have 21 days in which to decide whether he wishes to revalue his security. In the event of a revaluation, the trustee will have the option to redeem at the new value. If there is no revaluation then the trustee may proceed to redeem the security at the original value. The estate shall bear the cost of such redemption.

7.61 A secured creditor may at any time call upon the trustee in writing to elect whether or not he will exercise his power to redeem. Following such notice, the trustee has six months to decide whether to exercise the power of redemption.

7.62 A trustee who is dissatisfied with the original or revised valuation may require that any property comprised in the security be offered for sale on such terms as may be agreed or as the court may direct. If the sale is by auction, then the trustee on behalf of the estate, or the creditor on his own behalf, may appear and bid, but this rule shall not apply if the security has been revalued and the revaluation approved by the court.

7.63 If a creditor who has valued his security subsequently realises it (whether or not at the instance of the trustee), the net amount realised shall be substituted for the value previously put by the creditor on the security, and that amount shall be treated in all respects as the amended valuation made by him.

(d) Cases of dispute

7.64 In cases of dispute, the prudent trustee should take expert advice as to the value and method of sale before exercising this right against the wishes of the creditor. If the creditor is likely to challenge his actions, the trustee may wish to get the directions of the court under section 303. I.R. 6.197–6.199 contain special rules dealing with mortgaged property.

7.65 A person claiming to be the legal or equitable mortgagee of land belonging to the bankrupt may apply to the court for an order directing that the land be sold (I.R. 6.197(1)).

(e) Accounts and inquiries

7.66 The court, if satisfied as to the applicant's title, may direct accounts to be taken and inquiries made as to the principal, interest and costs due under the mortgage and, where the mortgagee has been in possession of all or part of the land, the rents and profits, dividends, interest or other proceeds received by him or on his behalf (I.R. 6.197(2)).

7.67 For the purpose of these accounts and inquiries and of making title to the purchaser, any of the parties may be examined by the court, and shall produce on oath before the court all such documents in their custody or under their control relating to the estate of the bankrupt as the court may direct. The court may authorise the service of interrogatories on any party (I.R. 6.197(3)).

7.68 In any proceedings between a mortgagor and mortgagee, or the trustee of either of them, the court may order accounts to be taken and inquiries made in like manner as in the Chancery Division of the High Court (I.R. 6.197(4)).

7.69 The court may order that the land may be sold and any party bound by the order and in possession of the land or part of it or in receipt of the rent and profits therefrom may be ordered to deliver up possession to the purchaser or such person as the court may direct. The court may permit the person having the conduct of the sale to sell the land in such manner as he thinks fit. Alternatively, the court may direct that the land be sold as directed by the order (I.R. 6.198).

(f) Court directions

7.70 The court may give directions (under I.R. 6.198(3)):

(i) appointing the persons to have the conduct of the sale;

(ii) fixing the manner of sale (whether by contract conditional on the court's approval, private treaty, public auction, or otherwise);
(iii) settling the particulars and conditions of sale;
(iv) obtaining evidence of the value of the property, and fixing a reserve or minimum price;
(v) requiring particular persons to join in the sale and conveyance;
(vi) requiring the payment of the purchase money into court, or to trustees or others;
(vii) if the sale is to be by public auction, fixing the security (if any) to be given by the auctioneer, and his remuneration.

The court may direct that, if the sale is to be by public auction, the mortgagee may appear and bid on his own behalf (I.R. 6.198(4)).

7.71 The proceeds of the sale shall be applied first in payment of the expenses of the trustee in connection with the application to the court, of the sale and of costs arising from taking of accounts and making of inquiries as directed by the court and secondly in payment of the amount due to any mortgagee for principal, interest and costs. Any balance shall be retained by or paid to the trustee (I.R. 6.199(1)).

7.72 The mortgagee is entitled to prove for dividend in respect of any shortfall but not so as to disturb any dividend already declared (I.R. 6.199(2)).

5. AFTER-ACQUIRED PROPERTY

7.73 The treatment of after-acquired property is determined by I.A. 1986, s.307 and I.R. 6.200–6.202.

7.74 The trustee may by notice in writing claim for the benefit of the bankrupt's estate any property acquired by, or devolved upon, the bankrupt after the commencement of his bankruptcy. The rule does not extend to exempt assets dealt with in paragraphs 7.48–7.55 above or to property devolving upon the bankrupt after discharge unless the court, in making an order discharging him under section 280, makes a condition with respect to such property. Upon service of such a notice, the property concerned shall vest in the trustee as part of the bankrupt's estate. The trustee is, however, not entitled to property acquired from the bankrupt in good faith, for value and without notice of the bankruptcy. A banker is also protected in respect of any transaction entered into in good faith and without such notice. Thereby section 307 perpetuates the rule in *Cohen v. Mitchell* (1890) 25 Q.B.D. 262 that transactions by the bankrupt with any person dealing bona fide and for value are, until the trustee intervenes, valid against the trustee.

7.75 A notice must be given by the trustee within 42 days of the day on which he became aware that the property had been acquired by or devolved upon the bankrupt (s.309(1)).

7.76 An award from the Criminal Injuries Compensation Board in respect of physical injury has been held to belong to the debtor and not vest in the trustee notwithstanding that there had been an expectation of an award at the time of the bankruptcy order (*Re a Bankrupt* (No. 145 of 1995) [1996] B.P.I.R. 238).

Duty of bankrupt

7.77 Where, at any time after the commencement of the bankruptcy, any property is acquired by or devolves upon the bankrupt or there is an increase in his income, then the bankrupt shall within 21 days give notice of the fact to the trustee in accordance with section 333 and I.R. 6.200. Within 42 days of such notice, the bankrupt shall not dispose of the property without the trustee's consent. Perhaps unrealistically the Rules provide that if the bankrupt does dispose of property without this consent, he shall forthwith disclose to the trustee the name and address of the disponee and provide any other information which may be necessary to enable the trustee to trace and recover the property. It seems rather unlikely that a bankrupt will dispose of property in contravention of the Rules and then assist the trustee to recover it.

7.78 The rule does not apply to property dealt with by the bankrupt in the ordinary course of his business but, if he is carrying on business, he must submit at least six-monthly information to the trustee as to goods or services bought and sold and the profit or loss. The trustee may require further details including the accounts of the business (I.R. 6.200(5)).

7.79 Where the property has been disposed of in contravention of the rule, the trustee may, within 28 days of becoming aware of the disponee's identity and address, serve upon him a notice claiming the property as part of the estate.

7.80 Expenses incurred by the trustee in acquiring title to after acquired property shall be paid out of the estate.

6. INCOME PAYMENTS ORDER

Trustee's application

7.81 It is an established principle that, as regards the bankrupt's personal income, the trustee is only entitled to the excess of that which is necessary for the support of the bankrupt and his family. Income for this purpose comprises earnings in respect of any office or employment as well as profits from carrying on a business. Under section 310, the trustee may make application to the court claiming for the bankrupt's estate such part of his income as shall exceed the amount necessary for meeting the reasonable and domestic needs of the bankrupt and his family. Notice of the application and of the time and place fixed for the hearing shall, in accordance with I.R. 6.189, be sent (see App. I, Form T) by the trustee to the bankrupt at least 28 days before the day so fixed together with a copy of his application and a short statement of the grounds on which it was made. The notice shall inform the bankrupt that:

(a) unless at least seven days before the date fixed for the hearing he sends to the court written consent to an order being made in the terms of the application, he is required to attend the hearing; and
(b) if he attends he will be given an opportunity to show the court why the order should not be made, or an order should be made otherwise than applied for by the trustee.

7.82 Before issuing such a notice, the trustee will consider whether the debtor's income is sufficient to warrant such action. It is not intended to leave the debtor destitute and section 310(2) provides that the court shall not make an income payments order the effect of which would be to reduce the income of the bankrupt below what appears to the court to be necessary for meeting the reasonable domestic needs of the bankrupt and his family. Practitioners vary in their views as to the amount of income it is reasonable for a bankrupt to retain and this will vary with the circumstances of the debtor and even the geographical area in which he resides. Having ascertained that the debtor has sufficient income to enable him to contribute to the estate, the trustee should endeavour to negotiate voluntary contributions before serving formal notice.

As a result of the decision in *Re Landau* [1997] B.P.I.R. 229 (discussed at para. 7.95–7.99) below it will be seen that rights under retirement annuity and pension policies may be assets vesting in a trustee and not require an income payments order.

7.83 The court may make an income payments order (Form 6.65 or 6.66 (see App. I, Forms U and V)), a sealed copy of which shall be sent to the bankrupt by the trustee as soon as it is made (I.R. 6.190). The order may require a person making payments of income to pay the amount claimed by the trustee to him instead of the bankrupt. A copy of the order shall be sent to the person concerned. A person receiving notice of an income payments order must immediately comply with the requirement to pay to the trustee income that would otherwise be payable to the bankrupt. He may, however, deduct the appropriate fee towards the clerical and administrative costs of complying with the order. He shall give the bankrupt a written statement of the amount deducted by him. He must give notice to the trustee if at any time he is no longer liable to make any payments of income to the bankrupt, or ceases to be liable having made payments in compliance with the order (I.R. 6.192).

7.84 Income payments shall not be required after the bankrupt's discharge except to the extent that the court may so order (s.310(6)).

7.85 The trustee should keep the amount of contributions under review in the light of any changes in the debtor's income and at an early stage should remind the bankrupt of his duty under section 333(2) and I.R. 6.200(1) to advise him of any increase in his income within 21 days of his becoming aware thereof. He should also be told that failure to comply without reasonable excuse renders him guilty of contempt of court (s.333(4)). This enables the trustee to apply to the court under I.R. 6.193 for the order to be varied. However, the debtor may himself apply for a review, presumably when his circumstances are reduced, and for the order to be varied or discharged.

7.86 Where the trustee makes the application, he must give notice to the bankrupt in accordance with the procedures set out in I.R. 6.189, described above. If an application to review the order is made by the bankrupt it shall be accompanied by a short statement of the grounds on which it is made (I.R. 6.193).

7.87 The court, if it thinks that no sufficient cause is shown for the application, may dismiss it but will not do so until the applicant has been given an opportunity to attend the court for an *ex parte* hearing of which he has been given at least seven days' notice. If it is not to be dismissed in this way, the court shall fix a venue for the application to be heard.

7.88 At least 28 days before the hearing, the applicant shall send to the trustee or the bankrupt (whichever is not himself the applicant) notice of the venue, accompanied by a copy of the application. The trustee may appear and be heard on the application but, whether or not he intends to do so, he may, not less than seven days before the date fixed for the hearing, file a written report of any matters which he considers ought to be drawn to the court's attention. The trustee shall send a copy of such report to the bankrupt.

7.89 Sealed copies of any order made on the application shall, forthwith after the order is made, be sent by the court to the trustee, the bankrupt and the payer if other than the bankrupt.

7. BOOK DEBTS AND RECEIVABLES

7.90 The trustee has a duty to collect all moneys due to the bankrupt's estate and in the event of default he may make use of any of the powers which would have been available to the bankrupt as a creditor. He may take legal proceedings including the issue of a winding-up or bankruptcy petition as the case may be.

7.91 The debtor should have disclosed to the trustee details of all debts due to his estate and details should have been set out in the statement of affairs (Chap. 3). However, if the trustee suspects that there have been transactions resulting in an indebtedness to the estate which has not been disclosed to him, he may raise questions at the public examination of the debtor (see Chap. 3) or utilise the other investigative powers open to him including the examination of all relevant records as mentioned in the introduction to this Chapter.

7.92 As mentioned in Chapter 4, the trustee will require the sanction of the creditors' committee or the D.T.I. to bring any legal proceedings or refer to arbitration, or compromise any debts.

A trustee is not bound to pursue every debt if he forms the opinion that the costs of doing so will outweigh any benefit. In particular a trustee may find that he could be faced with heavy costs in pursuing an overseas debt. Recognition of the rights of an English trustee in bankruptcy will vary from one overseas jurisdiction to another, although nowadays many countries, particularly in Europe, will recognise his title. He may, however, find himself handicapped, even in the more friendly jurisdictions, where the main creditor in the bankruptcy is the Inland Revenue since an overseas court will not normally assist in recovering debts effectively due to the Revenue. (See, for example, *Re Tucker* [1988] F.L.R. 378, Royal Court of Jersey.) It may sometimes be possible to obtain leave for issue of a writ to be served out of the court's jurisdiction under RSC, Ord. 11 (and formerly r. 86 of the Bankruptcy Rules 1952). However, the facts of the case must be such that the trustee's claim falls within Ord. 11, r. 1 (*Re Jogia (A Bankrupt), ex p. Trustee v. D. Pennellier & Co. Ltd* [1988] 2 All E.R. 328). Within the United Kingdom, section 426 provides for qualified co-operation between courts exercising jurisdiction in relation to bankruptcy so that, subject to certain provisions, an order made by a court in any part of the United Kingdom may be enforced in any other part. In a European context, a number of proposed bankruptcy conventions have been drafted over the years but none put into effect. However, as economic and political links between countries within the European Community strengthen, it may be expected that the courts will increasingly recognise the status of practitioners from other jurisdictions, thereby facilitating the task of the trustee in trying to realise assets abroad.

7.93 If the trustee receives notice that the debts have been assigned to a third party, he should examine the validity of the assignment carefully before, on the one hand, acknowledging the validity thereof or, on the other, expending time and money in collecting debts due to a third party. In particular the trustee should consider the timing and circumstances of the assignment and whether it is a voidable disposition of the bankrupt's property (see Chap. 9).

7.94 The trustee also has certain rights to recover moneys paid prior to the bankruptcy order which constitute a preference of one creditor over the general body of creditors or voidable dispositions of the bankrupt's property. This subject is examined in Chapter 9.

8. PENSIONS

7.95 Until recently there existed a diversity of views amongst insolvency practitioners, when acting as trustees in bankruptcy, as to the treatment of pension rights. The more hawkish would seek to sweep up any lump sum element as an asset of the estate and pursue ongoing rights, *e.g.* retirement annuities, by seeking an income payments order. The more benign trustee, from the debtor's point of view, would regard the debtor's reasonable pension rights as of a personal nature and sacrosanct. Philosophically, trustees would balance their duty to maximise realisations for creditors against that to act with due fairness towards the debtor.

7.96 The position has to some extent been clarified by the Pensions Act 1995 although the prime objectives of that statute are not insolvency related and were designed, in the aftermath of the Maxwell affair, to regulate the duties of trustees and employers in order to protect pension benefits.

7.97 In principle it may be argued that pension rights are assets of the debtor's estate, albeit payable at some future date, and vest in a trustee in bankruptcy just as surely as a debtor's savings in, for example, a bank deposit. Thus to protect participants against consequences of bankruptcy, a regular feature of occupational pension schemes, although less frequently found amongst personal pension schemes, was the inclusion of a "forfeiture clause" whereby pension rights should automatically cease on bankruptcy leaving the payment of benefits to the discretion of the scheme trustees, effectively creating a discretionary trust secure from the grasp of a trustee in bankruptcy. Whereas in the past, the effectiveness of forfeiture clauses may have been in some doubt, their effect in relation to occupational schemes is now to be secured by the Pensions Act 1995 section 92(2)(b) which has yet to come into effect. Section 92 makes it clear that where there is an approved occupational pension scheme, then unless there have been "excessive contributions" (see below) made by the bankrupt in the period immediately before bankruptcy, the trustee has no right to the pension for the benefit of the creditors of the estate. The Government at the time of writing has the matter under review in the light of the decision in *Re Landau* (see below) and the proposed implementation on April 1, 1997 has been deferred. The Act does not deal with forfeiture clauses relating to personal pension plans notwithstanding the encouragement given to such schemes in recent years. Thus the security of section 92 will be of limited benefit to potential bankrupts since, by the nature of their occupations, those contributing to personal pension plans are more likely to be at risk of becoming bankrupt than those in occupational schemes. This is a matter that may be clarified in later legislation but in the meantime forfeiture clauses are being inserted into personal pension plans in the hope that they may prove valid. Some policy holders may decide to switch to schemes involving such clauses but should consider the commercial and taxation implications of making changes.

7.98 Whilst the Inland Revenue has announced that forfeiture clauses in personal pension plans are acceptable for the purposes of tax relief, it remains to be seen whether they can successfully be challenged in the courts by a trustee in bankruptcy.

7.99 If a trustee in bankruptcy considers that contributions to an occupational scheme have been excessive, to the extent of diverting funds from creditors, the Pensions Act 1995 at section 95 specifically provides that a trustee in bankruptcy may apply to the court for an order for their recovery under I.A. 1986, s.342(1)(a).

The Pensions Act 1995, however, only protects a bankrupt if he is a member of an Inland Revenue approved occupational pension scheme. Personal pension plans and retirement annuity contracts are, from the point of view of the bankrupt, treated in a much harsher manner. This is a result of the decision in *Re Landau (a Bankrupt)* [1997] B.P.I.R. 229 where the debtor had taken out a retirement annuity contract prior to his bankruptcy order, which did not become payable until after his discharge. The court held that the policy vested in the trustee in bankruptcy being a contractual right existing at the date of the bankruptcy order. This enabled the trustee to obtain not only the lump sum payable to the bankrupt but also the annuity and the learned judge specifically held that section 310 (income payments order) did not apply. Accordingly no allowance could be made to the bankrupt for the normal domestic needs of himself or his family. This would appear at first sight to be a very harsh decision albeit correct in law because it places the bankrupt pensioner in a much worse position than the bankrupt who is in full time employment in that the latter would be able to obtain at least sufficient after an income payments order to cover his reasonable domestic needs and those of his family. It remains to be seen whether this decision will be changed on appeal or whether trustees will be forced by amending legislation or the rule in *ex parte James* (see above) to leave the bankrupt sufficient for such domestic needs.

7.100 Whilst the Pensions Act 1995 seeks to enhance the security of future pensioners, it may have the effect of creating a greater awareness amongst insolvency practitioners of their rights and duties and a more consistent approach.

7.101 In the somewhat rare event that a debtor was the proprietor of a business which itself operated an occupational scheme for its employees, the trustee in bankruptcy will have a duty to see that such a scheme is properly administered or wound up and may be obliged to appoint independent trustees. This situation is more common in matters of corporate insolvency and reference may be made to the authors' work *Voluntary Liquidation and Receivership: A Practical Guide* (3rd ed., FT Law & Tax, 1991) at pp. 52–54.

Chapter 8
CREDITORS' CLAIMS AND BANKRUPTCY COSTS

We must never assume that which is incapable of proof—G. H. Lewes.

Even the hard-pressed debtor and his family will normally recognise that the insolvency practitioner's first duty is to the creditors. His main objective is to receive the maximum net realisation possible in the shortest practicable time and to return to creditors, in their proper order of priority, as much money as possible as quickly as possible. **8.01**

If there is a deed or a voluntary arrangement (see Chap. 5) this objective is seldom forgotten as there is the minimum of formality to distract from the main purpose. This Chapter and the next set out the rights of creditors in a bankruptcy and the trustee's duties in dealing with claims. It should be noted, however, that under a deed or voluntary arrangement the right of a creditor to claim and the order of priority will usually be the same as in bankruptcy. There will, however, normally be no need for a formal proof of debt (see paras 8.04–8.28 below) nor a right to recover dispositions, preferences or other items as described in Chapter 9. **8.02**

A trustee in bankruptcy is required to attend to a number of formalities which are unnecessary under less formal arrangements (for example, the lodgment of moneys in the Insolvency Services Account at the Bank of England) and it becomes all too easy for him to lose sight of his main objectives. Without neglecting his statutory duties, the trustee should continuously ask himself the question: "How will this help the creditors?" **8.03**

1. Proof of Debt

Any person who wishes to establish his rights as a creditor in a bankruptcy must do so by completing a proof of debt (App. I, Form Y) but a different form is utilised if the creditor is a government department. The requirements are set out in section 322 and I.R. 6.96–6.107. **8.04**

The proof of debt establishes the creditor's right to vote at meetings and, more importantly, to participate in distributions. **8.05**

(a) Contents of proof

The proof of debt will specify (I.R. 6.98): **8.06**

(i) the creditor's name and address;
(ii) the total amount of his claim as at the date of the bankruptcy order;
(iii) whether or not that amount includes outstanding uncapitalised interest (see paras 8.54–8.58 below);
(iv) whether or not the claim includes V.A.T.;
(v) whether the whole or any part of the debt is preferential (see paras 8.35–8.38 below);

(vi) particulars of how and when the debt was incurred by the debtor;
(vii) particulars of any security held, the date when it was given and the value which the creditor puts upon it (see paras 8.29–8.34 below); and
(viii) the name, address and authority of the person signing the proof (if other than the creditor himself).

8.07 Forms for this purpose shall be distributed to creditors, by the O.R. or trustee, accompanying whichever of the following is first issued (I.R. 6.97):

(i) a notice under section 293(2) that no creditors' meeting is to be called;
(ii) a notice calling a meeting of creditors;
(iii) a notice sent by the O.R. where the court has issued a certificate of summary administration; or
(iv) where a trustee is appointed by the court, the notice of his appointment sent by him to creditors.

8.08 The O.R. shall decide upon the value at which a proof shall be admitted for voting at the first meeting of creditors or any adjournment thereof (see Chap. 4) and the trustee may consider proofs for voting at any subsequent meeting which he may convene (see Chap. 4).

8.09 The trustee, or the O.R. if there is no trustee, shall consider the amounts at which proofs shall rank for dividend purposes, for which purpose he must settle the list of creditors.

8.10 The proof shall specify any documents by reference to which the debt can be substantiated but it is not essential that such documents be attached. However, the trustee, or the convener or chairman of any meeting, may call for any document or other evidence to be produced to him where he thinks it necessary for the purpose of substantiating the whole or any part of the claim made in the proof.

8.11 If he thinks it necessary, the trustee may require the claim to be verified by affidavit (at App. I, Form Z) notwithstanding that a proof of debt has already been lodged.

8.12 Unless the court otherwise directs, every creditor must bear his own costs of proving his debt but the trustee's costs shall fall upon the estate (I.R. 6.100).

8.13 Where a proof relates to a contingent debt or for any other reason does not bear a certain value, the trustee shall estimate the value or he may seek the directions of the court under section 303. It is advisable to agree the amount with the creditor wherever possible but in the event of disagreement it will be open to the creditor to appeal to the court.

8.14 So long as the proofs are in his hands, the trustee shall allow them to be inspected, at all reasonable times, by any creditor who has submitted a proof (unless rejected), the bankrupt or a person acting on behalf of a creditor or the bankrupt (I.R. 6.101).

8.15 A proof of debt in respect of a moneylending transaction made before January 27, 1980, where the creditor at the time of the transaction was a licensed moneylender, shall have endorsed on or annexed to it a statement setting out in detail the particulars mentioned in the Moneylenders Act 1927, s.9(2) (I.R. 6.102).

8.16 Once a trustee takes over the estate from the O.R. there shall be transmitted to him the proofs thus far received together with an itemised list. Thereafter the proofs shall be handled by the trustee (I.R. 6.103).

(b) Admittance of proofs for voting purposes

8.17 In the interests of speed, proofs are likely to be admitted for voting purposes at the first meeting, without in-depth examination. Greater care is, however, required on the trustee's part before admitting claims for dividend. For this purpose the trustee will compare the claims with the debtor's statement of affairs and other books and records. In cases of doubt he may pursue inquiries of the debtor, the creditor or third parties but in principle the onus lies upon the creditor to evidence his claim. Where the trustee is unable to admit the claim for the amount quantified in the proof, it is desirable that any amended amount be agreed with the creditor in writing. A suggested form of assent, which is not a statutory form, is given at Appendix I, Form AA which it is suggested be attached to the proof.

8.18 In cases of disagreement, the trustee may formally reject the proof by preparing a written statement of his reasons for rejecting the claim in whole or in part and sending it to the creditor.

8.19 The onus is then upon the creditor, if dissatisfied with the trustee's decision, to apply to the court for that decision to be reversed or varied and this he must do within 21 days. Notice of the creditor's application must be sent to the trustee who shall deliver the proof in question to the court for filing together with a copy of his rejection. The court shall fix a time and place for the hearing of the application, giving notice to the creditor and the trustee. The court may expunge or reduce the amount claimed.

8.20 A trustee other than the O.R. is not liable for the costs of the application unless the court so orders. The O.R., however, cannot be personally liable.

8.21 If the amount claimed in a proof is increased, this has no effect with respect to distributions already made (I.R. 11.8) but if the proof is reduced, the creditor is liable to repay to the estate any amounts overpaid. In practice it is unlikely that a trustee will pay dividends to a creditor until the amount of the claim has been settled either by agreement or order of the court or 21 days have expired since his partial rejection.

8.22 Unless the court otherwise orders, a proof in respect of money owed on a bill of exchange, promissory note, cheque or other negotiable instrument or security cannot be admitted unless that instrument or security is produced (I.R. 6.108).

8.23 A secured creditor may prove for any unsecured balance of his claim if he realises his security, or for the full amount if he surrenders his security for the general benefit of creditors (I.R. 6.109). There are special rules affecting secured creditors discussed below.

8.24 There must be deducted from any claim such trade or other discounts as would have been available to the bankrupt excluding discount for prompt settlement.

8.25 The claims of overseas creditors should be converted to sterling at the official exchange rate prevailing at the date of the bankruptcy order. The official exchange rate is defined as the middle market rate at the Bank of England as published for the date in question. In the absence of any such published rate, it is such rate as the court determines. Dissatisfaction is sometimes expressed by creditors whose currency strengthens against the pound prior to the payment of a dividend but comment is seldom heard when the movement is in the other direction.

8.26 If a creditor is entitled to rent or other periodical payments, he may prove for amounts due and unpaid up to the date of the bankruptcy order. Where payment was accruing, the creditor may prove for so much as would have fallen due at the date of the bankruptcy order, if accruing from day to day.

8.27 The creditor may also prove for damage sustained in consequence of the operation of a disclaimer of onerous property. The question of disclaimer, and the position of landlords is further considered in Chapter 9.

8.28 A creditor may prove for a debt which is payable at some future date although not yet due at the date of the bankruptcy order but dividends paid before the due date may be subject to a reduction under a formula set out in I.R. 11.13.

2. SECURED CREDITORS

8.29 A secured creditor may realise his security and prove for the balance, surrender his security, or he may place a value on his security and prove for the balance. Thereafter the valuation may be varied by agreement with the trustee or leave of the court but if the creditor has voted in respect of the unsecured balance or he was the petitioning creditor and put a value on the security for that purpose, he may only revalue with the leave of the court.

Realisation of security

8.30 In practice most secured creditors will seek to realise their security before resorting to a bankruptcy petition and will usually find it prudent to forgo their voting rights rather than prejudice their security.

8.31 A creditor who omits to disclose his security for the purpose of his proof of debt shall be deemed to have surrendered it to the general benefit of creditors unless the court grants relief on the grounds that the omission was inadvertent or the result of an honest mistake, when the proof may be amended on such terms as may be just (I.R. 6.116).

8.32 Normally it may be expected that the secured creditor will wish to recover his money by redeeming the security and accounting to the trustee for any surplus or, in the alternative, by agreement with the creditor, if there is expected to be a surplus, the trustee may sell the security concerned, accounting to the creditor for the amount of his claim. In other cases the security may be some item that the debtor or his family wish to retain, in which event the debtor's spouse or some third party may seek to acquire the security from the creditor for its proper value.

8.33 Rule 6.139 provides that where the trustee sells assets on behalf of a secured creditor, he is entitled to take for himself, out of the proceeds of sale, a sum of remuneration equivalent to that chargeable by the O.R. in such circumstances. However, it is not entirely clear how much remuneration would be chargeable by the I.Reg. 36 refers to the O.R.'s remuneration in respect of property charged but only whilst acting as liquidator or provisional liquidator.

8.34 This contrasts with regulation 21 of the 1986 regulations, where a scale specified also extended to the O.R. acting as trustee.

3. PREFERENTIAL CREDITORS

The relevant date

8.35 Creditors having preferential rights are set out in Schedule 6 to the Act which also applies to other forms of insolvency administration. As certain time limits are prescribed it is necessary to establish the "relevant date" which is normally the date of the bankruptcy order. However, if at the date of the order there was an interim receiver appointed under section 286, the relevant date is the date on which the interim receiver was first appointed after the presentation of the bankruptcy petition.

8.36 In the case of a voluntary arrangement, where the debtor is not an undischarged bankrupt, the date will be that of the interim order made under section 252.

8.37 The principal classes of preferential claim are moneys owed to the Inland Revenue for income tax deducted at source (but not assessed taxes), V.A.T., car tax, betting and gaming duties, social security and pension scheme contributions and remuneration of employees. The taxation aspects are discussed in paragraphs 8.64–8.68.

8.38 Full details appear in Appendix IV which sets out the contents of Schedule 6 to the Act.

4. UNSECURED CREDITORS

8.39 Strictly speaking an unsecured creditor is one whose claim is not secured. Colloquially the expression is taken to exclude preferential creditors and refers to those whose claims, unless they have a deferred status, rank *pari passu* for dividend after preferential claims have been discharged in full.

8.40 If the debtor was in business as a sole trader then his business and domestic debts will have equal standing as there is no separation of his business and domestic estates. Different considerations apply if the debtor was in partnership and these are discussed in Chapter 6.

8.41 Unsecured creditors have the right to submit proofs of debt discussed above and must do so if they are to be included for dividend purposes.

8.42 The unsecured balance of the claim of any secured creditor (see above) will rank *pari passu* with other unsecured claims.

8.43 Interest on claims accrued after the bankruptcy order will be paid only after the claims have been paid in full. However, the claims themselves may include amounts of pre-bankruptcy interest and this subject is discussed in paragraphs 8.54–8.58 below.

8.44 Section 329 provides that the claim of any person who is the debtor's spouse at the commencement of the bankruptcy, whether or not the spouse at the time credit was provided, shall rank after payment of other creditors and interest thereon. As financial and domestic problems tend to be inter linked, debtors are frequently in the throws of divorce proceedings. An award made against the bankrupt in the family division of the court is not provable *pari passu* with unsecured creditors. It is not clear whether legal costs relating to bankruptcy proceedings are provable.

8.45 It seems only fair to the other creditors that a spouse's interests should be deferred.

8.46 Trade creditors incurring bad debts as a result of a bankruptcy, or for that matter a voluntary arrangement or deed, will normally be entitled to relief for both taxation and V.A.T. purposes. The rules relating to V.A.T. on bad debts have changed in recent Finance Acts and full details for the procedures for obtaining such relief are set out in V.A.T. leaflet 7600/18/91 which provides that such relief is available one year after the bad debt is suffered.

5. SET-OFF

8.47 Where before the commencement of the bankruptcy there have been mutual credits, mutual debts and other mutual dealings between the bankrupt and any creditor of the bankrupt proving or claiming to prove "for a bankruptcy debt", an account shall be taken of what is due from each party to the other in respect of mutual dealings and the sums due from one party shall be set off against the sums due from the other (s.323).

(a) Mutual dealings

8.48 The expression "mutual dealings" is interpreted widely and whenever a debt is due from a party who is also a creditor, it is in practice difficult for the trustee to establish that there is no right of set-off. The question of set-off and mutual dealings is further clarified in the discussion in *Stein v. Blake* [1995] 2 B.C.L.C. 94, where the House of Lords held that set-off is automatic at the date of bankruptcy without any formal procedural step. Where the net amount is in favour of the bankrupt, the net balance is an asset which a trustee may be entitled to assign. Bankruptcy set-off had a much wider scope than legal set-off and applied to any claim out of mutual credits or other mutual dealings before the bankruptcy including liabilities which at the time of the bankruptcy might have been subject to contingency. Set-off will not arise where one party acts in two capacities, as principal, on the one hand and, on the other, as trustee or agent for a third party. There also is an exception that no set-off shall arise if, at the time that a debt became due to the other party, such party had notice that a bankruptcy petition was pending. This seems a little hard on the other party who might not have been under such notice at the time that the transaction giving rise to the debt was entered into.

8.49 The parties cannot contract out of the right of set-off (*National Westminster Bank Ltd v. Halesowen Presswork & Assemblies Ltd* [1972] A.C. 785).

(b) Crown set-off

8.50 It is important to note, particularly if the bankrupt was in business, that government departments have a right to implement Crown set-off. Although court authority is required for set-off to apply between one government department and another (Crown Proceedings Act 1947, s.35) it seems likely that this would normally be given. In *Re D. H. Curtis (Builders) Ltd* [1978] Ch. 162, the Customs and Excise were held entitled to set off against their obligation to repay a V.A.T. refund, claims by the Inland Revenue and the Department of Health and Social Security. Likewise it can be expected that if, for example, a bankrupt has manufactured curtains for the Ministry of Defence, the debt due may be set off against the Inland Revenue's claim for outstanding P.A.Y.E. It was held in *R.A. Cullen Ltd v. Nottingham Health Authority, The Times*, August 1, 1986, that a regional health authority in entering into a contract to carry out plumbing work on hospital premises was exercising its function on behalf of the Secretary of State for Health and Social Security and thereby acting as an agent of the Crown. The outstanding sums due under the plumbing contract could therefore be set off against unpaid National Insurance contributions.

8.51 Normally a creditor will be able to set off, against his claim debts due from the creditor to the bankrupt as at the commencement of the bankruptcy but cannot set off against subsequent amounts due from him to the bankrupt. However the Secretary of State for Social Security has been held entitled to recover money by making deductions from prescribed benefits when the intended recipient of those benefits became bankrupt (*R. v. Secretary of State for Social Security, ex p. Taylor; R. v. Same, ex p. Chapman* [1997] B.P.I.R. 505). In one case a debt arose from a Social Security Fund loan but the deductions were made from income support. In the second case the debt arose from overpaid income support, whereas deductions were made from retirement pension. The court held that the bankrupts in these cases were not entitled to the full amount of income support or retirement pension and accordingly the Secretary of State was not pursuing a remedy which should have been curtailed by section 285(3). The same principle can apply to other creditors in respect of overpayments. For example, in *Bradley-Hole v. Cusen* [1953] 1 Q.B. 300 a tenant was entitled to deduct an overpayment of rent from subsequent instalments.

8.52 A similar decision was made in Scotland in the first division of the Inner House of the Court of Sessions in *Mulvey v. Secretary of State for Social Security* [1997] B.P.I.R. 125. In a judicial review, the court held that upon an individual's bankruptcy, any right to receive income support did not vest in his trustee and the Department of Social Security was entitled to set off a social fund loan that pre-dated the sequestration.

8.53 Where a company is indebted to the estate and is associated with a company that is a creditor, a set-off will sometimes be attempted. A group of companies does not have the same wide powers as the Crown and the trustee should resist such attempts.

6. INTEREST

8.54 A creditor with a contractual right to interest may include such interest in his proof of debt accrued up to the date of the bankruptcy order (s.322(2)).

Interest on claim for periods before the bankruptcy order

8.55 In the following circumstances, laid down in I.R. 6.113, a creditor may include interest on his claim for periods before the bankruptcy order although such right was not previously reserved or agreed:

(i) if the debt is due by virtue of a written instrument and payable at a certain time, interest may be claimed for the period from that time to the date of the bankruptcy order;
(ii) if a demand for payment was made in writing, before presentation of the bankruptcy petition, by or on behalf of a creditor giving notice, that interest would be payable from the date of the demand to the date of payment.

8.56 The rate of interest that can be claimed under this rule is that ruling under section 17 of the Judgments Act 1838, at the date of the bankruptcy order or any lower rate specified in the written demand.

8.57 A creditor may prove for interest not yet due but a dividend payable before that time is subject to the discounting provisions contained in I.R. 11.13.

8.58 There is a right of all creditors including preferential creditors to receive interest accrued after the date of the bankruptcy order once claims of preferential and unsecured creditors, but excluding the spouse's claims, have been paid in full. This right arises under section 328(4) and the rate shall be the greater of that specified in section 17 of the Judgments Act 1838 at the commencement of the bankruptcy and the rate applicable to that debt apart from the bankruptcy.

7. TAXATION

8.59 The income of a bankrupt received and retained by him during the period of bankruptcy is treated as the income of the individual. He is required to make any necessary returns and to pay the appropriate tax thereon to the Inland Revenue.

8.60 Income received and retained for the benefit of creditors and expenses of the estate by the trustee during the period of bankruptcy is for tax purposes the income of the trustee. The trustee is required to make a return of the income and account for the tax to the Inland Revenue prior to distribution to the creditors.

8.61 Notwithstanding that assets of a bankrupt are held under the control of a trustee they are treated for the purposes of capital gains tax as retained by the bankrupt. Any tax arising as the result of the disposal of such assets is calculated as if the bankrupt had disposed of the assets although the tax is actually payable by the trustee (*Re McMeekin* Q.B. (N.I.) 1973; 48 T.C. 725; [1974] S.T.C. 429.

8.62 In the event that a bankrupt dies, assets held or acquired by the trustee are treated as though they had been acquired by the personal representative of the deceased.

8.63 Penalties awarded against an insolvent person in proceedings commenced before the relevant date are provable in the bankruptcy. Where there are other creditors the Inland Revenue would not in practice prove for penalties as this could prejudice other creditors. Any compromise of penalties agreed by the trustee must also be agreed by the bankrupt (*Re Hurren (a bankrupt)*; *The Trusteee v. I.R.C. and Hurren* [1983] 1 W.L.R. 183.

Debts relating to taxation which are preferential

8.64 In accordance with I.A. 1986, s.386 and Sched. 6, the following debts relating to taxation are preferential:

(i) sums due from the bankrupt at the relevant date in respect of deductions he was liable to make under the P.A.Y.E. system from emoluments paid during the 12 months immediately before the relevant date. Any repayments of income tax the bankrupt was liable to make during the same period may be deducted;

(ii) sums due from the bankrupt at the relevant date in respect of deductions from sub-contractors he was liable to make for the same period;

(iii) sums due from the bankrupt at the relevant date on account of Class 1 or Class 2 National Insurance Contributions becoming due in the immediately preceding 12 months;

(iv) sums that have been assessed on (and are due from) the bankrupt in respect of Class 4 National Insurance Contributions up to April 5 immediately before the relevant date. These sums must not, taken together, exceed any one year's assessment and must be due to the Board rather than to the Secretary of State for Health and Social Security (or, in Northern Ireland, to the relevant department of the Northern Ireland Office). Class 4 contributions are due directly to the Secretary of State where they are payable by a person who, while being in employment, is nevertheless categorised as being a self-employed earner;

(v) any V.A.T. which is referable to the period of six months before the relevant date;

(vi) car tax, betting, gaming and bingo duty due for the period of 12 months next before the relevant date.

8.65 The relevant date varies according to whether an interim receiver of the debtor's property has been appointed at any time between the presentation of the petition for bankruptcy and the making of the bankruptcy order. Where there has been such an interim receiver the relevant date is the date he was first appointed. Where there has been no interim receiver, the relevant date is the date the bankruptcy order is made.

8.66 For V.A.T. purposes, if a taxable person becomes bankrupt or incapacitated, from that date until some other person is registered in respect of the taxable supplies made or to be made by that taxable person or until the incapacity ceases, the Commissioners may treat any person carrying on the business as a taxable person. Any person who commences to carry on the business must inform the Commissioners within 21 days in writing, stating the date on which the bankruptcy or incapacity begins. If no person carries on the business the normal procedures for cancellation or registration will apply.

8.67 It is understood that Customs do not intend raising default surcharge assessments in respect of post-relevant date returns. However, the surcharge already levied in respect of the insolvent's trading, but unpaid at the relevant date, will be claimed as a non-preferential element of the debt due to Customs.

8.68 The amount of any penalty, surcharge or interest assessed under V.A.T.A. 1994, s.76 is recoverable as if it were tax due and is not VAT as such. Therefore, it is not preferential even if it relates to the six month period prior to the relevant date. The amount of such penalty, etc., may be combined with an assessment for the appropriate accounting period.

8. COSTS

8.69 Before creditors can receive any money, the estate must realise sufficient funds to discharge the costs including those of the petitioner, O.R. and D.T.I. as well as the fees and expenses of the trustee. In a small bankruptcy such costs may absorb a high proportion of the realisations. The debtor who anticipates an ultimate surplus following realisations of his assets will find that bankruptcy has been an expensive exercise. In addition to all these costs, interest will have been paid to the creditors and yet his estate will have been granted no interest on moneys held in the Insolvency Services Account. On the contrary the D.T.I. will have charged a fee for looking after the money.

Order of priority

8.70 If there is not enough money to pay all the creditors then the order of priority, as set out in I.R. 6.224, is as follows:

(a) expenses properly chargeable or incurred by the O.R. or trustee in preserving, realising or getting in any of the assets of the bankrupt, including those incurred in acquiring title to after-acquired property;

(b) any other expenses incurred or disbursements made by the O.R. or under his authority, including those incurred or made in carrying on the business of a debtor or bankrupt;

(c) (i) the fee payable under any order made under I.A. 1986, s.415 for the performance by the O.R. of his general duties as such;

(ii) any repayable deposit lodged by the petitioner under such an order except where the deposit is applied in payment of an insolvency practitioner's appointment under a debtor's petition;

(d) any other fees payable under a section 415 order including those payable to the O.R. and any remuneration payable to him;
(e) the cost of any security provided by an interim receiver, trustee or special manager;
(f) the remuneration of any interim receiver;
(g) any deposit lodged on an application for the appointment of an interim receiver;
(h) the costs of the petitioner, and of any person appearing on the petition whose costs are allowed by the court;
(j) the remuneration of any special manager;
(k) any allowance authorised under I.R. 6.63 towards expenses incurred by the bankrupt in employing some person to assist in the preparation of the statement of affairs or accounts;
(l) any allowance made, by order of the court, towards costs of an application for release from the obligation to submit a statement of affairs, or for an extension of time for submitting such a statement;
(m) any necessary disbursements by the trustee, in the course of his administration, including reasonable travelling expenses directly incurred by members of the creditors' committee or their representatives in respect of their attendance at the committee meetings or otherwise on committee business, as shall be allowed by the trustee;
(n) the remuneration or emoluments of any person (including the bankrupt) who has been employed by the trustee to perform any services for the estate as required or authorised by the Act or Rules;
(o) the remuneration of the trustee not exceeding the amount which would be payable under the O.R.'s scale (see Chap. 4);
(p) the amount of any capital gains tax on chargeable gains accruing on the realisation of any assets of the bankrupt (without regard to whether the realisation is effected by the trustee, a secured creditor or a receiver or manager appointed to deal with a security);
(q) any balance of remuneration, in excess of the O.R.'s scale, due to the trustee which may have been authorised under the various arrangements discussed in Chapter 4.

(Note that above paras (a) to (q) are numbered as per I.R. 6.224, thus omitting (i).)

8.71 Court fees in bankruptcy proceedings, previously contained in the Bankruptcy Fees Order 1984, have been incorporated into the Supreme Court Fees Order and County Court Fees Order as appropriate.

8.72 It seems that it is not the practice of the O.R.'s Department, in respect of its costs, to issue V.A.T. invoices but this is understood not to cause a problem as regards V.A.T. compliance as long as the practitioner can produce a letter from the O.R. setting out his charges.

8.73 It will be noted that the trustee's remuneration comes towards the end of this list and for this reason prospective trustees would be well advised to consider, before accepting an appointment, whether the assets are likely to be sufficient to cover prior costs. In cases of doubt the practitioner may like to suggest that the trusteeship be left in the capable hands of the O.R. Without such caution, trustees can unwittingly become philanthropists in the smaller administrations.

8.74 The costs of a shorthand writer, if appointed by an order of the court made at the instance of the O.R. in connection with an examination, rank in priority to those costs specified in paragraph 8.70(a) above. However, the costs of a shorthand writer appointed in any other case rank after those costs mentioned in paragraph (l) and before disbursements mentioned in paragraph (m) above.

8.75 The costs of an examination held under the order of a court, applying special provisions for a debtor unfit to undergo a public examination, shall rank in priority to the costs specified in paragraph 8.70(a) above.

9. PRIORITY

8.76 Usually there are insufficient funds to pay all creditors in full and the trustee will utilise the moneys first in discharging the costs in the order of priority set out in paragraph 8.70 above.

Priority of debts

8.77 Thereafter the priority is governed by sections 328 and 329 as follows:

(i) preferential claims ranking *pari passu* (see paras 8.35–8.38 above);
(ii) unsecured creditors (see paras 8.39–8.46) other than those with a specific deferred status;
(iii) interest on preferential and unsecured claims at the greater of the rate applicable to the debt in question or that specified in section 17 of the Judgments Acts 1838 at the commencement of the bankruptcy (see paras 8.54–8.58);
(iv) debts due to a person who was the bankrupt's spouse at the commencement of the bankruptcy.

Any surplus is then returned to the bankrupt and in such circumstances he may seek annulment of the bankruptcy order (see Chap. 10).

10. DIVIDENDS

8.78 The trustee is required by section 324 to declare and distribute dividends among the creditors whenever he has sufficient funds in hand for the purpose subject to the retention of such sums as may be necessary for the expenses of the bankruptcy. In practice the trustee may find that whilst he has realised sufficient funds and possibly all the assets likely to be available, a distribution may be delayed if a number of claims are not quantified. In particular he will wish to make sure that there are sufficient funds to discharge preferential claims before declaring a dividend to other creditors.

8.79 In calculating the distribution, the trustee shall make provision for:

(i) bankruptcy debts which appear to him to be due to persons who, by reason of the distance of their place of residence, may not have sufficient time to tender and establish their proofs;
(ii) bankruptcy debts which are the subject of claims which have not yet been determined; and
(iii) disputed proofs and claims.

(a) Intention to declare a dividend

8.80 Before declaring a dividend, the trustee shall, in accordance with I.R. 11.2, give notice of his intention to do so. It should be sent to every possible creditor who has not proved his debt including creditors mentioned in the statement of affairs or otherwise known to the trustee. It is advisable to distribute this notice widely to any person who has indicated a possible claim even if the basis of such claim is regarded as doubtful.

8.81 Notice of intended dividend must state the latest date up to which proofs may be lodged, which shall be the same for each creditor and shall be not less than 21 days from the date of the notice.

8.82 The notice shall contain a statement of the trustee's intention to declare a dividend (specified as interim or final) within four months of the latest date for proofs. The trustee may postpone or cancel the dividend if:

(i) he rejects a proof in whole or in part and an application to the court is pending for his decision to be varied (see paras 8.17–8.28 above); or
(ii) an application is made to the court to expunge a proof or reduce the amount claimed.

Where an application is pending to vary, expunge or reduce a proof of debt, a dividend may not be declared without leave of the court (I.R. 11.5). In giving leave, the court may direct a provision to be made in respect of the proof in question.

8.83 Within seven days of the latest date for submitting proofs, the trustee must deal with every proof received either by admitting or rejecting, in whole or in part, or, if further examination is needed, by setting aside sufficient funds in declaring the dividend. The trustee is not obliged to deal with proofs lodged after the last date for proving; but he may do so, if he thinks fit (I.R. 11.3).

8.84 If the procedure is not delayed by application to court to amend proofs or other circumstances, the trustee may proceed to declare the dividend at any time before the expiration of the four-month period. Alternatively he should declare the dividend within four months of the outcome of any application to court to amend the proof or vary his decision.

(b) Requirements of notice

8.85 Once he is ready to declare the dividend, the trustee must in accordance with I.R. 11.6 give notice of dividend to all creditors who have proved. No form is prescribed in the Rules but a suggested notice appears at Appendix I, Form BB. The notice must give the following details:

(i) the amount realised from the sale of assets indicating, so far as practicable, amounts raised by the sale of particular assets;
(ii) payments made by the trustee in the administration of the estate;
(iii) provision (if any) made for unsettled claims, and funds retained for particular purposes;
(iv) the total amount to be distributed, and the rate of dividend; and
(v) whether, and if so when, any further dividend is expected to be declared.

The dividend, which may be sent by post, may be distributed simultaneously with the notice declaring it. Alternatively arrangements may be made with any creditor for payment in another way or to be held for his collection. The form of authority, which used to be necessary under earlier Rules, is no longer required and the procedure is thereby simplified.

8.86 On completing the administration, the trustee must give notice to creditors of intention to declare the final dividend or that no dividend or no further dividend will be declared (section 330).

8.87 Once a dividend has been calculated, the trustee shall in accordance with I.Reg. 23 make application to the D.T.I. for payment instruments which shall be entered in the records in total.

8.88 Normally a creditor shall not receive a dividend unless his proof has been submitted and admitted (see paragraphs 8.04–8.28 above), although in exceptional circumstances the court may order that creditors or any class of them may be entitled to receive a distribution from the estate without being required to prove their debts. Such exception might occur in a bankruptcy with a substantial number of creditors who may have difficulty in obtaining the information with which to submit their claims but it can be taken from the bankrupt's records where the costs of putting all creditors to strict proof would be substantial and unnecessary.

8.89 On vacating office the trustee shall return to the D.T.I. any unclaimed dividend payment instruments after endorsing them with the word "cancelled" (I.Reg. 23(4)).

8.90 If, after the payment of a dividend, the amount claimed by a creditor is increased, that creditor is not entitled to disturb the distribution (I.R. 11.8) as it would clearly be impracticable to ask other creditors to refund moneys for this purpose. However, he is entitled to be paid out of any money available for further dividends, in respect of any dividend which he failed to receive, before money is applied to payment of additional dividends. On the other hand if a creditor's proof is withdrawn or expunged he is liable to repay to the trustee any dividends that have been overpaid.

8.91 In computing the final dividend, the trustee must make provision for all claims and final costs that will arise in order to complete the administration and his notice of intended final dividend must state that the date then specified for lodgment of proofs is the final date.

Chapter 9
PROTECTION OF CREDITORS

No stranger to trouble myself, I am learning to care for the unhappy—Virgil.

9.01 At least in theory, it is a general concept that bankruptcy and other insolvency procedures should achieve equity between the creditors by removing a scramble for the assets and enabling the insolvency practitioner to realise the assets and distribute them *pro rata* to the creditors. Whilst there are exceptions to this general principle, the Act gives substantial powers to the trustee, and in some instances to the creditors themselves, to take steps first to ensure that as far as possible the assets find their way into the trustee's hands and secondly to limit the circumstances in which a particular creditor can benefit to the detriment of the others.

1. Private Examination of Bankrupt and Others

Who may be summoned

9.02 At any time after a bankruptcy order has been made the court may, on the application of the O.R. or the trustee, summon to appear before it:

(i) the bankrupt or his spouse or former spouse;
(ii) any person known or believed to have any property comprised in the bankrupt's estate in his possession or to be indebted to the bankrupt;
(iii) any person appearing to the court to be able to give information concerning the bankrupt or his dealings, affairs or property (I.A. 1986, s.366(1)).

The court may in cases (ii) and (iii) above require the person to submit an affidavit to the court containing an account of his dealings with the bankrupt or to produce any documents in his possession or under his control relating to the bankrupt's dealings, affairs or property.

9.03 The court has very wide powers under this section to bring people before it including the power of arrest or seizure of documents, money, records or other property (s.366(3), (4)).

9.04 A person brought before the court under section 366 may be examined on oath, either orally or by interrogatories, about the bankrupt or his dealings, affairs and property (s.367(4)).

9.05 Further powers are granted to the court by section 367 relating to an examination under section 366. The court is empowered following examination of evidence under section 366 to order up delivery of any property which that person has in his possession to the trustee or to the O.R. If it appears to the court on consideration of the evidence that any person is indebted to the bankrupt it may order the payment of all or part of that debt to the O.R. or to the trustee (s.367(2)).

9.06 By virtue of section 368 these provisions will also apply where an interim receiver has been appointed to act (see Chap. 3).

9.07 For the purpose of this examination, or indeed for a public examination under section 290, the court may, on the application of the O.R. or the trustee, order an Inland Revenue official to produce to the court his files relating to the bankrupt, his tax returns, etc. (see Chap. 4).

9.08 The power to order a private examination of individuals, including the bankrupt, is a restatement with modifications of the provisions formerly contained in B.A. 1914, s.25.

It has, in the words of the learned authors of *Muir Hunter on Personal Insolvency*, "long provided a most valuable weapon for the Official Receiver or the trustee to use to assist in the administration of the estate".

9.09 The wording of section 366 and the connected section 367 which deals with the court's enforcement powers under section 366 mirrors that contained in the corresponding sections 236 and 237 which relate to corporate insolvency and allow liquidators and other "office-holders" to inquire into company dealings. Accordingly, many of the cases which are discussed below, and which seek to define and interpret the rights of liquidators and others in respect of corporate insolvencies, are also applicable to personal bankruptcy.

9.10 The powers now contained in sections 366 and 367 are a re-statement, albeit with substantial modifications, of the provisions formerly contained in B.A. 1914. Again, to quote the same authority:

> "The powers contained in this section are directed to enabling the court to assist a trustee, who in general comes to the affairs of the bankrupt as a stranger, and with no personal knowledge of the case, to discover the truth of the circumstances relating to this property, dealings and affairs, with as little expense and as much expedition as possible, and with a particular view to the recovery of assets and the ascertainment of the validity of creditors' claims." (*Muir Hunter on Personal Insolvency*, para. 3–351/1.)

9.11 B.A. 1914 had been the subject of considerable judicial interpretation and it is thought that, although there are differences, these tenets of interpretation apply equally to I.A. 1986, s.366 *et seq*. However, this has been to some extent overshadowed by the spate of cases within the last few years, in particular the decisions in *Re Cloverbay Ltd (No. 2)* [1991] Ch. 90 and *Re Bishopsgate Investment Management Ltd* [1992] B.C.C. 222 and *Re British and Commonwealth Holdings plc (Nos. 1 and 2)* [1992] Ch. 342; [1993] A.C. 426. These cases will be analysed below.

9.12 The scope of examination is wide and the trustee's powers extend to examining the bankrupt even after his discharge (*Re Coulson* [1934] Ch. 45) and may extend to the personal representatives after the bankrupt's death.

9.13 If the trustee seeks to examine a person other than the bankrupt or his spouse, he must usually demonstrate that he has first attempted to obtain the relevant information by other means, *e.g.* a letter or questionnaire, and without success (*Re Rolls Razor Ltd (No. 2)* [1970] 1 Ch. 576). A pre-examination questionnaire is not, however, essential in the case of the bankrupt or his spouse. The court is unlikely to refuse the trustee the right to examine simply because he had failed to serve a questionnaire, although it is generally regarded as good practice for him to indicate to the proposed examinee the general areas which examination will cover, particularly in complex cases. The normal procedure is for the trustee to first attempt to obtain information by means of a private interview with the bankrupt, his spouse, or the proposed examinee.

9.14 The power to order an examination of the bankrupt or others has always been discretionary. A number of cases which had been decided under the provisions of successive Companies Acts relating to powers of liquidators and others to conduct examinations were applicable in bankruptcy cases too.

This is still the case now that all the relevant provisions have been incorporated into one statute. Indeed, all of the recent cases (see above) which lay down guidelines as to the court's discretion to allow examination relate to corporate rather than individual insolvency.

9.15 In general it had been held that the power to examine must not be abused by the trustee, that he must prove the need to examine, and that it must not be used in any oppressive, vexatious, or unfair way, in particular not to give him any special advantage in prospective litigation. In particular, decisions such as *Re Bletchley Boat Co. Ltd* [1974] 1 W.L.R. 630 and *Re Castle New Homes Ltd* [1979] 1 W.L.R. 1075 had limited the scope of the trustee's powers (see also *Re Franks* [1892] 1 Q.B. 546). It is an abuse of power for an office holder (trustee or liquidator) to use the process of examination for an ulterior motive: *Re PFTZM (In Liquidation)* [1995] B.C.C. 280.

9.16 However, from a number of recent cases, including those referred to above, it is clear that the courts will interpret the examination provisions more generously in favour of trustees than they would in favour of liquidators and receivers. To quote Hoffmann J. in the context of a corporate insolvency:

> "Persons who have had what is perhaps no more than a misfortune to be involved in the affairs of an insolvent company owe a public duty to assist the liquidator to investigate the affairs of the company in the interest of creditors." (*Re J. T. Rhodes Ltd* [1987] B.C.L.C. 77.)

9.17 The courts had formerly refused to allow an examination to proceed in cases where the liquidator or trustee had commenced or was definitely contemplating litigation on the basis that to do so would give the insolvency practitioner an unfair advantage. However, in *Re Cloverbay Ltd (No. 2)* (see above) the principles behind the exercise of the court's discretion were fully reviewed by the court which stated that a different view would be taken on the enlarged jurisdiction to examine under the Insolvency Act. This was a case involving a limited company where the administrators sought an order for further private examination of the company's bankers. It was clear that the administrators had not made a final decision whether or not to commence proceedings. Guidelines were laid down by the Vice-Chancellor. These may be summarised as follows:

(a) the court had an absolute discretion, not in any way limited by the statute;

(b) the case of *Re Castle New Homes Ltd* (see above) was disapproved. It was not appropriate to consider what an office-holder's intentions were because they were difficult to establish by objective evidence;

(c) the office-holder had to establish a reasonable requirement for the relevant information rather than an absolute need for it;

(d) if making an order would be oppressive or vexatious it would normally be refused. To that extent the law has not changed, but if the degree of oppression is small, the balance would come down in favour of making an order for examination;

(e) an examination could be ordered even where the office-holder had issued and served proceedings. It was a matter entirely for the court's unfettered discretion and a suggestion was made that the court adopt a more practical approach.

9.18 These principles were further refined and approved by the House of Lords in the later case of *Re British and Commonwealth Holdings plc (Nos. 1 and 2)* [1993] A.C. 426. The Court again affirmed the necessity of giving "great weight" to the views of the office-holder. He, whether trustee, liquidator or receiver, would have a detailed knowledge of the problems which exist in relation to the affairs of the company (or individual) and the information required. The court adopted the dictum of Buckley J. in *Re Rolls Razor Ltd* [1968] 3 All E.R. 698 that the purpose of such proceedings was:

> "to enable the court to help the liquidator to discover the truth of the circumstances connected with the affairs of the company . . . in order that he may be able, as effectively as possible, and with as little expense as possible, and with as much expedition as possible, to complete his function as liquidator."

9.19 An appeal to the House of Lords was unanimously dismissed. Lord Flynn said:

> "I am therefore of the opinion that the power of the court to make an order under section 236 is not limited to documents which can be said to be needed 'to reconstitute the state of the company's knowledge' even if that may be one of the purposes most clearly justifying the making of an order."

Lord Flynn pointed out that no such restriction had been imposed in the *Cloverbay* guidelines (para. 9.17 above) but the courts had to balance the inconvenience to those involved with the need for the insolvency practitioner to obtain full disclosure. The latter interest predominated in this instance but it was an exceptional case involving need to investigate all aspects of the financial collapse.

9.20 A clear implication of these cases is that the court looks at what might be described as the "public policy" issues in giving the liquidator, administrative receiver or trustee the maximum possible latitude in conducting his inquiries and in imposing on directors and others the "public duty" (see *Re J. T. Rhodes Ltd*) to answer questions.

9.21 The privilege against self-incrimination by a person whose examination is sought has recently come under scrutiny. Whereas a bankrupt was always under an obligation to disclose information concerning his estate to his trustee and had no privilege against self-incrimination (*Re Firth, ex p. Schofield* [1877] 6 Ch.D. 23), other witnesses who might have knowledge about the affairs or business of a bankrupt or those of an insolvent limited company were allowed a wider discretion to oppose examination on the grounds of possible self-incrimination. However, in *Bishopsgate Investment Management Ltd v. Maxwell* [1992] 2 W.L.R. 991 the Court of Appeal refused to allow Mr Kevin Maxwell to rely upon the privilege against self-incrimination to refuse to answer questions put to him by the provisional liquidator of Bishopsgate Investment Management Limited. As the court put it, to allow such privilege would effectively defeat the purposes of sections 235 and 236 of the Act. The decision in this case would clearly be applicable, not only in the case of bankrupts, who, as it has been said, have to co-operate and answer questions put by the trustee, but to those who may have a detailed knowledge of the bankrupt's business and affairs and who cannot now rely upon the privilege against self-incrimination in refusing to answer the trustee's reasonable questions.

9.22 A solicitor who has acted for the debtor (presumably this must apply to accountants too) may also be summoned to answer questions put by the trustee. In these cases it is usual for the trustee to issue a questionnaire and if the solicitor unreasonably refuses to answer the same then examination may be ordered (*Re A Debtor (No. 472 of 1950)* [1958] 1 W.L.R. 283). Solicitors might be able to rely upon some professional privilege although the decision in *Re Aveling Barford Ltd* [1989] B.C.L.C. 122 would indicate that the opportunities for claiming legal professional privilege against answering questions are limited.

9.23 The court's enforcement powers under section 366 are contained in section 367. If it appears to the court, on consideration of any evidence contained under section 366 or 367, that any person has in his possession property comprised in the bankrupt's estate, the court may, on the application of the O.R. or the trustee, order that person to deliver the whole or any part of the property to the O.R. or trustee (s.237(1)).

9.24 Section 367(2) goes on to state that if it appears to the court, on consideration of any evidence that is obtained, that any person is indebted to the bankrupt, then, on the application of the O.R. or the trustee, the court may make an order to pay such moneys to the O.R. or trustee. However, this is not to be read as a general power to assist the trustee with regard to disputed debt collection. Quite clearly if the trustee wishes to claim a debt on behalf of the estate, and that debt is subject to any dispute, he must use the normal procedures in the High Court or County Court for the collection of the same.

9.25 The provisions as to examination also have extra-territorial aspects. Section 367(3) states that the court may, if it thinks fit, order that any person who if within the jurisdiction of the court would be liable to be summoned to appear before it under section 366 should be examined in any part of the United Kingdom where he may be for the time being, or in any place outside the United Kingdom. However, in *Re Tucker (A Bankrupt), ex p. Tucker* [1988] 1 All E.R. 603 the Court of Appeal held that, on its true construction, these provisions did not mean that there was jurisdiction over British subjects resident abroad. The Court set aside orders made by the Registrar, on application of the trustee, for the issue of a summons under what was then B.A. 1914, s.25 requiring the debtor's brother, a British subject living in Belgium, to produce documents, to attend at court for examination and authorising service of the summons on the brother in Belgium. The Court also refused to exercise its discretion to make an order for the examination of the brother in Belgium before an examiner appointed by the English court. This decision clearly gives rise to problems. As one writer has put it:

> "In view of the increasingly international trend in modern dealings and business, *Tucker*... is a highly inconvenient decision." (Roger Gregory, *Bankruptcy of Individuals* (2nd ed.), CCH Editions Limited.)

9.26 It is, however, suggested by *Muir Hunter on Personal Insolvency* that the extra-territorial operation of another section of the Act, section 426, and Designation Orders made thereunder (see Co-Operation of Insolvency Court (Designation of Relevant Countries and Territories) Order 1986 (S.I. 1986 No. 2123)) may mean that, in the event of a foreign country being "designated", examination of witnesses abroad could be conducted by the foreign court. It is not intended to discuss this matter in detail but readers should refer to the discussion in *Muir Hunter on Personal Insolvency*, *op cit.*, paras. 3–353 and 3–479 *et seq.*

2. TRANSACTIONS AT AN UNDERVALUE

9.27 Section 339 of the Act allows the trustee to apply to the court to set aside a transaction at an undervalue entered into by the bankrupt within five years prior to the presentation of the petition if the bankrupt was insolvent at the time of the transaction or became insolvent as a result of it.

9.28 A bankrupt enters into a transaction with a person (including a corporate person) at an undervalue if:

(i) he makes a gift to that person or otherwise receives no consideration;
(ii) he enters into a transaction in consideration of marriage; or
(iii) he enters into the transaction for a consideration in money or money's worth which is significantly less in value than that provided by the bankrupt (s.339(3)).

9.29 If the transaction is entered into less than two years before presentation of the petition, the insolvency of the bankrupt does not have to be proved by the trustee. Otherwise the trustee must show that the bankrupt was insolvent at the time of the transaction or that he became insolvent as a result of it. However, insolvency is presumed in the case of a transaction at an undervalue with an "associate" unless the transaction is with an employee (s.341(2)). A very wide interpretation is given to "associate" in section 435 and because of its importance in interpreting various sections of the Act and Rules this is reproduced in essence in Appendix V. In *Re Kumar (a Bankrupt)* [1993] 1 W.L.R. 224 there was a transfer by a debtor to his wife of a joint tenancy in the matrimonial home. The only consideration was her assumption of liability for the mortgage. The transfer was set aside on the basis that the interest in the equity which was given to the wife far exceeded in value the size of the mortgage commitments which she had taken over.

9.30 Insolvency is defined in section 341(3)—an individual is insolvent if he is unable to pay his debts as they fall due or the value of his assets is less than the amount of his liabilities, taking into account contingent or prospective liabilities.

Application of the provision

9.31 In the application of this provision, unlike the case where a preference is alleged (see paras 9.32–9.47 below), there is no examination of the motives or intention of the bankrupt. The mere fact that the transaction is at an undervalue, provided the other conditions are satisfied, is sufficient to enable the trustee to apply to the court to have it set aside.

3. PREFERENCES

9.32 Section 340 gives the trustee power to apply to the court to set aside any preference given by the bankrupt during the "relevant time" as defined by section 341.

9.33 A preference is given if the debtor, when he is insolvent, does anything or suffers anything to be done which has the effect of putting one of his creditors or a surety or a guarantor of his debts or liabilities into a position which, in the event of his bankruptcy, will be better than if that thing had not been done. However, the court must be satisfied that the debtor was "influenced by a desire" to put that person in a better position in the bankruptcy than would otherwise have been the case.

9.34 The period during which a transaction may be attacked as a preference depends upon the circumstances and the type of transaction involved:

(i) in the case of a transaction which is also a transaction at an undervalue the trustee may go back to five years before presentation of the petition;
(ii) in the case of a transaction not at an undervalue but which is entered into with "an associate" of the debtor (see App. V) he may go back up to two years before presentation of the petition;
(iii) in the case of a transaction other than the above the period is six months prior to presentation of the petition.

Again, the debtor must be insolvent at the time of the transaction or must have become insolvent as a consequence of it and insolvency is defined as with transactions at an undervalue.

(a) "Influenced by a desire"

9.35 Of crucial importance is the proof that the debtor was "influenced by a desire" to place his creditor in a better position than the creditor would have been were it not for the transaction complained of. The rationale behind the law as to preferences is that ordinary unsecured and non-preferential creditors should be treated on an equal basis, with distributions made *pari passu*. A preference offends against this in advancing one particular unsecured creditor above his fellows—hence the trustee is empowered to redress the situation and recoup the advantage from that preferred creditor. Where the preferred person is an associate that influence is presumed unless the contrary is shown (s.340(5)) but in other cases the onus is upon the trustee or O.R. to prove such influence upon the mind of the debtor. However, the fact that something has been done in pursuance of a court order will not itself prevent it being regarded as a preference (s.340(6))—presumably to prevent orders obtained by some form of collusion between the debtor and the creditor being preferred.

9.36 The wording of section 340 mirrors that of section 239, which relates to preferences in corporate insolvencies and allows a liquidator in similar circumstances to set aside a transaction in favour of one of the company's creditors. Accordingly judicial interpretation of section 340 will be along the same lines as that used in respect of section 239 and a leading modern case, *Re M.C. Bacon Ltd* [1990] B.C.C. 78 (see below), must therefore form the basis of interpretation of section 340.

9.37 However, before examining that case to see what changes have taken place in the law relating to preferences, it is worthwhile looking at the historical context. Under B.A. 1914 for a preference to be proved, a trustee or liquidator had to show that there was in effect a dominant intention to prefer.

To quote an early edition of *Palmer's Company Law* (23rd ed.), a liquidator had to prove that "the substantial effectual or dominant view in the mind of the company, acting by its directors, was to prefer the creditor at a time when the company was unable to pay its debts as they became due".

9.38 Similar reasoning was applied to test the mind of the debtor. In practice this test proved extremely difficult, involving an examination of the state of mind of the individual or corporate debtor. If it could be shown that payment had been made under pressure, say, threatened litigation or closure of an account, then preference, or fraudulent preference as it was then known, was not provable.

9.39 I.A. 1986, in replacing the relevant provisions of the former C.A. 1985 and B.A. 1914 in one statute, introduced the phrase "influenced ... by a desire". In *Re M.C. Bacon Ltd* which, so far as the writers are aware, was the first reported case relating to preferences under the Act, Millett J. made it clear that the old tenets of interpretation would not apply. After discussing the old case law and its terminology under successive Companies Acts and B.A. 1914 he stated:

> "Section 44(1) has been replaced and its language has been entirely recast. Every single word of significance, whether in the form of a statutory definition or in its judicial exposition, has been jettisoned ... 'view', 'dominant', 'intention' and even 'to prefer' have all been discarded. These are replaced by 'influenced', 'desire', and 'to produce in relation to that person the effect mentioned in subsection (4)(b)'."

9.40 As the learned judge explained, the question of whether or not the debtor had been influenced by such desire involved a completely different test from that which had been used previously. With the removal of the requirement in the old law to establish a "dominant intention to prefer" a different type of test was involved:

> "intention could not remain the relevant test. Desire has been substituted ... intention is objective, desire is subjective. A man can choose the lesser of two evils without desiring either ... a man is not to be taken as *desiring* all the necessary consequences of his actions ... it will

still be possible to provide assistance to a company in financial difficulty provided that the company is actuated only by proper commercial considerations. Under the new régime a transaction will not be set aside as an avoidable preference unless the company positively wished to improve the creditor's position in the event of its own insolvent liquidation."

9.41 The wording of the sections (239 and 340) moreover requires only that desire should have *influenced* the decision. As the learned judge put it:

"that requirement is satisfied if it was one of the factors which operated on the mind of those who made the decision. It need not have been the only factor, or even the decisive one."

9.42 In *Re M.C. Bacon Ltd* the liquidator was not able to establish that the directors of the company were influenced by the necessary desire to prefer. M.C. Bacon Ltd had gone into creditors' voluntary liquidation in August 1987 owing its unsecured creditors in excess of £329,000. The overdraft, which stood at £235,000, was secured by a debenture which had been entered into in May 1987, within the six-month period required for an unconnected creditor. The liquidator's application that the debenture should be set aside either as a preference or as a transaction at an undervalue failed.

9.43 With regard to preference the learned judge, after considering the facts as mentioned above, said that, in deciding to grant the debenture, the directors were not influenced by any desire except to avoid the bank calling in the company's overdraft and to continue trading. Their actions were not influenced by desire to improve the bank's position as a creditor in the event (which happened) of the company's insolvent liquidation. In this case the bank's support was necessary to enable the company to continue trading. This was applied in *Re Ledingham-Smith (a Bankrupt)* [1993] B.C.L.C. 635 when a payment by the debtor of arrears of fees which were due to his former accountants did not satisfy the criteria under section 340(4). The debtor was influenced in this case not by a desire to prefer, but by a desire to retain the accountants' services in order to ensure that they continued to advise him about his financial affairs during a particularly difficult period.

9.44 The court in *Re M.C. Bacon Ltd* went on to say that the debenture was not a transaction at an undervalue:

"the granting of a debenture was not a gift, nor was it without consideration. The consideration consisted of the bank's forbearance from calling in the overdraft and its honouring of cheques and making of fresh advances to the company during the continuance of the facility . . . [s.238(4)] requires a comparison to be made between the value obtained by the company for the transaction, and the value of the consideration provided by the company."

9.45 It has been mentioned that where the person alleged to have been preferred is an "associate" (see App. V for definition) then the presumption is that the debtor was influenced by a desire to prefer (see, *e.g. Re D.K.G. Contractors Ltd* [1990] B.C.C. 903). However, even in the case of an associate the presumption as to the desire to prefer may be rebutted as happened in *Re Beacon Leisure Ltd* [1991] B.C.C. 213. In that case the learned judge accepted the evidence by two directors of the company that they had not, when paying certain rent to the landlord who was also co-director and shareholder (clearly an associate), been influenced by a wish to prefer him.

(b) Powers of the court to adjust the position of the parties

9.46 If a preference or transaction at an undervalue is proved by the trustee or O.R. the court has wide powers under section 342 to adjust the position of the parties; it may, *inter alia*:

(i) require property transfer to be vested in the trustee as part of the estate;
(ii) require any money to be so vested if it represents the proceeds of sale of such property;
(iii) release or discharge any security given by the bankrupt;
(iv) require a person to pay a sum of money to the trustee in respect of benefits received.

9.47 However, an order shall not prejudice the position of a person who has acquired an interest in property, from the person preferred, in good faith and for value without notice of the relevant circumstances (s.342(2)), as amended by the Insolvency (No. 2) Act 1994.

4. Extortionate Credit Transactions

9.48 By section 343 the trustee is empowered to apply to the court to make an order in respect of an extortionate credit transaction provided it was entered into no more than three years before the commencement of the bankruptcy. Bankruptcy commences at the date of the adjudication.

9.49 The transaction is extortionate if, having regard to the risk accepted by the provider of the credit, the terms require grossly exorbitant payments to be made (whether conditionally or not) or otherwise grossly contravene the ordinary principles of fair dealing.

9.50 The burden of proof in this case is on the provider of the credit. It is presumed that unless the contrary is shown the transaction is extortionate (s.343(3)).

Powers of the court

9.51 The powers of the court are again very wide (s.343(4)). The court may set aside the whole or any part of any obligation created by the transaction or vary the terms, or the terms of any security held, or order payments to be made to the trustee. It may require any person to surrender property held as security to the trustee or direct accounts to be taken between any persons.

5. Avoidance of General Assignments of Book Debts

9.52 I.A. 1986, s.344 provides that where a person is engaged in business and makes a general assignment of his existing or future book debts and he is subsequently adjudged bankrupt, the assignment is void against his trustee as regards book debts which were not paid before the presentation of the petition unless the assignment has been registered under the Bills of Sale Act 1878.

9.53 Assignment is defined to include an assignment by way of security or a charge over book debts. It is also provided that a "general assignment" does not include:

(a) an assignment of book debts due at the date of the assignment from a specified debtor or of debts becoming due under a specified contract; or

(b) an assignment of book debts included either in a transfer of a business made in good faith and for value or in an assignment of assets for the benefit of creditors generally.

6. CONTRACTS TO WHICH THE BANKRUPT IS A PARTY

9.54 Section 345 applies where a person has made a contract with an individual who is later adjudged bankrupt. It allows the other party to apply to the court to discharge his obligations under the contract on such terms as to payment by the applicant or the bankrupt of damages for non-performance as the court shall think equitable.

9.55 Damages payable by the bankrupt by virtue of an order under this section are provable as a bankruptcy debt (s.345(2)).

9.56 Where an undischarged bankrupt is a contractor in respect of any contract jointly with another person that person may sue or be sued in respect of the contract without the joinder of the bankrupt (s.345(4)).

7. JUDGMENT CREDITORS

9.57 A creditor who has obtained judgment against the bankrupt may clearly put himself in an advantageous position over other creditors if he is able to execute his judgment against the goods, land or debts of the bankrupt and retain the proceeds of such execution before division of the estate amongst other creditors. It is likely in such a case that the judgment creditor may obtain payment in full rather than a small dividend, if anything, out of the estate after the payment of the trustee's costs and expenses. This would of course conflict with the general rule in distribution of insolvent estates (whether corporate or personal) which is that creditors of the same class should be treated equally and it can therefore lead to what one eminent judge has called "an unseemly scramble" between creditors in their desire to obtain and execute judgment before their competitors (*per* Lord Brightman in *Roberts Petroleum Ltd v. Kenny (Bernard) Ltd* [1983] 2 A.C. 192). With a view to avoiding such a scramble certain provisions of the Act set out the circumstances in which a judgment creditor is allowed to retain the benefit of any execution levied by him.

9.58 It will be recalled (see Chap. 2) that by virtue of I.A. 1986, s.285, the court is empowered to stay any action, execution or other legal process against an individual where there is a bankruptcy petition pending or after adjudication. That section also provides that after the making of a bankruptcy order no creditor of the bankrupt in respect of a debt provable in the bankruptcy shall have any remedy against the property or person of the bankrupt in respect of that debt or, before his discharge, commence any action or any other legal proceedings except with the leave of the court and on such terms as the court may impose. That is, however, subject to the provisions as to enforcement procedures in section 346 (below) and section 347 (limited right of distress—see below). Nor do these provisions in any way affect the right of a secured creditor to enforce his security (s.285(4)).

9.59 Subject to this, where a creditor has before the commencement of the bankruptcy either issued execution against the goods or land of the bankrupt, or attached a debt due to the bankrupt, the creditor is not entitled, against either the trustee or the O.R., to retain the benefit of the execution or attachment or any sums paid to avoid it, unless the execution or attachment is completed or the sums paid before the commencement of the bankruptcy (s.346(1)). The bankruptcy commences when the order adjudging the person bankrupt is made (s.278(a)).

9.60 Section 346(5) provides that execution against goods is completed by seizure and sale or by the making of a charging order under the Charging Orders Act 1979, s.1, that execution against land is completed by seizure, by the appointment of a receiver or by the making of a charging order under section 1 as above and that an attachment of a debt is completed by the receipt of the debt.

9.61 Accordingly if execution is incomplete, the claims of the judgment creditor will usually be defeated. In the case of those orders which are made in two stages, *e.g.* a garnishee or charging order where there is a "nisi" stage before the orders are made absolute, the court has held (for similar provisions under the Companies Acts) that a garnishee order nisi or a charging order nisi should be set aside where, in those cases, winding up supervened, in order to achieve equality amongst creditors (*Wilson D. (Birmingham) Ltd v. Metropolitan Property Developments Ltd* [1975] 2 All E.R. 814; *Roberts Petroleum Ltd v. Kenny (Bernard) Ltd*, above).

9.62 These restrictions are not absolute: the court does have a discretion by virtue of section 346(6) to set aside the rights conferred on the trustee or O.R. to such extent and on such terms as it thinks fit, but there is clear authority to the effect that such powers will only be used in exceptional cases: *e.g.* where a creditor has been induced to delay taking action by some form of fraud (*Re Redman (Builders) Ltd* [1964] 1 W.L.R. 541; *Re Caribbean Products (Yam Importers) Ltd* [1966] Ch. 331).

Special provisions

9.63 Special provisions apply by virtue of section 346(2)–(4) in respect of goods which have been taken in execution where, before the completion of the execution, notice is given to the sheriff or bailiff that the debtor has been adjudged bankrupt. The sheriff must then on request deliver the goods or any money recovered to the O.R. or to the trustee, but the costs of execution are a first charge on the goods or money so delivered and the trustee or O.R. may sell such goods or part of them to satisfy the charge.

9.64 If the sheriff levies execution for a sum beyond £500, and the goods are sold or money paid to avoid sale, the sheriff is obliged by section 346(3) to keep the balance for 14 days. If notice is then served on him during that time that a petition has been filed on which a bankruptcy order is made, he must keep the balance for 14 days, or, if later, so long as the petition is pending. When the bankruptcy order is made, any balance must be paid over to the trustee or O.R. but the costs are retained as a first charge on that balance.

9.65 I.R. 12.19 specifies that any notice under section 346 to the sheriff, etc. must be in writing and delivered by hand or sent by recorded delivery to the under-sheriff or other officer charged with the execution.

9.66 Protection against a trustee's claims under section 346 is given to a person who acquires goods from the sheriff or bailiff in good faith under a sale. Such goods cannot be reclaimed (s.346(7)).

8. LEASEHOLD PROPERTY

(a) Disclaimer

9.67 A leasehold property may be a potential asset or a potential liability.

The trustee will be wary of the potential asset that may turn out to be a liability which will absorb the other realisations in the estate or, worse still, render him personally liable. For these reasons he will examine carefully the implications of adopting any property or contract. Fortunately for him it is usually possible to disclaim onerous property, leaving the other party with no remedy other than to claim as an unsecured creditor against the estate. **9.68**

Disclaimer in bankruptcy is governed by I.A. 1986, ss.315–321; and I.R. 6.178–186. **9.69**

The trustee may disclaim any unprofitable contract or any other property comprised in the bankrupt's estate which is unsaleable or not readily saleable or is such that it may give rise to a liability to pay money or perform any other onerous act. **9.70**

Probably the most common example is a leasehold property which a trustee is unable to assign on satisfactory terms. He might, however, in rare circumstances wish to disclaim a freehold property if a contract for sale would imply onerous obligations. For example, the property may carry with it obligations under environmental protection legislation. **9.71**

(b) Notice of disclaimer

For this purpose the trustee must deliver to the court a notice of disclaimer (App. I, Form W). The effect of the disclaimer is to determine, as from the date thereof, the rights, interests and liabilities of the bankrupt and his estate in respect of the property disclaimed and to discharge the trustee from all personal liability. The notice shall clearly identify the property disclaimed and shall be delivered in two copies, each of which shall be endorsed by the court with the date of delivery. One copy of the notice so endorsed shall be returned to the trustee. Within seven days of its return, the trustee shall send copies of the endorsed notice, in the case of a leasehold property, to any underlessee or mortgagee or, in the case of a dwelling-house, to any person known to be in occupation or claiming a right to occupy. A notice or copy notice to be served on any person under the age of 18 in relation to the disclaimer of property in a dwelling-house is sufficiently served if sent or given to a parent or guardian of that person. In every case a copy shall be sent to any person known to the trustee to claim an interest in the disclaimed property or to be under any liability in respect of the property. In the case of an unprofitable contract, the trustee shall give copies of the notice to such persons as are known to be parties to it, or have interests therein. If it subsequently comes to the trustee's notice that some other person was entitled to receive notice, the trustee shall forthwith send to that person a copy unless the person has already been made aware of the disclaimer or, on account of the lapse of time, no useful purpose would be served. **9.72**

The trustee shall deliver to the court, for filing, reports as to the persons to whom he has sent or given copies of the notice of disclaimer. **9.73**

The leave of the court is required for the disclaimer of property which has been claimed by the trustee as after-acquired property (see Chap. 7), personal property exceeding a reasonable replacement value or tenancies subject to a vesting notice under section 308A. In such circumstances the trustee may apply for that leave *ex parte* and his application must be accompanied by a report giving particulars of the property proposed to be disclaimed, setting out the reasons why, having claimed the property, he then seeks leave to disclaim and specifying the persons who have been informed of his intention to make the application. **9.74**

The trustee shall enclose copies of any consents to the disclaimer to which he may wish to refer in his report. **9.75**

On considering such application, the court may order that notice of the application be given to persons who would be entitled to apply for a vesting order if the property were disclaimed. **9.76**

9.77 Any person sustaining loss or damage in consequence of the operation of a disclaimer is deemed to be an unsecured creditor of the bankrupt to the extent of the loss or damage (s.315(5)). Disclaimer does not, however, release an original lessee or assignor of a lease, who would otherwise be liable in the event of the tenant's default (*Hindcastle Ltd v. Barbara Attenborough Associates Ltd*, [1996] B.P.I.R. 595, reversing the decision in *Stacey v. Hill* [1901] 1 K.B. 660).

9.78 In *MEPC Plc v. Scottish Amicable Life Assurance Society and another: Neville Richard Eckley (Third Party)* [1996] B.P.I.R. 447, the trustee in bankruptcy had filed a notice of disclaimer in the prescribed form but stating that he disclaimed "the licence to assign . . . relating to the lease". Presumably the trustee intended to disclaim the lease itself and it would indeed have been impossible for him to have disclaimed the obligations whilst enjoying the property. The assignor sought to establish that there had been no valid disclaimer. The Court of Appeal held that the disclaimer had been effective to disclaim the lease and such was the original intention of the trustee. Whilst this judgment may be of some comfort to trustees, faced with a complexity of assignments and other documents connected with the lease, they would be well advised to see that disclaimers are correctly worded in the first instance.

(c) 28–day notice

9.79 A person having an interest in a property, particularly a landlord of a leasehold property, may give a 28-day notice to the trustee under section 316 requiring the trustee to decide whether or not to disclaim (App. I, Form X). If the trustee does not then disclaim within 28 days of the notice, he is deemed to have adopted that contract or property and shall not be entitled to issue notice of disclaimer. Thereafter he cannot change his mind and must accept the obligations relating to the property. The trustee should therefore act promptly upon receipt of any document which could be construed as a 28-day notice, otherwise he may run the risk of personal liability. The section is a useful provision for landlords or other parties, who can be considerably disadvantaged if trustees take a long time to decide whether to adopt a leasehold interest or other contract.

9.80 If a 28-day notice is served upon the trustee in respect of a property that can be disclaimed only with leave of the court, as explained above, then the trustee may within 28 days of the notice make his application to the court for leave to disclaim. The court shall extend the time allowed under section 316 for giving notice of disclaimer to a date not earlier than that fixed for the hearing of the application.

(d) Vesting orders

9.81 As previously stated, a disclaimer of leasehold property does not take effect unless a copy of the notice has been served, so far as the trustee is aware of their addresses, on any person claiming under the bankrupt as underlessee or mortgagee and, in the case of a dwelling house, on every person in occupation or claiming a right to occupy. In such cases an application may be made to the court for a vesting order under section 320 by any person who claims an interest in the disclaimed property or is under a liability in respect of the property disclaimed, not being a liability discharged by the disclaimer, or by any person who is entitled to be an occupant of a dwelling-house. The court may make an order on such terms as it thinks fit, vesting the disclaimed property in, or ordering its delivery to, a person entitled to it or subject to a liability thereunder, or trustee of such persons or to an occupant or person entitled to occupy. A vesting order need not be completed by any conveyance, assignment or transfer.

9.82 Any application for a vesting order must be made within three months of the applicant becoming aware of the disclaimer or receiving a copy of the notice of disclaimer, whichever is the earlier. The procedure is set out in I.R. 6.186.

9.83 Section 321 contains rules concerning the vesting of leasehold properties. It states that the court shall not make an order vesting disclaimed leasehold property in any person, except subject to the same liabilities and obligations as the bankrupt was subject to under the lease on the date that the bankruptcy petition was presented and also, if the court thinks fit, subject to obligations that would apply to an assignee. The same section then goes on to state that if no person is willing to accept these conditions, the property may be vested in any person who is liable to perform the covenants of the lease and the court may vest the property in such a person freed and discharged from all encumbrances and interests created by the bankrupt. In *Re Yarmarine (IW) Ltd* [1992] B.C.C. 29 a surety made application for a vesting order under section 181 which applies following disclaimer by a liquidator and is similar to section 320. In this case the company had not been wound up but had been struck off for failure to file returns and the lease had been disclaimed by the Treasury Solicitor. The court held that, whilst a disclaimer by the Treasury Solicitor is in some respects similar to a disclaimer by a liquidator, this was not sufficient for section 181 to apply, and the court had no jurisdiction to make a vesting order.

9.84 The trustee in disclaiming property may, without prejudice to his other obligations, give notice of the disclaimer to any person who in his opinion ought, in the public interest or otherwise, to be informed of it.

9.85 If it appears to the trustee that some person claims or may claim an interest in a property to be disclaimed, he may give notice to that person to declare within 14 days whether he claims any interest and, if so, the nature and extent thereof (I.R. 6.184). Failing compliance with the notice, a trustee is entitled to assume that the person concerned has no interest in the property as will prevent or impede its disclaimer.

9.86 Any disclaimer of property by the trustee is presumed valid and effective, unless it is proved that he has been in breach of his duty with respect to the giving of notice of disclaimer or otherwise (I.R. 6.185).

9.87 Many bankrupts, but few if any landlords, tend to the misapprehension that disclaimer brings to an end any claim by the landlord other than entitlements accrued up to the date of the disclaimer. Whilst the debtor and the trustee have no obligation for ongoing rent, the landlords are entitled to claim against the bankrupt's estate in respect of damages suffered in consequence of the disclaimer (s.315(5)). The complexity of such claims is amply-demonstrated by the case of *Re Park Air Services Plc (Christopher Moran Holdings Limited v. Bairstow* [1997] 3 All E.R. 193. At first instance (reported at [1996] B.P.I.R. 377). Although this was a case involving a members voluntary liquidation, and the landlord's claim arose under section 178(6), the principles apply equally to bankruptcy. No less than seven different possible bases were put forward for calculation of the loss and damage suffered by the landlord and sums between £200,000 and £5.3 million were submitted on the basis of expert evidence. Ferris J. had decided that the damages payable were worked out by taking a capital value calculated by reference to future rent, and other payments (*e.g.* insurance rent), reduced by "market risk rate" to assess the present value of payments due in the future. Deducted from that was a "residual amount" for the value of the lease, that is what could be obtained on a re-letting.

The concept of "market risk" resulted in a lower figure for the landlord which consequently appealed to the Court of Appeal. The landlord argued that the damages payable should be the difference between:

(a) the total of all sums payable by the tenant until the end of the term of the lease; and

(b) the total of all sums payable by new tenants on re-lettings of the premises during the same period

and that there should be no discount for early payment but, the landlord should receive the benefit of the cost of repairs caused by any breach of the tenant's repairing obligations, which the landlord might need to make in order to effect a re-letting. The absence of any discount for early payment means, in the words of one commentator that there was a "remarkable windfall" for the landlord and the Court of Appeal decision has been criticised on that basis (see an excellent article by Andrew Pickin in *Insolvency Intelligence* (1997) July/August. It certainly means that trustees in bankruptcy and liquidators will have a much harder job in defeating large claims from landlords, particularly in respect of over-rented premises. The authors understand that an appeal to the House of Lords is pending.

9.88 Landlord have a number of potential remedies. Their right to levy distress is dealt with below. They may also re-enter the premises and forfeit the lease for non-payment of rent. It was held in *Razzaq v. Pala, The Times*, June 6, 1997, that forfeiture for non-payment of rent by a bankrupt is not the enforcement of a security by a secured creditor but the exercise of the right of forfeiture. However, in this case, although the landlord had validly re-entered the premises on non-payment of rent by the tenant, in view of the tenant's promise to pay, before re-entry, and his payment very shortly after forfeiture, and the hardship occasioned by the loss of his business premises and means of livelihood, the court granted relief from forfeiture and an order that possession be restored.

9.89 During the recession of the early 1990s, insolvency practitioners became conditioned into regarding all leases as potential liabilities to be promptly disclaimed. However in more buoyant times, trustees should consider whether leasehold properties are potential assets either to be sold at a premium or, as presumably happened in the *Razzaq v. Pala* case, to be utilised by the bankrupt and enable him to make contributions. The right to apply to the court for relief against forfeiture can be useful in such circumstances.

9. LANDLORDS: DISTRESS FOR RENT

9.90 Landlords may be in an even more advantageous position than judgment creditors. Distress is a simple and relatively cheap remedy for the collection of rent. It does not require a court order, only the payment of commission to a certificated bailiff who may be instructed to levy distress as soon as rent is even one day overdue.

9.91 By virtue of section 347, the landlord in a bankruptcy retains a limited right of distress. He is allowed to distrain upon the goods and effects of an undischarged bankrupt for rent due but only for six months' rent prior to the commencement of the bankruptcy. This right is given even if the property has vested in the trustee (s.347(9)) and is without prejudice to the landlord's right to prove for any bankruptcy debt in respect of outstanding rent (s.347(10)).

Limitations on landlord's rights to distress

9.92 There are, however, two limitations on the landlord's rights:

(i) where the distress is against the lessee to whom a petition relates and an order is subsequently made, any amount of distress for the period exceeding six months or if relating to a period after the levy of distress is held for the benefit of the estate (s.347(2)); and

(ii) the distress will be postponed to the preferential creditors. If there are insufficient assets in the estate to pay them, the landlord will be obliged to surrender goods or money to the trustee to pay the preferential creditors and, although the landlord will then be able to rank as a preferential creditor himself, the goods surrendered will be exempt from his claims (s.347(3), (4)).

10. TRANSACTIONS DEFRAUDING CREDITORS

9.93 Sections 423 to 425 of the Act, which appear under the title "Provisions against debt avoidance", effect a repeal and reconstitution of L.P.A. 1925, s.172. This provision of ancient origin (it can be traced back to a 16th century statute) had allowed the court to set aside fraudulent conveyances, being those intended to defraud creditors, made before the commencement of the bankruptcy.

9.94 Section 423 widens the former provisions of L.P.A. 1925, s.172 and specifically includes payments of money rather than simply fraudulent conveyances. The section relates to companies as well as individuals and, as with so many other provisions of I.A. 1986, the principles of interpretation will be the same in individual as they are in corporate insolvency. Moreover, there is clearly harmonisation with the sections of the Act relating to preferences and transactions at an undervalue making it easier for trustees to show that there has been a transaction defrauding creditors.

9.95 Those transactions which may be attacked are:

(i) transactions where the individual who later becomes bankrupt makes a gift or otherwise receives no consideration;
(ii) transactions entered into in consideration of marriage;
(iii) transactions entered into at an undervalue (as defined above).

9.96 If the court is satisfied that the debtor entered into such a transaction for the purpose:

(i) of putting assets beyond the reach of a person who is making, or may at some time make, a claim against him; or
(ii) of otherwise prejudicing the interests of such a person in relation to the claim which he is making or may make,

the court may then make an order restoring the position to what it would have been if the transaction had not been entered into, and protecting the interests of persons who are the victims of the transaction (s.423(1), (2)).

9.97 The reference to a protection being given to persons who "may at some time" make a claim against the debtor gives statutory force to a line of cases decided under section 172 and its predecessors which protected future or contingent creditors, *e.g.* where a man about to go into a business or trade conveyed most of his property away so that it was out of the reach of future trade creditors should the business be unsuccessful. The courts then held that the transaction could be impeached notwithstanding that the debts, which were subsequently avoided, did not exist at the time of the conveyance (*Mackay v. Douglas* [1872] L.R. 14 Eq. 106; *ex p. Russell* (1882) 19 Ch.D. 588).

9.98 Notwithstanding the heading to section 423, "Transactions defrauding creditors", it is no longer necessary (as it was under L.P.A. 1925, s.172) to show that there was "intent" to defraud creditors. The significant change is that the court is required to find only that the debtor entered into the transaction "*for the purpose of* ... " putting assets beyond the reach of creditors. The effect of this change is that even a transaction entered into with an honest motive may be impeached.

9.99 In *Arbuthnot Leasing International Ltd v. Havelet Leasing Ltd (No. 2)* [1990] B.C.C. 636 Scott J. reversed the transaction at the behest of a judgment creditor, Arbuthnot Leasing, where the defendant company, Havelet Leasing, had transferred the bulk of its income to an associated company for insufficient consideration. The learned judge accepted the evidence from the managing director of Havelet that the transaction had been carried out on legal advice and without any dishonest motive in that he carried out the transaction in what he believed to be the best interests of the company and its other creditors. Nevertheless it was carried out for the purpose of avoiding the judgment in favour of Arbuthnot and ought to be reversed.

9.100 In the later case of *Chohan v. Saggar* [1992] B.C.C. 306, on appeal [1994] B.C.C. 134, it was held that for section 423 to apply the trustee had to show that it was a *dominant* purpose of the debtor to remove assets out of the reach of creditors. With respect to the learned judge, this is a curious interpretation inconsistent with the approach adopted by the court in construing the law as to preferences (see *M.C. Bacon Ltd* above and see the comments by Sealy and Milman, *op. cit.*, p. 457). The state of mind or belief of the *recipient* of the transaction is, however, irrelevant in determining the issue which relates to the motives of the debtor (*Moon v. Franklin* [1996] B.P.I.R. 198).

"Victims of transaction"

9.101 Section 423 gives certain rights to "the victim of the transaction" who is defined in section 423(5) as a person who is, or is capable of being, prejudiced by the transaction. By section 424(1) the classes of person who can apply for an order under section 423 where the debtor has been adjudged bankrupt are described as:

(i) the trustee or the O.R. or, with the leave of the court, the victim of the transaction;
(ii) where the victim is bound by a voluntary arrangement approved under the Act, the supervisor of the voluntary arrangement or the victim of the transaction; or
(iii) in any other case, the victim of the transaction.

The representative nature of the action under sections 423–425 is recognised by section 424(2) which provides that an application made under section 424(1) is to be treated as made on behalf of every victim of the transaction. The victim of a transaction may include, as in *Moon v. Franklin* (above), persons who are suing the debtor for professional negligence or any litigant who is proceeding against the debtor, in which he has a chance of a successful recovery.

9.102 The powers given to the court under these sections are wide and are contained in section 425. They include orders requiring any property transferred as part of the transaction to be vested in any person; similar orders in respect of the proceeds of sale of property; release or discharge in whole or in part of security given by the debtor; requiring persons to pay money over in respect of benefits received from the debtor; providing for the release or discharge of surety or guarantor liabilities or the revival of obligations released under the transaction. The court also has very wide powers to order discovery, even of privileged documents in the hands of a solicitor, which tend to show that the debtor had "iniquitous purposes" in respect of the transactions (*Barclays Bank Plc v. Eustice* [1995] B.C.C. 978).

9.103 An order may affect the property of or impose an obligation on any person, whether or not he is the person with whom the debtor entered the transaction, but there is a saving (section 425(2)) in respect of persons acquiring property from a person other than the debtor in good faith and for a value without notice.

9.104 One important feature of section 423 which contrasts with the rights given to a trustee under sections 339 and 340 is that there is no time limit so that the trustee can if necessary investigate a transaction even if it had been made 10 years before the bankruptcy. There is, however, some doubt, following the decision in *Re Farmizer (Products) Limited* [1995] 2 B.C.L.C. 462 (subsequently upheld by the Court of Appeal) as to whether a claim for relief under section 423 may become statute-barred by reason of the Limitation Act 1980. (See discussion in *Muir Hunter* at para. 3–467).

11. LIENS

9.105 A lien over goods or documents of the bankrupt may exist in favour of a person or company who has supplied services to the bankrupt and remains unpaid either wholly or in part. It is a potentially valuable right allowing the holder of the lien to frustrate the ability of the trustee to get in the assets of the bankrupt and therefore may constitute a valuable bargaining counter in the hands of the holder of the lien. The trustee may well choose to settle with the particular creditor to get the lien released.

9.106 Liens over goods may be general or specific, a general lien giving the holder the right to retain possession until all his claims have been met whether or not in relation to the specific goods being held. General liens are difficult to establish at common law although those held by bankers or solicitors and warehousemen have been recognised. Moreover, a general lien may always be created by specific agreement between the parties.

9.107 Specific liens are much more common as they give the holder rights to retain possession until work done on the goods is paid for, *e.g.* work done by a garage on a vehicle.

9.108 A lien does not automatically carry with it the power of sale, although many contractual liens have this right built in to give the holder additional protection. However, at common law the power of sale is limited although a statutory right of sale has been given in many cases, *e.g.* to carriers. Liens do not generally arise in the hands of employees who have retained goods belonging to the bankrupt against their claims for unpaid wages.

Limitation of rights

9.109 The rights of holders of liens are in one case severely limited by the Act. By section 349, a lien or other right to retain possession of any of the books, papers or other records of a bankrupt is unenforceable to the extent that its enforcement would deny possession of such books, etc., to the O.R. or trustee. However, this does not apply to a lien on documents, which give title to property and are held as such so that the right, say, of an equitable mortgagee, who has possession of such documents by deposit of deeds, is protected.

Chapter 10
THE BANKRUPT

I will pay you some, and, as most debtors do, promise you infinitely—William Shakespeare, *Henry IV, Pt 2.*

1. Disabilities

10.01 Bankruptcy has never been a comfortable state although in some well-publicised bankruptcies the bankrupts seemed to have lived—indeed seem to continue living—to a standard which might be envied by their solvent contemporaries.

10.02 Bankruptcy has always carried with it a certain social stigma, if not worse. As Stephen Aris has graphically put it, referring to 19th century views, "society so disapproved of those who could not pay their debts that prison was the usual fate" (*Going Bust: Inside the Bankruptcy Business* (Andre Deutsch, 1985)) and although somewhat less Draconian provisions prevail nowadays there do remain disabilities and offences which are peculiar to bankruptcy law. Even if the element of disgrace has largely disappeared there are still very real obstacles preventing bankrupts leading a normal life at least in so far as financial matters are concerned.

(a) Public office

10.03 A bankrupt cannot sit in the House of Lords or be elected for the House of Commons. These disqualifications last until discharge or annulment (I.A. 1986, s.427). Nor can a bankrupt be a justice of the peace or a member of a local authority or of certain statutory authorities.

(b) Company directorships

10.04 An undischarged bankrupt may not act as a director of or directly or indirectly take part in or be concerned in the promotion, formation or management of a company, except with the leave of the court (Company Directors' Disqualification Act 1986, s.11(1)). Breach of this section is an offence. The court for this purpose is the court by which he was adjudged bankrupt. Notice of intention to apply for leave must be served on the O.R. and it is the duty of the O.R., if he is of the opinion that it is contrary to the public interest that the application should be granted, to attend on the hearing of the application and oppose it (*ibid.* s.11(3)). It has been held that the offence of acting as a director while being an undischarged bankrupt is an absolute offence. The fact that the defendant genuinely believes that his bankruptcy has been discharged is irrelevant, save in mitigation (*R v. Brockley* [1994] B.C.C. 131).

10.05 An application for leave under section 11 must be supported by an affidavit identifying the company, giving the details as set out in I.R. 6.203 regarding the company and the manner and capacity in which the applicant proposes to take part or be concerned in its promotion, formation or management and must also give details of any emoluments and other benefits he is likely to obtain. The O.R. must also deliver a report to the court, and the bankrupt has the opportunity of making representations disputing or denying any statements made therein (I.R. 6.204). The O.R. and the trustee may appear on the hearing of the application and may make representations and put to the bankrupt such questions as the court may allow.

10.06 The prohibition upon a bankrupt becoming a company director is not there to punish the bankrupt; its objective is purely to protect the public (*Re Altim Pty Ltd* [1968] 2 N.S.W.R. 762, a decision of the New South Wales Supreme Court). Nevertheless the desire to protect the public is so strong that it will only be in exceptional cases that a bankrupt is given leave to act as a company director (*Re McQuillan* (1989) 5 B.C.C. 137).

(c) Engaging in business

10.07 The offences created by section 360 of the Act relating to obtaining credit and engaging in business in a name other than that in which he was adjudged bankrupt effectively stop a bankrupt engaging in business on his own account as do the restrictions on bank accounts (para. 10.08 below) and after-acquired property imposed by section 307 (Chap. 7).

(d) Bank accounts

10.08 There is no direct statutory provision prohibiting an undischarged bankrupt from holding a bank account. However, in practice this would not be a feasible exercise. First, it is an offence for a bankrupt to obtain credit over a prescribed amount without disclosing his status. Secondly, section 307, although giving limited protection to bankers, allows the trustee to claim for the estate all after-acquired property including any credit balance in a bank account.

(e) Other disqualifications

10.09 An undischarged bankrupt is not qualified to act as an insolvency practitioner (I.A. 1986, s.390(4)) nor is he allowed to act as a trustee of a charity without the permission of the court or a waiver from the charity commissioners (Charities Act 1993, s.72) and similar provisions apply in respect of pension schemes governed by the Pensions Act 1995, s.29.

10.10 There may be a number of "professional" disqualifications *e.g.* inability to practice as a solicitor, barrister or chartered accountant without the leave of the relevant professional body. It is impossible to provide a full list in this text and reference should be made to the rules of the appropriate professional body. However, the inability to practice one's profession while being an undischarged bankrupt will obviously make a voluntary arrangement a much more attractive proposition for such a person and possibly for the creditors too if that is perceived as a way of maximising his earnings potential.

2. DUTIES IN RELATION TO THE TRUSTEE

10.11 Bankruptcy serves to relieve the debtor, to a large extent, of his obligations to creditors. In return the bankrupt is obliged to act in good faith towards the trustee of his property. As mentioned in the introduction to Chapter 7, the bankrupt must make full disclosure of his property and his dealings therein. He must also disclose his income and advise the trustee of any change of his circumstances or change of address.

10.12 The bankrupt is entitled to retain only those assets necessary for the continuation of his trade or for the maintenance of himself and his family. Even so it was noted in Chapter 7 that the trustee may require the sale of expensive items and substitute reasonable replacements. Likewise the bankrupt is only entitled to retain such part of his income as is reasonably necessary for his own and his family's maintenance.

10.13 I.A. 1986, s.333 imposes upon the bankrupt certain specific duties in relation to the trustee:

(i) to give to the trustee such information as to his affairs, to attend upon the trustee and to do all such other things as the trustee may reasonably require;
(ii) within 21 days of an increase in his income or any property acquired by him or devolved upon him, to give notice to the trustee.

The duties in paragraph 10.11 above continue to apply after the bankrupt's discharge. Whilst the discharge brings to an end the obligation to account for income or newly-acquired property, except to the extent that the court may order otherwise, the trustee's task of realising the assets in the bankruptcy does not cease and the bankrupt still has a duty to co-operate.

10.14 A failure by the bankrupt, without reasonable excuse, to comply with the obligations imposed by section 333 renders him guilty of a contempt of court and liable to be punished accordingly.

10.15 The trustee assumes all the powers of the bankrupt in relation to the estate. He may accordingly take legal action to recover debts or assets. In many respects his powers are wider than those of the bankrupt. He may recover preferences and other transactions (see Chap. 9) and may frequently sell the matrimonial home against the wishes of the spouse as it is the creditors' interests that predominate (Chap. 7).

10.16 Mention was made in the introduction to Chapter 7 of the trustee's investigative powers. He may also ask questions at a public (Chap. 3) or private (Chap. 9) examination of the bankrupt. If the bankrupt has failed to co-operate, the trustee may oppose his discharge (see paras 10.52–10.65 below).

Offences by the bankrupt

10.17 The Act stipulates a number of instances in which the wrongdoing bankrupt may be guilty of an offence; namely, for non-disclosure (s.353), concealment of property (s.354), concealment of books and papers and falsification (s.355), false statements (s.356), fraudulent disposal of property (s.357), absconding (s.358), fraudulent dealing with property obtained on credit (s.359), obtaining credit or engaging in business without disclosing his status (s.360), failure to keep proper books of accounts of a business (s.361) and gambling or rash and hazardous speculations which materially contribute to his insolvency (s.362).

10.18 In practice not all bankrupts will be models of rectitude in fulfilling their obligations. Frequently a bankrupt changes his address or even goes abroad permanently without advising the trustee or the O.R. Contributions from income, whether voluntary or pursuant to a court order, if not the subject of an income payments order, tend to be erratic and the time required to collect them can easily outweigh their value.

10.19 When it comes to the matrimonial home, the resourceful bankrupt will find many obstacles to place in the trustee's path. These have included the introduction of a friendly party as a tenant, who then theoretically obtains rights on the property and can object to its sale or at least diminish its value. Other bankrupts are less than readily available when it comes to the service of proceedings. The authors have even known one bankrupt who posed as his own fictitious brother alleging that the real bankrupt was "somewhere in Greece or perhaps in Cyprus!"

3. OFFENCES

(a) General

10.20 Bankruptcy is not and never has been a criminal offence *per se*. However, it has always hovered on the fringes of the criminal law so might have been regarded as having had quasi-criminal status. Indeed in the 18th century bankrupts could be, and on rare occasions were, sentenced to death for concealment of their effects. Even in the 19th century when imprisonment for debt was widespread, bankruptcy had very serious consequences for the individual.

10.21 A number of offences are set out in sections 350 to 362; essentially a restatement in modern form of the codification which took place in the B.A. 1914.

Proceedings

10.22 Proceedings for offences under I.A. or I.R. may not be instituted except by the D.T.I. or by or with the consent of the D.P.P. (s.350(5)).

10.23 Proceedings may not be instituted after annulment and the bankrupt is not guilty of an offence in respect of anything done after discharge but proceedings may be commenced against a discharged bankrupt for an offence committed prior to his discharge.

10.24 It is not a defence for a bankrupt to say that anything relied upon in whole or in part as constituting the offence was done outside England and Wales.

10.25 As far as penalties are concerned, the list of possible penalties is set out in a convenient form in Schedule 10 to the Act in relation to offences under the Act and in I.R., Sched. 5 in relation to offences under the Rules.

(b) Defence of innocent intention

10.26 Section 352 of the Act, which applies in the case of some of the offences, provides a defence of innocent intention if the bankrupt can prove that, at the time of the conduct constituting the offence, he had no intention to defraud or to conceal the state of his affairs. The effect is that for those offences where the section 352 defence is not available, the offence is one of absolute liability, but even where the section 352 defence applies the onus of proof is on the bankrupt.

10.27 In the various offences under this part of the Act there is a statement whether the section 352 defence of innocent intention will apply.

(c) Non-disclosure

10.28 As mentioned in Chapter 7, it is an offence under section 353 if the bankrupt does not, to the best of his knowledge and belief, disclose all his property to the O.R. or the trustee or if he fails to inform them of any disposal of property which would have formed part of his estate with full details of such disposal.

10.29 The latter provision does not, however, apply to any disposal in the ordinary course of a business carried on by the bankrupt or to any payment of the ordinary expenses of himself or his family. The section 352 defence is available in respect of this offence.

(d) Concealment of property

10.30 It is an offence under section 354 if a bankrupt does not deliver up possession to the O.R. or the trustee, or as they may direct, of any property in his estate which is in his possession or under his control. It is similarly an offence to conceal any debt due to or from him, or to conceal any property in value not less than £500 or where in the 12 months before the petition or in the period between presentation of the petition and adjudication (described in the Act as "the initial period") he did anything which would have been an offence of concealment of a debt or property had the bankruptcy order been made immediately before he did it. The section 352 defence is available.

10.31 He is also guilty of an offence under section 354(2) if he removes, or in the initial period removed, property in value not less than £500 which he would have had to deliver up to the trustee or O.R. Again the section 352 defence will apply.

10.32 Under section 354(3), he is guilty of an offence if without reasonable excuse he fails, on being required to do so by the O.R. or the court, to account for the loss of any substantial part of his property in the 12 months prior to the petition or in the initial period or to give a satisfactory explanation of any such loss. Here the section 352 defence is not available.

(e) Concealment of books and papers: falsification

10.33 A bankrupt is guilty of an offence under section 355(1) if he does not deliver up to the O.R. or trustee, or as they may direct, all books, papers and other records relating to his estate or his affairs. The section 352 defence applies to this offence.

10.34 He is guilty of an offence under section 355(2) if he prevents, or in the initial period prevented, the production of any such books or papers or records or conceals, destroys, mutilates or falsifies or permits such acts to be done to any such books and papers and records; or if he makes or causes the making of false entries in such documents, or in the 12 months before the petition, or in the initial period, he did anything which would have been an offence under section 355(2)(b) and (c) had the bankruptcy order been made immediately before he did this. The section 352 defence applies to this offence.

10.35 The bankrupt will be guilty of an offence under section 355(3) if he disposes of, or alters, or makes any omission, or causes or permits such disposal, etc., in any book, document or record relating to his estate or affairs, or if in the months before the petition, or in the initial period, he did anything which would have been such an offence if the order had been made before he did it. The section 352 defence applies.

(f) False statements

10.36 The bankrupt is guilty of an offence under section 356(1) if he makes or has made any material omission in any statement relating to his affairs. The defence under section 352 applies.

10.37 He is also guilty of an offence under section 356(2), to which there is no defence under section 352, if:

(i) he knows or believes that a false debt has been proved by any person and fails to inform the trustee as soon as practicable;

(ii) he attempts to account for any part of his property by fictitious losses or expenses;
(iii) he attempts at any meeting of his creditors in the 12 months before the petition or at any time in the initial period (whether or not at such a meeting) to account for property by fictitious losses or expenses; or
(iv) he has made false or fraudulent statements or representations to creditors for the purpose of obtaining their consent to any matter relating to his affairs or his bankruptcy.

(g) Fraudulent disposal of property

10.38 The bankrupt is guilty of an offence under section 357(1) if he makes any gift or transfer of, or charge on, his property within the period of five years before the commencement of the bankruptcy. The reference to making a transfer of, or any charge on, any property includes causing or conniving at the levying of any execution against that property. The defence under section 352 applies.

10.39 He is also guilty of an offence under section 357(3) if he has concealed or removed any of his property within two months before or at any time after there has been a money judgment against him which remains unsatisfied. The defence under section 352 is available. A bankrupt defendant who is guilty of fraudulent disposal of property contrary to section 357(3) could expect to receive a custodial sentence even if of previous exemplary character. The Court of Appeal so held in *Regina v. Mungroo, The Times*, July 3, 1997, in which the bankrupt, having had a long and excellent army career, left the service and failed to disclose his gratuity of £31,000 which he used to pay off gambling debts and debts to members of his family and for an extension to the family home. Their Lordships entirely agreed with the Recorder, who in passing sentence had observed, "Those who stand to gain from the release of bankruptcy but conceal their assets, try to have their cake and eat it, attack the whole basis on which the bankruptcy legislation is founded".

(h) Absconding

10.40 The bankrupt is guilty of an offence under section 358 if he leaves or attempts or makes preparations to leave England and Wales with any property the value of which is not less than £500 and of which he is required to deliver up possession to the O.R. or trustee, which period also extends to six months before the petition or during the initial period. The defence under section 352 applies. It is sometimes suggested that an undischarged bankrupt cannot leave the jurisdiction of the court without the permission of his trustee or O.R., even to the extent that the O.R. or trustee could impound his passport. This is not, in the writers' view correct. An undischarged bankrupt is perfectly able to move around freely and go abroad, even permanently, but he commits a criminal offence if he removes or attempts to remove property in the circumstances described above. It is therefore suggested that if the O.R. or trustee gets wind of the fact that the bankrupt is proposing to remove assets from the jurisdiction he should apply to the court for a Mareva type injunction or some other order preventing the bankrupt from removing himself and property from the jurisdiction. The trustee can probably prevent the bankrupt from leaving the jurisdiction if his express purpose is to avoid examination under section 366 (*c.f.* the enforcement powers in s.367).

(i) Fraudulent dealing with property obtained on credit

10.41 The bankrupt is guilty of an offence under section 359(1) if in the 12 months before the petition, or in the initial period, he disposed of any property which he had obtained on credit and which was not paid for at the time he disposed of it. The defence under section 352 applies.

10.42 An offence is also committed under section 359(2) by any person who, within 12 months before the petition or in the initial period, acquired or received property from the bankrupt knowing or believing that the bankrupt owed money on the property and that the bankrupt did not intend or was unlikely to be able to pay the money he owed. There is, however, protection available if the disposal, acquisition or receipt of the property was in the ordinary course of a business carried on by the bankrupt.

10.43 In inquiring whether property is disposed of in the ordinary course of business the court may have regard in particular to the price paid for the property (section 359(4)) so that sales at an obvious undervalue would clearly be suspect.

(j) Obtaining credit; engaging in business

10.44 Section 360(1) makes it an offence for the bankrupt either alone or jointly with any other person to obtain credit, in excess of £250, without giving the person from whom the credit is obtained information about his status. It is also an offence to engage (whether directly or indirectly) in any business under a name, other than that in which he was adjudged bankrupt, without disclosing to all persons with whom he enters into any business transaction the name in which he was so adjudged.

10.45 Credit is widely defined by section 360(2) to include goods sold under an H.P. agreement or conditional sale or where the bankrupt is paid in advance for the supply of goods or services.

10.46 The defence under section 352 does not apply to this offence and it therefore creates a very serious disability for a bankrupt in attempting to engage in any form of business.

(k) Failure to keep proper accounts of business

10.47 The bankrupt is guilty of an offence under section 361(1) where he has been engaged in any business for any of a period of two years before the petition and has failed to keep proper accounting records throughout that period and throughout any part of the initial period, or he has not preserved all the accounting records which had been kept.

10.48 There is no offence, however, if his unsecured liabilities when adjudged do not exceed £20,000 or if he proves that in the circumstances in which he carried on business the omission was honest and excusable.

10.49 Section 361(3) further defines proper accounting records to include records of entries of cash paid and received on a daily basis and statements of annual stocktaking. The defence under section 352 does not apply.

(l) Gambling

10.50 The bankrupt is guilty of an offence under section 362 if he has in the two years before the petition materially contributed to, or increased the extent of, his insolvency by gambling, or by rash and hazardous speculations, or has in the initial period lost any part of his property by such means. The section 352 defence does not apply.

(m) False representations

10.51 It is an offence under I.R. 5.30 for a debtor to make any false representation or to commit any other fraud for the purpose of obtaining the approval of his creditors to a proposal for a voluntary arrangement under Part VIII of the Act.

4. DISCHARGE

(a) Duration of bankruptcy

10.52 I.A. 1986 substantially changed the rules as to discharge from bankruptcy. Instead of automatic discharge being the exception, it became the norm. However, automatic discharge may be suspended (see below) in certain circumstances which in theory should prevent abuses of the automatic discharge provisions.

10.53 The Act provides that:

(i) the bankruptcy commences with the day on which the order is made and continues until discharge (s.278);
(ii) there is an overriding discretion for the court to suspend automatic discharge where there are breaches of any statutory obligations by the bankrupt (see below);
(iii) automatic discharge applies after three years. However, the court may suspend the running of the period for any breach of the bankrupt's obligations under the Act.

(b) Discretionary grounds

10.54 This applies where a person has previously been an undischarged bankrupt at any time in the period of 15 years ending with the commencement of the present bankruptcy. Discharge is then only by way of an order of the court made under section 280(1) of the Act. An application under this section may only be made by the bankrupt, after the end of a period of five years from the commencement of the bankruptcy.

Court's powers

10.55 The court's powers to discharge the bankrupt are set out in section 280(2) and are discretionary. The court may:

(i) refuse the discharge;
(ii) give an absolute discharge; or
(iii) make an order for discharge subject to conditions in respect of any income which may become due to the bankrupt or in respect of any property acquired by him.

The court may also make the order have an immediate effect, or have its effects suspended for a period of time, or until conditions laid down in the order are fulfilled.

Procedure

10.56 The procedure on an application under section 280 is governed by I.R. 6.217–6.218. A sample form of application is included at Appendix I, Form DD. Notice must be given to the O.R. and a sum deposited to cover the O.R.'s costs of the application.

10.57 The court will then fix a venue for the hearing giving notice of at least 42 days to the O.R. and to the bankrupt. The O.R. must also give notice to the trustee and to every creditor who, to his knowledge, has a claim outstanding against the estate which has not been satisfied.

10.58 The O.R. is also obliged to make a report to the court under I.R. 6.218 which will deal *inter alia* with any failure by the bankrupt to comply with his obligations under the Act, the circumstances surrounding the present and any previous bankruptcy, particulars of distribution and any other relevant matters according to the O.R.'s discretion. The bankrupt is entitled to file a notice in court disputing any matters in the O.R.'s report.

(c) Automatic discharge

Application to suspend the running of time

10.59 This applies in the case of a summary administration after two years and in any other case after three years (section 279(1)(b)). The O.R. may, however, apply to the court to suspend the running of time if he alleges the bankrupt has failed, or is failing, to comply with any of his obligations under the Act and, if so satisfied, the court may suspend the period or alternatively impose conditions before the time starts to run. This is a very wide power as technically any breach of a statutory obligation by the bankrupt may lead to the suspension of time running for the automatic discharge provisions.

10.60 Where the O.R. does make an application to the court for suspension of the automatic discharge provisions, I.R. 6.215 and 6.216 apply. Again, the O.R. must file a report with the court setting out his reasons for making the application and the bankrupt may file a notice disputing any of the O.R.'s statement.

10.61 Where the court has made an order suspending the discharge, the bankrupt may apply under I.R. 6.216 for this suspension to be lifted, but the O.R. or trustee may appear on this application and object.

10.62 Where a bankrupt is discharged, on whatever basis, the court must on his application issue to him a certificate of discharge and he may require the D.T.I. to give notice of the discharge in the *Gazette* or in any newspaper in which the bankruptcy was advertised or in both (I.R. 6.220).

(d) Effect of discharge

10.63 The effect of discharge of the bankrupt is twofold:

(i) to release the bankrupt from the various disabilities for which an undischarged bankrupt suffers (see paras 10.01–10.08 above);
(ii) to release the bankrupt personally from all the "bankruptcy debts" (see paras 10.79–10.81 below), whether proved or provable.

10.64 The effect of discharge is formally stated in section 281: where a bankrupt is discharged, the discharge releases him from all the bankruptcy debts, but has no effect:

(i) on the functions (so far as they remain to be carried out) of the trustee; or
(ii) on the operation, for the purposes of the carrying out of those functions, of the provisions of the Act generally; and, in particular, discharge does not affect the right of any creditor of the bankrupt to prove in the bankruptcy for any debt from which the bankrupt is released (s.281(1)).

10.65 Section 281 goes on to state that:

(i) discharge does not affect the right of any secured creditor of the bankrupt to enforce his security for the payment of a debt from which the bankrupt is released (s. 281(2));
(ii) discharge does not release the bankrupt from any bankruptcy debt which he incurred in respect of, or forbearance in respect of which was secured by means of, any fraud or fraudulent breach of trust to which he was a party (s.281(3));
(iii) discharge does not release the bankrupt from any liability in respect of a fine imposed for an offence or from any liability under a recognisance except, in the case of a penalty imposed for an offence under an enactment relating to the public revenue or of a recognisance, with the consent of the Treasury (s.281(4));

(iv) discharge does not, except to such extent and on such conditions as the court may direct, release the bankrupt from any bankruptcy debt which:
(a) consists in a liability to pay damages for negligence, nuisance or breach of a statutory, contractual or other duty, or to pay damages by virtue of Part I of the Consumer Protection Act 1987, being in either case damages in respect of personal injuries to any person; or
(b) arises under any order made in family proceedings (s.281(5));

(v) discharge does not release the bankrupt from such other bankruptcy debts, not being debts provable in his bankruptcy, as are prescribed (s.281(6)). In this respect reference should be made to I.R. 6.223 to the effect that discharge does not release the bankrupt from any obligation arising under a confiscation order made under section 1 of the Drug Trafficking Offences Act 1986, section 1 of the Criminal Justice (Scotland) Act 1987 or C.J.A. 1988, s.71;

(vi) discharge does not release any person other than the bankrupt from any liability (whether as a partner or co-trustee of the bankrupt or otherwise) from which the bankrupt is released by the discharge, or from any liability as surety for the bankrupt, or as a person in the nature of such a surety (s.281(7)).

5. ANNULMENT

10.66 The court has power, under section 282 of the Act, to annul a bankruptcy order if at any time it appears to the court:

(i) that, on any ground existing at the time the order was made, the order ought not to have been made; or
(ii) that, to the extent required by I.R., the bankruptcy debts and expenses have all, since the making of the order, been either paid or secured to the satisfaction of the court.

10.67 The bankruptcy order may be annulled whether or not the bankrupt has been discharged. I.R. 6.206 states that the application must specify whether it is made on the grounds under (i) or (ii) above and must be supported by affidavit evidence. A form of application is to be found at Appendix I, Form EE.

10.68 The Court of Appeal has considered the power to annul in *Royal Bank of Scotland v. Farley* [1996] B.P.I.R. 638 (reported at first instance as *Re A Debtor (No. 64 of 1992)* [1994] 1 W.L.R. 264).

10.69 This revealed in the words of Hoffmann L.J. a not uncommon situation, namely:

> "[One] . . . in which a bankrupt allows judgment against him to go by default, makes no attempt to set aside the statutory demand, is adjudicated bankrupt and then seeks to litigate the question of whether there was a debt in the first place . . ." (at 641).

The facts of this case and judgments are instructive as to the limits of section 282(1)(a).

10.70 In June 1990 the creditor, Royal Bank of Scotland (RBS) obtained judgment against the debtor. In October 1991 it served a statutory demand and a bankruptcy petition was presented in February 1992. In April 1992 a bankruptcy order was made. Shortly thereafter the debtor applied to annul the bankruptcy. In July 1992 judgment against him was set aside (that is after the bankruptcy order had been made) but RBS appealed. In August 1992 while this appeal was pending, the district judge annulled the bankruptcy order on the debtor's application. The matter was further appealed by RBS to Harman J. who allowed their appeal against the annulment (report at [1996] B.P.I.R. 478). He set aside the annulment order on the basis that under the Act there was no ground existing *at the time the bankruptcy order was made* enabling the court to grant an annulment. The debtor appealed to the Court of Appeal which dismissed his application.

10.71 In dismissing the application the Court of Appeal held:

(i) that the bankruptcy court had jurisdiction to go behind a default judgment and enquire as to whether there really was a debt. If it could be shown by evidence subsequent to the bankruptcy order that the debt upon which the petition was founded did not exist, then there could in a sense be a relation back to the time of the order within section 282(1)(a) allowing an annulment.

(ii) at the time when the bankruptcy order was made, there was a judgment against the bankrupt and no application pending to set aside the judgment debt upon which the petition was based. The bankrupt himself had no locus standi to apply to set aside the judgment after a bankruptcy order had been made (applying *Heath v. Tang* [1993] 1 W.L.R. 1421, CA).

(iii) The Court of Appeal considered that the bankruptcy procedure had adequate safeguards built into it to enable a bankrupt to challenge the existence of a debt. The bankrupt could make an application to set aside the statutory demand. Moreover if a bankrupt has a bona fide appeal or application to set aside judgment which is in existence at the time when the petition comes on to be heard, it was in the words of Hoffmann L.J. "the invariable practice" to adjourn the hearing of the petition until that application or appeal had been decided (see at 641). In the words of Hoffmann L.J.:

> ". . . it merely leads to wasteful litigation which is inevitably at the expense of the petitioner if a further opportunity to litigate the matter is provided after the bankruptcy order has been made" (at 641/642).

(iv) It is moreover also suggested (see *Sealy and Milman*, at p. 344) that the court's overriding power to review its own procedures contained in section 375 will ensure that no injustice to the debtor results.

10.72 The trustee or the O.R. must be given 28 days' notice of the application and served a copy together with any affidavit in support.

10.73
10.74 Where an application is made on the grounds that the debts and expenses of the bankruptcy are all paid or secured, the trustee or O.R. must file a full report in court dealing with the circumstances leading to the bankruptcy, the extent of the assets and liabilities both at the date of the order and at the date of the application, details of creditors known who have claims that have not proved and any other relevant matters which the trustee or O.R. sees fit to put before the court. The report must include particulars of the extent (if any) to which the debts and expenses of the bankruptcy have been paid or secured and the report must also state whether the O.R. or trustee considers the security satisfactory. If the report is made by a trustee who is not the O.R., he must send a copy of the report to the O.R., who may himself file an additional report.

Notice to creditors

10.75 Notice must be given to all creditors who have not proved, and the court may give directions to the trustee as to notifying creditors or advertising and the application may be adjourned for this purpose (I.R. 6.209): see, *e.g. Re Robertson (A Bankrupt)* [1989] 1 W.L.R. 1139. All bankruptcy debts which have been proved must have been paid in full, save that if a debt is disputed or a creditor who has proved can no longer be traced, the bankrupt must give some security in the form of a bond or money paid into court adequate to satisfy any sum that may be found due. The former bankrupt may require the D.T.I. to give notice of the making of an order of annulment in the *Gazette* or in any newspaper in which the bankruptcy order was advertised, or in both (I.R. 6.213).

10.76 Annulment does not release the trustee from any accounting duties imposed by the Act or Rules and he must submit his final account as soon as practicable after the annulment (I.R. 6.214). The trustee will be released from such time as the court may determine, having regard to whether he has complied with the duty as to his final account and as to whether any security given in respect of a disputed debt has been, or will be, released (I.R. 6.214(4)).

10.77 Where the court annuls a bankruptcy order, any sale or other disposition of property, payment made or other thing done under the Act, or by or under the authority of the O.R. or trustee, is valid but if any of the bankrupt's estate is then vested in the trustee, it shall vest in such person as the court may appoint or, in default of any appointment, it will revert to the bankrupt on terms as the court may direct (s.282(4)).

Annulment following I. V.A.

10.78 Annulment may also follow the acceptance by creditors of a Case 1 proposal for a voluntary arrangement, where the court exercises its discretion under section 261(1)(a) (see Chap. 5).

6. THE BANKRUPTCY DEBTS

10.79 Both section 281 (discharge) and section 282 (annulment) refer specifically to payment of "the bankruptcy debts". These are defined specifically in section 382(1) as any of the following:

(a) any debt or liability to which the bankrupt is subject at the commencement of the bankruptcy;
(b) any debt or liability to which the bankrupt may become subject after the commencement of the bankruptcy (including after his discharge from bankruptcy) by reason of any obligation incurred before the commencement of the bankruptcy; and
(c) any interest provable as mentioned in section 322(2) of the Act.

10.80 Section 382(2) and (3) states that liability in tort may be a bankruptcy debt and that both contingent and unliquidated liabilities may form the basis of a bankruptcy debt.

10.81 However, an obligation arising under an order made in family or domestic proceedings is specifically excluded from the list of provable debts by I.R. 12.3(2)(a) which means that the spouse who is owed the money is able to take proceedings against the bankrupt notwithstanding section 285(3) (see Chap. 2) and discharge will not release the bankrupt from liability to the spouse, except in so far as the bankruptcy court directs such release (s.281(5)).

Chapter 11
DEATH AND THE INSOLVENT ESTATE

He that dies pays all debts—William Shakespeare, *The Tempest.*

11.01 Death provides no sanctuary for the unfortunate debtor against the demands of his creditors. The Inland Revenue in particular will continue to pursue a debtor's estate for years after his death. A combination of bad tax planning, particularly in the area of inheritance tax, prior to death and careless administration following death could involve the insolvency of quite wealthy estates.

11.02 Death does not discriminate and attacks not only the debtor but also the trustee and almost all persons having dealings with his estate. The implications are discussed in the various heads below.

1. Death of a Creditor

11.03 The general rule is that life goes on despite the creditor's death.

11.04 In the absence of any contractual arrangement to the contrary, the executor or administrator of a creditor's estate, like a liquidator or trustee of a corporate creditor, assumes all the rights of the creditor against the debtor including the right to petition for a bankruptcy order (Chap. 1).

Death after the commencement of the bankruptcy

11.05 If the creditor dies after commencement of the bankruptcy, the executor or administrator should send to the trustee for notation copy probate or letters of administration. Subject to satisfying himself as to the appointment of the personal representative, the trustee will recognise that person as being entitled to vote at creditors' meetings, and to receive dividends and such information as the creditor would have been entitled to receive.

11.06 Before declaring a dividend, the trustee will give notice of intended dividend and notice of dividend (see Chap. 8) to the personal representative of any deceased creditor who has not proved.

2. Death of the Trustee

11.07 The second-named author has frequently been appointed to replace a deceased trustee and on occasions has been the third trustee in a series. He is therefore conscious that trustees are not immortal and has designated colleagues to take control of the files in the event of his death.

11.08 Upon the death of a trustee, other than the O.R., his personal representative has a duty under I.R. 6.143 to give notice specifying the date of death to the O.R. If the deceased trustee was a partner in a firm of insolvency practitioners, notice may be accepted by the O.R. from a partner in that firm who is himself a qualified insolvency practitioner or a member of one of the recognised professional bodies (see Chap. 4). In practice it will be a partner who gives notice in the majority of cases and usually, although not inevitably, a partner will be appointed as the next trustee.

11.09 Notice may also be given by any person producing to the O.R. the relevant death certificate or a copy of it.

11.10 The O.R. shall give notice to the court under section 299(3)(a) for the purpose of fixing the date of the deceased trustee's release.

11.11 The procedure for filling a vacancy in the office of trustee is discussed in Chapter 4.

11.12 Similar considerations will apply upon the death of a trustee under a deed of arrangement or the supervisor of a voluntary arrangement (see Chap. 5). It is usual for a deed to give power to the creditors to appoint a new trustee but failing that the court has power to make an appointment under the Trustee Act 1925. Such power shall be exercised either by the High Court or by the court having jurisdiction in bankruptcy in the district in which the debtor resided or carried on business at the date of execution of the deed.

11.13 The court also has power to appoint an insolvency practitioner to fill the vacancy upon the death of the supervisor of a voluntary arrangement.

3. Death of the Debtor

11.14 Where a debtor, by or against whom a bankruptcy petition has been presented, dies, the proceedings in the matter are, unless the court otherwise orders, continued as if he were alive but with modifications set out in A.I.E.D.P.O., Sched. 2. The principal modification is that, where the order was made otherwise than on a debtor's petition and the debtor has subsequently died without submitting a statement of affairs to the O.R., the personal representative or other such person as the court, on the application of the O.R., may direct shall submit to the O.R. a statement of the deceased debtor's affairs containing particulars of assets and liabilities (App. I, Form FF). The statement shall be submitted within 56 days of the request or such longer period as the court may allow.

Funeral and testamentary expenses

11.15 The reasonable funeral and testamentary expenses have priority over the preferential creditors (A.I.E.D.P.O. 5(2)). However, after notice of final dividend has expired the trustee may declare the dividend without regard to funeral expenses of which he has not already been given notice.

11.16 If a debtor dies after a presentation of the bankruptcy petition but before service, the court may order the service to be effected on his personal representative or such other person as it thinks fit.

11.17 Clearly no examination of the bankrupt can proceed. The trustee retains, however, the right to seek information from the debtor's spouse or other parties in order to realise the assets of the estate. The trustee's power to deal with assets including after-acquired property will take precedence over that of an executor or administrator who has no power to deal with the bankrupt's property.

11.18 Death before the bankruptcy order is considered in paragraphs 11.21–11.32 below. If the bankrupt dies after the bankruptcy order, no inheritance tax is likely to arise as the whole of his estate would have already passed to the trustee. However, a liability could still accrue from lifetime gifts within seven years of the date of the death although the donee of those gifts would normally have the primary liability.

11.19 The transfer of assets to the trustee is not a voluntary disposition and is not, therefore, a transfer for value for inheritance tax purposes. In practice it would seem most unlikely that a bankrupt will have sufficient assets to trigger an inheritance tax charge in any event.

11.20 The bankrupt will not obtain his discharge but it is still possible for the bankruptcy order to be annulled on payment of all liabilities and costs and the trustee will account to the debtor's personal representative in respect of any surplus.

4. INSOLVENCY ARISING AFTER DEATH

11.21 It is not unknown for the personal representative of a debtor, on finding that he has an insolvent estate on his hands, to put a proposal to the creditors that they receive a *pro rata* settlement. Such an arrangement will frequently be found acceptable if it promises a better and speedier return than would be expected on the formal bankruptcy of an estate. It is recommended that, in the majority of deceased insolvent estates, the personal representative and creditors co-operate in this way without involvement of a formal insolvency procedure. Indeed A.I.E.D.P.O., art. 4 envisages just such arrangements and provides that the same provisions as may be in force under the law of bankruptcy shall apply to the respective rights of secured and unsecured creditors, to debts and liabilities provable, to the valuation of future and contingent liabilities and to the priorities of debts and other payments. It is further provided that the reasonable funeral, testamentary and administration expenses shall have priority over preferential creditors. Furthermore the personal representative is not required to be an authorised insolvency practitioner, provided that the matter is not dealt with in bankruptcy, *i.e.* an insolvency administration order has not been made in such cases.

11.22 A personal representative may present a debtor's petition although frequently it will be found that no person has sought probate or letters of administration and a creditor will petition for an insolvency administration order against the estate. The court may, in accordance with I.R. 6.16, order that service be effected on the debtor's personal representatives or on such other persons as it thinks fit. The administration proceeds much like any other bankruptcy.

11.23 Section 421 gives the Lord Chancellor, with the concurrence of the Secretary of State, power to introduce secondary legislation on this subject. In exercise of this power, A.I.E.D.P.O. specifies the provisions of I.A. 1986 which apply to the administration in bankruptcy of the insolvent estates of deceased persons. It also specifies provisions where the estate of a deceased person is insolvent, which apply to the administration otherwise than in bankruptcy of the estate.

(a) Procedure for the presentation of a petition

11.24 The procedure for the presentation of a petition is similar to that which would apply if the debtor were alive, save that it is known as "an insolvency administration petition", and is likely to result in "an insolvency administration order". The petition may be presented by a creditor or, in the case of a debtor's petition, the personal representative of the deceased.

Following the insolvency administration order, the personal representative or, if there is no such person, such individual as the court may direct on the application of the O.R. shall submit to the O.R. a statement of the deceased's affairs (App. I, Form FF). It shall be submitted within 56 days of the O.R.'s request or such longer period as the court may allow. **11.25**

The Inland Revenue may have a charge in respect of unpaid tax or interest on any property. Where the chargeable transfer is made on death, personal or movable property situated in the United Kingdom which was beneficially earned by the deceased immediately before his death and vests in his personal representatives is, however, not subject to the Inland Revenue charge. For this purpose, "personal property" includes leaseholds and undivided shares in land held on trust for sale, whether statutory or not, and the question whether any property was beneficially owned by the deceased is to be determined without regard to the inheritance tax rules on interests in possession (I.H.T.A. 1984, s.237). The charges cease on the sale of the property but will then apply to the property representing it (I.H.T.A. 1984, s.238). **11.26**

(b) Life policies

The trustee of a deceased's estate should consider whether any life policies will thereby benefit the estate and make the appropriate claims. The question of pensions and life policies is discussed at Chapter 7. **11.27**

The death can sometimes be an unexpected windfall for the creditors but, as the debtor is not available to give explanations or complete a statement of affairs, it may take longer than usual to agree the taxation and other liabilities. In these circumstances it seems a little unfair on creditors that no exception can be made to the requirement, regretted in Chapter 4, that the moneys must be paid into the Insolvency Services Account and that no interest can accrue for the benefit of creditors.

The O.R. is under no duty to investigate the conduct and affairs of the deceased debtor unless he thinks fit but must make such report (if any) to the court, as he thinks fit. **11.28**

As in the case of deaths after the bankruptcy petition, the trustee shall out of available assets discharge the reasonable funeral, testamentary and administration expenses of the personal representative, or other person who has incurred them, in priority to the preferential claims. **11.29**

Where the court has made an interim order, in connection with a voluntary arrangement, the nominee shall give notice to the court of the death of the debtor and the court shall discharge the order. **11.30**

If the debtor dies before the creditors' meeting being held in connection with a voluntary arrangement, and if the debtor was an undischarged bankrupt at the date of his death, then the personal representative should give notice of the death to the trustee and the O.R. and no such meeting shall be held. **11.31**

A.I.E.D.P.O. sets out other modifications that make the procedure compatible with the circumstances following the death, and the Schedules to that Order contain various forms. **11.32**

5. DEATH OF A COMMITTEE MEMBER

The death of a committee member is not one of the circumstances mentioned in I.R. 6.158 as giving rise to the automatic termination of that person's membership of the committee. **11.33**

11.34 I.R. 6.156 indicates that a committee member may be represented by another person duly authorised. Although it is not specifically stated in the Rules, it can be presumed that a personal representative would be so authorised. If there is no such representative willing to continue as a committee member, then the vacancy may be filled by the trustee or a meeting of creditors as discussed in Chapter 4.

11.35 Where an individual who attends meetings on behalf of a corporate body dies, then his place may be filled by that body authorising another person in writing.

6. DEATH OF TESTATORS AND OTHERS

11.36 Where the trustee and the debtor are both happily alive, the trustee will consider whether there are any other parties whose deaths might in some way benefit the estate.

11.37 The names that first spring to mind are those wealthy relatives minded to mention the bankrupt in their wills. However, it is unlikely that such persons will be beneficially disposed towards the creditors and they have a habit of changing their wills in favour of others who have put their financial affairs on a sounder basis.

11.38 Of greater interest to the trustee will be the bankrupt's residual entitlements under a trust or following the death of a life tenant where the original testator died before the bankruptcy order and can no longer change his mind. However, the prudent testator might make a general provision that any person becoming bankrupt will cease to be a beneficiary.

11.39 Such interests will be of the nature of after-acquired property, the subject of section 307, discussed in Chapter 7. The bankrupt has a duty to make full disclosure but the trustee is advised to make his own inquiries in case there are matters which have slipped the bankrupt's memory. Frequently the bankrupt's solicitor, accountant or banker may be a source of reliable information.

11.40 Other parties may die, indebted to the bankrupt's estate, and the trustee will claim against their personal representatives.

11.41 The death of the bankrupt's spouse will remove some of the emotional issues from the trustee's application for an order for the sale of the matrimonial home. The personal representative, however, is entitled to claim the share which would have devolved upon the deceased spouse.

11.42 Other deaths may affect the bankruptcy administration; they include the trustee's clerk who has lost the file of proofs of debt, and the trustee's solicitor who is inconsiderate enough to die before completing the matters on which he was instructed. The list is almost endless and the reader will be able to add his own favourites. The majority will not give rise to insurmountable problems but they help establish the principle that the private individual, as well as the professional man, who keeps a simple written record of his dealings instead of relying entirely on his memory greatly assists the task of his successors.

Chapter 12
CLOSING PROCEDURES, RELEASE AND COSTS

So may a thousand actions, once afoot, end in one purpose—William Shakespeare, *Henry V.*

12.01 For the trustee the act of closing the bankruptcy can be like parting with an old friend, particularly if the administration has been long and complex involving the trustee in applications to court to obtain contributions to the estate, possession of after-acquired property and the matrimonial home. The trustee has built up a fund of knowledge which is about to become redundant. The authors have traced no formal record as to the longest-running bankruptcy but they are aware of at least one administration that lasted for more than 21 years and thereby came of age. Bankruptcy has tended to be the most protracted form of insolvency administration. The average bankruptcy probably takes longer to complete than the average corporate insolvency because, although the value of the assets is usually smaller, the collection of contributions to the estate and the sale of the matrimonial home usually take longer to complete than the disposal of a company's assets. Indeed the administration may be so lengthy that the authors have devoted a chapter to the effects of death upon bankruptcy (Chap. 11).

1. Closing Procedures

12.02 Nevertheless a day will come in every bankruptcy when the trustee can close the administration. The closing procedures can commence when all assets have been realised and all creditors' claims agreed. It is useful to have a simple checklist of the final steps to be taken since if a mistake is uncovered, after the trustee has distributed all the funds, he may find himself making good the error out of his own pocket and thereby losing any profit that he expected to make on his remuneration. A suggested checklist is attached at Appendix VI.

12.03 The trustee shall realise all the assets but he is not obliged to sell items where the costs of realisations are likely to exceed the proceeds. Furthermore he is not required to realise assets if in his opinion this would needlessly protract the trusteeship (s.330(1)).

12.04 If the bankrupt's home has not been realised, the trustee shall have regard to the provisions of section 332 whereby, before the bankruptcy is closed, either:

(i) the court makes an order imposing a charge on the property under section 313 for the benefit of the bankrupt's estate; or
(ii) the court declines to make such an order; or
(iii) the Secretary of State issues to the trustee a certificate stating that it would be inappropriate or inexpedient for such an application to be made in the case in question.

12.05 If the court has ordered the bankrupt to make payments to the estate whether under an income payments order described in Chapter 7 or on a conditional discharge described in Chapter 10, the trustee may wish to apply to the court to have such order varied if the further sums likely to be collected would be small in proportion to creditors' claims but would needlessly protract the bankruptcy.

2. DRAFT FINAL ACCOUNT

12.06 The trustee should prepare a projected draft final account making provision for the costs of administration as detailed in Chapter 8, including the costs of the final circulars to creditors and of holding the final meeting. He should provide for all future costs up to the time of obtaining his release including the storage of the bankrupt's books and records during that period.

12.07 If there is a final distribution to be paid to the creditors, the trustee should give notice in the manner described in Chapter 8. Unclaimed dividends should be handled as described in that Chapter.

12.08 The trustee will obtain approval for the final amount of his remuneration as described in Chapter 4, and he will probably wish to send a final report to the creditors' committee under I.R. 6.163.

12.09 Once the final dividend has been paid and all costs of the bankruptcy discharged, the trustee will be able to draw up his final account (see Chapter 4) up to the date of his application for release.

3. FINAL GENERAL MEETING

12.10 A trustee, other than the O.R., shall then summon a final general meeting of the bankrupt's creditors in accordance with section 331 and I.R. 6.137 at which the creditors shall receive a report on the trustee's administration and determine whether he should be granted his release. Notice of the meeting may be dispatched at the same time as notice of the final dividend but the meeting shall be adjourned if, by that date, the administration is not complete for all practical purposes. It is not normally necessary to gazette or advertise the notice of meeting.

12.11 With effect from the time of his release, a trustee is discharged from all liability both in respect of acts or omissions of his in the administration of the bankrupt's estate and otherwise in relation to his conduct as trustee (I.A. 1986, s.299(5)). However, this section also provides that the release will not prevent the exercise by the court of its powers under section 304 to hold the trustee liable for any misapplication of funds, misfeasance or breach of fiduciary or other duty in the carrying out of his functions.

12.12 The statutory provisions distinguish between the O.R. as trustee and other trustees. The Act and Rules also make the manner and timing of release dependent upon how and why the trustee's office has been terminated.

12.13 Creditors who have proved their debts, and the bankrupt himself, shall be given at least 28 days' notice of the final meeting. The trustee shall prepare and lay before the meeting a report including a summary of his receipts and payments and a statement that he has reconciled his account with that held by the D.T.I. The creditors may question the trustee with respect to any matter contained in his final report and may resolve against him having his release.

12.14 After the meeting the trustee shall give notice, accompanied by a copy of the report, to the court that the final meeting has been held and whether or not he has been given his release. A copy of the notice shall be sent by the trustee to the O.R.

12.15 In the majority of cases no quorum will be present at the final meeting which will usually be treated as no more than a formality. The Rules have provided for this possibility and it is indicated in I.R. 6.137(5) that if no quorum is present the trustee shall report accordingly to the court and the creditors will be deemed to have not resolved against the trustee having his release. If creditors have not resolved against the trustee's release, or if the trustee dies, release is effective from the time that the court is given notice (s.299(3)(a)).

12.16 In the rare event of creditors attending the meeting and opposing the trustee's release, the trustee must seek his release from the Secretary of State. When the Secretary of State gives his release, he shall certify it accordingly and send the certificate to the O.R. who shall deliver it to the court for filing. A copy thereof shall be sent by the Secretary of State to the trustee whose release is effective from the date of the certificate. Presumably if creditors have opposed the release, they will be able to make representations to the Secretary of State who will no doubt make appropriate inquiries and call upon the trustee to clear up any defects in the administration before the release is granted.

12.17 If creditors have resolved against the trustee's release, or removed him, or the trustee has been removed by the court or the D.T.I., or if the trustee has vacated office by reason of having ceased to be a qualified insolvency practitioner under section 298(6), release will be effective when the D.T.I. so determines (s.299(3)(b) and I.R. 6.135).

12.18 When the D.T.I. gives release in respect of a trustee who has been removed or has resigned, a certificate will be sent by the D.T.I. to the former trustee and also to the O.R. to be filed with the court. Release is effective from the date of the certificate (I.R. 6.135).

12.19 If, when the trustee resigns, the creditors' meeting resolves in favour of his release, then it should be effective when the O.R. files notice of resignation with the court (I.R. 6.127 and 6.135).

12.20 Upon an annulment of a bankruptcy order, the trustee's release, if not previously granted, will be determined by the court (s.299(4)).

12.21 Once the trustee has obtained his release, he will return the books and papers relating to the bankruptcy, including his own administration files, to the O.R.

12.22 In accordance with the Insolvency Practitioners Regulations 1990, reg. 20, the trustee shall, however, be required to retain for a period of 10 years from the date of his release the record set out in Schedule 3 of the Regulations.

12.23 Where the O.R. acts as trustee, he shall have his release on giving notice to the D.T.I. that the administration is complete (s.299(2)). He is not required to convene a final meeting of creditors but shall apply to the Secretary of State for his release and shall send to all creditors who have proved their debts, notice of his intention to apply for release together with a summary of his receipts and payments. When the Secretary of State has given the O.R. his release, he shall give notice to the court that he has done so (I.R. 6.136).

12.24 Alternatively the O.R. may be released on the appointment of a person in his stead to act as trustee. In such circumstances section 299(1) provides that where a trustee is appointed by a general meeting of creditors, or by the D.T.I., release takes effect when notice is given by the O.R. to the court. Alternatively, when a trustee is appointed by the court, release of the O.R. shall be effective at such time as the court shall determine.

4. VOLUNTARY ARRANGEMENT

12.25 In a voluntary arrangement, if there is no bankruptcy order, there will be no particular formality for the supervisor to obtain release other than as may be agreed with the creditors as part of the arrangement. It is to be expected that the supervisor will report the outcome to the creditors and circulate his final account. If there is a bankruptcy, then the formalities mentioned above must be observed. Not more than 28 days after completion of a voluntary arrangement, the supervisor shall send to all creditors and to the debtor a notice, in accordance with I.R. 5.29, that the arrangement has been fully implemented. With the notice there should be sent a copy of the supervisor's report summarising all receipts and payments and explaining any difference between the actual implementation and the proposal approved at the creditors' meeting. The supervisor shall, within the 28 days, send to the D.T.I. and the court a copy of the notice and the report. The period of 28 days may be extended by the court.

12.26 A trustee under a deed of arrangement is not required to convene a final meeting but will file his final return of receipts and payments with the registrar of deeds.

Chapter 13
SCOTLAND

By D. H. Chaplin and R. R. McIlvride
Anderson Fyfe, Solicitors, Glasgow

Come let me know what it is that makes a Scotchman happy—Samuel Johnson.

The law of bankruptcy in Scotland is statutory. The Bankruptcy (Scotland) Act 1985 (the 1985 Act) repealed the earlier Act of 1913 and introduced a number of new provisions, particularly in relation to the appointment of the trustee in bankruptcy. The 1985 Act was subsequently amended, in part, by the Bankruptcy (Scotland) Act 1993. This Chapter seeks to give a brief summary of the principal provisions of the 1985 Act as amended. Sections referred to are sections of the 1985 Act unless otherwise indicated. **13.01**

Scottish law is a system of law fundamentally different from that of England and, while there are some similarities in bankruptcy procedures in the two countries, there are a number of significant differences. There is, for example, no office of O.R. in Scotland, and there is no direct Scottish equivalent to the English voluntary arrangement governed by Part VIII of I.A. 1986. It should be noted that I.A. 1986 applies in relation to bankruptcy matters to England only. **13.02**

1. TERMINOLOGY

Some Scottish legal terms have no direct equivalent in English law but the following list may assist in relation to terms used in this Chapter. **13.03**

Arrestment: the process of attachment of goods or funds held by third parties under an obligation to account to the debtor for them. An arrestment can be lodged before or after a decree is obtained. **13.04**

Charge: a formal notice of the existence of a decree served by an officer of the court on a debtor. A charge "expires" 14 days after service if the sum due under the decree remains unpaid, and the expiry of a charge is a necessary precondition to future diligence. **13.05**

Decree: judgment. **13.06**

Debtor: the term used in the 1985 Act to denote a bankrupt. **13.07**

Diligence: any step in the process of enforcing a decree. **13.08**

Heritable property: broadly speaking, land and buildings. **13.09**

Poinding: the procedure by which moveables (*i.e.* chattels) belonging to the debtor are attached under a decree and placed under restrictions pending a warrant sale. **13.10**

Sequestration: the process of bankruptcy. **13.11**

Warrant sale: the process of sale by order of the court under a decree in order to recover funds to satisfy a decree. **13.12**

2. THE INTERIM TRUSTEE

13.13 The 1985 Act introduced in Scotland the office of interim trustee. An interim trustee must be appointed in every sequestration. A list of interim trustees, who are required to be qualified insolvency practitioners, is kept by the Accountant in Bankruptcy who has a general administration role in bankruptcy (section 1A). There is no O.R. in Scotland, and the duties of the Accountant in Bankruptcy are not analogous to those of the O.R. except in relation to his general administrative role.

13.14 The Act provides that a debtor requires the concurrence of a creditor in order to petition for his own sequestration. The practice arose, however, following on the passing of the 1985 Act, for debtors to grant trust deeds for behoof of creditors (similar to the English assignments for the benefit of creditors) which included a power for the trustee under the trust deed to petition for the sequestration of the debtor without requiring to show further cause to the court. The trustee would petition for sequestration immediately on the granting of the trust deed so that the debtor achieved the same result as he would have done by a petition in his own name, but without the need to find a creditor to concur in the petition. As the 1985 Act, as originally enacted, provided for public funds to be made available to pay the fees and outlays of the interim trustee and permanent trustee in a sequestration where the debtor's assets were insufficient to cover those costs, these trust deed petitions accounted for the greater part of Scottish sequestrations following on the 1985 Act, with a corresponding increase in the level of government expenditure on trustees' fees, which rose to a total of £18.5 million in 1991–1992. The greater part of the trust deed petitions were cases in which the amount of assets was small and the debts were exclusively consumer debts. The main changes made by the 1993 Act were intended to make a saving in this expenditure by restricting the circumstances in which a trustee under a trust deed could petition for sequestration, and by making public funds available to meet the costs of sequestration only where the Accountant in Bankruptcy is appointed trustee in the sequestration. The 1993 Act also introduced a simplified sequestration procedure ("summary administration") applicable where the aggregate amount of the debtor's liabilities does not exceed £20,000 and the aggregate amount of the debtor's assets does not exceed £2,000.

Functions

13.15 The functions of the interim trustee are, *inter alia*, to safeguard the debtor's estate pending the appointment of a permanent trustee, to ascertain the state of the debtor's assets and liabilities, and to administer the sequestration pending the appointment of a permanent trustee. The court may, on cause shown, or if the debtor consents, appoint an interim trustee before the award of sequestration if the debtor's estate requires immediate protection.

3. THE PERMANENT TRUSTEE

13.16 If the case is not subject to "summary administration" a permanent trustee is elected by the creditors at a meeting of creditors and the appointment is confirmed on an application to the court. His functions are, *inter alia*, to recover, manage and realise the debtor's estate, to distribute it among the creditors, and to inquire into the reasons for the insolvency.

4. COMMISSIONERS

13.17 Commissioners may be elected by the creditors at the meeting of creditors. Their duties include advising the permanent trustee, supervising his intromissions, and granting him authority, where appropriate, to exercise certain powers, such as carrying on the business of the debtor and taking part in legal proceedings in relation to the debtor's estate. Their function is broadly equivalent to that of the creditors' committee set up under the English legislation (I.A. 1986, s.301).

5. PETITIONS FOR SEQUESTRATION

(a) Debtor petition

13.18 The debtor himself can petition provided he has the formal concurrence of a creditor to whom he is indebted to the extent of at least £1,500 or, without the concurrence of a creditor, where (a) the total amount of his debts is at least £1,500; (b) no award of sequestration has been made against him in the preceding five years; and (c) he is either "apparently insolvent" within the meaning of section 7 of the 1985 Act (see para. 13.21 below) or he has granted a trust deed for the benefit of his creditors and the trustee under the trust deed has been unsuccessful in making the trust deed "protected".

A trustee acting under a trust deed granted by the debtor conveying his estate to the trustee for the benefit of the creditors generally can also petition. However, as a result of the amendments introduced by the 1993 Act, a trustee under a trust deed can only petition for the debtor's sequestration where he can advise the court either that the debtor has failed to comply with his obligations under the trust deed or to co-operate with the trustee, or that an award of sequestration is in the best interests of the creditors.

(b) Creditor petition

13.19 A creditor can petition or consent to a petition by the debtor only if the debt due by the debtor is not less than £1,500.

(c) Provisions

13.20 There are detailed provisions for the sequestration of trusts, partnerships and limited partnerships (s.6).

13.21 A debtor's apparent insolvency occurs (s.7) where:

(i) he grants a trust deed (similar to the English "deed of arrangement");
(ii) a charge for payment of a debt expires without payment;
(iii) the debtor gives notice to his creditors that he has ceased to pay his debts in the ordinary course of business;
(iv) on the occurrence of various other events specified in the Act, unless it is shown that the debtor was able and prepared to pay his debts as they became due; or
(v) a creditor has served on the debtor by an officer of the court a demand in the prescribed form (Bankruptcy (Scotland) Regulations 1985 (S.I. 1985 No. 1925)) requiring the debtor to pay a debt of not

less than £750, and within three weeks of service the debtor has not either complied with the demand or returned by recorded delivery post a written denial in the prescribed form set out in the Regulations. This is similar to the English procedure set out in I.A. 1986, s.268 and similar considerations apply to the competence of the demand. It must, for example, relate to a liquid debt, (*i.e.* one that is ascertained, or capable of early ascertainment) and a debt that is not the subject of a bona fide dispute.

13.22 A petition for sequestration of a living debtor can be granted only if apparent insolvency was constituted within the immediately preceding four months. A petition for the sequestration of the estate of a deceased debtor can be presented at any time by an executor or trustee administering the estate or by a creditor where the deceased was rendered "apparently insolvent" within the four months prior to death. A creditor's petition is competent without apparent insolvency having been established but in those circumstances cannot be presented until at least six months have elapsed since the date of death.

6. JURISDICTION

13.23 The Court of Session (the Scottish superior court in Edinburgh) has jurisdiction over an individual debtor if the debtor had an established place of business in Scotland, or was habitually resident in Scotland at any time in the year immediately preceding the date of presentation of the petition, and over a partnership if it had an established place of business in Scotland during that period, or was constituted or formed under Scots law, and at any time carried on business in Scotland. In Scotland a partnership is a separate legal person from the individual members of the partnership, and a partnership can accordingly be sequestrated without the partners necessarily being sequestrated at the same time.

13.24 The Sheriff Court has jurisdiction if the debtor had an established place of business in the Sheriffdom, or was habitually resident there during the relevant period. The Sheriff Court has equivalent jurisdiction to that of the Court of Session in relation to partnerships. Sheriff Courts are inferior to the Court of Session. Scotland is divided into Sheriffdoms, which are further subdivided into Sheriff Court Districts, each with its own Sheriff Court, usually situated in a major town.

7. THE AWARD OF SEQUESTRATION

13.25 The application for sequestration is made by petition. The following rules apply:

(a) where the petition is presented by the debtor, the court will award sequestration forthwith (s.12(1));
(b) where the petition is presented by a creditor, or by a trustee acting under a trust deed, the court will grant a warrant to cite the debtor to appear before the court on a fixed date to show cause why sequestration should not be awarded. If the debtor does not appear on this date, and in any event does not show cause why sequestration

should not be awarded, and if he does not pay, satisfy, or produce evidence of payment, or give security for payment of the debt, then the court must award sequestration on that date.

8. PROCEDURE ON SEQUESTRATION

13.26 On making an award of sequestration the court appoints an interim trustee if no interim trustee was appointed prior to the award of sequestration. In the petition for sequestration the petitioning creditor will have nominated an insolvency practitioner in private practice or the Accountant in Bankruptcy. The nominee will almost invariably be appointed interim trustee by the court. Where the petition for sequestration was presented by a creditor or a trustee under a trust deed, the interim trustee must formally notify the debtor of the appointment. If the interim trustee wishes to carry on the business of the debtor he must apply to the court for power to do so.

13.27 A copy of the order granting sequestration is sent by the clerk of court to the Accountant in Bankruptcy. A further copy is sent to the keeper of the Register of Inhibitions and Adjudications, who records the sequestration in the Register to give notice to anyone searching the Register of the sequestration, and to restrain the debtor from voluntary dealings with his heritable property. The Register of Inhibitions and Adjudications is routinely searched prior to the settlement of conveyancing transactions.

13.28 The interim trustee must publish a notice in the *Edinburgh Gazette*, stating that sequestration has been awarded, and inviting the submission of claims by creditors (s.15(6)).

9. RECALL OF SEQUESTRATION

13.29 Recall is by petition to the Court of Session only. The debtor, a creditor, the interim trustee, the permanent trustee, or the Accountant in Bankruptcy, or any person having an interest, may apply for recall but must do so within ten weeks after the date of the award of sequestration unless recall is sought on the following grounds:

(a) the debtor has paid his debts in full or given sufficient security for their payment;
(b) a majority in value of the creditors reside in a country other than Scotland; or
(c) one or more other awards of sequestration have been granted.

10. FURTHER DUTIES OF THE INTERIM TRUSTEE

13.30 The interim trustee must obtain a list of assets and liabilities from the debtor, prepare a preliminary statement of affairs of the debtor's affairs, and prepare a report for the meeting of creditors, which must be held within 60 days (or such longer period as the Sheriff may allow) after the award of sequestration if the Accountant in Bankruptcy has not been appointed interim trustee.

Notice of the meeting is given by the interim trustee to all known creditors, who submit claims entitling them to vote at the meeting.

Where the Accountant in Bankruptcy has been appointed interim trustee, he must advise the creditors within 60 days of the award of sequestration whether he intends to call a meeting of creditors. The meeting may be held at such time and place as the Accountant in Bankruptcy determines. The Accountant in Bankruptcy must call a meeting of creditors when requested to do so by not less than one quarter in value of the debtor's creditors.

11. THE MEETING OF CREDITORS

13.31 At the meeting, the interim trustee acts as chairman. He considers the creditors' claims and accepts or rejects the claims, in whole or in part, for the purposes of voting. He reports on the debtor's assets and liabilities, and indicates whether, in his opinion the debtor's assets are unlikely to be sufficient to pay any dividend whatsoever to creditors. In cases where the debtor's assets are likely to be insufficient to allow payment of a dividend, an application will almost certainly be made to the court for a certificate of summary administration and the sequestration will therefore be regulated by the simplified procedure applicable to such cases.

13.32 The creditors vote at the meeting to elect the permanent trustee. The interim trustee reports the proceedings to the court and, in the absence of any relevant objections in terms of section 25, the court confirms the appointment of the permanent trustee. A permanent trustee who was not previously the interim trustee requires to advertise his appointment in the *Edinburgh Gazette*. Where the Accountant in Bankruptcy is the interim trustee, and no permanent trustee is elected at the meeting of creditors, the Accountant in Bankruptcy is the interim trustee, and no permanent trustee is elected at the meeting of creditors, the Accountant in Bankruptcy or his nominee will be appointed permanent trustee by the court. In cases where the interim trustee is not the Accountant in Bankruptcy, and no permanent trustee is elected at the meeting of creditors, the interim trustee will be appointed by the court as permanent trustee. If the interim trustee does not himself become permanent trustee, he must hand over everything in his possession in relation to the sequestration to the permanent trustee, and the interim trustee then ceases to act (s.26).

12. SUMMARY ADMINISTRATION

13.33 A simplified procedure for the administration of "small asset" sequestrations was introduced by the 1993 Act. An application to the court for a certificate of summary administration can be made where the aggregate amount of the debtor's liabilities does not exceed £20,000 and the aggregate amount of the debtor's assets does not exceed £2,000. Where a certificate of summary administration is granted by the court the permanent trustee's duties, and the normal procedure regulating sequestrations, are modified in terms of Schedule 2 and Schedule 2A to the 1985 Act. An application to the court for a certificate of summary administration can be made by the Accountant in Bankruptcy (a) not later than seven days after the award of sequestration where a debtor has petitioned for his own sequestration (s.12) or (b) where the Accountant in Bankruptcy has been appointed interim trustee and has decided not to call a meeting of creditors (s.21A) or (c) where the Accountant in Bankruptcy is interim trustee and no permanent trustee is elected at the meeting of creditors (s.24). Where a certificate of summary administration is granted by the court on an application by the Accountant in Bankruptcy in any of those circumstances, the Accountant in Bankruptcy or his nominee will be appointed by the court as permanent trustee. In any case where the Accountant in Bankruptcy is not the interim trustee, and no permanent trustee is elected at the meeting of creditors, the interim trustee is obliged to report accordingly to the court and in those circumstances the court will grant a certificate of summary administration and appoint the interim trustee as permanent trustee (s.24). An interim trustee may also apply to the court for a certificate of summary administration if a permanent trustee has been elected at the meeting of creditors (s.25) but in that case the court cannot grant a certificate of summary application before confirming the appointment of the permanent trustee elected at the meeting of creditors (s.23).

13. Vesting of Estate in Permanent Trustee

13.34 The debtor's estate vests in the permanent trustee for the benefit of the creditors by virtue of the trustee's act and warrant issued by the court following confirmation of the permanent trustee's appointment. Property exempted by law from poinding for the purpose of protecting the debtor and his family and property held on trust are exempt from vesting. Property acquired subsequently by the debtor will also vest in the permanent trustee if it is property which would have vested in the permanent trustee by virtue of his act and warrant had it been acquired by the debtor by the date the act and warrant was granted.

14. Income of the Debtor

13.35 The permanent trustee may apply to the court to have a suitable amount fixed for the maintenance of the debtor and his family. If the debtor's income is in excess of the total amount fixed, the court must order the balance to be paid to the permanent trustee (s.32). Unless an order is made by the court, the debtor retains his income.

15. Protection of Creditors—Gratuitous Alienations (s.34)

13.36 An alienation of property by the debtor is challengeable if it was made to the prejudice of his creditors and if it was made on a "relevant day" (as defined in s.74). A relevant day in relation to an "associate" (a relative or person connected with the debtor as defined by s.76) is any day within the period of five years prior to the date of sequestration. In relation to any person not an associate, a relevant day is a day within two years prior to the date of sequestration. An alienation is challengeable by a creditor or by the permanent trustee, and the remedy open to the court is to grant a decree of reduction setting aside the alienation, and restoring the property or money in lieu to the debtor's estate. The defences open to the debtor are that, at any time after the alienation, his assets exceeded his liabilities or that the alienation was made for adequate consideration, or that the alienation was a birthday, Christmas, or other conventional gift, or a gift for charitable purposes which having regard to all the circumstances it was reasonable for the debtor to make.

16. Protection of Creditors—Unfair Preferences (s.36)

13.37 If the debtor enters into a transaction which creates a preference in favour of a creditor to the prejudice of the general body of creditors not more than six months prior to sequestration, the transaction is challengeable by a creditor or the permanent trustee. As in the case of gratuitous alienations the remedy is to apply to the court for a decree of reduction, or for restoration of the property alienated, or for payment of the value of the asset transferred. The debtor's defences are:

(a) that the transaction was in the ordinary course of trade or business;
(b) that the transaction was a payment in cash (including a cheque which has not been endorsed) for a debt which, when it was paid, had become payable (unless the transaction was collusive); or
(c) that the transaction was one whereby the parties undertook reciprocal obligations (unless the transaction was collusive). In this context the "reciprocal obligations" must have resulted in the debtor having received equivalent value for the asset transferred to the creditor.

17. Common Law Remedies

13.38 There are similar remedies available to the trustee or to a creditor at common law in relation to gratuitous alienation or unfair preferences.

18. Effect of Sequestration on Diligence

13.39 In sequestrations the law attempts to "equalise" the rights of creditors. The law here is complex and a full explanation would require a detailed discussion of the Scots law of diligence which is beyond the scope of this Chapter. The following general summary should be taken as an introduction only to the subject and reference should be made to any of the standard texts on diligence for a complete explanation.

13.40 All arrestments and poindings executed within 60 days prior to apparent insolvency or within four months after it rank equally (Sched. 7, para. 24). Sequestration is equivalent in effect to an arrestment or a poinding. If sequestration occurs (a) within four months of an arrestment or poinding, or (b) within four months of the debtor having been made apparently insolvent, and the apparent insolvency itself was within 60 days of an arrestment or poinding, then the sequestration is equivalent to an arrestment or poinding on behalf of all the creditors. The effect is, of course, that the arresting and poinding creditors have no better right than the trustee on behalf of all the creditors.

13.41 The effect of sequestration is also to cut down prior diligence. An arrestment or poinding 60 days before sequestration in general terms is ineffectual, although the creditor retains a preference for the expenses (*i.e.* costs) of the decree and of the diligence (s.37).

19. "DATE OF SEQUESTRATION"

13.42 For the purposes of the provisions relating to gratuitous alienations, unfair preferences and the effect of sequestration on diligence the date of sequestration is the date on which the petition for sequestration was presented and not the date on which the award of sequestration was made by the court.

20. ADMINISTRATION OF THE ESTATE

13.43 The permanent trustee carries out his duties in realising the estate in terms of the detailed provisions contained in section 39. If there are no commissioners, he requires the concurrence of the Accountant in Bankruptcy to exercise various functions.

21. THE DEBTOR'S FAMILY HOME

13.44 In terms of section 40, the permanent trustee must, before he disposes of any interest in the debtor's family home, obtain "the relevant consent", or, if he cannot obtain this, the authority of the court. "The relevant consent" means the consent of the spouse of the debtor, if he or she occupies the family home, or, if the debtor occupies the family home with a child, the consent of the debtor. The court, in granting any application for authority to dispose of a right or interest in the family home, will have regard, *inter alia*, to the needs and financial resources of any spouse or child, the interests of the creditor, and the length of time during which the family home was used as a residence for the debtor or his family.

22. EXAMINATION OF THE DEBTOR

13.45 The permanent trustee may request the debtor to appear before him to give information relating to his assets, his conduct, or his business affairs, and may obtain an order of the court requiring the debtor to attend court for a private examination. There are similar provisions in relation to the debtor's wife. The trustee can also apply for a public examination before the sheriff. A public examination, unlike a private examination, is advertised, and is held in open court. A creditor can ask questions only at a public examination. There are provisions for apprehending the debtor by an officer of the court in Scotland, or in any other part of the United Kingdom, if he fails to attend for examination before the court. Examination before the court is taken on oath.

23. CLAIMS

13.46 Detailed provisions are set out in section 48 in relation to the form of claims to be submitted. The permanent trustee adjudicates on claims and distributes funds in the following order:

- (a) the interim trustee's outlays and remuneration;
- (b) the permanent trustee's outlays and remuneration;
- (c) the petitioning creditor's expenses;
- (d) preferred debts;
- (e) ordinary debts;
- (f) interest on preferred debts from sequestration until payment;
- (g) interest on ordinary debts from sequestration until payment;
- (h) postponed debts, of which the principal category is loans made to the debtor by the debtor's spouse.

24. ACCOUNTING BY THE PERMANENT TRUSTEE

13.47 The permanent trustee is required to make up an account of his intromissions with the debtor's estate in respect of each period of 26 weeks (an accounting period), commencing with the date of sequestration. Within two weeks after the end of an accounting period the permanent trustee must submit his accounts of intromissions for audit to the commissioners or Accountant in Bankruptcy.

25. DISCHARGE OF DEBTOR

13.48 Section 54 of the Act provides for the automatic discharge of the debtor on the expiry of three years from the date of sequestration. The object of this section is to ensure that bankrupts do not remain undischarged indefinitely. Before the 1985 Act a discharge was granted only on the application of the debtor to the court. The permanent trustee can apply to the court for a deferment of the discharge for a period not exceeding two years. The permanent trustee can repeat his application for deferment.

13.49 The effect of the discharge is that the debtor is discharged of all debts and obligations contracted by him in the United Kingdom at the date of sequestration with certain limited exceptions (s.55). The principal exceptions are any obligation of the debtor to pay aliment (maintenance) to a spouse, former spouse, or child and any debt for which a creditor holds security.

26. OFFENCES BY THE DEBTOR

13.50 A list of offences is set out in section 67. These include a false statement in relation to the debtor's assets or business affairs to any creditor, or to any person concerned with the administration of the estate; the destruction by the debtor of any part of his estate, or of any records relating to it; the falsification of documents by the debtor; and the obtaining of credit to the extent of £250 or more without giving the person from whom credit is obtained information about the debtor's status as a bankrupt.

27. DIVIDEND PROCEDURES

13.51 Detailed provisions regarding the payment of dividends are set out in section 53.

28. CLOSING PROCEDURES

13.52 Closing procedures and the provisions for discharge of the trustee are similar in general principle to the procedures set out in Chapter 12.

Chapter 14
NORTHERN IRELAND

By John G. Gordon
Napier & Sons, Solicitors and Insolvency Practitioners, Belfast

I can get no remedy against this consumption of the purse—William Shakespeare, *Henry IV, Pt 2.*

1. Historical Background

14.01 Today's law of personal insolvency in Northern Ireland had its beginnings in a period in history when Ireland was part of the United Kingdom of Great Britain and comprised both Northern Ireland and the Republic of Ireland. In many instances separate legislation for Ireland was enacted at Westminster. It applied to the whole of the island. The Irish Bankrupt and Insolvent Act 1857 (c.60), the Debtors Act (Ireland) 1872 (c.57) and the Bankruptcy (Ireland) Amendment Act 1872 (c.58) were all enacted prior to partition of the country in 1921.

14.02 After partition these statutes were followed by the Bankruptcy Amendment Act (Northern Ireland) 1929 (c.1) and the Bankruptcy (Amendment) Act (Northern Ireland) 1963 (c.23). These were enacted by the Parliament of Northern Ireland which was suspended in 1972.

14.03 Since the suspension of the Northern Ireland Parliament, legislation which applies solely to Northern Ireland has been enacted by Order in Council at Westminster. Two such Orders have been made in bankruptcy matters—the Bankruptcy Amendment (Northern Ireland) Order 1980 and the Insolvency (Northern Ireland) Order 1989. With the exception of the 1989 Order, the previous enactments have over the years been referred to as the "Bankruptcy Acts".

14.04 There were also the Deeds of Arrangements Act (1887) (c.57) and the Deeds of Arrangement (Amendment) Act (1890) (c.24) which as their titles suggest facilitated arrangements between debtors and creditors.

14.05 To harmonise the insolvency law of England and Wales with that of Northern Ireland, the Insolvency (Northern Ireland) Order 1989 commenced on October 1, 1991 (see App. VIII).

14.06 The period of two years between 1989 and 1991 was spent by the Insolvency Rules Committee adapting the English Rules, Regulations and forms to provide Northern Ireland with a similar practice and procedure in implementing the legislation.

14.07 The Insolvency Regulations (Northern Ireland) 1991 mirror the English Regulations to such an extent that the equivalent English regulation is cited at the end of each Northern Ireland regulation.

14.08 This is of invaluable assistance to practitioners in that it enables them to refer to the English periodicals and textbooks for guidance and understanding. Northern Ireland practitioners tend to rely on the experience of their colleagues in England and Wales as there is no reported case law relating to insolvency cases in Northern Ireland to date.

14.09 The other subordinate legislation such as the Insolvency Practitioners Regulations (Northern Ireland) 1991 and the Insolvency Regulations (Northern Ireland) 1991 are all similar to their English counterparts and as their title suggests make regulations in respect of accounts, records, the authorisation of insolvency practitioners and the level of security to be given by the practitioner to maintain that authorisation.

14.10 The Insolvent Partnerships Order (Northern Ireland) 1991, like its English equivalent the Insolvent Partnerships Order 1986, has introduced a radical change in the application of insolvency law to partnerships and their members. The legislation which is of a primary nature in Northern Ireland and subordinate nature in England has been heavily criticised by practitioners. The result is that a new draft Order is being prepared in England and it is widely expected that when the new Order is eventually introduced in England, Northern Ireland will follow relatively quickly with its own Order suitably adapted. It is, however, worth noting that in Northern Ireland to date there has been no compulsory winding-up of a partnership or its members. The evidence suggests that this is because of the complicated nature of the legislation.

2. INSOLVENCY PRACTITIONERS

14.11 Despite the similarities between the legislation serving both jurisdictions, there are still a number of real differences in the law as it applies in Northern Ireland. The concept of insolvency practitioners has been introduced in Northern Ireland. Part XII of the Insolvency (Northern Ireland) Order 1989 deals specifically with the qualifications of insolvency practitioners and imposes restrictions on unqualified persons acting as, *inter alia*, trustees in bankruptcy. This is identical to sections of I.A. 1986.

14.12 The Insolvency Practitioners Regulations (Northern Ireland) 1991 stipulate those bodies recognised to grant authorisation to insolvency practitioners. These are the same as those bodies listed at Chapter 4 under Qualifications (paras 4.04–4.13) but substituting the Law Society of Northern Ireland for the Law Society of Scotland. This means that there is practical reciprocation save that practitioners licensed by the Law Society of Northern Ireland are unable to act in respect of cases relating to other parts of the United Kingdom.

14.13 The procedure for obtaining authorisation as an insolvency practitioner in Northern Ireland is similar to that in Great Britain. The recognised professional bodies may authorise members of those bodies to be insolvency practitioners provided that the professional bodies are satisfied of the fitness of such persons and their experience in insolvency matters. Currently in Northern Ireland there is no practical examination as in England and Wales but it is expected that examinations will commence by January 1, 1994.

14.14 The second method of obtaining authorisation is similar in both jurisdictions. In Great Britain it is by application to the D.T.I. and in Northern Ireland it is by application to the Department of Economic Development. However, in Great Britain any would-be insolvency practitioner who is refused authorisation or has his authorisation subsequently withdrawn may appeal to the Insolvency Practitioners Tribunal set up under I.A. 1986. There is no equivalent provision in Northern Ireland and the only redress for an aggrieved applicant would be to have the decision judicially reviewed.

3. JURISDICTION

14.15 The High Court of Justice in Northern Ireland is vested with sole jurisdiction in all insolvency matters (art. 239 of the Insolvency (Northern Ireland) Order 1989). Unlike England and Wales there is no County Court jurisdiction. All matters relating to personal insolvency are undertaken by the Master in Bankruptcy, who will, *inter alia*, hear applications in respect of rights of occupation of the matrimonial home under Part IV of the Family Law (Miscellaneous Provisions) (Northern Ireland) Order 1984 and proceedings under the Partition Act 1868.

4. ENFORCEMENT OF JUDGMENTS

14.16 Judgments are enforced under the provisions of the Judgments Enforcement Act (Northern Ireland) 1969, as amended by the Judgments Enforcement (Northern Ireland) Order 1981. There is no equivalent legislation in England and Wales. Under section 3 of this Act the Enforcement of Judgments Office was set up to enable all judgments to which the Act applied to be enforced. The Office is provided with significant powers relating to debt recovery, and may issue an instalment order, an order of seizure of goods, an order charging land, an order for delivery of possession of land, an order for delivery of goods, a charging order on funds, stocks or shares, an order appointing a receiver, an attachment of debts order, an order for payment by a garnishee and an attachment of earnings order. The method of enforcement is in the discretion of the Office and an applicant for enforcement may not require the use of any particular method. If, after an exhaustive process of investigation of an individual's personal circumstances, the Office decides that a particular judgment cannot be enforced within a reasonable time by any enforcement order, the Office issues to the creditor and to the debtor a notice of unenforceability. The same procedure will follow in respect of a partially enforced judgment where it appears to the Office to be reasonably practical, and a notice of unenforceability is issued for the balance remaining due. If the Office then concludes that a money judgment in respect of which a notice of unenforceability has been issued cannot within a reasonable time be enforced, it may grant a certificate of unenforceability.

14.17 Where a certificate of unenforceability is granted in respect of a money judgment against a debtor, no further action is taken by the Office in relation to the application for enforcement of that judgment or any application for enforcement of any other money judgment. No further applications for enforcement will be accepted.

14.18 Under the previous insolvency law and prior to October 1991, a certificate of unenforceability constituted an act of bankruptcy. Under the new Order a notice of unenforceability is one of the grounds listed under article 242(1)(d) of the Order upon which a creditor's petition for bankruptcy may be presented. A sheriff's or bailiff's return of an unsatisfied execution is the equivalent in England and Wales.

14.19 There is provision in the Judgments Enforcement (Northern Ireland) Order 1981 for application to be made for stay of enforcement in cases of insolvency. Under article 14 of the Order the Office has power to stay enforcement on the grounds that, having regard to the liabilities of the debtor, the property of the debtor ought, in the opinion of the Office, to be administered for the benefit of all creditors. The Office in applying this article may stay enforcement for a period of six weeks. The grounds for issuing such an order are that there is a reasonable likelihood that the debtor will enter into an arrangement with his creditors generally or a petition to the court to make a bankruptcy order will be presented by or against him. The major benefit to insolvents with assets is that this provision can act as a form of protection to enable an application for an interim order to be made. The experience to date has been that very few individual voluntary arrangements have been made where there have been no applications in the Enforcements of Judgments Office against the particular debtor.

5. THE LAW SOCIETY OF NORTHERN IRELAND

14.20 The Law Society of Northern Ireland has always had a special place in legislation applying to Northern Ireland. Successive governments at Westminster have recognised this and have continued to safeguard that position. The legislation governing the conduct of solicitors is contained in the Solicitors (Northern Ireland) Order 1976 as amended.

14.21 Article 238(1)(d) of the Insolvency (Northern Ireland) Order 1989 provides that a petition for a bankruptcy order may be made: "where in the case of a solicitor, the Law Society of Northern Ireland has been appointed his attorney by virtue of Part 3 of the Solicitors (Northern Ireland) Order 1976."

14.22 Under article 36 of the Solicitors (Northern Ireland) Order 1976, if the Law Society Council has reasonable cause to believe that a solicitor has been guilty of dishonesty in connection with his practice, the Council may pass a resolution stating the same and the provisions of Schedule 1 to the Order shall apply in relation to that solicitor. Schedule 1 empowers the Society to take control of all moneys held by that solicitor or his firm. In the event that the solicitor fails to comply with the requirements of the resolution and subsequent notice, a judge of the High Court may, on the application of the Society, appoint the Society to act as the attorney of the solicitor in question.

14.23 These powers are used by the Society when the need arises. The experience has been that it has never been necessary for the Society to petition for the bankruptcy of a particular solicitor. In most circumstances where default has occurred and the provisions of Schedule 1 have been applied, the solicitor has usually adjudicated himself bankrupt or voluntarily given the Law Society power of attorney.

14.24 It is therefore unlikely that the powers under article 238(1)(d) of the Insolvency (Northern Ireland) Order 1989 will be invoked and the High Court asked to make a bankruptcy order on the petition of the Law Society. However, the fact that the power exists is a powerful deterrent that enables the Society to regulate the conduct of solicitors in a most effective manner. There is no equivalent legislative provision in England and Wales.

6. CONVEYANCING

14.25 Due to the differences between the two jurisdictions in respect of land law it has been necessary to enact for Northern Ireland separate provisions to provide for the registering of bankruptcy petitions and bankruptcy orders. In Northern Ireland, especially in urban areas, a considerable amount of land is unregistered and deeds of conveyance are registered in the Registry of Deeds. There is a Land Registry similar to the Land Registry in England and Wales and it deals, as its title suggests, with all registered land. There is no separate land charges registry in Northern Ireland as there is in England.

14.26 Schedule 9 of the Insolvency (Northern Ireland) Order 1991 provides specific amendments to the Land Registry Act (Northern Ireland) 1970 and the Registration of Deeds Act (Northern Ireland) 1970. Subordinate legislation has also been brought in to govern the registration of bankruptcy petitions and bankruptcy orders and the registration of a bankrupt's rights of occupation.

14.27 The Insolvency (Registration of Deeds) Regulations (Northern Ireland) 1991 contain the Rules and forms to enable the various orders to be registered. When application is made for a bankruptcy order under a creditor's petition, the court registers the petition in the Registry of Deeds in accordance with section 3A(1) of the Registration of Deeds Act (Northern Ireland) 1970 and where a petition is filed, and it appears to the master that the person against whom it is presented is the registered owner of any land, the master shall give notice of the presentation of the petition to the Registrar of Titles in accordance with section 67A(1) of the Land Registration Act (Northern Ireland) 1970 (see r. 6.012 of the Insolvency Rules (Northern Ireland) 1991).

14.28 Where a bankruptcy petition is heard and a bankruptcy order is made (irrespective on whose application) the Official Receiver registers the bankruptcy order in the Registry of Deeds in accordance with section 3B(1) of the Registration of Deeds Act (Northern Ireland) 1970. However, he does not file the order with the Registrar of Titles in the Land Registry where a trustee is appointed. That obligation falls to the trustee (see r. 6.043 of the Insolvency Rules (Northern Ireland) 1991).

14.29 The procedure by which bankruptcy petitions and orders are filed with the Registrar of Titles is dealt with under the Land Registration (Amendment No. 3) Rules (Northern Ireland) 1991.

7. DEEDS OF ARRANGEMENT

14.30 Under Part VIII of the Insolvency (Northern Ireland) Order 1989, a new system of deeds of arrangement has been introduced in Northern Ireland. The new procedure is modelled on the English Deeds of Arrangement Act 1914 as amended by I.A. 1986.

14.31 The law in Northern Ireland prior to the 1989 Order was the Deeds of Arrangement Act 1887 which at that time governed England, Wales and Ireland. After 1914 the Act only applied to Ireland. The main benefit of the new legislation (see arts. 210–225 of the Order) is that a deed of arrangement which has been entered into no longer constitutes an act of bankruptcy as the concept of "act of bankruptcy" has now been abolished.

14.32 As in England and Wales the provision of security by a trustee under a deed of arrangement means that all trustees must be insolvency practitioners. To date there have been no deeds of arrangement registered in Northern Ireland. The use and success of an individual voluntary arrangement will probably ensure that that continues to be the case.

8. RECENT DEVELOPMENTS

14.33 The Insolvency (No. 2) Act 1994, dealing with the adjustment of certain transactions regarding the sale of land, was extended to Northern Ireland in order to cover certain amendments to the Insolvency (N.I.) Order 1989. The Pensions (N.I.) Order 1995 has inserted an article for the recovery of excessive pension contributions.

14.34 The law relating to partnership insolvency has remained in line with that applicable to England and Wales described at Chapter 6. The Insolvent Partnerships Order (N.I.) 1995, which came into operation on September 1, 1995, revoked the Insolvent Partnerships Order (N.I.) 1991 and follows closely the Insolvent Partnerships Order 1994.

Chapter 15
REPUBLIC OF IRELAND

By Jane Marshall
McCann FitzGerald, Solicitors, Dublin

Annual income twenty pounds, annual expenditure nineteen nineteen six, result happiness. Annual income twenty pounds, annual expenditure twenty pounds ought and six, result misery—Charles Dickens, *David Copperfield.*

15.01 A long overdue reform of the Irish law of personal insolvency was introduced by the Bankruptcy Act, 1988 (the Act). Procedural rules contained in Statutory Instrument No. 79 of 1989 complement the Act. This review summarises the reformed law and procedure. (For a detailed review see Sanfey and Holohan, *Bankruptcy Law and Practice in Ireland* (Round Hall Press, 1991); Forde, *Bankruptcy Law in Ireland* (Mercier Press, 1990))

15.02 All bankruptcy matters come within the jurisdiction of the High Court (the court) and the administration of most bankruptcy cases is supervised by the Official Assignee in Bankruptcy, an officer of the court. The bankruptcy process can only be triggered by the commission of an act of bankruptcy. Section 7 of the Act lists these as making an assignment for the benefit of creditors, making a fraudulent conveyance, gift, delivery or transfer of property, conveying or charging property in a manner that would constitute a fraudulent preference, leaving the jurisdiction with intent to defeat or delay creditors, filing a declaration of insolvency, suffering the seizure and sale of property by way of execution, or most commonly, failure to satisfy a debt of IR £1,500 or more following service of a bankruptcy summons.

1. The Bankruptcy Summons and Adjudication

15.03 The most common type of bankruptcy petition is one grounded upon a bankruptcy summons. (See generally ss.8–17 of the Act and rr. 10–44.) As a preliminary step the creditor should serve notice on the debtor demanding payment of a liquidated sum within four days. If the demand is not satisfied, the creditor may then apply to the court office for a bankruptcy summons by lodging a copy of the notice and an affidavit verifying his debt. The summons sets out details of the debt, states the consequences of non-payment and advises the debtor that he may file an affidavit within 14 days of service disputing the fact of indebtedness or claiming that he had already sought court protection prior to service of the summons. A sealed copy of the summons must be served personally on the debtor within 28 days of its issue. If not served, the court may extend the time for service. The debtor may apply to the court to dismiss the bankruptcy summons. The court also retains a general discretion to dismiss a bankruptcy summons and is obliged to do so "if satisfied that an issue will arise for trial". However if 14 days pass with no such application being made and without the debt being paid or otherwise satisfactorily secured or compounded, the debtor has committed an act of bankruptcy and the creditor may proceed to petition for the debtor's adjudication.

15.04 The creditor must satisfy the court that the debtor or his business or property is within its jurisdiction, that the debt is a liquidated sum of IR£1,500 or more and that it is legally enforceable. The petition must be presented within three months of an act of bankruptcy having been committed without the debtor having meanwhile paid the debt. If a petition is presented by a secured creditor, his security must be disclosed to the court and he must state either his willingness to give up the security in the event of adjudication, or estimate the value of his security, in which case his debt will be deemed to be the unsecured shortfall (s.11).

15.05 The petition, which is verified by the creditor's affidavit, states details of the debt and that it is still outstanding and provides an undertaking to advertise the requisite public notices and indemnify the Official Assignee with regard to any costs awarded to him by the court. The sum of IR£500 must be lodged with the Official Assignee to cover his costs, fees and expenses. The petition, containing notice of the hearing date, must be served personally on the debtor, at least seven days before the hearing. Where at the hearing the court is satisfied that all the requirements of section 11 have been met, it is obliged to make an adjudication order (s.14). This order is served on the bankrupt by the bankruptcy inspector, a member of the Official Assignee's staff.

15.06 The debtor has an opportunity within 14 days of being served with the adjudication order to show cause why the court should annul its order. The show cause application is limited to grounds which show the failure of the creditor to comply with section 11. The petitioning creditor and Official Assignee must be given notice of the application which is made on affidavit.

15.07 The next step involves the statutory sitting. A sealed summons to attend is served personally on the bankrupt by the petitioning creditor and the bankrupt is obliged to attend. The sitting is advertised by the petitioner at least 10 days beforehand and at least two clear days before the sitting, the bankrupt is obliged to file a sworn statement of affairs in a prescribed form with the Official Assignee. At the sitting, the creditors can decide (by a majority vote in value) to appoint their own assignee to represent them in the administration of the estate (s.18) or (by a majority vote of three-fifths of the creditors in number and value) to appoint a trustee (having the powers of the Official Assignee) and a committee of inspection to wind up the estate (ss.110–114).

15.08 The Act also provides for presentation of a petition by the debtor himself. He must provide the court with details of his assets so that the court can be satisfied that they are worth at least IR£1,500 (s.15).

2. Consequences of Adjudication

15.09 Once the time limit for showing cause has expired, the fact of adjudication must be published in *Iris Oifigiuil* (the official gazette) and at least one daily newspaper circulating in the area where the bankrupt resides. All property (other than "excepted articles" to the value of IR£2,500, or such further amount as the court may allow), automatically vests in the Official Assignee (see generally ss.44–56). All after-acquired property also vests in the Official Assignee if and when he claims it. The bankrupt's salary may be attached although the court retains a discretion in these matters, having regard to the personal needs of the bankrupt and his family (s.65). A bankrupt may not obtain credit for IR£500 or more without stating that he is a bankrupt (s.129). He is also prohibited from acting as a director or otherwise managing a company (s.183 of the Companies Act, 1963) and from holding elected representative office (ss.41–42 of the Electoral Act, 1993).

15.10 The bankrupt's property is placed beyond the reach of all creditors (s.139), other than secured creditors, who may realise their security without submitting to the bankruptcy process. The sheriff must surrender any seized property or proceeds obtained by him within 21 days of receiving notice of adjudication (s.50). Unless there is a contrary provision in a partnership agreement to which the bankrupt is party, the partnership relationship is dissolved upon his adjudication (s.33 of the Partnership Act, 1890). Similarly a joint tenancy is severed and the Official Assignee becomes a tenant-in-common with the remaining co-tenants.

3. THE OFFICIAL ASSIGNEE

15.11 Unless the creditors take the uncommon initiative of voting to appoint a trustee, bankruptcies are administered by the Official Assignee, (see generally ss.60–69). The Official Assignee is an officer attached to the High Court and appointed under section 3 of the Court Officers Act, 1926 and Schedule 8 to the Courts (Supplemental Provisions) Act, 1961. His duties are to get in and realise the property, to ascertain the debts and liabilities and to distribute the assets in accordance with the Act. He may bring, continue and defend legal proceedings relating to the bankrupt's property and is also free to seek directions of the court regarding the discharge of his duties. He is personally liable for all costs incurred but, provided he can show that he acted bona fide, he is entitled to be indemnified from the bankrupt's assets.

15.12 Third parties are required to deliver up money and securities which have vested in the Official Assignee (s.66). He is required to take an inventory of all the bankrupt's assets and has wide-ranging powers of seizure (ss.27 and 62). Money or securities received are lodged with his account at the Central Bank of Ireland (s.69(3)). The Official Assignee does not have the power to carry on the bankrupt's business although the court may appoint a receiver and manager of the property for that purpose (s.73).

15.13 The Official Assignee may determine the manner in which the debtor's property may be sold and he may pass good title (s.55). By virtue of the Family Home Protection Act, 1976, certain protections are extended to a spouse whose name does not appear on the title of the "family home". Before such property may be disposed of, section 61(4) and (5) provides that court approval must be obtained. The court may postpone sale of the family home having taken account of the "interests of the creditors and of the spouse and dependants of the bankrupt as well as . . . all the circumstances of the case". In view of the wide discretion vested in the court, it is clear that it may postpone a sale but it does not have power ultimately to refuse to authorise the sale of a "family home".

15.14 The Official Assignee may disclaim any unprofitable contracts, unsaleable land or leasehold property if it is burdened with onerous covenants (s.56). In the latter case, the Official Assignee is discharged of any personal liability in respect of the property and any affected party may prove for damages in the bankruptcy. A guarantor of the bankrupt's liability remains liable notwithstanding the disclaimer (*Tempany v. Royal Liver Trustees Ltd* [1984] I.L.R.M. 273). The application to disclaim must be made within 12 months of the adjudication or being notified of the existence of the property or contract. An interested party may require the Official Assignee to elect whether or not he wishes to disclaim and, if he fails to elect, he is deemed to have adopted the lease or contract.

15.15 The Supreme Court decided in *Re Casey* [1991] I.L.R.M. 385 that adjudication acts as a novation of the bankrupt's contracts so that the Official Assignee becomes entitled to exercise the bankrupt's rights thereunder unless he elects to disclaim, and mere notification of the adjudication does not in itself constitute a disclaimer.

4. INVESTIGATING THE BANKRUPT'S AFFAIRS

15.16 The Official Assignee has a number of investigative powers relating to transactions prior to adjudication which may have placed assets beyond the reach of creditors (see generally ss.21, 57–59). He may examine under oath the bankrupt and others who have had dealings with the bankrupt and his property. The court may summon parties to attend for examination and to produce relevant documents. The examination may be conducted in private and the examinee is entitled to legal representation. The aims of the examination are to understand what led to the bankruptcy, whether a proper statement of affairs has been presented, whether grounds exist for challenging third party transactions and whether criminal offences may have been committed. The examinee is obliged to answer questions which may incriminate him but answers given are not admissible as evidence against that person in any subsequent civil or criminal proceedings.

15.17 The principle of fraudulent preference may be invoked to invalidate transactions entered into within six months prior to the date of adjudication. For the benefit conferred on a creditor to be returned, the Official Assignee must establish that the debtor's dominant intention was to prefer that creditor over others. The court will be entitled to draw inferences from the evidence to determine the dominant intention of the debtor. The action may fail where it is established that the debtor's will was overborne by pressure from a demanding creditor. On the other hand the rights of purchasers or incumbrancers who take the debtor's property in good faith for valuable consideration are unlikely to be challenged by the Official Assignee.

15.18 The term "settlement" is very broadly defined as including any conveyance or transfer, other than for valuable consideration or in consideration of marriage, of money, goods, things in action and real or personal property whether in Ireland or elsewhere and all other rights arising out of the property. Such "settlement" or voluntary transfer made by the bankrupt within two years prior to adjudication is void and the property may be recovered by the Official Assignee. A settlement made within five years prior to adjudication is void unless the recipient can prove that the bankrupt was solvent at the date of receipt (s.59).

15.19 In addition to the provisions of the Act dealing with voluntary settlements, the Conveyancing Act (Ireland) 1634 may be invoked by the Official Assignee. The court has stated that "the class of fraud which is contemplated and against which the Statute is directed is one in which the debtor attempts to defeat his creditors by bogus or colourable transactions under which the debtor retains a benefit to himself" (*per* Overend J. in *Rose v. Greer* [1945] I.R. 503). The Official Assignee must establish an intent to delay, hinder or defraud creditors or the circumstances must themselves raise a presumption of fraud. (See further Sanfey and Holohan, *Bankruptcy Law and Practice in Ireland*, *op. cit.*, at para. 8.15).

15.20 A sale of property at a price substantially under market value is void in certain circumstances. The transaction must have been preceded by the commission of an act of bankruptcy and have occurred within three months prior to adjudication. The transaction may nonetheless stand if bona fide entered into when the other party did not have notice of the act of bankruptcy (s.58).

5. COMPOSITIONS AND ARRANGEMENTS

15.21 The most discreet means of dealing with personal insolvency is by arrangement outside of court. This is a contractual arrangement by deed whereby the debtor's assets are transferred to a trustee for sale and distribution to creditors in an agreed amount following payment of all costs and expenses and preferential debts. The trustee has power to pay his agents, require proof of debt and choose the manner of realisation. For his part, the debtor contracts with the trustee and each creditor that he will make full disclosure and facilitate the sale through the trustee as his attorney. The creditors in return agree to release the debtor but not necessarily his guarantors. Although the transfer to the trustee constitutes an act of bankruptcy (see para. 15.02), by joining in the deed of arrangement the creditors are estopped from petitioning for adjudication. The practical difficulty for the debtor is the requirement to secure the co-operation of all creditors.

15.22 A debtor may also make a formal arrangement with his creditors, with court approval. The Act (ss.87–109) enables a debtor to seek court protection from creditors whereupon a preliminary creditors' meeting is called to consider a statement of affairs. There follows a private sitting of the court before which a sworn statement of affairs must be filed with the Official Assignee together with the offer to creditors and minutes of the preliminary meeting. The offer requires approval by the court and three-fifths of the creditors in number and value voting at the meeting. Although this procedure protects the debtor from bankruptcy he may be adjudicated if his offer is not accepted or his statement of affairs is found to be untrue (s.105).

15.23 At any time after adjudication the bankrupt may apply to court for an order staying the realisation of assets to enable him to put an offer of composition to creditors. Ten days notice by post and advertisement must be given to creditors convening a meeting before the court. The notice must specify the composition terms. To bind all creditors the composition must be approved by the court and by three-fifths of the creditors in number and in value voting at the meeting (ss.38–39). On lodging sufficient funds or securities to enable the Official Assignee to implement the composition, the bankrupt may obtain a discharge from the court.

6. PROOF OF DEBTS AND DISTRIBUTION

15.24 The Act permits proof of almost every type of debt or claim (s.76 and Sched. 1). The Official Assignee notifies all known creditors of the date by which proof of their debts must be submitted to him and this notice must also be published in *Iris Oifigiuil* and appropriate newspapers (r. 65). An affidavit may be required in some cases (Sched. 1, r. 7).

15.25 Unliquidated claims may be assessed upon application to the court (s.75(4)). Contingent debts must be estimated as at the date of adjudication and if the contingency materialises prior to submission of proof then the actual amount is admitted. Post-adjudication interest or any other consideration in lieu of interest cannot be claimed on any debt unless ultimately there is a surplus (s.86). A creditor cannot prove twice in respect of what is essentially the same debt, as where, for example, the debtor has given separate covenants to pay (*Deering v. Bank of Ireland* (1886) 12 H.L.C. 20), nor may two parties claim in respect of the same debt; thus for example a creditor and the surety may not claim against the bankrupt (*Re Fenton* [1931] 1 Ch. 85). Where the parties traded with each other in the same capacity so that mutuality exists between them, one debt may be set off against the other so that only the net balance, if any, is provable in the bankruptcy (Sched. 1, r. 17).

15.26 Once the Official Assignee has realised sufficient assets to pay expenses, fees, costs, preferential creditors and pay a dividend to unsecured creditors, he reports to the court for orders as to the distribution of the estate (s.82). Authorisation is sent to the Central Bank of Ireland to pay a dividend to creditors on production by them of a notice sent to them by the Official Assignee.

15.27 The order of priority for distribution is as follows (ss.80–81):

(a) administrative costs;
(b) superpreferential debt (unpaid social insurance deductions made from employees' remuneration);
(c) preferential debts (a variety of taxes, social insurance contributions and employee entitlements);
(d) ordinary creditors;
(e) deferred creditors, including certain partnership debts and beneficiaries whose settlements have been avoided.

7. DISCHARGE

15.28 The Act provides for the bankrupt's discharge (ss.41 and 85) if a successful composition has been effected or when payment of expenses, fees, costs and preferential debts has been made and unsecured creditors have received full payment including interest or they have all consented to the discharge. The court may also discharge the bankrupt if it is satisfied that the estate has been fully realised, provision made for expenses, fees, costs and preferential payments and other creditors have received at least 50 pence in the pound or the case has subsisted for 12 years. It is also possible to annul the adjudication if it can be established that the order should not have been made in the first place.

8. ORDERS IN AID OF FOREIGN COURTS

15.29 Pursuant to Section 142 of the Act, on receipt of a request from a bankruptcy court in England, Wales, Scotland, Northern Ireland, the Isle of Man or the Channel Islands, the Irish High Court may act in aid of the foreign court and exercise the same jurisdiction and authority as in an Irish bankruptcy.

APPENDIX I

Table of Forms and Precedents

FORM A

Rule 6.1 **Form 6.1**

Statistory Demand under section 268(1)(a) of the Insolvency Act 1986
Debt for Liquidated Sum Payable Immediately

In the ______ No. ______ of 19 ______ No. ______ of 19 ______
IN BANKRUPTCY
Re

Warning

- This is an **important** document. You should refer to the notes entitled "How to comply with a statutory demand or have it set aside".
- If you wish to have this demand set aside you must make application to do so **within 18 days** from its service on you.
- If you do not apply to set aside **within 18 days** or otherwise deal with this demand as set out in the notes **within 21 days** after its service on you, you could be made bankrupt and your property and goods taken away from you.
- Please read the demand and notes carefully. If you are in any doubt about your position you should seek advice **immediately** from a solicitor or your nearest Citizens Advice Bureau.

Demand

To ______

Address ______

______

This demand is served on you by the creditor:

Name ______

Address ______

______

The creditor claims that you owe the sum of £ full particulars of which are set out on page 2, and that it is payable immediately and to the extent of the sum demanded, is unsecured.

The creditor demands that you pay the above debt or secure or compound for it to the creditor's satisfaction

[The creditor making this demand is a Minister of the Crown or a Government Department and it is intended to present a bankruptcy petition in the High Court in London].

[Delete if appropriate]
Signature
of individual ______

Name
(BLOCK LETTERS) ______

Date ______

*I am authorised to make this demand on the creditor's behalf

Position with or relationship to creditor: ______

Address ______

Tel. No. ______

Ref. ______

N.B. The person making this demand must complete the whole of pages 1, 2 and parts A, B and C on page 3

Notes for Creditor

- If the creditor is entitled to the debt by way of assignment, details of the original creditor and any intermediary assignees should be given in part C on page 3.
- If the amount of debt includes interest not previously notified to the debtor as included in the debtor's liability, details should be given, including the grounds upon which interest is charged. The amount of interest must be shown separately.
- Any other charge accruing due from time to time may be claimed. The amount or rate of the charge must be identified and the grounds on which it is claimed must be stated.
- In either case the amount claimed must be limited to that which has accrued due at the date of the demand.
- If the creditor holds any security the amount of debt should be the sum the creditor is prepared to regard as unsecured for the purposes of this demand. Brief details of the total debt should be included, and the nature of the security and the value put upon it by the creditor, as at the date of the demand, must be specified.
- If signatory is a solicitor or other agent of the creditor the name of his/her firm should be given.

* Delete if signed by the creditor himself

Form 6.1 cont.

Particulars of Debt

(These particulars must include (a) when the debt was incurred, (b) the consideration for the debt (or if there is no consideration the way in which it arose) and (c) the amount due as at the date of this demand.)

Notes for Creditor
Please make sure that you have read the notes on page 1 before completing this page.

Note:
If space is insufficient continue on page 4 and clearly indicate on this page that you are doing so.

Form 6.1 cont.

Part A

Appropriate Court for setting aside demand

Rule 6.4(2) of the Insovlency Rules 1986 states that the appropriate court is the court to which you would have to present your own bankruptcy petition in accordance with Rule 6.40(1) and (2). In accordance with these rules on present information the appropriate Court is [the High Court of Justice] [court] (address)

Any application by you to set aside this demand should be made to that court.

Part B

The individual or individuals to whom any communication regarding this demand may be addressed is/are:

Address

Tel. No.

Reference

Part C

For completion if the creditor is entitled to the debt by way of assignment

	Name	Date(s) of Assignment
Original creditor		
Assignees		

(ACT WITHIN 18 DAYS)

How to comply with a statutory demand or have it set aside

If you wish to avoid a bankruptcy petition being presented against you, you must pay the debt set out on page 1, particulars of which are set out on page 2 of this notice, within the period of **21 days** after its service upon you. Alternatively, you can attempt to come to a settlement with the creditor. To do this you should:

- inform the individual (or one of the individuals) named in part B above immediately that you are willing and able to offer security for the debt to the creditor's satisfaction; or
- inform the individual (or one of the individuals) named in part B immediately that you are willing and able to compound for the debt to the creditor's satisfaction.

If you dispute the demand in whole or in part you should:

- contact the individual (or one of the individuals) named in part B immediately

THERE ARE MORE IMPORTANT NOTES ON THE NEXT PAGE.

Form 6.1 cont.

If you consider that you have grounds to have this demand set aside or if you do not quickly receive a satisfactory written reply from the individual named in part B whom you have contacted you should **apply within 18 days** from the date of service of this demand on you to the appropriate court shown in part A above to have the demand set aside.

Any application to set aside the demand (Form 6.4 in Schedule 4 to the Insolvency Rules 1986) should be made within 18 days from the date of service upon you and be supported by an affidavit (Form 6.5 in Schedule 4 to those Rules) stating the grounds on which the demand should be set aside. The forms may be obtained from the appropriate court when you attend to make the application.

Remember!—	From the date of service on you of this document (a) you have only 18 days to apply to the court to have the demand set aside, and (b) you have only 21 days before the creditor may present a bankruptcy petition

FORM B

Rule 6.1 **Form 6.2**

Statotory Demand under section 268(1)(a) of the Insolvency Act 1986

Debt for Liquidated Sum Payable Immediately Following a Judgment or Order of the Court

In the ______ No. ______ of 19 ______ No. ______ of 19 ______

IN BANKRUPTCY

Re

Warning

- This is an **important** document. You should refer to the notes entitled "How to comply with a statutory demand or have it set aside".
- If you wish to have this demand set aside you must make application to do so **within 18 days** from its service on you.
- If you do not apply to set aside **within 18 days** or otherwise deal with this demand as set out in the notes **within 21 days** after its service on you, you could be made bankrupt and your property and goods taken away from you.
- Please read the demand and notes carefully. If you are in any doubt about your position you should seek advice **immediately** from a solicitor or your nearest Citizens Advice Bureau.

Demand

To ______

Address ______

______

This demand is served on you by the creditor:

Name ______

Address ______

______

The creditor claims that you owe the sum of £ full particulars of which are set out on page 2, and that it is payable immediately and to the extent of the sum demanded, is unsecured.

By a Judgment/Order of the ______ Court in proceedings entitled, (case) ______ Number ______ between ______ Plaintiff and ______ Defendant it was adjudged/ordered that you pay to the Plaintiff creditor the sum of £ ______ and £ ______ for costs

The creditor demands that you pay the above debt or secure or compound for it to the creditor's satisfaction

[The creditor making this demand is a Minister of the Crown or a Government Department and it is intended to present a bankruptcy petition in the High Court in London].

[Delete if appropriate]

Signature ______

Name (BLOCK LETTERS) ______

Date ______

*I am authorised to make this demand on the creditor's behalf.

Position with or relationship to creditor: ______

Address ______

Tel. No. ______

Ref. No. ______

N.B. The person making this demand must complete the whole of pages 1, 2 and parts A, B and C on page 3

Notes for Creditor

- If the creditor is entitled to the debt by way of assignment, details of the original creditor and any intermediary assignees should be given in part C on page 3.
- If the amount of debt includes interest not previously notified to the debtor as included in the debtor's liability, details should be given, including the grounds upon which interest is charged. The amount of interest must be shown separately.
- Any other charge accruing due from time to time may be claimed. The amount or rate of the charge must be identified and the grounds on which it is claimed must be stated.
- In either case the amount claimed must be limited to that which has accrued due at the date of the demand.
- If the creditor holds any security the amount of debt should be the sum the creditor is prepared to regard as unsecured for the purposes of this demand. Brief details of the total debt should be included, and the nature of the security and the value put upon it by the creditor, as at the date of the demand, must be specified.
- Details of judgment or order should be inserted, including details of the Division of the Court or District Registry and court reference, where judgment is obtained in the High Court.
- If signatory is a solicitor or other agent of the creditor the name of his/her firm should be given.

* Delete if signed by the creditor himself

Form 6.2 cont.

Particulars of Debt

(These particulars must include (a) when the debt was incurred, (b) the consideration for the debt (or if there is no consideration the way in which it arose) and (c) the amount due as at the date of this demand.)

Notes for Creditor
Please make sure that you have read the notes on page 1 before completing this page.

Note:
If space is insufficient continue on page 4 and clearly indicate on this page that you are doing so.

Form 6.2 cont.

Part A

Appropriate Court for setting aside demand

Rule 6.4(2) of the Insolvency Rules 1986 states that the appropriate court is the court to which you would have to present your own bankruptcy petition in accordance with Rule 6.40(1) and (2).

Any application by you to set aside this demand should be made to that court, or, if this demand is issued by a Minister of the Crown or a Government Department, you **must** apply to the High Court to set aside if it is intended to present a bankruptcy petition against you in the High Court (see page 1).

In accordance with these rules on present information the appropriate Court is [the High Court of Justice] [court] (address).

Part B

The individual or individuals to whom any communication regarding this demand may be addressed is/are:

____

Address ____________________

____

Tel. No. ____________________

Part C

For completion if the creditor is entitled to the debt by way of assignment

	Name	Date(s) of Assignment
Original creditor		
Assignees		

THERE ARE MORE IMPORTANT NOTES ON THE NEXT PAGE

How to comply with a statutory demand or have it set aside

If you wish to avoid a bankruptcy petition being presented against you, you must pay the debt set out on page 1, particulars of which are set out on page 2 of this notice, within the period of **21 days** after its service upon you. However, if the demand follows (includes) a judgment or order of a County Court, any payment must be made to that County Court (quoting the Case No.). Alternatively, you can attempt to come to a settlement with the creditor. To do this you should:

- inform the individual (or one of the individuals) named in part B above immediately that you are willing and able to offer security for the debt to the creditor's satisfaction; or
- inform the individual (or one of the individuals) named in part B immediately that you are willing and able to compound for the debt to the creditor's satisfaction.

If you dispute the demand in whole or in part you should:

- contact the individual (or one of the individuals) named in part B immediately.

If you consider that you have grounds to have this demand set aside or if you do not quickly receive a satisfactory written reply from the individual named in part B whom you have contacted you should **apply within 18 days** from the date of service of this demand on you to the appropriate court shown in part A above to have the demand set aside.

Any application to set aside the demand (Form 6.4 in Schedule 4 to the Insolvency Rules 1986) should be made within 18 days from the date of service upon you and be supported by an affidavit (Form 6.5 in Schedule 4 to those Rules) stating the grounds on which the demand should be set aside. The forms may be obtained from the appropriate court when you attend to make the application.

Remember!—	From the date of service on you of this document (a) you have only 18 days to apply to the court to have the demand set aside, and (b) you have only 21 days before the creditor may present a bankruptcy petition.

FORM C

Rule 6.4 **Form 6.4**

Application to Set Aside a Statutory Demand

(TITLE)

(a) Insert name and address of person to attend hearing

Let (a)

attend before the Registrar as follows:—

Date ____________________

Time ____________________ hours

Place ____________________

(b) Insert name of debtor

on the hearing of an application by (b)

the applicant for an order that the statutory demand dated be set aside.

(c) Insert date

The grounds on which the applicant claims to be entitled to the order are set out in the affidavit of the applicant sworn on (c) a copy of which affidavit accompanies this application.

(d) State the names and addresses of the persons to be served

The names and addresses of the persons upon whom this application should be served are:— (d)

(e) State the applicant's address for service

The applicant's address for service is:— (e)

Dated ____________________

Signed ____________________
(Solicitor for the) Applicant

If you do not attend, the Court may make such order as it thinks fit

FORM D

Rule 6.4

Form 6.5

Affidavit in Support of Application to Set Aside Statutory Demand

(TITLE)

(a) Insert name address and description of person making the oath

I (a) ____________________

____

____

____

make oath and say as follows:—

(b) Insert date

1. That on (b) ____________ the statutory demand exhibited hereto and marked "A" came into my hands.

(c) Insert one of the 8 following alternatives or if none of them are applicable state grounds on which you consider the statutory demand should be set aside

(1) "Do not admit the debt because . . ." [here state grounds] or

(2) "Admit the debt but not that it is payable immediately" [state reason], or

(3) "Admit the debt as to £ , and that this is payable but that the remainder is not immediately payable. I am prepared to pay the amount of £ immediately" [state reason], or

(4) "Admit the debt and am prepared to secure or compound for it to the creditor's satisfaction by . . . ." [state nature of satisfaction], or

(5) "Say that the debt is a secured debt" [give full details of security and its value], or

(6) "Have a counter-claim (or set-off or cross demand) for £ being a sum equal to (or exceeding) the claim in respect of" [here state grounds of counterclaim etc.], or

2. That I (c)

Form 6.5 cont.

(7) "Say that execution on the Judgment of the Court has been stayed" [give details], or

(8) "Say that the Demand does not comply with the Insolvency Rules in that .... " [state reason]

Sworn at

FORM E

Rule 6.6 **Form 6.7**

Creditor's Bankruptcy Petition on Failure to Comply with a Statutory Demand for a Liquidated Sum Payable Immediately

(TITLE)

(a) Insert full name(s) and address(es) of petitioner(s).

I/We (a) ____________________

____

____

(b) Insert full name, place of residence and occupation (if any) of debtor

petition the court that a bankruptcy order may be made against (b) ____________________

____

(c) Insert in full any other name(s) by which the debtor is or has been known

[also known as (c) ____________________]

(d) Insert trading name (adding "with another or others", if this is so), business address and nature of business

[and carrying on business as (d) ____________________

____

____________________]

(e) Insert any other address or addresses at which the debtor has resided at or after the time the petition debt was incurred

[and lately residing at (e) ____________________

____

____________________]

(f) Give the same details as specified in note (d) above for any other businesses which have been carried on at or after the time the petition debt was incurred

[and lately carrying on business as (f) ____________________

____

____________________]

and say as follows:—

1. The debtor has for the greater part of six months immediately preceding

(g) Delete as applicable

the presentation of this petition (g) [resided at] [carried on business at]

____

(h) Or as the case may be following the terms of Rule 6.9.

within the district of this court (h)

(j) Please give the amount of debt(s), what they relate to and when they were incurred. Please show separately the amount or rate of any interest or other charge not previously notified to the debtor **and the reasons why you are claiming it**

2. The debtor is justly and truly indebted to me[us] in the aggregate sum of £(j) ________

3. The above-mentioned debt is for a liquidated sum payable immediately and the debtor appears to be unable to pay it.

Form 6.7 cont.

(k) Insert date of service of a statutory demand

4. On (k) ______________________ a statutory demand was served upon the debtor by

(l) State manner of service of demand

(l) ______________________
in respect of the above-mentioned debt. To the best of my knowledge and belief the demand has neither been complied with nor set aside in accordance with the Rules and no application to set it aside is outstanding

(m) If 3 weeks have not elapsed since service of statutory demand give reasons for earlier presentation of petition

(m)

5. I/We do not, nor does any person on my/our behalf, hold any security on the debtor's estate, or any part thereof, for the payment of the above-mentioned sum

OR

(n) Delete as applicable

I/We hold security for the payment of (n) [part of] the above-mentioned sum. I/We will give up such security for the benefit of all the creditors in the event of a bankruptcy order being made.

OR

I/We hold security for the payment of part of the above-mentioned sum and I/we estimate the value of such security to be £ This petition is not made in respect of the secured part of my/our debt.

Endorsement

This petition having been presented to the court on ______________________
it is ordered that the petition shall be heard as follows:—

Date ______________________

Time ______________________ hours

Place ______________________

(p) Insert name of debtor

and you, the above-named (p) ______________________, are to take notice that if you intend to oppose the petition you must not later than 7 days before the day fixed for the hearing:

(i) file in court a notice (in Form 6.19) specifying the grounds on which you object to the making of a bankruptcy order; and

(ii) send a copy of the notice to the petitioner or his solicitor.

(q) Only to be completed where the petitioning creditor is represented by a solicitor

The solicitor to the petitioning creditor is:— (q)

Name ______________________

Address ______________________

____

Telephone Number ______________________

Reference ______________________

FORM F

Rule 6.6 **Form 6.9**

Creditor's Bankruptcy Petition Where Execution or Other Process on a Judgment has been Returned in Whole or Part

(TITLE)

(a) Insert full name(s) and address(es) of petitioner(s).

I/We (a) ______________________________

____

(b) Insert full name, place of residence and occupation (if any) of debtor

petition the court that a bankruptcy order may be made against (b) ______________

____

____

(c) Insert in full any other name(s) by which the debtor is or has been known

[also known as (c) ______________________________]

(d) Insert trading name (adding "with another or others", if this is so), business address and nature of business

[and carrying on business as (d) ______________________________

______________________________]

(e) Insert any other address or addresses at which the debtor has resided at or after the time the petition debt was incurred

[and lately residing at (e) ______________________________

______________________________]

(f) Give the same details as specified in note (d) above for any other businesses which have been carried on at or after the time the petition debt was incurred

[and lately carrying on business as (f) ______________________________

____

______________________________]

and say as follows:—

(g) Delete as applicable

1. The debtor has for the greater part of six months immediately preceding the presentation of this petition (g) [resided at] [carried on business at] _

____

(h) Or as the case may be following the terms of Rule 6.9.

within the district of this court (h)

2. The debtor is justly and truly indebted to me[us] in the aggregate sum of

(j) Please give the amount of debt(s), what they relate to and when they were incurred. Please show separately the amount or rate of any interest or other charge not previously notified to the debtor **and the reasons why you are claiming it.**

£(j) ______

3. The above mentioned debt is for a liquidated sum payable immediately and the debtor appears to be unable to pay it.

Form 6.9 cont.

(k) Insert date on which judgment was obtained

4. On (k) ______________ judgment was obtained in (g) [the High Court of Justice ________ Division] [______________ County Court]. [or as the case may be] on an action the short title and reference to the record whereof is "A " V. "B " Number ______ in the sum of £ ________ following which execution was issued at the ________

(l) Insert date of execution

court in respect of the debt and on (l) ________ the sheriff/county court (g) [made a return] [endorsed upon the writ a statement] to the effect that the execution was unsatisfied (g) [as to the whole] [as to part] and the above-mentioned debt represents the amount by which the execution was returned unsatisified.

5. I/We do not, nor does any person on my/our behalf, hold any security on the debtor's estate, or any part thereof, for the payment of the above-mentioned sum.

OR

I/We hold security for the payment of (g) [part of] the above-mentioned sum. I/We will give up such security for the benefit of all the creditors in the event of a bankruptcy order being made

OR

I/We hold security for the payment of part of the above-mentioned sum and I/we estimate the value of such security to be £ This petition is not made in respect of the secured part of my/our debt.

Endorsement

This petition having been presented to the ccurt on ______________

it is ordered that the petition shall be heard as follows:—

Date ______________

Time ______________ hours

Place ______________

(m) Insert name of debtor

and you, the above-named (m) ______________ are to take notice that if you intend to oppose the petition you must not later than 7 days before the day fixed for the hearing:

(i) file in court a notice (in Form 6.19) specifying the grounds on which you object to the making of a bankruptcy order; and

(ii) send a copy of the notice to the petitioner or his solicitor.

(n) Only to be completed where the petitioning creditor is represented by a solicitor.

The solicitor to the petitioning creditor is:— (n)

Name ______________

Address ______________

____

Telephone Number ______________

Reference ______________

FORM G

Rule 6.12 **Form 6.13**

Affidavit of Truth of Statements in Bankruptcy Petition

(TITLE)

(a) Insert name, address and description of person making oath

I (a) ______________________________

____

____

make oath and say as follows:—

[1. I am the petitioner. The statements in the petition now produced and shown to me marked "A" are true to the best of my knowledge, information and belief.

(b) If petition is based upon a statutory demand, and more than 4 months have elapsed between service of the demand and presentation of the petition, give reason(s) for delay and explanation of circumstances which have contributed to the late presentation of the petition.

2. (b)]

OR

(c) State the capacity eg. director, secretary, solicitor etc.

[1. I am (c) ______________________________ of the petitioner; or

(d) Delete as applicable

2. I am duly authorised by the petitioner to make this affidavit on (d) [its] [his] behalf.

(e) State means of knowledge of matters sworn to in the affidavit

3. I have been concerned in the matters giving rise to the presentation of the petition and I have the requisite knowledge of the matters referred to in the petition because (e)

4. The statements in the petition now produced and shown to me marked "A" are true to the best of my knowledge, information and belief.

5. (b)]

Sworn at

FORM H

Rule 6.21 **Form 6.19**

Notice by Debtor of Intention to Oppose Bankruptcy Petition

(TITLE)

(a) Insert name

Take note that I (a) ______________________________
intend to oppose the application to make a bankruptcy order on the following grounds:—

____

____

____

Dated ____

To the court
and to the [solicitors for] the petitioner.

FORM I

Rule 6.23 **Form 6.20**

Notice of Intention to Appear on Bankruptcy Petition

(TITLE)

In the matter of a bankruptcy petition filed

(a) Insert date

on (a) ______________________________

to be heard on (a) ______________________________

(b) Insert full name and address, or if a firm, the name of the firm and address

I (b) ______________________________

____

____

(c) State amount and nature of debt eg. goods supplied

(d) Delete as applicable

a creditor of the above-named debtor in respect of (c) ______________ intend to appear on the hearing of the above-mentioned petition and to (d) [support] [oppose] the petition.

Signed ______________________________

Dated ______________________________

Name in BLOCK LETTERS ______________________________

(e) If creditor's solicitor or other agent please give name and address of firm

Position with or relationship to creditor (e) ______________________________

____

____

____

Telephone No ______________________________

Reference No ______________________________

(f) Insert name(s) and address(es) of petitioner(s)

To (f) ______________________________

____

____

____

FORM J

Rule 6.37 **Form 6.27**

Debtor's Bankruptcy Petition

(TITLE)

(a) Insert full name, address and occupation (if any) of debtor

I (a) ____
____
____]

(b) Insert in full any other name(s) by which the debtor is or has been known

also known as (b) ____

(c) Insert former address or addresses at which the debtor may have incurred debts or liabilities still unpaid or unsatisfied

[lately residing at (c) ____]

(d) Insert trading name (adding "with another or others", if this is so), business address and nature of the business.

[and carrying on business as (d) ____
____
____]

(e) Insert any former trading names (adding "with another or others", if this is so), business address and nature of the business in respect of which the debtor may have incurred debts or liabilities still unpaid or unsatisfied

[and lately carrying on business as (e) ____
____
____
____
____]

request the court that a bankruptcy order be made against me and say as follows:—

(f) Delete as applicable

1. I have for the greater part of six months immediately preceding the presentation of this petition (f) [resided at] [carried on business at] ________________
____

within the district of (f) [this court] [(j) county court. I am presenting my petition to this court, as it is the nearest full-time county court to (j) county court, for the following reasons:

(g) State reasons

(g)

]

2. I am unable to pay my debts.

3. (f) That within the period of five years ending with the date of this petition:—

(i) I have not been adjudged bankrupt

OR

(h) Insert date

(j) Insert name of court

I was adjudged bankrupt on (h) in the (j)

Form 6.27 cont.

(k) Insert number of bankruptcy proceedings

Court No. (k)

(ii) I have not (f) [made a composition with my creditors in satisfaction of my debts] or (f) [entered into a scheme of arrangement with creditors] (S.16 BA 1914)

OR

On (h) I (f) [made a composition] [entered into a scheme of arrangement] with my creditors.

(iii) I have not entered into a voluntary arrangement

OR

On (h) I entered into a voluntary arrangement

(iv) I have not been subject to an administration order under Part VI of the County Courts Act 1984

OR

On (h) an administration order was made against me in the (j) county court.

4. A statement of my affairs is filed with this petition.

Date ______________________________

Signature ______________________________

Complete only if petition not heard immediately

Endorsement

This petition having been presented to the court on ____________________ it is ordered that the petition shall be heard as follows:—

Date ______________________________

Time ____________________ hours

Place ______________________________

FORM K

Rule 6.59 **Form 6.33**

Insolvency Act 1986

Statement of Affairs (Creditor's Petition)

NOTE: These details will be the same as those shown at the top of your petition

In the ______________________

In Bankruptcy No __________ of 19 ______

Re ______________________

The 'Guidance Notes' Booklet tells you how to complete this form easily and correctly

Show your current financial position by completing all the pages of this form which will then be your Statement of Affairs.

Affidavit

This Affidavit must be sworn before a Solicitor or Commissioner of Oaths or an officer of the court duly authorised to administer oaths when you have completed the rest of this form

(a) Insert full name and occupation

I (a) ______________________

(b) Insert full address

of (b) ______________________

Make oath and say that the attached pages exhibited hereto and marked __________ are to the best of my knowledge and belief a full, true and complete statement of my affairs as at ______________ the date of the bankruptcy order made against me.

Sworn at ______________________

Date ______________________ Signature(s) ______________

Before me ______________________

____

A Solicitor or Commissioner of Oaths or Duly authorised officer

Before swearing the affidavit the Solicitor or Commissioner is particularly requested to make sure that the full name, address and description of the Deponent are stated, and to initial any crossings-out or other alterations in the printed form. A deficiency in the affidavit in any of the above respects will mean that it is refused by the court, and will need to be re-sworn.

Form 6.33 cont.

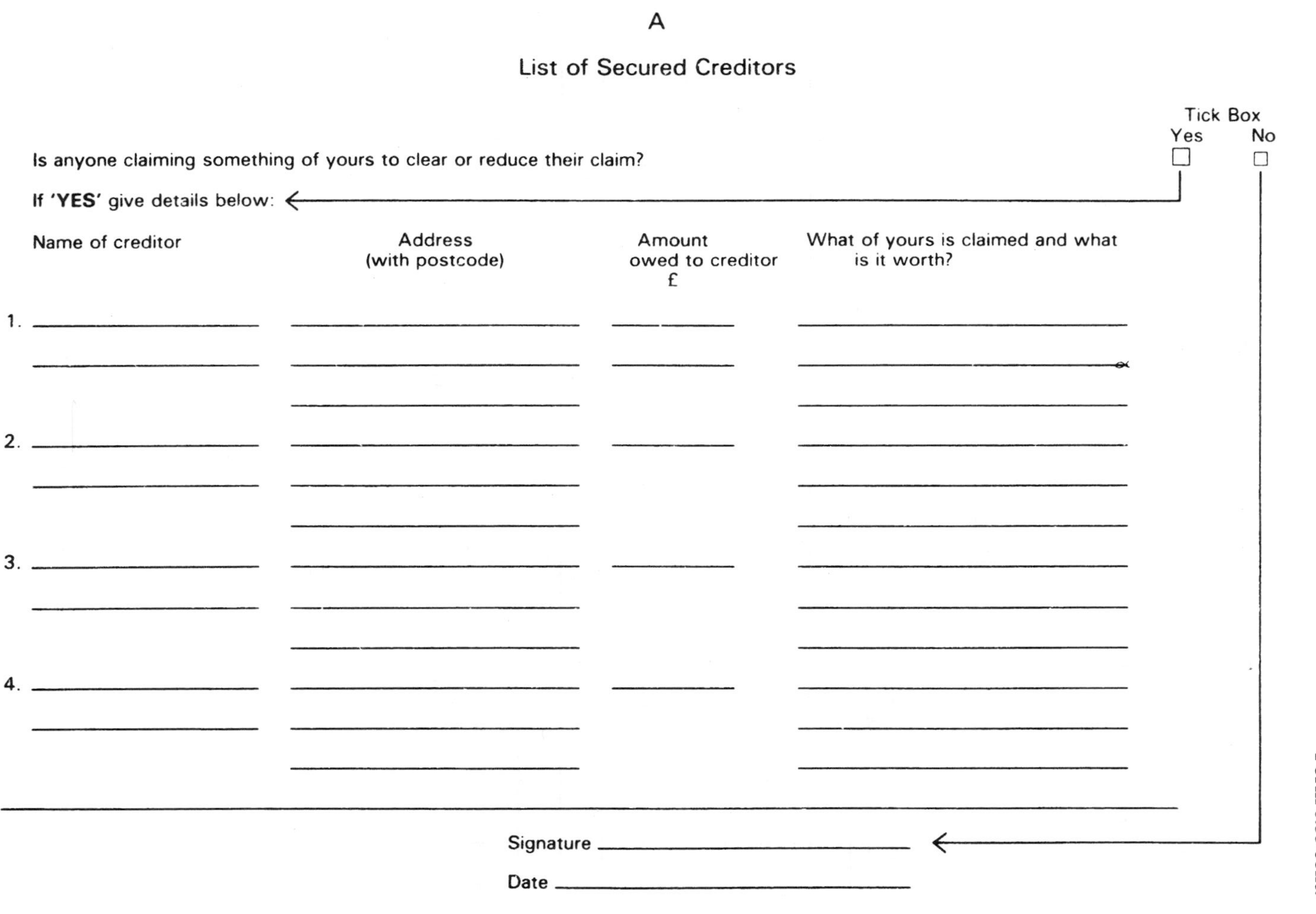

A

List of Secured Creditors

Is anyone claiming something of yours to clear or reduce their claim?

Tick Box

Yes ☐ No ☐

If **'YES'** give details below:

Name of creditor	Address (with postcode)	Amount owed to creditor £	What of yours is claimed and what is it worth?
1.			
2.			
3.			
4.			

Signature ______

Date ______

Form 6.33 cont.

B

List of Unsecured Creditors

1. No.	2 Name of creditor or claimant	3 Address (with postcode)	4 Amount the creditor says you owe him/her £	5 Amount you think you owe £

Signature ____________________ Date ____________________

Form 6.33 cont.

C

Assets

Now show anything else of yours which may be of value:

	£
a) Cash at bank or building society	
b) Household furniture and belongings	
c) Life policies	
d) Money owed to you	
e) Stock in trade	
f) Motor vehicles	
g) Other property (see Guidance Notes):	
TOTAL	

Signature ______________________ Date ______________

FORM L

Rule 7.2 **Form** 7.1

Originating Application

(TITLE)

Between

Applicant ______________________________

and

Respondent ______________________________

(a) Insert name and address of respondent

Let (a) attend

before the Judge/Registrar on:—

Date ______________________________

Time ______________________________ hours

Place ______________________________

(b) Insert name of applicant

On the hearing of an application by (b)
the applicant for an order in the following terms:—

(c) State the terms of the order to which the applicant claims to be entitled

(c)

The grounds on which the applicant claims to be entitled to the order are:—

(d) Set out grounds or refer to an affidavit in support

(d)

The names and addresses of the persons upon whom it is intended to serve this application are:—

(e) State the names and addresses of the persons intended to be served

(e)

OR

It is not intended to serve any person with this application.

(f) State the applicant's address for service

The applicant's address for service is: (f)

Dated ______________________________

Signed: ______________________________
(SOLICITOR FOR THE) APPLICANT

If you do not attend, the court may make such order as it thinks fit.

FORM M

Rule 7.2 **Form 7.2**

Ordinary Application

(TITLE)

Between

Applicant ______________________________

and

Respondent ______________________________

Take notice that I intend to apply to the Judge/Registrar on:

Date ______________________________

Time ______________________________ hours

Place ______________________________

(a) State nature and grounds of application

for (a)

Signed: ______________________________
(SOLICITOR FOR THE) APPLICANT

My/Our address for service is:—

(b) Give the name(s) and address(es) of the person(s) (including the respondent) on whom it is intended to serve the application

To: (b)

OR

It is not intended to serve any person with this application

If you do not attend, the court will make such order as it thinks fit

FORM N

Rule 6.128 **Form 6.45**

Order of Court Giving Trustee Leave to Resign

(TITLE)

Mr Registrar in chambers

(a) Insert full name, address and description of applicant

Upon the application of (a)

And upon hearing

And upon reading the evidence

(b) Insert full name and address of trustee

It is ordered that (b)

the trustee of the above-named bankrupt's estate be at liberty to resign from office.

(c) Insert details of any further order in the matter

[And it is ordered that (c)

]

And it is ordered that the release of (b)

(d) State the date from which the trustee's release is effective

as trustee of the above-named bankrupt's estate shall be effective from (d)

Dated ______________________________

FORM O

Rule 6.132

Form 6.48

Rule 6.132

Order of Court Removing Trustee or Directing Trustee to Summon a Meeting of Creditors for the Purpose of His Removal

(TITLE)

Mr Registrar in chambers

(a) Insert full name, address and description of applicant

Upon the application of (a)

And upon hearing

And upon reading the evidence

(b) Insert full name and address of present trustee

It is ordered that (b)

the trustee of the above-named bankrupt's estate be removed from office.

OR

It is ordered that (b)

(c) Insert date

the trustee of the above-named bankrupt's estate do summon a meeting of the above-named bankrupt's creditors on or before (c) for the purpose of considering his removal from office.

(d) Delete as applicable

(e) Insert details of any further order in the matter

(d) [And it is ordered (e)

]

Dated ______________________________

FORM P

DATED 19

— TO —

Assignment

FOR THE BENEFIT OF CREDITORS.

This Assignment is made the day of 19

Between

(hereinafter called " the Debtor ") of the first part

(hereinafter called " the Trustee ") of the second part

and

(hereinafter called " the Committee ") of the third part and the SEVERAL PERSONS COMPANIES AND PARTNERSHIP FIRMS whose names and addresses are set forth in the Schedule hereto being respectively CREDITORS of the Debtor and all other (if any) persons who are now Creditors of the Debtor and shall assent hereto in writing or otherwise (all of which parties are hereinafter called " the Creditors " which expression shall where the context admits include the persons respectively deriving title under them) of the fourth part WHEREAS :

(1) The Debtor is indebted to the Creditors respectively in divers sums of money which the Debtor is unable to pay in full and he has proposed to make such provision for the payment thereof as is hereinafter contained :

(2) The Creditors have agreed to accept such proposal and to enter into the covenants on their part hereinafter contained :

(3) The Committee have agreed to act as a Committee of Inspection.

NOW in pursuance of the said agreement and for the consideration aforesaid THIS DEED WITNESSES as follows :—

1. THE Debtor as Beneficial Owner hereby conveys assigns and appoints unto the Trustee (and as to real estate) in fee simple

ALL AND SINGULAR the real and personal estate whatsoever and wheresoever which belongs to the Debtor beneficially except as follows :—

(a) Leasehold property held for years (not being a mortgage term) or for any less term ;

(b) Land the title to which is registered under the Land Registration Acts 1925 and 1936 ;

(c) All shares standing in the name of the Debtor which are not fully paid up or to the holding of which some liability is attached ; and

(d) The Debtor's tools of trade (if any) and the necessary wearing apparel and bedding of the Debtor and his family ;

AND ALSO (by way of conveyance and not of exception) all property whether real or personal which the Debtor now has any power by deed or writing (otherwise than by Will only) to appoint as he may think fit

TO HOLD as to real estate Unto the Trustee in fee simple And as to personal estate Unto the Trustee absolutely UPON TRUST to call in collect and receive such parts of the property as can be realised in that manner and to sell and convert into money such parts thereof as shall not consist of money either by public auction or private contract TOGETHER with full power for the Trustee with the leave of the Committee to bring defend compromise or abandon any action or other proceeding relating to the estate or any part thereof and to give time for the payment of any debts owing to the Debtor and to accept payment thereof by instalments composition or otherwise and to abandon any debts which shall be considered bad AND out of the money to be so realised—

(i) In the first place to pay the expenses of the collection realisation and conversion into money of the said estate ;

(ii) Secondly to pay all costs charges and expenses of or preliminary or incidental to the preparation execution and registration of this deed (including the convening and holding of any meeting of the Creditors held before the execution of this deed and the negotiations therefor and the investigation of the Debtor's affairs) and of carrying this deed into effect including the professional charges of the Trustee (to which the Trustee shall be entitled in the same manner as if the Trustee were not a Trustee and had been employed to perform the services rendered by the Trustee) ;

(iii) Thirdly to pay such rates taxes wages and other claims or such part thereof respectively as would have been payable in priority to all other debts if a receiving order had on the date hereof been made against the Debtor and the Debtor had on that date been adjudged a bankrupt ;

(iv) Subject as aforesaid to divide the residue of the said money amongst all the Creditors rateably in proportion to the amounts of their respective debts in the same manner as if the estate of the Debtor had been administered in bankruptcy and by such dividends and at such times as the Committee shall direct ;

(v) And if there shall be any surplus of the said money Upon Trust to pay such surplus to the Debtor.

2. PROVIDED that if any Creditor shall hold any mortgage charge or lien on the property of the Debtor or any part thereof as a security for a debt owing by the Debtor such Creditor shall (subject to the verification or determination thereof in case of dispute in the manner hereinafter provided) be entitled to participate in the division of the estate of the Debtor to the extent of the balance only of such debt after deducting the value of such security.

3. THE Debtor hereby irrevocably appoints the Trustee and every other person who shall hereafter be duly appointed a trustee hereunder and each of them and the substitute of every such Trustee to be his Attorney in his name and on his behalf or otherwise to execute any deed or document or to do any act which shall be necessary for effectuating the purposes of this deed and in particular for effecting any assurance of property and shares as are hereinafter authorised to be effected or agreed to be made and also to demand sue for recover and receive any debt or other thing in action owing or belonging to the Debtor.

4. (1) NOT less than twenty-one days nor more than two months before declaring any dividend the Trustee shall give notice of the intention so to do in the " London Gazette " and such other newspaper as shall be directed by the Committee and such notice shall specify the time within which notice of any debt owing by the Debtor to any of the Creditors shall be given to the Trustee which shall be not less than twenty-one days from the date of such notice.

(2) THE Trustee upon the expiration of the time named in the said notice shall be at liberty to distribute the assets of the Debtor or any part thereof amongst the persons entitled thereto having regard only to the claims of which the Trustee shall then have had notice.

(3) THE Trustee shall not be liable for the assets or any part thereof so distributed to any person of whose claim the Trustee shall not have had notice or of whose claim the amount or the particulars or value of the securities (if any) held in respect thereof shall not have been duly verified or determined or whose claim shall in any particular be disputed but any Creditor of whose claim the Trustee shall not have had notice or of whose claim the amount or the particulars or value of the securities (if any) held in respect thereof shall not have been verified or determined or whose claim shall in any particular be disputed shall on giving notice of his claim to the Trustee and on the same being duly verified or determined (in case of dispute as hereinafter provided) be entitled to be paid out of any assets for the time being in the hands of the Trustee the amount of any dividends which such Creditor shall have failed to receive before such assets shall be applied in the payment of any future dividends but such Creditor shall not be entitled to disturb the distribution of any dividend declared before the notice to the Trustee of such Creditor's claim or before the verification or determination thereof in the manner hereinafter provided (as the case may be).

5. IF there shall be any dispute as to the value of the security held by any Creditor the same shall be determined by arbitration in the manner hereinafter provided and such determination shall be final.

6. THE Trustee shall have power to require the amount of any debt or claim and the particulars and value of any security held by any of the Creditors to be verified by statutory declaration or in such other manner as the Trustee shall require or to admit such debt or claim and the particulars and value of any such security upon such information and vouchers if any being furnished and produced as the Trustee may require or can obtain for the satisfaction of the Trustee.

7. IF any Creditor shall not within twenty-one days after notice in writing expressing the requirements of the Trustee as to the statement or verification of the debt or claim or of the particulars or value of the securities (if any) of such Creditor shall have been given to such Creditor or left at or posted to the last known place of abode occupation or business of such Creditor comply with the requirements of the Trustee such Creditor shall (unless the Trustee shall otherwise determine as to the whole or any part of the debt or claim) be excluded from the benefit of the dividends declared after the expiration of such period of twenty-one days :

PROVIDED that if such Creditor shall within the said period of twenty-one days by notice in writing to the Trustee require and consent to any dispute with reference thereto being determined by arbitration the rights of the Creditor and the Trustee respectively with respect to the matter in dispute shall be as shall be determined by such arbitration notwithstanding that the said period of twenty-one days shall have expired before the dispute shall have been so determined.

8. (1) THE Trustee shall have power at the cost of the trust estate from time to time to summon General Meetings of the Creditors for the purpose of ascertaining their wishes or otherwise and it shall be the duty of the Trustee to summon Meetings at such times as the Creditors by resolution may direct or whenever requested in writing so to do by Creditors entitled to one-fourth in value of the assets or by the Committee and any such Meeting shall be summoned by notices sent not less than three days before the day appointed for the Meeting to the Creditors of whose debts the Trustee shall have had notice and all resolutions passed by the majority in number of Creditors entitled to three-fourths in value of the assets present or represented at any such Meeting shall be binding on the Creditors.

(2) THE notices summoning any such Meeting shall be deemed to have been duly served if left at or sent by prepaid post letter addressed to the last known address of the person to be served therewith and any resolution duly passed as aforesaid at any such Meeting shall be valid if the said notices shall have been so left or sent notwithstanding that some of the Creditors shall not have received such notice.

9. (1) ALL money to be received by the Trustee shall forthwith be paid to a separate trust account to be opened in the name of the Debtor's estate at the Trustee's Bankers or at such other Bank as shall be directed by the Committee or by a resolution passed at a meeting of the Creditors.

(2) THE Trustee (besides sending to each of the Creditors such statements of the accounts and proceedings as are required by Section fourteen of the Deeds of Arrangement Act 1914) shall at such times as the Committee shall require furnish and transmit to the Committee a statement of account showing the receipts and payments and of any other matters necessary to show the position of the administration of the estate and submit the accounts and vouchers to the Committee for audit.

10. THE Trustee may with the consent of the Committee carry on the business of the Debtor so far as may be necessary for the beneficial winding up of the estate and make such allowances to the Debtor for his services in the winding up of the estate and with the like consent postpone the sale of the property of the Debtor or any part thereof for such time as may be deemed expedient.

11. (1) ANY Trustee may be removed from office and a new Trustee appointed in his place pursuant to a resolution passed by a majority in number and three-fourths in value of the Creditors present or represented at any General Meeting called in the manner aforesaid by the Committee.

(2) THE statutory power of appointing a new Trustee shall be vested in and exercisable by the members of the Committee pursuant to any such resolution but a purchaser or other person dealing with the Trustee for money's worth shall not be concerned to see that any deed of appointment expressed to be made in accordance with a resolution is so made.

12. IF any member of the Committee shall die or go to reside abroad or desire to be discharged or become unfit or incapable of acting it shall be lawful for a majority in number and three-fourths in value of the Creditors present or represented at a Meeting to be summoned for that purpose to appoint one or more Creditors or some other eligible persons to be members of the Committee in the place of such member of the Committee so dying or going to reside abroad or desirous of being discharged or becoming unfit or incapable of acting as aforesaid and any persons so appointed as aforesaid may exercise the powers hereby conferred as fully and effectually as if they had been hereby constituted members of the Committee and on any such appointment the number of such Committee may be increased or reduced.

13. THE act decision or determination of a majority of the Committee upon or with respect to any question matter or thing falling to be decided determined or done by them hereunder shall be as valid as that of the whole Committee and binding and conclusive upon all parties claiming or entitled hereunder.

14. THE expressions "the Trustee" and "the Committee" respectively include the Trustee and the Committee of Inspection respectively for the time being under this deed.

15. THE Debtor hereby covenants with the Trustee that the Debtor :—

(i) Will make a full and true discovery to the Trustee of all the estate and effects belonging to or capable of being applied for the Creditors' use by the Debtor and of the names and addresses of all the Creditors of the Debtor and the amounts of their respective debts and if required by the Trustee verify the same by statutory declaration or otherwise.

(ii) Will give such further inventory of his property and particulars of his Creditors and Debtors and of the debts owing to and from them respectively and submit to such examination as to his property or his Creditors and attend such Meetings of his Creditors or the Committee and wait at such times on the Trustee and generally do all such acts and things in relation to his property and the distribution of the proceeds thereof amongst his Creditors as may be reasonably required by the Trustee.

(iii) Will aid to the utmost of his power the realisation of his property and the distribution of the proceeds thereof amongst his Creditors.

16. (1) THE Debtor shall stand possessed of all leasehold property (not being property held for a term of years by way of mortgage) registered land and shares belonging to him and hereinbefore expressed to be excepted from the foregoing conveyance IN TRUST for the Trustee absolutely or in fee simple according to the nature of the premises and to deal with and dispose of the same and the income thereof in such manner as the Trustee shall direct.

(2) THE Debtor hereby covenants with the Trustee to execute a transfer of all registered land belonging to the Debtor at the cost of the trust estate to the Trustee and cause the Trustee to be registered as proprietor thereof and also (if so required) to transfer or sub-demise or charge by way of legal mortgage to the Trustee or as he may direct any other property of the Debtor not included in the foregoing conveyance and to apply for and use his best endeavours to obtain all requisite licences to assign sub-demise or charge any leasehold or other property.

(3) THE Trustee shall have the same powers of disposition over and other powers with respect to the said excepted property and shares as are hereby conferred on the Trustee with respect to the real and personal estate hereinbefore conveyed to the Trustee.

17. (1) IN addition to all the powers hereinbefore conferred or which are by law conferred on trustees for sale the Trustee shall have all the like powers and discretions as are given to the trustee of a bankrupt's estate by the Bankruptcy Act 1914 or any statutory modification thereof and shall with the permission or consent of the Committee have all the like powers and discretions as are by the same Act given to or to be exercisable by the trustee of a bankrupt's estate with the permission of the Committee of Inspection appointed under that Act.

(2) THE Trustee shall have power to pay in full or make such arrangements with any Creditor of whose debts the total amount is under pounds as the Trustee shall think fit.

18. (1) IN consideration of the premises the Creditors do and each of them doth hereby respectively release the Debtor from all debts claims and demands whatsoever which the Creditors or any of them respectively now may have or but for this release might hereafter have against the Debtor in respect of any debt contract transaction matter or thing incurred done or suffered before the date hereof:

(2) PROVIDED that if the title of the Trustee to the estate and effects hereinbefore assured or agreed to be held by the Debtor in trust or any part thereof shall fail by reason of the Debtor's bankruptcy or by reason of the conveyance assignment appointment or trust thereof hereinbefore contained being or becoming void then the release hereinbefore contained shall thereupon become void.

(3) THE release to the Debtor hereinbefore contained shall not prevent any of the Creditors from suing any other persons who may have become bound as sureties for the Debtor or who are in any manner liable for the payment of any debts of the Debtor but the Creditors and each of them shall have the same remedies against any such sureties or other persons as the Creditors might have had if this deed had not been made.

19. IF any dispute or difference shall arise between the Trustee and the Creditors or any of them as to any matter or thing which it is hereby provided shall or may be determined by arbitration or touching any clause matter or thing whatsoever herein contained or the operation or construction thereof or any matter or thing in any way connected with this deed or the rights duties or liabilities of the Trustee or the Creditors or any of them under or in connexion with this deed then and in every such case the dispute or difference shall be referred to two Arbitrators one to be appointed by each party in difference and in case of their disagreement then to an Umpire to be chosen by the Arbitrators before entering on the consideration of the matters referred to them and this deed shall be deemed to be a submission to arbitration within the meaning of the Arbitration Act 1950.

IN WITNESS whereof the parties hereto have hereunto set their hands and seals the day and year first above written.

SIGNED SEALED AND DELIVERED
by the above-named

in the presence of

L.S.

SIGNED SEALED AND DELIVERED
by the above-named

in the presence of

L.S.

THE SCHEDULE

SIGNATURE OF CREDITOR	SEAL	ADDRESS AND BUSINESS	AMOUNT OF DEBT			DATE OF EXECUTION	SIGNED, SEALED AND DELIVERED IN THE PRESENCE OF
			£	S.	D.		

NOTE:—This Deed must be duly registered under the Deeds of Arrangement Act 1914, within seven days after the first execution thereof by the Debtor or any Creditor and if it relates to land must also be registered under the Land Charges Act 1925. In the case of registered land a separate transfer will be required.

FORM Q

Dear Sir/Madam,

YOUR AFFAIRS

I refer to my appointment as trustee of your property under a deed of arrangement dated ....

I am summarising hereunder the consequences of a deed of arrangement, your position in relation to your assets, to myself and to creditors and finally my powers and responsibilities.

The consequences of a deed of assignment under the Deeds of Arrangement Act, 1914

1. By executing the deed, you transferred all the assets you possessed at the date of the deed to me as trustee for the benefit of your creditors. From that date, I became the legal owner of all your assets, though as trustee for your creditors, and as a consequence you can no longer sell, transfer or in any way deal with the assets. Thus, you could not sue any of your debtors in your own name or instruct solicitors or any agent to act for you in any matter relating to the assets. Thus, if you instructed solicitors to issue proceedings, or to continue proceedings already issued, it would be a good defence for the debtor to cite the deed of assignment as the grounds for withholding payment, and the court will be bound to dismiss such proceedings because the legal title on the book debts no longer vests in you.

2. You are now incapable of giving a valid receipt for a purchaser for value of any of your assets, or to any of the debtors. Therefore, any attempt by you to assign the book debts to third parties will be null and void and the assignees will not acquire a valid title to the debts.

3. By executing the deed of assignment, you transferred your [50%] interest in the freehold property to me and consequently, your wife and I are now joint owners of the property.

4. The deed of assignment relieves you from your liability to the creditors who have assented to the deed, and such creditors no longer have the right to seek recovery of their claims from you and must rely on the assets realised and distributed by me as trustee.

5. In relation to your assets and your liabilities at the date of the deed of assignment, your position is identical to the position of a bankrupt in that the trustee alone has the right to deal with your assets and liabilities.

The powers and responsibilities of a trustee

As trustee, I have the legal right and responsibility to realise all your assets for the benefit of the creditors. This confers on me the right to employ solicitors, [with the agreement of the creditors' committee] to recover the debts due to your estate and to issue proceedings against the debtors in my own name. In this connection you may make suggestions regarding the debtors, but the ultimate decision as to whether to pursue a debt, or to abandon it, is mine and mine alone, although, in making such decisions, I would obviously be guided by the advice of my solicitors and the views of the committee.

In relation to the freehold property, I have the legal right to realise your share of the equity in the property, either by sale to your wife or failing that, by sale of the property. In relation to the sale, I have all the powers of a trustee in bankruptcy and can therefore apply to the court for an order of vacant possession and sale of the property.

[Having accepted your wife's offer of £ at the rate of £ per month, in consideration of my forbearance from realising your interest in the property and, provided the terms of the offer and of my acceptance are complied with, I cannot exercise the right of sale in order to realise your interest.]

[In the event of default in complying with the terms of the offer and my acceptance, my right to take the necessary steps to realise your interest in the property will come into play. However, the amount already received in compliance with the terms of the offer cannot be refunded, or be considered as part payment of your interest in the property, since my forbearance from realising that interest is the consideration for the payments.]

Contributions to the estate

I would refer to your undertaking to pay to me as trustee such proportion of your future salary or income as shall be agreed.

[I confirm our agreement that you will pay the sum of £ per month and your remittance should be sent to this office on the first day of each month.]

[I will be in contact with you to discuss the amount of contributions to be made in the circumstances.]

[I note that you are not in a position to pay contributions at present but I would ask you to contact me when personal circumstances change, failing which I shall be obliged to apply to the court for contributions in line with Section 310 of the Insolvency Act 1986.]
[Delete as applicable]

Yours faithfully,

FORM R

Rule 8.1 **Form 8.1**

Insolvency Act 1986

Proxy (Company or Individual Voluntary Arrangements)

(TITLE)

Notes to help completion of the form

Please give full name and address for communication

Name of creditor/member ______

Address ______

______

Please insert name of person (who must be 18 or over) or the "chairman of the meeting" (see note below). If you wish to provide for alternative proxy-holders in the circumstances that your first choice is unable to attend please state the name(s) of the alternatives as well

Name of proxy-holder ______

1 ______

______

2 ______

______

3 ______

______

Please delete words in brackets if the proxy-holder is only to vote as directed ie he has no discretion

I appoint the above person to be my/the creditor's/member's proxy-holder at the meeting of creditors/members to be held on ______, or at any adjournment of that meeting. The proxy-holder is to propose or vote as instructed below [and in respect of any resolution for which no specific instruction is given, may vote or abstain at his/her discretion].

______

Voting instructions for resolutions

*Please delete as appropriate

1. For the acceptance/rejection* of the proposed voluntary arrangement [with the following modifications:—]

Any other resolutions which the proxy-holder is to propose or vote in favour of or against should be set out in numbered paragraphs in the space provided below Paragraph 1. If more room is required please use the other side of this form.

______

______

______

______

______

______

This form must be signed

Signature ______ **Date** ______

Name in CAPITAL LETTERS ______

Only to be completed if the creditor/member has not signed in person

Position with creditor/member or relationship to creditor/member or other authority for signature ______

______

Remember: there may be resolutions on the other side of this form.

FORM S

APPLICATION BY TRUSTEE FOR SALE OF MATRIMONIAL HOME

IN THE HIGH COURT OF JUSTICE (OR COUNTY COURT)

IN BANKRUPTCY

Re: A.B a Bankrupt,
Ex Parte C.D. the Trustee in Bankruptcy
BETWEEN

C.D.
As Trustee in Bankruptcy of the Estate of A.B. A Bankrupt Applicant and
Sarah B. (Married Woman) First Respondent
and
A.B. (a Bankrupt) Second Respondent

Let Sarah B. (Married Woman) and A.B. a Bankrupt both of

attend before the Judge/Registrar on:

Date ....

Time .... hours

Place ....

On the Hearing of an application by C.D. as Trustee in Bankruptcy of the estate of the Bankrupt, the Applicant, for an Order in the following terms:—

1. A Declaration that the Applicant is beneficially entitled to a half interest (or the interest in—as the case may be) the property known as as the same is registered at H M Land Registry under title no. (or as the case may be)

2. An Order the said property be sold and that the Applicant do have conduct of the sale.

3. An Order directing that the Respondent (or both Respondents) do execute such Deeds or other assurances as may be necessary to transfer the title in the property for the Applicant (or as the case may be).

4. An Order that the Respondent (or both Respondents) do give up vacant possession of the property to the Applicant.

5. An Order that the net sale proceeds of the property be divided up in the following proportions:

6. Such further or other Order as to the Court shall seem just.

7. An Order that the First Respondents do pay the costs of and occasioned by this Application.

The grounds on which the Applicant claims to be entitled to the Order are set out in the Affidavit sworn by the Applicant on the day of 19 and filed herewith.

The names and addresses of the persons upon whom it is intended to serve this Application are:

Sarah B. of
A.B. of

The Applicant's address for service is c/o his Solicitors, Messrs XYZ of

Dated this day of 19
Signed
Solicitor for the Applicant

If you do not attend, the Court may make such Order as it thinks fit

---

(NOTE—Not part of the form. It is necessary to join the bankrupt as a respondent if he is in possession or joint possession of the property.)

FORM T

Rule 6.189 **Form 6.64**

Notice to Bankrupt of Application Under Section 310 of the Insolvency Act 1986 for Income Payments Order

(TITLE)

(a) Insert full name of bankrupt

To (a)

TAKE notice that I intend to apply to this court as follows:—

Date ______

Time ______ hours

Place ______

b) Insert total amount to be paid

(c) Insert intervals at which instalments are to be paid e.g weekly/monthly and amount to be paid in each instalment

(d) Delete as applicable

(e) Insert name, address and description of person who will make payments eg bankrupt's employer etc

(f) Insert date not less than 7 days before hearing

for an order under Section 310 of the Insolvency Act 1986 for the payment from your income to me as your trustee in bankruptcy, of (b) £ by (c) (d) [which it is intended will be paid to me by (e)

]

or such other order as the court thinks fit.

Attached is a statement of the grounds for this application. You are required to attend the hearing of my application unless by (f) , you send to the court and to me, using the tear-off forms below, written consent to the making of such order.

If you attend the hearing, you will be given an opportunity to show why the order should not be made, or why it should be in different terms.

Dated ______

Signed ______
Trustee

Name in BLOCK LETTERS ______

Address of Trustee ______

Form 6.64 cont.

Notice to Court. Consent of Bankrupt to Order Under Section 310 of the Insolvency Act 1986

(TITLE)

(a) Insert full name and address of bankrupt

I, (a)

(b) Insert name of trustee

the above-named bankrupt, consent to the making of an order under the terms of the application of (b)

Dated ______________________________

Signed ______________________________

Name in BLOCK LETTERS ______________________________

Detach here

- -

Detach here

Notice to Trustee. Consent of Bankrupt to Order under Section 310 of the Insolvency Act 1986

(a) Insert full name and address of bankrupt

I, (a)

the above-named bankrupt, consent to the making of an order under the terms of your application dated

Dated ______________________________

Signed ______________________________

Name in BLOCK LETTERS ______________________________

FORM U

Rule 6.190 **Form 6.65**

Order for Income Claimed Under Section 310(3)(a) of the Insolvency Act 1986

(TITLE)

Mr Registrar in chambers

Upon the application of (a)

And upon hearing

(b) [And upon the consent of the above-named bankrupt] and it appearing to the court that the sum of £(c) be paid by the above-named bankrupt by (d)

to the trustee until (e)

It is ordered that the above-named bankrupt do pay (d)

out of his income, the first of such instalments to be made on or before (f)

And it is ordered that the above-named bankrupt do send the payments to (g)

Dated ______________________________

(a) Insert full name and address of applicant

(b) Delete as applicable

(c) Insert total amount to be paid

(d) Insert intervals at which instalments are to be paid eg weekly/monthly and amount to be paid in each instalment

(e) Insert date to which order is to remain in force

(f) Insert date of first payment

(g) Insert name and address of trustee to whom payments are to be sent

FORM V

Rule 6.190 **Form 6.66**

Order for Income Claimed Under Section 310(3)(b) of the Insolvency Act 1986

(TITLE)

Mr Registrar in chambers

(a) Insert full name and address of applicant

Upon the application of (a)

And upon hearing

(b) Delete as applicable

(c) Insert total amount to be paid

(d) Insert intervals at which instalments are to be paid e.g weekly/monthly and amount to be paid in each instalment

(e) Insert date to which order is to remain in force

(f) Insert full name and address of payor

(g) Insert date of first payment

(h) Insert name and address of trustee to whom payments are to be sent

(b) [And upon the consent of the above-named bankrupt] it appears to the court that the sum of £(c) be paid by the above-named bankrupt by (d)

to the trustee until (e)

It is ordered that (f)

do take (d)
out of the above-named bankrupt's income, the first of such instalments to be paid on or before (g)

And it is ordered that (f)

do send the sums deducted to (h)

Dated ______________________

Note:

Under Rules 6.192(2) and 13.11 you are entitled to deduct the sum of 50p for each payment sent to the trustee, from the bankrupt's income towards the clerical and administrative costs of compliance with this order.

FORM W

Rule 6.178 **Form 6.61**

Notice of Disclaimer under Section 315 of the Insolvency Act 1986

(TITLE)

PART 1

(a) Insert date — On (a)

(b) Insert name of trustee — I (b) ______________________________

the trustee of the above-named bankrupt's estate disclaim all my interest in:

(c) Insert full particulars of property — (c)

Dated ______________________________

Signed ______________________________

Address ______________________________

____

____

Name in BLOCK LETTERS ______________________________

____

PART 2

(d) Insert name of court — This is a copy of a notice filed at the (d) Court
on (a)

Seal of the Court

____

PART 3 This is a copy of a notice of disclaimer filed by me at the
(d) Court

Signed ______________________________
Trustee

NOTE: 1. Part 1 is to be completed by the trustee and filed in court with a copy
Part 2 is to be completed by the court and returned to the trustee
Part 3 is to be completed by the trustee when sending out copy notice under Rule 6.179 or 6.180
2. The attention of a recipient of this notice is drawn to sections 315–321 of the Insolvency Act 1986.
3. Where the property concerned consists of land or buildings the nature of the interest should also be stated (*e.g.* whether freehold, leasehold etc.)

FORM X

Rule 6.183 **Form 6.62**

Notice to Elect

(TITLE)

(a) Insert name, address and particulars of interest in property (e.g landlord etc)

I (a)

(b) Insert details

of property comprising (b)

require the trustee to decide within 28 days of receiving this notice whether he will disclaim the above property or not and to notify me of his decision.

Dated ______________________

Signed ______________________

Name in BLOCK LETTERS ______________________

To the trustee of the above-named bankrupt's estate.

Address

FORM Y

Rule 6.96 Form 6.37

Proof of Debt–General Form

(TITLE)

Date of Bankruptcy Order No

1	Name of Creditor	
2	Address of Creditor	
3	Total amount of claim, including any Value Added Tax and outstanding uncapitalised interest as at the date of the bankruptcy order	£
4	Details of any documents by reference to which the debt can be substantiated. [Note: the official receiver or trustee may call for any document or evidence to substantiate the claim at his discretion]	
5	If the total amount shown above includes Value Added Tax, please show:— (a) amount of Value Added Tax (b) amount of claim NET of Value Added Tax	 £ £
6	If total amount above includes outstanding uncapitalised interest please state amount	£
7	If you have filled in both box 3 and box 5, please state whether you are claiming the amount shown in box 3 or the amount shown in box 5(b)	
8	Give details of whether the whole or any part of the debt falls within any (and if so which) of the categories of preferential debts under section 386 of, and schedule 6 to, the Insolvency Act 1986 (as read with schedule 3 to the Social Security Pensions Act 1975)	Category Amount(s) claimed as preferential £

Form 6.37 cont.

9	Particulars of how and when debt incurred	
10	Particulars of any security held, the value of the security, and the date it was given	
11	Signature of creditor or person authorised to act on his behalf	
	Name in BLOCK LETTERS	
	Position with or relation to creditor	

Admitted to vote for

£

Date

Official Receiver/Trustee

Admitted preferentially for

£

Date

Trustee

Admitted non-preferentially for

£

Date

Trustee

FORM Z

Rule 6.96, 6.99 **Form 6.39**

Affidavit of Debt

(TITLE)

(a) Insert full name, address and description of person making oath

I (a)

make oath and say:

(b) Delete as applicable

(1) That (b) [I am a creditor of the above-named bankrupt] [I am (c)

(c) State capacity eg director, secretary, solicitor etc

of (d)

(d) Insert full name and address of creditor

a creditor of the above-named bankrupt.

(e) State means of knowledge of matters sworn to in affidavit

I have been concerned in this matter (e)

and am authorised by the creditor to make this affidavit on its/his behalf]

(f) Insert name of bankrupt

(2) That the said (f)

(g) Insert date

on (g) the date of the bankruptcy order, was and still is justly and truly indebted (b) [to me] [to the said creditor] in the sum of £ as shown in the proof of debt exhibited hereto marked "A".

Sworn at

FORM AA

Trustee

In the High Court of Justice

In Bankruptcy

Re .... No. ....

I/We consent to the proof of debt for £

being admitted in the sum of £ and the balance is hereby withdrawn

Signed ....

Address ....

....

....

Dated ....

FORM BB

NOTICE OF DIVIDEND
under Rule 11.6 of
the Insolvency Rules 1986

IN THE

IN BANKRUPTCY No. of 19 .

RE
DIVIDEND of in the Pound

Trustee's
Address

19 .

NOTICE IS HEREBY GIVEN that a Dividend of in the Pound has been declared in this matter, and that a payable order for £.... being the amount payable to you in respect of the dividend is enclosed herewith.

A statement of realisations and payments is enclosed.

In making this distribution, provision has been made for dividends on unsettled possible claims of £.... and for the following possible expenditure.

[give details]

* A further dividend is expected to be declared
[* a. within...... months]
(* delete as appropriate)
[* b. but no date can be given]

* No further dividend is expected.

To .... (Signed) ....
Trustee

FORM CC

No. of 19

APPLICATION BY A TRUSTEE FOR LEAVE TO EXAMINE

IN THE HIGH COURT OF JUSTICE (OR COUNTY COURT)

IN BANKRUPTCY

Re: A.B. a Bankrupt
Ex Parte C.D. the Trustee in Bankruptcy
BETWEEN

C.D.
As Trustee in Bankruptcy of the Estate of A.B. A Bankrupt Applicant.
and
A.B. (a Bankrupt) Respondent

Let A.B. Bankrupt of
attend before the Judge/Registrar on:—

Date ....

Time .... hours

Place ....

On the Hearing of an application by C.D. as Trustee in Bankruptcy of the estate of the Bankrupt, the Applicant, for an Order in the following terms:—

1. That the Respondent be Ordered to appear before the Court for examination pursuant to s.366 of the Insolvency Act 1986 and rule 9.2(3)(a) of the Insolvency Rules 1986; or to answer interrogatories in respect of the following matters; or to submit Affidavits with the regard to the following matters; or to produce the following books, papers or other records (as the case may be).
2. For the appointment of one of the shorthand writers of this Court for the purpose of taking down in shorthand the evidence of the said A.B. and making a transcript of his notes thereof.
3. The costs of this Application be paid by the Respondent (or as the case may be).

The grounds on which the Applicant claims to be entitled to the Order are as set out in the Affidavit (or Report) of the Applicant sworn on the day of 19 and filed herewith (or in the Report filed herewith).

The names and addresses of the persons upon whom it is intended to serve this application are:—

A.B. of
or
It is not intended to serve any person with this application.

The Applicant's address for service is c/o his Solicitors XYZ & Co of

Dated
Signed

Solicitors for the Applicant

If you do not attend, the Court may make such Order as it thinks fit

---

(NOTES—Not part of the form.

1. The application may be made *ex parte* (r. 9.2).
2. The application may be for one or more of the purposes stated above (see r. 9.2) but the purpose must be stated.
3. The application must be accompanied by a brief statement of the grounds on which it is made, which may be an affidavit or report form.
4. Further details are dealt with in rules 9.2 to 9.6.
5. Persons other than the bankrupt may be summoned for examination—see I.A. 1986, s.366(1).)

FORM DD

No. of 19

APPLICATION BY A BANKRUPT FOR DISCHARGE

IN THE HIGH COURT OF JUSTICE (OR COUNTY COURT)

IN BANKRUPTCY

Re: A.B. a Bankrupt
BETWEEN

A.B.	Applicant
and	
(1) The Official Receiver and	First Respondent
(2) XYZ, Trustee in Bankruptcy	Second Respondent

Let the Official Receiver, in Bankruptcy of
attend before the Judge/Registrar on:—

Date ....

Time .... hours

Place ....

On the Hearing of an application by A.B, the Bankrupt, for an Order in the following terms:—

That the Applicant be granted his discharge from bankruptcy.

The grounds on which the Applicant claims to be entitled to the Order are:—

as set out in the affidavit of the Applicant sworn on the day of 19 and filed herewith.

The names and addresses of the persons upon whom it is intended to serve this application are:—

The Official Receiver TB, Trustee in Bankruptcy of

The Applicant's address for service is c/o his Solicitors S & Co of

Dated
Signed
Solicitor for the Applicant

If you do not attend, the Court may make such Order as it thinks fit

---

(NOTES—Not part of the form

1. Notice of application must be given to the O.R and the sum deposited with him to cover his costs (r. 6.217).
2. The O.R. must give notice to the trustee and to every creditor who has a claim outstanding to his knowledge (r. 6.217).
3. Further reference should be made to rules 6.215–6.230.

FORM EE

No. of 19

APPLICATION BY BANKRUPT FOR ANNULMENT

IN THE HIGH COURT OF JUSTICE (OR COUNTY COURT)

IN BANKRUPTCY

Re: A.B. A Bankrupt,
Ex parte A.B. A Bankrupt
BETWEEN

A.B A Bankrupt Applicant
and
C.D.
As Trustee in Bankruptcy of the Estate of A.B. A Bankrupt Respondent
The Official Receiver Respondent

Let C.D., the Trustee in Bankruptcy of A.B a Bankrupt of and the Official Receiver of attend before the Judge/Registrar on:—

Date ....

Time .... hours

Place ....

On the Hearing of an application by A.B, the Bankrupt, for an Order in the following terms:—

1. For an Order pursuant to s.282 of the Insolvency Act 1986 that and the Bankruptcy Order made herein on the day of be annulled on the grounds that:—
   (a) The Order ought not to have been made, or
   (b) That the debts and expenses of the bankruptcy have all been paid or secured
2. That the costs of this Application be provided for.

The grounds on which the Applicant claim to be entitled to the Order are:—

As set out in the Affidavit of the Applicant sworn herein on the day of 19 and filed herewith.

The names and addresses of the persons upon whom it is intended to serve this Application are:—

1. The Official Receiver of

2. C.D. the Trustee in Bankruptcy of the Estate of A.B. of

The Applicant's address for service is c/o XYZ & Co his Solicitors of

Dated
Signed
Solicitor for the Applicant

If you do not attend, the Court may make such Order as it thinks fit

---

(NOTES—Not part of the form

1. The application must state the grounds on which it is made (r. 6.206).
2. An affidavit must be filed stating the grounds.
3. Notice of the application must be given to the O.R. and if another trustee is appointed to that trustee (r. 6.206).)

FORM FF

Form 7

The Administration of Insolvent Estates of Deceased Persons Order 1986

Statement of Affairs (Deceased Insolvent)

NOTE: These details will be the same as those shown at the top of the petition

IN THE ____________________

IN BANKRUPTCY NO ________ OF 19 ____

RE ____________________

THE 'GUIDANCE NOTES' BOOKLET TELLS YOU HOW TO COMPLETE THIS FORM EASILY AND CORRECTLY

Show the financial position of the deceased debtor by completing all the pages of this form which will then be the Statement of Affairs.

Affidavit

THIS AFFIDAVIT MUST BE SWORN BEFORE A SOLICITOR OR COMMISSIONER OF OATHS OR AN OFFICER OF THE COURT DULY AUTHORISED TO ADMINISTER OATHS WHEN YOU HAVE COMPLETED THE REST OF THIS FORM

(a) Insert your full name and occupation

I (a) ____________________

____

(b) Insert your full address

of (b) ____________________

____

Make oath and say that the several pages marked ____________ are to the best of my knowledge and belief a full, true and complete statement of the affairs of the deceased debtor as at ____________ the date of the insolvency administration/bankruptcy order.

Sworn at ____________________

Date ____________________ Signature(s) ____________

Before me ____________________

____

A Solicitor or Commissioner of Oaths or Duly authorised officer

Before swearing the affidavit, the Solicitor, Commissioner or duly authorised officer is particularly requested to make sure that the full name, address and description of the deponent are stated, and to initial any crossings-out or other alterations in the printed form. A defect in the affidavit in any of the above respects will mean that it will be refused by the court, and will need to be re-sworn.

Form 7 cont.

A

Tick Box YES ☐ NO ☐

IS ANYONE CLAIMING SOMETHING OF THE DECEASED DEBTOR'S TO CLEAR OR REDUCE THEIR CLAIM?

If 'YES' give details below:

	Name of creditor	Address (with postcode)	Amount owed to creditor £	What property is claimed and what is it worth?
1.				
2.				
3.				
4.				

Signature ______________________

Date ______________________

Form 7 cont.

B

1. Has the deceased debtor any creditors under hire-purchase or conditional sale agreements?
If **'YES'** name the creditors and give a description of the goods subject to each agreement and the amount owed

Tick Box
YES ☐ NO ☐

2. Has the deceased debtor any liability under leasing agreements?
If **'YES'** name the creditors and give details of the property leased

YES ☐ NO ☐

3. Are any other creditors claiming title to goods that they supplied to the deceased debtor?
If **'YES'** name the creditor and give details of the goods claimed

YES ☐ NO ☐

Signature ______________________ Dated ______________

Form 7 cont.

C

LIST THE REST OF THE CREDITORS HERE

1 No.	2 Name of creditor or claimant	3 Address (with postcode)	4 Creditor's claim at date of death £	5 Creditor's claim at date of insolvency administration bankruptcy order £

Signature ______________________ Date ______________________

D

Form 7 cont.

	Tick	Box
1. Did the deceased have any personal bank accounts, including joint accounts?		
If '**YES**' state where they are and how much is in them now	YES ☐	NO ☐

2. Did the deceased have any business bank accounts, including joint accounts?	YES	NO
If '**YES**' state the name of the accounts, where they are and how much is in them now	☐	☐

3. Did the deceased have any building society accounts, or an interest in one?	YES	NO
If '**YES**' state where they are and how much is in them now	☐	☐

Signature ______________________ Dated __________

D1

Form 7 cont.

	Tick	Box
4. Are there any other savings? If '**YES**' state the amounts and where they are	YES ☐	NO ☐

____

____

____

____

____

____

____

____

5. Did the deceased debtor have any interest in any life policies? If '**YES**' state with whom they were effected, the policy numbers, and any value to the estate	YES ☐	NO ☐

____

____

____

____

____

____

____

____

6. Did the deceased debtor have an interest, of value, in any other policies or agreements? If '**YES**' state with whom they were effected, the policy or agreement numbers and the value to the estate	YES ☐	NO ☐

____

____

____

____

____

____

____

____

Signature ______________________________ Dated ______________

Form 7 cont.

E

List here any debts due to the estate

1 No.	2 Name of debtor	3 Address (with postcode)	4 Amount of debt £	5 Year debt incurred	6 Why has debt not yet been paid and what action has been taken to obtain payment	7 What evidence is there to confirm that the sum is owed	8 Amount now likely to be recovered £	9 Particulars of any securities held for debt

Signature ______________________ Date ______________

Form 7 cont.

F

Property

NOW SHOW ANYTHING OF THE DECEASED DEBTOR'S WHICH MAY BE OF VALUE AND IS NOT SHOWN ON ANOTHER PAGE:	£
a) Cash deposited with solicitor at	
b) Cash in hand	
c) Stock in trade at	
d) Machinery at	
e) Trade fixtures, fittings, utensils etc at	
f) Farming stock at	
g) Growing crops and tenant rights at	
h) Household furniture and effects at	
i) Stocks and shares in	
j) Any interests under wills etc	
k) Motor vehicles (give details)	
l) Bills of exchange, promissory notes etc available as assets	
m) Other property viz:—	
	£

Signature ______________________ Date ______________

Form 7 cont.

G

	Tick Box
1. Is there any claim against the estate for funeral, testamentary and administration expenses? If **'YES'** give details below.	YES ☐ NO ☐

____
____
____
____
____
____
____
____

2. Did the deceased debtor have any assets when he died which are not now shown in this statement of affairs? If **'YES'** list them below and state what has happened to them	YES ☐ NO ☐

____
____
____
____
____
____
____
____

Signature ______________________ Dated ______________

FORM GG

No. 13A. Deeds of Arrangement Rules 1925.

DEEDS OF ARRANGEMENT ACT 1914

In the matter of a Deed of Arrangement between

of

(A) Add description. (A)

and his Creditors, dated the day of 19
and registered under the Deeds of Arrangement Act 1914, on the
day of 19 .

Statement of Trustee's Accounts and of Proceedings under the Deed from the day of 19 , to the day of 19

RECEIPTS	£	PAYMENTS	£	£
Cash deposited by Debtor with Solicitor for costs of deed		Law Costs of preparation and registration of deed		
Cash at Bank at date of deed		Law Costs of Solicitor to Trustee		
Cash in hand at date of deed		Other Law Costs (3)		
Book debts				
Stock-in-Trade realised from sale by (1)		Accountant's charges		
Machinery realised from sale by (1) ..		Auctioneer's and Valuer's charges		
Trade fixtures, fittings, &c., realised from sale by (1)		Trustee's remuneration		
Furniture realised from sale by (1)		Possession		
		Incidental expenses		
Surplus from securities in hands of Creditors		Other costs and charges (3) ..		
Trading Receipts		Total costs and charges		
		Allowance to Debtor		
Other Property, viz.: realised from sale by (1)		Payments to Creditors, viz.:—	£	
		Rent from the day of 19 , to the day of 19		
Gross Receipts		Rates and Taxes		
Less: Trading payments .. £		Salaries and Wages		
Payments to redeem securities, viz.: (2)		Other preferential payments, viz. (3)		
		Dividend of in the £ on £		
£		Paid ..		
		Unpaid ..		
		Other payments (if any) (3)		
Net realisations		Total		
Balance due to Trustee (if any)		Balance in hand (if any)		
£		£		

(1) Insert gross proceeds of sale, and state how goods were sold, e.g., by auction, by valuation, or as the case may be.

(2) Here insert to whom payments made, nature of security redeemed, and amount of each payment, or annex schedule giving these particulars.

(3) Insert particulars or annex schedule.

(4) Insert name of Bank.

The total payments into the (4) Bank to the day of 19 , were £ and the total payments out of the said Bank to the day of 19 , were £

The amounts of the Assets and Liabilities at the time the Deed was executed as estimated by the Debtor were :—

Assets after deducting £ the value of securities held by Creditors and required to cover debts due to them £

Liabilities after deducting £ the amount covered by securities, £

(3) Insert particulars or annex schedule.

The nature and value of the assets unrealised are (3)

The causes which delay the termination of the winding up of the estate are (3)

The estate will probably be completely wound up within

The following special circumstances affect the costs of realisation and the administration of the estate, viz. (3)

.... Trustee.

Address ....

....

Date..

FORM HH

No. 3. DEEDS OF ARRANGEMENT RULES, 1925

Statutory Declaration by Trustee to be filed with Registrar as to Assents of Creditors.

IN THE MATTER of a Deed of Arrangement between

of

(1)

and his Creditors dated the day of

19 (2) (and registered under the Deeds of Arrangement Act, 1914, on the day of 19).

(1) Add description.

(2) Strike out words in brackets if deed has not been already registered.

I,

of

being the Trustee under the above-mentioned Deed of Arrangement, do solemnly and sincerely declare that the requisite majority in number and value of the Creditors of the said

, so far as the same are known to me, have assented to the said Deed of Arrangement.

And I make this solemn declaration conscientiously believing the same to be true and by virtue of the provisions of the Statutory Declarations Act, 1835.

Declared at
in the of
this day of 19

Before me,

A Commissioner for Oaths.

APPENDIX II

Table of Forms: Individual voluntary arrangement

FORM A

A Clennam Esq
Flat 6
Covent Garden
Magwitch
Dickenshire

Messrs Rugg & Bawkins
Pentonville
London

Dear Sirs,

I, ARTHUR CLENNAM, hereby instruct Rugg & Bawkins to prepare a proposal for a voluntary arrangement to be put forward to my creditors and I further authorise Rugg & Bawkins to enter into correspondence in order to obtain confidential information from any of my creditors.

Yours faithfully,

(A Clennam)

FORM B

(Specimen letter to creditors)

RUGG & BAWKINS,
PENTONVILLE,
LONDON

T Hardy Esq
Madding House
Egdon Heath
Wessex

(Date) 1997

Dear Sir,

ARTHUR CLENNAM OF FLAT 6, COVENT GARDEN, MAGWITCH, DICKENSHIRE (INDIVIDUAL VOLUNTARY ARRANGEMENT)

As insolvency practitioners, we are assisting Mr Clennam to prepare a proposal for a voluntary arrangement to be put forward to creditors pursuant to Part VIII of the Insolvency Act 1986.

In order that we may formulate such a proposal, a full list of his creditors is being compiled and we should be grateful to receive your claim at the earliest opportunity.

We shall write again enclosing Mr Clennam's proposal for your consideration in due course.

Yours faithfully,

Rugg & Bawkins

FORM C

(Specimen letter to Court)

RUGG & BAWKINS,
PENTONVILLE,
LONDON

The District Judge
Dickensian County Court
Copperfield Road
Magwitch
Dickenshire

1997

Dear Sir,

ARTHUR CLENNAM OF FLAT 6, COVENT GARDEN, MAGWITCH, DICKENSHIRE
PROPOSAL FOR A VOLUNTARY ARRANGEMENT

I attach herewith the following documents in respect of the above debtor:

1. Originating application (rule 7.2) for an interim order together with an affidavit.

2. A notice to intended nominee (rule 5.4) and confirmation to act as nominee and supervisor.

I also enclose a nominee's report to the Court pursuant to section 256, Insolvency Act 1986, debtor's proposal and a statement of affairs.

I recommend that a meeting of the creditors be summoned to consider the debtor's proposals and that the meeting should take place at The Pickwick Club, Strand, London WC on February 26, 1997.

Should you require any further information please contact Mr Robinson of my office as soon as possible.

Yours faithfully,

S Rugg
Nominee

FORM D

Rule 7.2 **Form 7.1**

ORIGINATING APPLICATION

IN THE DICKENSIAN COUNTY COURT

No. of 1997

Re: ARTHUR CLENNAM OF FLAT 6, COVENT GARDEN, MAGWITCH, DICKENSHIRE

Date:

Time:

Place:

On the hearing of ARTHUR CLENNAM the applicant for an order in the following terms:

An interim order under section 252 of the Insolvency Act 1986 in the terms as attached.

The grounds on which the applicant claims to be entitled to the order are set out in the affidavit attached.

The applicant's address for service is:

RUGG & BAWKINS
Pentonville
London

DATED day of 1997

SIGNED ....
ARTHUR CLENNAM

FORM E

IN THE DICKENSIAN COUNTY COURT

AFFIDAVIT TO ACCOMPANY APPLICATION TO THE COURT FOR AN INTERIM ORDER

I, ARTHUR CLENNAM OF FLAT 6, COVENT GARDEN, MAGWITCH, DICKENSHIRE, make oath and say as follows:

(a) My reasons for making application to the Court for an interim order are as follows:

(i) that I am insolvent, being unable to pay my debts as and when they fall due

(ii) that I intend to put forward proposals for a voluntary arrangement of my affairs in order that I may make orderly payments to my creditors.

(b) The following have commenced proceedings:

Plaintiff	*Court*	*Case No.*
Thomas Hardy	Wessex County Court	123 of 1996
Ebenezer Scrooge	Dickensian County Court	456 of 1996

(c) That no previous application for an interim order has been made by me, or in respect of me, during the last twelve months.

(d) That SEPTIMUS RUGG OF PENTONVILLE, LONDON, the nominee under the proposal referred to in paragraph (a) above, is a person who is qualified to act as an insolvency practitioner in relation to me and that he is willing to act in relation to the proposal. I attach hereto marked "A" my proposal for an individual voluntary arrangement and also marked "B" a copy of the notice to the intended nominee under the Insolvency Rules, rule 5.4 endorsed to the effect that he agrees so to act.

Sworn at)
this day of)
before me)
)
)
....) ....

SOLICITOR/
COMMISSIONER
OF OATHS

ARTHUR CLENNAM

FORM F

NOTICE TO INTENDED NOMINEE OF A PROPOSAL FOR A VOLUNTARY ARRANGEMENT

To: Septimus Rugg
Pentonville
London

NOTICE IS HEREBY GIVEN pursuant to the Insolvency Rules, rule 5.4 that I, ARTHUR CLENNAM OF FLAT 6, COVENT GARDEN, MAGWITCH, DICKENSHIRE, propose to make an application to the Dickensian County Court for an interim order, in accordance with the attached in order that my proposal for a voluntary arrangement of my affairs, a copy of which is attached hereto, may be considered.

NOTICE IS ALSO GIVEN that if you agree to act as nominee and supervisor of the voluntary arrangement you should sign the attached copy and return it to me at my address shown above.

SIGNED ....

ARTHUR CLENNAM

DATED ....

I, SEPTIMUS RUGG of RUGG & BAWKINS, PENTONVILLE, LONDON, acknowledge receipt of this notice and confirm that I agree to act as nominee and supervisor of the voluntary arrangement.

SIGNED ....

SEPTIMUS RUGG

DATED ....

This is the exhibit marked "B" referred to in the affidavit sworn before me this day of 1997.

SIGNED ....

A SOLICITOR

FORM G

NOMINEE'S REPORT TO THE COURT
PURSUANT TO SECTION 256, INSOLVENCY ACT 1986

IN THE DICKENSIAN COUNTY COURT No. of 1997

Re: ARTHUR CLENNAM OF FLAT 6, COVENT GARDEN, MAGWITCH, DICKENSHIRE

I, SEPTIMUS RUGG of RUGG & BAWKINS, PENTONVILLE, LONDON, the nominee under the proposal for a voluntary arrangement by ARTHUR CLENNAM report as follows:

(a) I attach hereto a copy of the debtor's proposal for a voluntary arrangement, together with a summary of his statement of affairs.

(b) In my opinion, the proposals put forward by the debtor provide for an orderly distribution of assets to his creditors in due order of priority and should provide a greater benefit for those creditors than would the debtor's bankruptcy. The success of the arrangement depends however upon the contribution from Mr D. Doyce referred to a paragraph (b) and upon the net earnings referred to at clause (c) meeting the debtor's expectations. Mr Doyce is abroad and I have been unable to interview him personally. I have, however, received a letter from Mr Doyce confirming his intention to make the contribution of £25,000 subject to approval of the proposal. Such confirmation may not necessarily be legally enforceable. I have examined the business forecast prepared by the debtor, which appears to be achievable based on past performance provided that the debtor's customers continue their loyalty to the debtor notwithstanding the voluntary arrangement.

(c) Whilst, in view of the substantial sum involved, every effort should be made to recover moneys due from Mr M. Murdle, no account has been taken in these arrangements of any possible recovery and no provision has been made for the costs of recovery action.

(d) I therefore recommend that a meeting of creditors be summoned to consider the debtor's proposals and that such meeting should take place at THE PICKWICK CLUB, STRAND, MAGWITCH, DICKENSHIRE on February 26, 1997 and that the date from which the interim order has effect should be extended for a further period of 28 days after that date, in order that the meeting may be held.

SIGNED ....

SEPTIMUS RUGG

DATED ....

FORM H

IN THE DICKENSIAN COUNTY COURT

IN THE MATTER OF THE INSOLVENCY ACT 1986

and

IN THE MATTER OF A PROPOSAL FOR A VOLUNTARY ARRANGEMENT

Re: ARTHUR CLENNAM of FLAT 6, COVENT GARDEN, MAGWITCH, DICKENSHIRE

I, Arthur Clennam, the above-named debtor, hereby submit my proposals for a voluntary arrangement.

In accordance with rule 5.3 of the Insolvency Rules 1986:

(a) A full disclosure of my assets and liabilities, with the exception of necessary household furniture and wearing apparel, is given in my statement of affairs lodged with this Court. The whole of my assets of any nature whatsoever to which I am entitled at the date hereof and to which I might become entitled up to the date of the approval of the creditors of the terms of this my proposed voluntary arrangement will be available for the benefit of my creditors.

I am the proprietor of the engineering firm trading as "Doyce & Clennam" at Bleeding Heart Yard, Magwitch, Dickenshire. I am of the opinion that my bankruptcy would result in the loss of income from this business which would thereby be detrimental to my creditors.

My colleague, Mr D. Doyce, has loaned to me the sum of £10,000 and will defer this loan to the interests of other creditors and provide further finance to the business to enable profits to be earned for the benefit of creditors as the basis of my monthly contributions to the scheme.

The property, at Flat 6, Covent Garden, Magwitch, Dickenshire, has been surrendered by me to Huffam Building Society, and there is no equity anticipated. The flat is in a Georgian Grade 1 listed building comprising six flats: it required considerable structural and maintenance work (surveyor's report available) of which my share would have been 19 per cent. of an estimated cost of £250,000. The survey of the property at the time of purchase was arranged by Huffam Building Society and this survey failed to identify these major works. Clearly I would not have proceeded with the purchase had I known the extent of the necessary works, hence the surrender of the property to Huffam Building Society. I believe that other leaseholders have taken similar action and when visiting Covent Garden I have noticed that major renovation work is being carried out at the property.

My business premises at Bleeding Heart Yard have been valued at £20,000 and are subject to a charge in favour of the Dickensian Bank Plc. Such property will not be sold as part of these arrangements in order that the business may continue to trade. The plant and machinery has also been valued for the purposes of my attached statement of affairs and such plant will be retained by me for the purposes of generating profits.

My Aston Martin motor vehicle will be sold for the benefit of creditors and the net proceeds after the acquisition of a modest motor vehicle will be available for distribution to my creditors.

Save as aforesaid there are no assets to be excluded from the arrangement.

(b) My colleague, Mr D. Doyce, will make a contribution of £25,000 for distribution to my creditors. There are no further assets other than those referred to above that are proposed to be included in this voluntary arrangement.

(c) Full disclosure of my known liabilities is made in my statement of affairs. Creditors will be paid in due order of priority. There are no associates of mine who rank as creditors (except my mother) and to the best of my knowledge and belief there are no circumstances giving rise to the possibility of claims under section 339 (transactions at an undervalue), 340 (preference), or 343 (extortionate credit transactions) of the Insolvency Act 1986. An early distribution shall be made out of moneys advanced by Mr Doyce and from the proceeds of sale of my motor vehicle. Further contributions shall be made from my net earnings to the extent of £600 per month commencing on March 1, 1997 for a period of two years (24 monthly payments).

I further propose to make such additional contributions from my income, after provision of necessary accommodation and subsistence expenses, as circumstances permit.

My mother, Mrs M. Clennam, has agreed to defer her claim to the claims of other creditors upon acceptance of this proposal. In the event of bankruptcy her claim will rank *pari passu* with the other creditors.

Preferential creditors shall be paid in full not later than July 31, 1997.

(d) No guarantees have been given of my debts by any other persons nor is it intended that they should do so.

(e) It is anticipated that the voluntary arrangement will take two years and six months to implement.

(f) Distributions to creditors will be made as funds become available but not before August 1997. I anticipate distribution to the creditors as follows:

August 1997 — 50p in the £
January 1998 — 6p in the £
January 1998 — 6p in the £

I have advanced over a period in total £800,000 to Michael Murdle, now of unknown address, and should this asset be realised the amount of realisation will be used for the benefit of the creditors and distributed accordingly. Any recovery from this source is uncertain.

(g) That the remuneration of the nominee be fixed at the sum of £2,350 inclusive of V.A.T. and expenses.

(h) That the premium on the supervisor's bond and properly incurred expenses be payable from the estate.

(j) No guarantees are to be given by any person other than myself and no security is to be given or sought, other than appears from my statement of affairs.

(k) Funds received by the supervisor shall be banked at Flintwinch Bank plc, Imperial House, London WC, pending distribution to creditors.

(l) Any surplus funds remaining after payment to the creditors in full, plus statutory interest, will be utilised first to repay all loans and advances received from my colleague, Mr D. Doyce, secondly to repay the loan from my mother, Mrs F. Clennam, which claim is to be deferred to other creditors, and the balance shall be returnable to myself upon termination of the arrangement.

(m) I undertake to keep my supervisor advised as to the financial aspects of any business undertaken and allow him facilities to monitor the financial arrangements.

(n) There will be no further credit facilities arranged as part of these proposals.

(o) The supervisor shall receive the moneys to be made available to creditors in accordance with my proposal and shall make payments to the creditors in accordance therewith. He shall exercise where appropriate the other powers afforded to him in this proposal.

(p) That Septimus Rugg, Chartered Accountant, of Rugg & Bawkins, of Pentonville, London, a qualified insolvency practitioner, be appointed supervisor of the aforesaid voluntary arrangement in order to administer the arrangement.

I further propose as follows:

(i) In the event of my failure to comply with the agreed terms of the voluntary arrangement, I fully understand that the supervisor or any creditor bound by the arrangement will be entitled to petition for my bankruptcy.

The supervisor, as a result of my non-compliance of the terms of this arrangement, shall have residual right to sell my assets as in bankruptcy and/or a right to petition for my bankruptcy.

That the supervisor shall retain sufficient funds from realisations or contributions to petition for my bankruptcy under section 264(1)(c) of the Insolvency Act 1986 should the arrangement be deemed to be in default, as defined in section 276 of the Act. It is proposed that £1,000 be retained to cover the petition fee and any time costs involved.

(ii) I verily believe that the voluntary arrangement offers the best prospects of maximising realisations for the benefit of my creditors. In addition, due to the statutory costs of voluntary arrangement being lower than those in bankruptcy, I believe that the creditors will receive distributions more quickly under these proposals than under an administration in bankruptcy and that the distributions to unsecured creditors will be greater under a voluntary arrangement than under an administration in bankruptcy.

(iii) Failure to pay monthly contributions within 28 days of the due dates is to be seen as failure of the arrangement.

(iv) The supervisor is to retain sufficient funds to petition for bankruptcy in the event of failure to comply with the terms of the arrangement.

(v) The supervisor is to review the level of voluntary contributions on a six-monthly basis with a view to obtaining a higher dividend for creditors.

(vi) Future tax liabilities shall be paid as and when due.

(vii) All outstanding accounts and returns including V.A.T. returns (if any) to be submitted within six months.

(viii) Supervisor's fees will be on time cost basis.

(ix) All legal costs incurred by H.M. Customs and Excise, if any, to date to be paid as part of the voluntary arrangement prior to any distribution to the creditors.

(x) Any legal costs incurred by the Official Receiver, if any, will form part of this voluntary arrangement and payable prior to any distribution to the creditors.

(xi) Should I at any time become beneficiary to, or receive, any sums by way of a "windfall" for a period of two years from the date of acceptance of this individual voluntary arrangement, I agree that such funds will be utilised and paid over to the supervisor of the voluntary arrangement for the benefit of the creditors.

(xii) The business assets including the leasehold property at Bleeding Heart Yard and all plant and equipment therein shall not immediately be sold but shall be retained by me in order that my business may continue for the benefit of creditors. Should profits not accrue for the benefit of creditors, my supervisor shall be entitled to sell those assets for creditors' benefit. In the meantime my supervisor shall register a caution with regard to the property and take such other steps as solicitors may advise to be appropriate to enable my supervisor to hold such assets in trust for the creditors under this scheme.

(xiii) I have to the best of my knowledge made a full disclosure to all my creditors as appears in my statement of affairs and the schedule thereto. However, in the event that any creditors have inadvertently been omitted from this list, my supervisor shall be authorised to admit the claims of such creditors and include them in any distribution.

It is proposed that the shortfall, if any, to the creditors as a result of implementing the voluntary arrangement shall not be treated as a gain and/or profit to me.

DATED THIS DAY OF 1997

SIGNED ....

FORM I

ARTHUR CLENNAM

Approximate Statement of Affairs as at January 31, 1997

	Book Value £	Estimated to Realise £
Leasehold property: Flat 6, Covent Garden	100,000	50,000
less: Fixed Charge—The Huffam Building Society	80,000	80,000
	20,000	(30,000)
Leasehold property: Bleeding Heart Yard	50,000	25,000
less: Fixed Charge—Dickensian Bank plc	40,000	40,000
Estimated surplus/(shortfall)	10,000	(15,000)
Plant and equipment	30,741	10,000
Furniture and effects	1,000	nil
Investments Murdle Trust	800,000	nil
Motor vehicle	100,000	80,000
	931,741	90,000
Less: Preferential Creditors		
P.A.Y.E.	5,748	
V.A.T.	16,032	
Wages and holiday pay	12,709	34,489
Estimated surplus as regards preferential creditors		55,511
Unsecured Creditors		
The Huffam Building Society (see above)	30,000	
Dickensian Bank plc (see above)	15,000	
Trade and expense	172,412	
D. Doyce—business loan	10,000	
Mrs. F. Clennam (mother)—loan	30,000	
Credit cards and personal liabilities	6,341	263,753
Estimated deficiency as regards unsecured creditors subject to realisation and costs		148,242

FORM J

(Specimen letter to creditors)

RUGG & BAWKINS,
PENTONVILLE,
LONDON

PRIVATE AND CONFIDENTIAL
TO ALL CREDITORS

1997

Dear Sir/Madam,

Re: ARTHUR CLENNAM OF FLAT 6, COVENT GARDEN, MAGWITCH, DICKENSHIRE

I wish to inform you that I, SEPTIMUS RUGG, am the nominee in a proposed voluntary arrangement under the Insolvency Act 1986. Pursuant to section 252 of this Act, application has been made to the Dickensian County Court for an interim order; the application was heard by the district judge on February ..., 1997 and the interim order was duly made; this has the effect of suspending bankruptcy proceedings to enable a meeting of the creditors to consider the attached proposals for the voluntary arrangement, which would be of more benefit to any creditor than bankruptcy.

I therefore attach for your attention a notice of the creditors' meeting to be held on February 26, 1997, together with a form of proxy. I also enclose a copy of the debtor's proposals together with the nominee's report to Court and the notice to intended nominee and a copy of the statement of affairs.

Before the date of the meeting, creditors should notify me of the amount and details of their claim and give particulars of any security held by them in respect of the debt. A notice of claim form is enclosed for this purpose and should be returned to me duly completed.

If you require any further information, please do not hesitate to contact Mr Robinson of my office.

Yours faithfully,

S RUGG
Nominee

FORM K

NOTICE OF CREDITORS' MEETING

IN THE MATTER OF THE INSOLVENCY ACT 1986

and

IN THE MATTER OF A PROPOSAL FOR A VOLUNTARY ARRANGEMENT

NOTICE IS HEREBY GIVEN that a meeting of the creditors of ARTHUR CLENNAM OF FLAT 6, COVENT GARDEN, MAGWITCH, DICKENSHIRE will be held at the PICKWICK CLUB, STRAND, MAGWITCH, DICKENSHIRE on February 26, 1997 at 11.30 a.m. in order to consider his proposals for a voluntary arrangement. Attached is a copy of the debtor's proposals together with a summary of his statement of affairs and the nominee's comments on the proposal.

The nominee's report has been delivered to the Dickensian County Court.

Attached hereto is a form of proxy for your use at the meeting, which should be lodged with the nominee before the start of the meeting.

SIGNED ....
SEPTIMUS RUGG—NOMINEE

Notes: Please refer to notes on next page

FORM L

NOTES:

1. Subject as follows, at the creditors' meeting for any resolution to be passed approving any proposal or modification, there must be a majority in excess of three-quarters in value of the creditors present in person or by proxy and voting on the resolution.

2. In the following cases there is to be left out of account a creditor's vote in respect of any claim or part of a claim:

   (a) where written notice of the claim was not given either at the meeting or before it to the chairman or the nominee;

   (b) where the claim or part is secured;

   (c) where the claim is in respect of a debt wholly or partly on or secured by a current bill of exchange or promissory note unless the creditor is willing to treat the liability to him on the bill or note of every person who is liable on it antecedently to the debtor and against whom a bankruptcy order has not been made (or in the case of a company which has not gone into liquidation) as security in his hands, and to estimate the value of the security and (for the purpose of entitlement to vote, but not of any distribution under the arrangement) to deduct it from his claim.

3. Any resolution is invalid if those voting against it include more than half in value of the creditors counting in these latter only those:

   (a) to whom notice of the meeting was sent;

   (b) whose votes are not to be left out of account under paragraph 2 above;

   (c) who are not, to the best of the chairman's belief, associates of the debtor.

4. Proxies may be lodged at any time prior to voting. Those sent by fax will be accepted, but hard copies should follow by post.

FORM M

Rule 8.1 **Insolvency Act 1986** **Form 8**

PROXY (COMPANY OR INDIVIDUAL VOLUNTARY ARRANGEMENTS)

Notes to held completion of the form

ARTHUR CLENNAM

Please give full name and address for communication

Name of creditor/member ______

Address ______

______

Please insert name of person (who must be 18 or over) or the "chairman of the meeting" (see note below). If you wish to provide for alternative proxy-holders in the circumstances that your first choice is unable to attend please state the name(s) of the alternatives as well

Name of proxy-holder ______

1 ______

______

______

2 ______

______

______

3 ______

______

______

Please delete words in brackets if the proxy-holder is only to vote as directed i.e. he has no discretion

I appoint the above person to be my/the creditor's/member's proxy-holder at the meeting of creditors/members to be held on Wednesday, February 26, 1997 at 11.30 a.m. or at any adjournment of that meeting. The proxy-holder is to propose or vote as instructed below [and in respect of any resolution for which no specific instruction is given, may vote or abstain at his/her discretion]

Voting instructions for resolutions

*Please delete as appropriate

1. For the acceptance/rejection* of the proposed voluntary arrangement [with such modifications as are approved by the meeting of creditors] [with the following modifications:]

Any other resolutions which the proxy-holder is to propose or vote in favour of or against should be set out in numbered paragraphs in the space provided below paragraph 1. If more room is required please use the other side of this form.

______

______

______

______

______

______

______

______

This form must be signed.

Signature ______ Date ______

Name in CAPITAL LETTERS ______

Only to be completed if the creditor/member has not signed in person.

Position with creditor/member or relationship to creditor/member or other authority for signature ______

Remember: There may be resolutions on the other side of this form.

FORM N

NOTICE OF CLAIM: INDIVIDUAL VOLUNTARY ARRANGEMENT

IN THE MATTER OF THE INSOLVENCY ACT 1986

IN THE MATTER OF ARTHUR CLENNAM OF FLAT 6, MAGWITCH, DICKENSHIRE

Name of creditor

Address of creditor

Total amount of claim
including V.A.T. £

Details of any documents by reference to which the debt can be substantiated

---

If the total amount shown above included V.A.T., please show:

(a) amount of V.A.T. £
(b) amount of claim NET of V.A.T. £

Particulars of how and when debt incurred

Particulars of any security held, the value of the security, and the date it was given

---

Signature of creditor or person authorised to act on his behalf

Name in BLOCK LETTERS

Position with or relation to creditor

Admitted preferentially/non-preferentially for

£

Nominee

Date

FORM O

ARTHUR CLENNAM

PROXIES FOR CREDITORS' MEETING
THE PICKWICK CLUB, STRAND, MAGWITCH,
DICKENSHIRE, AT 11.30 A.M.
ON FEBRUARY 26, 1997

CHAIRMAN GENERAL

£

PROXY-HOLDERS (REPRESENTED BY)

£

FORM P

ARTHUR CLENNAM

MEETING OF CREDITORS
HELD AT THE PICKWICK CLUB, STRAND, MAGWITCH, DICKENSHIRE
ON FEBRUARY 26, 1997 AT 11.30 A.M.

ATTENDANCE LIST

Creditor	Signature of Representative	Amount of Claim

FORM Q

(Specimen letter to Court)

RUGG & BAWKINS,
PENTONVILLE,
LONDON

The District Judge
Dickensian County Court
Bleak House
Copperfield Road
Magwitch
Dickenshire

1997

Dear Sir,

ARTHUR CLENNAM No. OF 1997
(INDIVIDUAL VOLUNTARY ARRANGEMENT)

I enclose herewith a report to the Court of the result of the creditors' meeting held on Wednesday, February 26, 1997 for your file records.

I also take this opportunity to enclose a copy of the updated approximate statement of affairs as at February 26, 1997.

I shall now proceed to implement the agreed proposals for the benefit of the creditors.

Yours faithfully,

S Rugg
Supervisor

FORM R

IN THE DICKENSIAN COUNTY COURT No. of 1997

REPORT TO THE COURT OF RESULT OF CREDITORS' MEETING

PURSUANT TO SECTIONS 257–259 INSOLVENCY ACT 1986

In the matter of a proposal for an Individual Voluntary Arrangement by ARTHUR CLENNAM OF FLAT 6, COVENT GARDEN, MAGWITCH, DICKENSHIRE, I, IAN JAMES ROBINSON, chairman (for and on behalf of SEPTIMUS RUGG) of the meeting of creditors held on Wednesday, February 26, 1997 at The Pickwick Club, Strand, London WC at 11.30 a.m., hereby report as follows:

(a) The proposal for a voluntary arrangement by ARTHUR CLENNAM was approved by the creditors with the following modifications:

(i)

(ii)

(b) The creditors present or represented voted as follows:

Creditor	*Value for Acceptance*	*Value for Rejection*

For acceptance of the proposal: %
For rejection of the proposal %

The proposal for a voluntary arrangement was accepted by the creditors in accordance with the Insolvency Rules 1986; rules 5.17 and 5.18.

(c) SEPTIMUS RUGG, FCA, FIPA, FSPI was confirmed as supervisor of the voluntary arrangement.

SIGNED ....

IAN JAMES ROBINSON—CHAIRMAN

DATED February 26, 1997

To the District Judge
Dickensian County Court
Bleak House
Copperfield Road
Magwitch
Dickenshire

The Creditors

FORM S

(Specimen letter to the Secretary of State)

RUGG & BAWKINS,
PENTONVILLE,
LONDON

The Secretary of State
Department of Trade and Industry
Commercial Union House
22 Martineau Square
Birmingham
B2 4UZ

1997

Dear Sir,

ARTHUR CLENNAM OF FLAT 6, COVENT GARDEN, MAGWITCH, DICKENSHIRE (INDIVIDUAL VOLUNTARY ARRANGEMENT)

I write to inform you that the following voluntary arrangement has been *approved* by the creditors:

Debtor:	ARTHUR CLENNAM
Date of approval by creditors:	FEBRUARY 26, 1997
Name and address of supervisor:	SEPTIMUS RUGG RUGG & BAWKINS PENTONVILLE LONDON
Court to which report filed:	DICKENSIAN COUNTY COURT BLEAK HOUSE COPPERFIELD ROAD MAGWITCH DICKENSHIRE

I enclose a cheque in the sum of £35 in accordance with Fee I of Part II of the Schedule to the Insolvency Fees Order 1986.

Yours faithfully,

S Rugg
Supervisor

FORM T

(Specimen letter to creditors)

RUGG & BAWKINS,
PENTONVILLE,
LONDON

TO ALL CREDITORS

1997

Dear Sir/Madam,

ARTHUR CLENNAM OF FLAT 6, COVENT GARDEN, MAGWITCH, DICKENSHIRE (INDIVIDUAL VOLUNTARY ARRANGEMENT)

Further to previous correspondence in this matter, I wish to inform you that at the creditors' meeting held on February 26, 1997 the voluntary arrangement was *approved* by the creditors.

I will now proceed to implement the agreed proposals. I should be obliged if you would let me have, if not already sent, a statement of your claim against the above debtor as at February 26, 1997.

If you require any further information, please do not hesitate to contact Mr Robinson of my office.

Yours faithfully,

S Rugg
Supervisor

APPENDIX III

County Courts with Bankruptcy Jurisdiction

Court	*Address*
ABERDARE	Crown Building, Green Street, Aberdare, Mid Glamorgan, CF44 7DW. Tel: 01685 87 4779
ABERYSTWYTH	Edalestone House, Queens Road, Aberystwyth, Dyfed, SY23 2HP. Tel: 01970 617597
AYLESBURY	2nd Floor, Heron House, 49 Buckingham Street, Aylesbury, Bucks, HP20 2NQ. Tel: 01296 393498
BANBURY	35 Parsons Street, Banbury, Oxford, OX16 8BW. Tel: 01295 265799
BARNSLEY	12 Regent Street, Barnsley, South Yorks, S70 2EW. Tel: 01226 203471
BARNSTAPLE	The Law Courts, 7th Floor, Civic Centre, North Walk, Barnstaple, Devon, EX31 1DY. Tel: 01271 72252
BARROW-IN-FURNESS	Government Buildings, Michaelson Road, Barrow-in-Furness, Cumbria, LA14 2EZ. Tel: 01229 820046 01229 827150
BATH	Cambridge House, Henry Street, Bath, Avon, BA1 1DJ. Tel: 01225 310282

BEDFORD	29 Goldington Road, Bedford, MK40 3NN. Tel: 01234 359322
BIRKENHEAD	76 Hamilton Street, Birkenhead, Merseyside, L41 5EN. Tel: 0151 647 8826/7 0151 647 9676
BIRMINGHAM	The Priory Courts, 33 Bull Street, Birmingham, B4 6DS. Tel: 0121 681 3000
BLACKBURN	64 Victoria Street, Blackburn, Lancs., BB1 6DJ. Tel: 01254 680640 01254 680654
BLACKPOOL	The Law Courts, Chapel Street, Blackpool, Lancs., FY1 5RJ. Tel: 01253 293178
BLACKWOOD	County Court Office, Blackwood Road, Blackwood, Gwent, NP2 2XB Tel: 01495 223197
BOLTON COMBINED COURT CENTRE	The Law Courts, Blackhorse Street, Bolton, Lancs., BL1 1SU. Tel: 01204 392881
BOSTON	Crown Buildings, Lincoln Lane, Boston, Lincs., PE21 8SG. Tel: 01205 366080.
BOURNEMOUTH COMBINED COURT CENTRE	The Courts of Justice, Deansleigh Road, Bournemouth, Dorset BH7 7DS Tel: 01202 502800

BRADFORD COMBINED COURT CENTRE	Bradford Law Courts, Exchange Square, Drake Street, Bradford, W. Yorks BD1 1JA. Tel: 01274 840274
BRIDGEND	Crown Buildings, Angel Street, Bridgend, Mid Glamorgan, CF31 4AS. Tel: 01656 55522
BRIDGWATER	Court House, Queen Street, Bridgwater, Somerset, TA6 3AP. Tel: 01278 422180
BRIGHTON	William Street, Brighton, Sussex, BN2 2LG. Tel: 01273 674421
BRISTOL	Greyfriars, Lewins Mead, Bristol, BS1 2NR. Tel: 0117 9294414
BURNLEY COMBINED COURT CENTRE	The Law Courts, P.O. Box 30, Hammerton Street, Burnley, Lancs., BB11 1XD. Tel: 01282 416899
BURTON-UPON-TRENT	65 Station Street, Burton-upon-Trent, Staffs, DE14 1BP. Tel: 01283 568241
BURY ST. EDMUNDS	Triton House, St. Andrews Street North, Bury St. Edmunds, Suffolk, IP33 1TR. Tel: 01284 753254
CAERNARFON	Llanberis Road, Caernarfon, Gwynedd, LL55 2RA Tel: 01286 678911

CAMBRIDGE	Three Crowns House 72–80 Hills Road, Cambridge CB2 1LA. Tel: 01223 354416
CANTERBURY COMBINED COURT CENTRE	The Law Courts, Chaucer Road, Canterbury, Kent, CT1 1ZA. Tel: 01227 819200
CARDIFF CF	(1) 2 Park Street, Cardiff, South Glam., CF1 1ET. (2) Welsh Water Authority Section 2 Park Street Cardiff, South Glam., CF1 1ET Tel: 01222 376400
CARLISLE COMBINED COURT SERVICE	Courts of Justice, Earl Street, Carlisle, Cumbria, CA1 1DJ. Tel: 01228 28182
CARMARTHEN	The Old Vicarage, Picton Terrace, Carmarthen, Dyfed, SA31 1BJ. Tel: 01267 236598/232351
CHELMSFORD	London House, New London Road, Chelmsford, Essex, CM2 0QR. Tel: 01245 264670 01245 281386 01245 350718 01245 256964
CHELTENHAM	The Court House, County Court Road, Cheltenham, Glos., GL50 1HB. Tel: 01242 519983.
CHESTER	1st Floor, Centurion House, 77 Northgate Street, Chester, CH1 2HB. Tel: 01244 312245

CHESTERFIELD	St Mary's Gate, Chesterfield, Derbys., S41 7TD. Tel: 01246 501200
COLCHESTER AND CLACTON	Falkland House, 25 Southway, Colchester, Essex, CO3 3EG. Tel: 01206 572743
COVENTRY COMBINED COURT CENTRE	140 Much Park Street, Coventry, West Midlands, CV1 2SN. Tel: 01203 536166
CREWE	The Law Courts, Civic Centre, Crewe, Cheshire, CW1 2DP. Tel: 01270 212255
CROYDON COMBINED COURT CENTRE	The Law Courts, Altyre Road, Croydon, CR0 3NE. Tel: 0181 681 2533
DARLINGTON	4 Coniscliffe Road, Darlington, Co. Durham, DL3 7RG. Tel: 01325 463224
DERBY COMBINED COURT CENTRE	The Morledge, Derby, DE1 2XE. Tel: 01332 622600
DEWSBURY	County Court House, Eightlands Road, Dewsbury, West Yorks, WF13 2PE. Tel: 01924 465860 (2 lines) 01924 466135
DONCASTER	74 Waterdale, Doncaster, South Yorks, DN1 3BT. Tel: 01302 365400 01302 323733
DUDLEY	Harbour Buildings, Waterfront West, Dudley Road, Brierley Hill, Dudley, West Midlands, DY5 1LN. Tel: 01348 480799

DURHAM	Hallgarth Street, Durham, DH1 3RG. Tel: 0191 386 7864
EASTBOURNE	4 The Avenue, Eastbourne, East Sussex, BN21 3SZ. Tel: 01323 735195
EXETER COMBINED COURT CENTRE	The Castle, Exeter, Devon, EX4 3PS. Tel: 01392 210655
GLOUCESTER COMBINED COURT CENTRE	Combined Court Building, Kimbrose Way, Gloucester, GL1 2DE. Tel: 01452 529351/2/3
GREAT GRIMSBY COMBINED COURT CENTRE	Town Hall Square, Gt Grimsby, South Humberside, DN31 1HX. Tel: 01472 45816
GREAT YARMOUTH	Havenbridge House, North Quay, Great Yarmouth, Norfolk, NR30 1HZ. Tel: 01493 843132
GUILDFORD	The Law Courts, Mary Road, Guildford, Surrey, GU1 4PS. Tel: 01483 34991
HALIFAX	Prescott Street, Halifax, West Yorks, HX1 2JJ. Tel: 01422 344700
HARROGATE	2 Victoria Avenue, Harrogate, North Yorks., HG1 1EL. Tel: 01423 503921
HASTINGS	The Law Courts, Bohemia Road, Hastings, East Sussex, TN34 1DX. Tel: 01424 435128

HAVERFORDWEST	Crown Buildings, Cherry Grove, Haverfordwest, Dyfed, SA61 2NN. Tel: 01437 765741/2
HEREFORD	First Floor, Barclays Bank Chambers, 1/3 Broad Street, Hereford, HR4 9BA. Tel: 01432 357233 01432 357571
HERTFORD	Sovereign House, Hale Road, Hertford, SG13 8DY. Tel: 01992 503954
HUDDERSFIELD	Queensgate House, Queensgate, Huddersfield, West Yorks., HD1 2RR. Tel: 01484 421043 01484 535085
IPSWICH	8 Arcade Street, Ipswich, Suffolk, IP1 1EJ. Tel: 01473 214256
KENDAL	Kendal Courthouse, Burneside Road, Kendal, Cumbria, LA9 4NF. Tel: 01539 721218
KIDDERMINSTER	10 Comberton Place, Kidderminster, Worcs., DY10 1QR. Tel: 01562 822480
KING'S LYNN	Chequer House, 12 King Street, Kings Lynn, Norfolk, PE30 1ES. Tel: 01553 772067
KINGSTON-UPON-HULL COMBINED COURT CENTRE	Lowgate, Kingston-upon-Hull, Humberside, HU1 2EX. Tel: 01482 586161

KINGSTON-UPON-THAMES	St. James Road, Kingston-upon-Thames, KT1 2AD. Tel: 0181 546 8843
LANCASTER	Mitre House, Church Street, Lancaster, Lancs, LA1 1UZ. Tel: 01524 68112/3
LEEDS COMBINED COURT CENTRE	The Courthouse, 1 Oxford Row, Leeds, LS1 3BG. Tel: 0113 2830040
LEICESTER	P.O. Box 3, 90 Wellington Street, Leicester, LE1 6ZZ. Tel: 0116 222 2323
LINCOLN COMBINED COURT CENTRE	360 High Street, Lincoln, LN5 7RL. Tel: 01522 883000
LIVERPOOL COMBINED COURT CENTRE	Queen Elizabeth II Law Courts, Derby Square, Liverpool, L2 1XA. Tel: 0151 473 7373
LLANGEFNI	County Court Buildings, Glanhwfa Road, Llangefni, Gwynedd, Tel: 01248 750225
LUTON	3rd Floor, Cresta House, Alma Street, Luton, Beds., LU1 2PU. Tel: 01582 35671
MACCLESFIELD	2nd Floor, Silk House, Park Green, Macclesfield, Cheshire, SK11 7NA. Tel: 01625 422872 01625 432492

MAIDSTONE COMBINED COURT CENTRE	The Law Courts, Barker Road, Maidstone, Kent, ME16 8EQ. Tel: 01622 202000
MANCHESTER	The Courts of Justice, Crown Square, Manchester, M60 9DJ. Tel: 0161 954 1800
MEDWAY	Anchorage House, High Street, Chatham, Kent, ME4 4DW. Tel: 01634 402881
MERTHYR TYDFIL COMBINED COURT CENTRE	The Law Courts, Glebeland Place, Merthyr Tydfil, Mid-Glamorgan, CF47 8BH. Tel: 01685 721322
MILTON KEYNES	351 Silbury Boulevard, Witon Gate East, Central Milton Keynes, MK9 2DT. Tel: 01908 668855
NEATH & PORT TALBOT	Forster Road, Neath, West Glamorgan, SA11 3BN. Tel: 01639 642267/8
NEWBURY	Kings Road West, Newbury, Berks, RG14 5AH. Tel: 01635 40928
NEWCASTLE-UPON-TYNE	The Law Courts, Quayside, Newcastle-upon-Tyne, NE1 3LA. Tel: 0191 201 2000
NEWPORT (I.o.W.)	1 Quay Street, Newport, I.o.W., PO30 5YT. Tel: 01983 526821

NEWPORT (Gwent)	Olympia House, 3rd Floor, Upper Dock Street, Newport, Gwent, NP9 1PQ. Tel: 01633 255267
NORTHAMPTON COMBINED COURT CENTRE	85–87 Lady's Lane, Northampton, NN1 3HQ. Tel: 01604 250131
NORWICH COMBINED COURT CENTRE	The Law Courts, Bishopgate, Norwich, NR3 1UR. Tel: 01603 610921/5
NOTTINGHAM COMBINED COURT CENTRE	60 Canal Street, Nottingham, NG1 7EJ. Tel: 0115 910 3500
OLDHAM	Church Lane, Oldham, Lancs, OL1 3AR. Tel: 0161 620 0425
OXFORD COMBINED COURT CENTRE	St Aldates, Oxford, OX1 1TL. Tel: 01865 264200
PETERBOROUGH COMBINED COURT CENTRE	Crown Buildings, Rivergate, Peterborough, PE1 1EJ. Tel: 01733 349161
PLYMOUTH COMBINED COURT CENTRE	The Law Courts, Armada Way, Plymouth, Devon, PL1 2ER. Tel: 01752 208284
PONTYPRIDD	Courthouse Street, Pontypridd, Mid Glamorgan, CF37 1JW. Tel: 01443 402471 01443 402135
PORTSMOUTH COMBINED COURT CENTRE	The Courts of Justice, Winston Churchill Avenue, Portsmouth, PO1 2EB. Tel: 01705 822281

PRESTON	The Law Courts, Openshaw Place, Ring Way, Preston, Lancs., PR1 2LL. Tel: 01772 832300
READING	160–163 Friar Street, Reading, Berks, RG1 1HE. Tel: 0118 959 9833
RHYL	Clwyd Buildings, Clwyd Street, Rhyl, Clwyd, LL18 3LA. Tel: 01745 330216
ROCHDALE	Fleece Street, Rochdale, Lancs, OL16 1ND. Tel: 01706 46862 01706 45377
ROMFORD	2a Oaklands Ave, Romford, Essex RM1 4DP. Tel: 01708 750677
ST. ALBANS	Victoria House, 117 Victoria Street, St Albans, Herts, AL1 3TJ. Tel: 01727 885 6925
SALFORD	Prince William House, Peel Cross Road, (off Eccles New Road), Salford, M5 2RR. Tel: 0161 745 7511
SALISBURY COMBINED COURT CENTRE	Alexandra House, St. John Street, Salisbury, Wilts, SP1 2PN. Tel: 01722 325444
SCARBOROUGH	9 Northway, Scarborough, North Yorks, YO11 2EH. Tel: 01723 366361

SCUNTHORPE	Crown Building, Comforts Avenue, Scunthorpe, South Humberside, DN15 6PR. Tel: 01724 280111
SHEFFIELD	50 Westbar, Sheffield, S3 8PH. Tel: 0114 2812400
SHREWSBURY	3rd Floor, Mardol House, Market Hall Buildings, Shoplatch, Shrewsbury, Salop, SY1 1HS. Tel: 01743 232650
SLOUGH	The Law Courts, Windsor Road, Slough, Berks, SL1 2HE. Tel: 01753 694280
SOUTHAMPTON COMBINED COURT CENTRE	The Courts of Justice, London Road, Southampton, Hants, SO9 5AF. Tel: 01703 228586
SOUTHEND	Tylers House, Tylers Avenue, Southend-on-Sea, Essex, SS1 2AW. Tel: 01702 601991
STAFFORD COMBINED COURT CENTRE	Victoria Square, Stafford, ST16 2QQ. Tel: 01785 255217
STOCKPORT	Heron House, Wellington Street, Stockport, Cheshire, SK1 3DJ. Tel: 0161 474 7707
STOKE-ON-TRENT COMBINED COURT CENTRE	Bethesda Street, Hanley, Stoke-on-Trent, Staffs, ST1 3BP. Tel: 01782 854000

STOURBRIDGE	7 Hagley Road, Stourbridge, West Midlands, DY8 1QL. Tel: 01384 394232
SUNDERLAND	The Court House, 44 John Street, Sunderland, Tyne and Wear, SR1 1RB. Tel: 0191 567 3691
SWANSEA	Government Buildings, St Mary's Square, Swansea, West Glamorgan, SA1 3LL. Tel: 01792 510200
SWINDON COMBINED COURT CENTRE	The Law Courts, Islington Street, Swindon, Wilts, SN1 2HG. Tel: 01793 614848
TAMESIDE	Scotland Street, Ashton-under-Lyne, Lancs, OL6 6SS. Tel: 0161 339 1711
TAUNTON COMBINED COURT CENTRE	Shire Hall, Taunton, Somerset, TA1 4EU. Tel: 01823 335972
TEESIDE COMBINED COURT CENTRE	The Law Courts, Russell Street, Middlesborough, Cleveland, TS1 2AE Tel: 01642 340000
TORQUAY AND NEWTON ABBOT	Nicholson Road, Torquay, Devon, TQ7 7AZ. Tel: 01803 616791
TRURO COMBINED COURT CENTRE	The Courts of Justice, Edward Street, Truro, Cornwall, TR1 2PB. Tel: 01872 222340
TUNBRIDGE WELLS	Merevale House, 42/46 London Road, Tunbridge Wells, Kent, TN1 1DP. Tel: 01892 515515

WAKEFIELD	Crown House, 127 Kirkgate, Wakefield, West Yorks, WF1 1JW Tel: 01924 370268
WALSALL	Bridge House, Bridge Street, Walsall, West Midlands, WS1 1JQ. Tel: 01922 432200
WARRINGTON COMBINED COURT CENTRE	Legh Street, Warrington, Cheshire, WA1 1UR. Tel: 01925 572192
WARWICK COMBINED COURT CENTRE	Northgate, Southside, Warwick, CV34 4RB. Tel: 01926 495428
WELSHPOOL AND NEWTOWN	The Mansion House, 24 Severn Street, Welshpool, Powys, SY21 7UX. Tel: 01938 552004
WEST BROMWICH	2nd Floor, Spencer House, 335/337 High Street, West Bromwich, West Midlands B70 8RF. Tel: 0121 500 5101
WEYMOUTH AND DORCHESTER COMBINED COURT SERVICE	2nd Floor, Westwey House, Westwey Road, Weymouth, Dorset, DT4 8TE. Tel: 01305 778684
WINCHESTER COMBINED COURT CENTRE	The Law Courts, The Castle, Winchester, Hants, SO23 9EL. Tel: 01962 841212
WOLVERHAMPTON COMBINED COURT CENTRE	Pipers Row, Wolverhampton, West Midlands, WV1 3LQ. Tel: 01902 481000

WORCESTER	The Shirehall, Foregate Street, Worcester, WR1 1EQ. Tel: 01905 730800
WORKINGTON	Langdale House, Gray Street, Workington, Cumbria, CA14 2PA. Tel: 01900 603967
WREXHAM	2nd Floor, 31 Chester Street, Wrexham, Clwyd, LL13 8XN. Tel: 01978 351738
YEOVIL	20 Hendford, Yeovil, Somerset, BA20 2QD. Tel: 01935 74133
YORK	Piccadilly House, 55 Piccadilly, York, YO1 1PL. Tel: 01904 629935

APPENDIX IV

SCHEDULE 6 (as amended) Section 386.

THE CATEGORIES OF PREFERENTIAL DEBTS

Category 1: Debts due to Inland Revenue

1. Sums due at the relevant date from the debtor on account of deductions of income tax from emoluments paid during the period of 12 months next before that date.

The deductions here referred to are those which the debtor was liable to make under section 203 of the Income and Corporation Taxes Act 1988 (pay as you earn), less the amount of the repayments of income tax which the debtor was liable to make during that period.

2. Sums due at the relevant date from the debtor in respect of such deductions as are required to be made by the debtor for that period under section 559 of the Income and Corporation Taxes Act 1988 (sub-contractors in the construction industry).

Category 2: Debts due to Customs and Excise

3. Any value added tax which is referable to the period of 6 months next before the relevant date (which period is referred to below as "the 6-month period").

For the purposes of this paragraph—

(a) where the whole of the prescribed accounting period to which any value added tax is attributable falls within the 6-month period, the whole amount of that tax is referable to that period; and
(b) in any case the amount of any value added tax which is referable to the 6-month period is the proportion of the tax which is equal to such proportion (if any) of the accounting reference period in question as falls within the 6-month period;

and in sub-paragraph (a) "prescribed" means prescribed by regulations under the Value Added Tax Act 1983.

4. The amount of any car tax which is due at the relevant date from the debtor and which became due within a period of 12 months next before that date.

5. Any amount which is due—

(a) by way of general betting duty or bingo duty, or
(b) under section 12(1) of the Betting and Gaming Duties Act 1981 (general betting duty and pool betting duty recoverable from agent collecting stakes), or
(c) under section 14 of, or Schedule 2 to, that Act (gaming licence duty),

from the debtor at the relevant date and which became due within the period of 12 months next before that date.

5A. The amount of any excise duty on beer which is due at the relevant date from the debtor and which became due within a period of 6 months next before that date.

5B. Any amount which is due by way of lottery duty from the debtor at the relevant date and which became due within the period of 12 months next before that date.

Category 3: Social security contributions

6. All sums which on the relevant date are due from the debtor on account of Class 1 or Class 2 contributions under the Social Security Contributions and Benefits Act 1992 or the Social Security (Northern Ireland) Act 1975 and which became due from the debtor in the 12 months next before the relevant date.

7. All sums which on the relevant date have been assessed on and are due from the debtor on account of Class 4 contributions under either of those Acts of 1975, being sums which—

(a) are due to the Commissioners of Inland Revenue (rather than to the Secretary of State or a Northern Ireland department), and
(b) are assessed on the debtor up to 5th April next before the relevant date,

but not exceeding, in the whole, any one year's assessment.

Category 4: Contributions to occupational pension schemes, etc.

8. Any sum which is owed by the debtor and is a sum to which Schedule 4 to the Pensions Schemes Act 1993 applies (contributions to occupational pension schemes and state scheme premiums).

Category 5: Remuneration, etc., of employees

9. So much of any amount which—

(a) is owed by the debtor to a person who is or has been an employee of the debtor, and
(b) is payable by way of remuneration in respect of the whole or any part of the period of 4 months next before the relevant date,

as does not exceed so much as may be prescribed by order made by the Secretary of State.

10. An amount owed by way of accrued holiday remuneration, in respect of any period of employment before the relevant date, to a person whose employment by the debtor has been terminated, whether before, on or after that date.

11. So much of any sum owed in respect of money advanced for the purpose as has been applied for the payment of a debt which, if it had not been paid, would have been a debt falling within paragraph 9 or 10.

12. So much of any amount which—

(a) is ordered (whether before or after the relevant date) to be paid by the debtor under the Reserve Forces (Safeguard of Employment) Act 1985, and
(b) is so ordered in respect of a default made by the debtor before that date in the discharge of his obligations under that Act,

as does not exceed such amount as may be prescribed by order made by the Secretary of State.

Interpretation for Category 5

13.—(1) For the purpose of paragraphs 9 to 12, a sum is payable by the debtor to a person by way of remuneration in respect of any period if—

(a) it is paid as wages or salary (whether payable for time or for piece work or earned wholly or partly by way of commission) in respect of services rendered to the debtor in that period, or
(b) it is an amount falling within the following sub-paragraph and is payable by the debtor in respect of that period.

(2) An amount falls within this sub-paragraph if it is—

(a) a guarantee payment under section 12(1) of the Employment Protection (Consolidation) Act 1978 (employee without work to do for a day or part of a day);
(b) remuneration on suspension on medical grounds under section 19 of that Act or remuneration on suspension on maternity grounds under section 47 of that Act;
(c) any payment for time off under [section 31(3) or 31A(4) of that Act (looking for work, etc; ante-natal care) or under section 169 of the Trade Union and Labour Relations (Consolidation) Act 1992 (trade union duties)]; or
(d) remuneration under a protective award made by an industrial tribunal under [section 189 of the latter Act] (redundancy dismissal with compensation).

14.—(1) This paragraph relates to a case in which a person's employment has been terminated by or in consequence of his employer going into liquidation or being adjudged bankrupt or (his employer being a company not in liquidation) by or in consequence of—

(a) a receiver being appointed as mentioned in section 40 of this Act (debenture-holders secured by floating charge), or
(b) the appointment of a receiver under section 53(6) or 54(5) of this Act (Scottish company with property subject to floating charge), or
(c) the taking of possession by debenture-holders (so secured), as mentioned in section 196 of the Companies Act.

(2) For the purposes of paragraphs 9 to 12, holiday remuneration is deemed to have accrued to that person in respect of any period of employment if, by virtue of his contract of employment or of any enactment that remuneration would have accrued in respect of that period if his employment had continued until he became entitled to be allowed the holiday.

(3) The reference in sub-paragraph (2) to any enactment includes an order or direction made under an enactment.

15. Without prejudice to paragraphs 13 and 14—

(a) any remuneration payable by the debtor to a person in respect of a period of holiday or of absence from work through sickness or other good cause is deemed to be wages or (as the case may be) salary in respect of services rendered to the debtor in that period, and
(b) references here and in those paragraphs to remuneration in respect of a period of holiday include any sums which, if they had been paid, would have been treated for the purposes of the enactments relating to social security as earnings in respect of that period.

Category 6: Levies on coal and steel production

15A. Any sums due at the relevant date from the debtor in respect of:

(a) the levies on the production of coal and steel referred to in Articles 49 and 50 of the ECSC Treaty, or
(b) any surcharge for delay provided for in Article 50(3) of that Treaty and Article 6 of Decision 3/52 of the High Authority of the Coal and Steel Community.

Orders

16. An order under paragraph 9 or 12—

(a) may contain such transitional provisions as may appear to the Secretary of State necessary or expedient;
(b) shall be made by statutory instrument subject to annulment in pursuance of a resolution of either House of Parliament.

APPENDIX V

Meaning of "associate"

INSOLVENCY ACT 1986, s.435

PART XVIII

INTERPRETATION

435.—For the purposes of this Act any question whether a person is an associate of another person is to be determined in accordance with the following provisions of this section (any provision that a person is an associate of another person being taken to mean that they are associates of each other).

(2) A person is an associate of an individual if that person is the individual's husband or wife, or is a relative, or the husband or wife of a relative, of the individual's husband or wife.

(3) A person is an associate of any person with whom he is in partnership, and of the husband or wife or a relative of any individual with whom he is in partnership: and a Scottish firm is an associate of any person who is a member of the firm.

(4) A person is an associate of any person whom he employs or by whom he is employed.

(5) A person in his capacity as trustee of a trust other than—

(a) a trust arising under any of the second Group of Parts or the Bankruptcy (Scotland) Act 1985, or
(b) a pension scheme or an employees' share scheme (within the meaning of the Companies Act).

is an associate of another person if the beneficiaries of the trust include, or the terms of the trust confer a power that may be exercised for the benefit of, that other person or an associate of that other person.

(6) A company is an associate of another company—

(a) if the same person has control of both, or a person has control of one and persons who are his associates, or he and persons who are his associates, have control of the other, or
(b) if a group of two or more persons has control of each company, and the groups either consist of the same persons or could be regarded as consisting of the same persons by treating (in one or more cases) a member of either group as replaced by a person of whom he is an associate.

(7) A company is an associate of another person if that person has control of it or if that person and persons who are his associates together have control of it.

(8) For the purposes of this section a person is a relative of an individual if he is that individual's brother, sister, uncle, aunt, nephew, niece, lineal ancestor or lineal descendant, treating—

(a) any relationship of the half blood as a relationship of the whole blood and the stepchild or adopted child of any person as his child, and
(b) an illegitimate child as the legitimate child of his mother and reputed father;

and references in this section to a husband or wife include a former husband or wife and a reputed husband or wife.

(9) For the purposes of this section any director or other officer of a company is to be treated as employed by that company.

(10) For the purposes of this section a person is to be taken as having control of a company if—

(a) the directors of the company or of another company which has control of it (or any of them) are accustomed to act in accordance with his directions or instructions, or
(b) be entitled to exercise, or control the exercise of, one third or more of the voting power at any general meeting of the company or of another company which has control of it;

and where two or more persons together satisfy either of the above conditions, they are to be taken as having control of the company.

(11) In this section "company" includes any body corporate (whether incorporated in Great Britain or elsewhere); and references to directors and other officers of a company and to voting power at any general meeting of a company have effect with any necessary modifications.

APPENDIX VI

Closing Check List

1. Obtain written confirmation from O.R. that there are no outstanding sums due to him for fees, disbursements or costs of anyone employed by him and no further charges will arise.
2. Obtain confirmation from D.T.I. insolvency section that all sums due to them have been charged to the estate and no further charges will arise.
3. Obtain written confirmation from any interim receiver, previous trustee or special manager that all fees, costs and expenses due to them or any person employed by them have been paid and they have no further claim on the estate.
4. Check costs of petition have been paid in full.
5. Check that any allowance for costs of statement of affairs has been paid.
6. Obtain confirmation from any solicitor, agent or other person employed by you that they have been paid and have no further charges to render.
7. Confirm with your file that any trading liabilities incurred by you have been paid.
8. Confirm any post appointment taxation has been agreed and paid including tax on any profits during trading, capital gains on sale, P.A.Y.E. and National Insurance deductions and not forgetting the amount due on final V.A.T. returns.
9. Confirm your own out of pocket expenses, travelling, postages, stationery, telephone and other miscellaneous items have been paid and ensure you retain sufficient funds to cover costs to be incurred.
10. Most important—trustee's own remuneration—check this has been drawn or adequate provision made.
11. Pay final dividend to creditors.
12. Consider application for a charge on the bankrupt's home, is not realised (ss.313, 332).
13. Send list of unclaimed dividends to D.T.I.
14. Summon final meeting (I.A. 1986, s.331 and I.R. 6.137).
15. Give notice to the court (copy to O.R.) that final meeting held.
16. If creditors oppose release, apply to D.T.I.
17. Return books and papers to O.R.

APPENDIX VII

Practice Notes and Directions

1. Practice note (Bankruptcy: Individual Voluntary Arrangements: Orders without attendance) (No. 1/91).
2. Practice note (Bankruptcy: Certificate of Debt) (No. 1/86).
3. Practice note (Bankruptcy: Petition) (No. 3/86).
4. Practice note (Bankruptcy: substituted service) (No. 4/86).
5. Practice note (Bankruptcy: statutory demand) (No. 5/86).
6. Practice note (Bankruptcy: statutory demand: setting aside) (No. 1/87).
7. Practice note: Preparation of affidavits and exhibits.

1. Practice Note (Bankruptcy: Individual Voluntary Arrangements: Orders without Attendance)

(No. 1/91)

---

1. In suitable cases the High Court registrars will normally be prepared to make orders under Part VIII of the Insolvency Act 1986 (individual voluntary arrangements) without the attendance of either party, provided there is no bankruptcy order in existence and (so far as is known) no pending petition. The cases are:–
   (1) A 14-day interim order with the application adjourned 14 days for consideration of the nominee's report, where the papers are in order and the nominee's signed consent to act includes a waiver of notice of the application or a consent by the nominee to the making of an interim order without attendance.
   (2) A standard order on consideration of the nominee's report, extending the interim order to a date 7 weeks after the date of the proposed meeting, directing the meeting to be summoned and adjourning to a date about 3 weeks after the meeting. Such an order may be made without attendance if the nominee's report has been delivered to the Court and complies with s.256(1) of the Insolvency Act 1986 and rule 5.10(2) and (3) of the Insolvency Rules 1986 and proposes a date for the meeting not less than 14 nor more than 28 days after the date of the "hearing".
   (3) A "concertina" order, combining orders as under (1) and (2) above. Such an order may be made without attendance if the initial application for an interim order is accompanied by a report of the nominee and the conditions set out in (1) and (2) above are satisfied.
   (4) A final order on consideration of the chairman's report. Such an order may be made without attendance if the chairman's report has been filed and complies with rule 5.22(2). The order will record the effect of the chairman's report and discharge the interim order.
2. Provided that the conditions as under 1(2) and (4) above are satisfied and that the appropriate report has been lodged with the court in due time the parties need not attend or be represented on the adjourned hearing for consideration of the nominee's report or of the chairman's report (as the case may be) unless they are notified by the court that attendance is required. Sealed copies of the order made (in all four cases as above) will be posted by the court to the applicant or his solicitor and to the nominee.
3. The procedure outlined above is designed to save time and costs but is not intended to discourage attendance.
4. Practitioners are reminded that whenever a document is filed the correct case number, code and year (eg 123/10/92) should appear at the top right-hand corner. A note should be attached stating the date and time of the next hearing (if any).

Chief Bankruptcy Registrar

1991

---

2. Practice Note (Bankruptcy: Certificate of Debt)

(No. 1/86)

On the hearing of a petition for a bankruptcy order, to satisfy the court that the debt on which the petition is founded has not been paid or secured or compounded for the court will normally accept as sufficient a certificate signed by the person representing the petitioning creditor in the following form:

> "I certify that I have/my firm has made inquiries of the petitioning creditor(s) within the last business day prior to the hearing/ adjourned hearing and to the best of my knowledge and belief the debt on which the petition is founded is still due and owing and has not been paid or secured or compounded for (save as to)
>
> "Signed .... Dated ...."

For the convenience of practitioners this Certificate will be printed on the attendance slips. It will be filed after the hearing. A fresh certificate will be required on each adjourned hearing.

This practice note will take effect on December 29, 1986, when the Insolvency Act 1986 and Insolvency Rules 1986 come into effect, in respect of all petitions heard on or after that date whether or not presented and filed earlier.

November 25, 1986

3. Practice Note (Bankruptcy: Petition)

(No. 3/86)

To help practitioners to complete the new forms of a creditor's bankruptcy petition, attention is drawn to the following points:

1. The petition does not require dating, signing or witnessing.

2. In the title it is only necessary to recite the debtor's name e.g. Re John William Smith or Re J. W. Smith (male). Any alias or trading name will appear in the body of the petition. This also applies to all other statutory forms other than those which require the "full title."

3. Where the petition is based on a statutory demand, only the debt claimed in the demand may be included in the petition, [*except that interest or other charges which have accrued since the date of the demand to the date of the petition may be added: see the Insolvency Rules 1986, rule 6.8–(1)(c), read with rule 6.1(4).*]

4. When completing paragraph 2 of the petition, attention is drawn to rule 6.8–(1)(*a*) to (*c*), particularly where the "aggregate sum" is made up of a number of debts.

5. Date of service of the statutory demand (paragraph 4 of the petition):

(a) In the case of personal service, the date of service as set out in the affidavit of service should be recited and whether service is effected *before/after* 16.00 hours on Monday to Friday or *before/after* 12.00 hours on Saturday: see R.S.C., Ord. 65, r. 7.

(b) In the case of substituted service (otherwise than by advertisement), the date alleged in the affidavit of service should be recited. (As to the date alleged see *Practice Note (Bankruptcy: Substituted Service)* [1987] 1 W.L.R. 82.)

(c) In the strictly limited case of substituted service by advertisement under rule 6.3 of the Insolvency Rules 1986, the date to be alleged is the date of the advertisement's appearance or, as the case may be, its first appearance: see rules 6.3–(3) and 6.11–(8) of the Insolvency Rules 1986.

6. There is no need to include in the preamble to or at the end of the petition details of the person authorised to present the petition.

7. Certificates at the end of the petition:

(a) The period of search for prior petitions has been reduced to *three* years.

(b) Where a statutory demand is based wholly or in part on a county court judgment, the following certificate, which replaces the affidavit of county court search, is to be added:

> "I/We certify that on the day of 19 I/We attended on the County Court and was/were informed by an officer of the Court that no money had been paid into Court in the action or matter v. Plaint No. pursuant to the Statutory demand."

This certificate will not be required when the demand also requires payment of a separate debt, not based on a county court judgment, the amount of which exceeds the bankruptcy level (at present £750).

8. Deposit on petition:

The deposit will now be taken by the court and forwarded to the official receiver. The petition fee and deposit should be handed to the Supreme Court Accounts Office, Fee Stamping Rooms, who will record the receipt and will impress two entries on the original petition, one in respect of the court fee and the other in respect of the deposit. Cheque(s) for the whole amount should be made payable to "H.M. Paymaster General."

December 18, 1986

---

4. Practice Note (Bankruptcy: Substituted Service)

(No. 4/86)

Statutory demands

1. The creditor is under an obligation to do all that is reasonable to bring the statutory demand to the debtor's attention and, if practicable, to cause personal service to be effected. Where it is not possible to effect prompt personal service, service may be effected by other means such as first class post or insertion through a letter box.

2. Advertisement can only be used as a means of substituted service where (a) the demand is based on a judgment or order of any court; (b) the debtor has absconded or is keeping out of the way with a view to avoiding service; and (c) there is no real prospect of the sum due being recovered by execution or other process.

As there is no statutory form of advertisement, the court will accept an advertisement in the following form:

STATUTORY DEMAND

(Debt for liquidated sum payable immediately following a Judgment or Order of the Court)

To (block letters)
of

TAKE NOTICE that a Statutory Demand has been issued by
Name of creditor
Address

The creditor demands payment of £ the amount now due on a Judgment/Order of the (High Court of Justice Division) (. . . County Court) dated the day of 19

The Statutory Demand is an important document and it is deemed to have been served on you on the date of the first appearance of this advertisement. You *must* deal with this demand within 21 days of the service upon you or you could be made bankrupt and your property and goods taken away from you. If you are in any doubt as to your position, you should seek advice *immediately* from a solicitor or your nearest Citizen's Advice Bureau.

The Statutory Demand can be obtained or is available for inspection and collection from:

Name
Address

(Solicitor for) the creditor
Tel. No. Reference

You have only 21 days from the date of the first appearance of this advertisement before the creditor may present a bankruptcy petition.

3. In all cases where substituted service is effected, the creditor must have taken all those steps which would suffice to justify the court making an order for substituted service of a petition. The steps to be taken to obtain an order for substituted service are set out below. Practitioners are reminded that failure to comply with the requirements of this practice note may result in the court declining to file the petition: rule 6.11(5)(*a*) of the Insolvency Rules 1986.

Order for substituted service of a bankruptcy petition

4. In most cases, the following evidence will suffice to justify an order for substituted service:

(a) One personal call at the residence and place of business of the debtor where both are known or at either of such places as is known. Where it is known that the debtor has more than one residential or business address, personal calls should be made at all addresses.

(b) Should the creditor fail to effect service, a first class prepaid letter should be written to the debtor referring to the call(s) the purpose of the same and the failure to meet with the debtor, adding that a further call will be made for the same purpose on the day of 19 at hours at (place). At least two business days notice should be given of the appointment and copies of the letter sent to all known addresses of the debtor. The appointment letter should also state that (i) in the event of the time and place not being convenient, the debtor is to name some other time and place reasonably convenient for the purpose; (ii) (statutory demands) if the debtor fails to keep the appointment the creditor proposes to serve the debtor by [advertisement] [post] [insertion through a letter box] or as the case may be, and that, in the event of a bankruptcy petition being presented, the court will be asked to treat such service as service of the demand on the debtor; (iii) (petitions) if the debtor fails to keep the appointment, application will be made to the court for an order for substituted service either by advertisement, or in such other manner as the court may think fit.

(c) In attending any appointment made by letter, inquiry should be made as to whether the debtor has received all letters left for him. If the debtor is away, inquiry should also be made as to whether or not letters are being forwarded to an address within the jurisdiction (England and Wales) or elsewhere.

(d) If the debtor is represented by a solicitor, an attempt should be made to arrange an appointment for personal service through such solicitor. Practitioners are reminded that the rules provide for a solicitor accepting service of a statutory demand on behalf of his client but there is no similar provision in respect of service of a bankruptcy petition.

(e) The supporting affidavit should deal with all the above matters including all relevant facts as to the debtor's whereabouts and whether the appointment letter(s) have been returned.

5. Where the court makes an order for substituted service by first class ordinary post, the order will normally provide that service be deemed to be effected on the seventh day after posting. Practitioners serving a statutory demand by post may consider using the same method of calculating service.

December 18, 1986

---

5. Practice Note (Bankruptcy: Statutory Demand)

(No. 5/86)

---

1. Rule 6.11(3) of the Insolvency Rules 1986 provides that, if the statutory demand has been served personally, the affidavit of service must be made by the person who effected that service. Rules 6.11(4) provides that, if service of the demand (however effected) has been acknowledged in writing, the affidavit of service must be made by the creditor or by a person acting on his behalf. Rule 6.11(5) provides that, if neither paragraphs (3) or (4) apply, the affidavit msut be made by a person having direct knowledge of the means adopted for serving the demand.

2. Form 6.11 (affidavit of personal service of the statutory demand).

This form should only be used where the demand has been served personally and acknowledged in writing: rule 6.11(4). If the demand has not been acknowledged in writing, the affidavit should be made by the process server and paragraphs 2 and 3 (part) of Form 6.11 should be omitted: rule 6.11(3).

3. Form 6.12 (affidavit of substituted service of the statutory demand).

This form can be used whether or not service of the demand has been acknowledged in writing. Paragraphs 4 and 5 (part) provide for the alternatives. Practitioners are reminded, however, that the appropriate person to make the affidavit may not be the same in both cases. If the demand has been acknowledged in writing, the appropriate person is the creditor or a person acting on his behalf. If the demand has not been acknowledged, that person must be someone having direct knowledge of the means adopted for serving the demand.

Practitioners may find it more convenient to allow process servers to carry out the necessary investigation whilst reserving to themselves the service of the demand. In these circumstances paragraph 1 should be deleted and the following paragraph substituted: "1. Attempts have been made to serve the demand, full details of which are set out in the accompanying affidavit of ..."

December 31, 1986

---

6. Practice Note (Bankruptcy: Statutory Demand: Setting Aside)

(No. 1/87)

Application to set aside statutory demand

1. The application (Form 6.4) and affidavit in support (Form 6.5) exhibiting a copy of the statutory demand must be filed in court within 18 days of service of the statutory demand on the debtor. Where service is effected by advertisement in a newspaper the period of 18 days is calculated from the date of the first appearance of the advertisement: see *Practice Note (Bankruptcy: Substituted Service),* [1987] 1 W.L.R. 82 [*see (No. 4/86), supra*]. Three copies of each document must be lodged with the application to enable the court to serve notice of the hearing date on the applicant, the creditor and the person named in Part B of the statutory demand.

2. Where, to avoid expense, copies of the documents are not lodged with the application, any order of the registrar fixing a venue is conditional upon copies of the documents being lodged on the next business day after the registrar's order otherwise the application will be deemed to have been dismissed.

3. Where the statutory demand is based on a judgment or order, the court will not at this stage go behind the judgment or order and inquire into the validity of the debt nor, as a general rule, will it adjourn the application to await the result of an application to set aside the judgment or order.

4. When the debtor (a) claims to have a counterclaim, set off or cross demand (whether or not he could have raised it in the action in which the judgment or order was obtained) which equals or exceeds the amount of the debt or debts specified in the statutory demand or (b) disputes the debt (not being a debt subject to a judgment or order) the court will normally set aside the statutory demand if, in its opinion, on the evidence there is a genuine triable issue.

Applications for an extension of time to apply to set aside a statutory demand

5. Each term two judges of the Chancery Division will sit to hear insolvency cases, one of whom ("the bankruptcy judge") will be primarily concerned to hear cases affecting individual debtors.

After the expiration of 18 days from the date of service of the statutory demand, the debtor must apply for an extension of time if he wishes to apply to set aside the demand. The application for extension of time and (if necessary) to restrain the presentation of a bankruptcy petition should be made to the bankruptcy judge, but in cases of urgency and where the bankruptcy judge is not available the application may be made to the judge hearing ordinary motions. (This requirement will appear in a practice direction to be published.)

Paragraphs 1 and 2 of Form 6.5 (affidavit in support of application to set aside statutory demand) should be used in support of the application for extension of time with the following additional paragraphs:

> "3. That to the best of my knowledge and belief the creditor(s) named in the demand has/have not presented a petition against me.
> "4. That the reasons for my failure to apply to set aside the demand within 18 days after service are as follows: ...
> "5. Unless restrained by injunction the creditor(s) may present a bankruptcy petition against me."

(The fee on the application will be £15).

January 6, 1987

---

7. Practice Note: Affidavit and Exhibits

Practitioners are reminded of the rules relating to the title of and preparation of affidavits and exhibits:

1. Every affidavit must be entitled in the cause or matter **[RSC, Ord. 41, r. 1(1)]**
2. Every affidavit must be bound in book form **[RSC, Ord. 41, r. 1(5)]**
3. Binding must not be with thick plastic strips or anything which hampers filing **[Practice Direction (Evidence: Documents) [1983] 1 W.L.R. 922]**
4. Marking each affidavit and each exhibit must be marked as follows:

   At the top right hand corner of the first page of every affidavit, and also on the backsheet, there must be written in clear permanent dark blue or black marking:
   (i) the party on whose behalf it is filed
   (ii) the initials and surname of the deponent
   (iii) the number of the affidavit in relation to the deponent

(iv) the identifying initials and number of each exhibit to the affidavit; and

(v) the date when sworn. *For example:* 2nd Dft: E. W. Jones: 3rd: 24.7.82. E. W. J. 3, 4 and 5.

The text of the above Practice Direction is fully set out in the *Supreme Court Practice 1997* (the *White Book*) at p. 708, para. [41/11/2].

The Court may decline to read any affidavit and/or exhibits not properly prepared.

January 1997

APPENDIX VIII

Insolvency (Northern Ireland) Order 1989

TABLE OF DERIVATIONS AND CORRESPONDENCES

In this Table the following abbreviations are used:

C.O. = Companies (Northern Ireland) Order 1986 (N.I.6)
I.A. = Insolvency Act 1986 (c.45)
D.O.A. = Deeds of Arrangement Act 1914 (c.47)

Article of Insolvency (N.I.) Order 1989	Title of Provision	Derivation	Corresponding Provision of Insolvency Act 1986
PART VIII: CHAPTER 1: DEEDS OF ARRANGEMENT			
209	Deeds of arrangement to which this Chapter applies	D.O.A., ss.1, 2, 30(2)	
REGISTRATION OF DEEDS OF ARRANGEMENT			
210	Registrar and deputy registrar	New provision	
211	Mode of registration	D.O.A., s.5	
212	Form of register	D.O.A., s.6	
213	Rectification of register	D.O.A., s.7	
AVOIDANCE OF DEEDS OF ARRANGEMENT			
214	Avoidance of unregistered deeds of arrangement	D.O.A., s.2.	
215	Avoidance of deeds of arrangement unless assented to by a majority of creditors	D.O.A., s.3	
216	Deeds otherwise void or voidable	D.O.A., s.24(3) (part)	
PROVISIONS AS TO TRUSTEES			
217	Notice to creditors of avoidance of deed	D.O.A., s.20	
218	Trustee acting when deed of arrangement void	D.O.A., s.12	
219	Protection of trustees under void deeds	D.O.A., s.19	
220	Payment of expenses incurred by trustees	D.O.A., s.21	
221	Security by trustee	D.O.A., s.11(1), (2), (5)	
222	Transmission of accounts	D.O.A., ss.13(1), (2) (part), 14	
223	Preferential payment to creditor	D.O.A., s.17	
MISCELLANEOUS			
224	Applications to the High Court	D.O.A., s.23	

Article of Insolvency (N.I.) Order 1989	Title of Provision	Derivation	Corresponding Provision of Insolvency Act 1986
225	Inspection of register, etc., certified copies and evidence	D.O.A., ss.9 (part), 13(3), 25 (part)	

PART VIII: CHAPTER II: VOLUNTARY ARRANGEMENTS

MORATORIUM FOR INSOLVENT DEBTORS

226	Interim order of High Court	I.A., s.252	s.252
227	Application for interim order	I.A., s.253	s.253
228	Effect of application	I.A., s.254	s.254
229	Cases in which interim order can be made	I.A., s.255	s.255
230	Nominee's report on debtor's proposal	I.A., s.256	s.256
231	Summoning of creditors' meeting	I.A., s.257	s.257

CONSIDERATION AND IMPLEMENTATION OF DEBTOR'S PROPOSAL

232	Decisions of creditors' meeting	I.A., s.258	s.258
233	Report of decisions to High Court	I.A., s.259	s.259
234	Effect of approval	I.A., s.260	s.260
235	Effect where debtor an undischarged bankrupt	I.A., s.261	s.261
236	Challenge of meeting's decision	I.A., s.262	s.262
237	Implementation and supervision of approved voluntary arrangement	I.A., s.263	s.263

PART IX: CHAPTER 1: BANKRUPTCY PETITIONS; BANKRUPTCY ORDERS

PRELIMINARY

238	Who may present a bankruptcy petition	I.A., s.264	s.264
239	Conditions to be satisfied in respect of debtor	I.A., s.265	s.265
240	Other preliminary conditions	I.A., s.266	s.266

CREDITOR'S PETITION

241	Grounds of creditor's petition	I.A., s.267	s.267
242	Definition of "inability to pay", etc., the statutory demand	I.A., s.268	s.268
243	Creditor with security	I.A., s.269	s.269
244	Expedited petition	I.A., s.270	s.270
245	Proceedings on creditor's petition	I.A., s.271	s.271

DEBTOR'S PETITION

246	Grounds of debtor's petition	I.A., s.272	s.272
247	Appointment of insolvency practitioner by the High Court	I.A., s.273	s.273
248	Action on report of insolvency practitioner	I.A., s.274	s.274
249	Summary administration	I.A., s.275	s.275

OTHER CASES FOR SPECIAL CONSIDERATION

250	Default in connection with voluntary arrangement	I.A., s.276	s.276
251	Petition in respect of a solicitor	Unique N.I. provision	

Article of Insolvency (N.I.) Order 1989	Title of Provision	Derivation	Corresponding Provision of Insolvency Act 1986
COMMENCEMENT AND DURATION OF BANKRUPTCY: DISCHARGE			
252	Commencement and continuation	I.A., s.278	s.278
253	Duration	I.A., s.279	s.279
254	Discharge by order of the High Court	I.A., s.280	s.280
255	Effect of discharge	I.A., s.281	s.281
256	Power of High Court to annul bankruptcy order	I.A., s.282	s.282
PART IX: CHAPTER II: PROTECTION OF BANKRUPT'S ESTATE AND INVESTIGATION OF HIS AFFAIRS			
257	Restriction on dispositions of property	I.A., s.284	s.284
258	Restrictions on proceedings and remedies	I.A., s.285	s.285
259	Power to appoint interim receiver	I.A., s.286	s.286
260	Receivership pending appointment of trustee	I.A., s.287	s.287
261	Statement of affairs	I.A., s.288	s.288
262	Investigatory duties of Official Receiver	I.A., s.289	s.289
263	Public examination of bankrupt	I.A., s.290	s.290
264	Duties of bankrupt in relation to Official Receiver	I.A., s.291	s.291
PART IX: CHAPTER III: TRUSTEES IN BANKRUPTCY			
TENURE OF OFFICE AS TRUSTEE			
265	Power to make appointments	I.A., s.292	s.292
266	Summoning of meeting to appoint first trustee	I.A., s.293	s.293
267	Power to call creditors' requisition meeting	I.A., s.294	s.294
268	Failure of meeting to appoint trustee	I.A., s.295	s.295
269	Appointment of trustee by Department	I.A., s.296	s.296
270	Special cases	I.A., s.297	s.297
271	Removal of trustee; vacation of office	I.A., s.298	s.298
272	Release of trustee	I.A., s.299	s.299
273	Vacancy in office as trustee	I.A., s.300	s.300
CONTROL OF TRUSTEE			
274	Creditors' committee	I.A., s.301	s.301
275	Exercise by Department of functions of creditors' committee	I.A., s.302	s.302
276	General control of trustee by the High Court	I.A. s.303	s.303
277	Liability of trustee	I.A., s.304	s.304
PART IX: CHAPTER IV: ADMINISTRATION BY TRUSTEE			
PRELIMINARY			
278	General functions of trustee	I.A., s.305	s.305

Article of Insolvency (N.I.) Order 1989	Title of Provision	Derivation	Corresponding Provision of Insolvency Act 1986
ACQUISITION, CONTROL AND REALISATION OF BANKRUPT'S ESTATE			
279	Vesting of bankrupt's estate in trustee	I.A., s.306	s.306
280	After-acquired property	I.A., s.307	s.307
281	Vesting in trustee of certain items of excess value	I.A., s.308	s.308
282	Time-limit for notice under article 280 or 281	I.A., s.309	s.309
283	Income payments order	I.A., s.310	s.310
284	Acquisition by trustee of control	I.A., s.311	s.311
285	Obligation to surrender control to trustee	I.A., s.312	s.312
286	Charge on bankrupt's home	I.A., s.313	s.313
287	Powers of trustee	I.A., s.314	s.314
DISCLAIMER OF ONEROUS PROPERTY			
288	Disclaimer (general power)	I.A., s.315	s.315
289	Notice requiring trustee's decision	I.A., s.316	s.316
290	Disclaimer of leaseholds	I.A., s.317	s.317
291	Disclaimer of dwelling-house	I.A., s.318	s.318
292	Disclaimer of land subject to rent-charge	I.A., s.319	s.319
293	High Court order vesting disclaimed property	I.A., s.320	s.320
294	Order under article 293 in respect of leaseholds	I.A., s.321	s.321
DISTRIBUTION OF BANKRUPT'S ESTATE			
295	Proof of debts	I.A., s.322	s.322
296	Mutual credit and set-off	I.A., s.323	s.323
297	Distribution by means of dividend	I.A., s.324	s.324
298	Claims by unsatisfied creditors	I.A., s.325	s.325
299	Distribution of property *in specie*	I.A., s.326	s.326
300	Priority of debts	I.A., s.328	s.328
301	Preferential charge on goods distrained	I.A., s.347 (3), (4)	s.347 (3), (4)
302	Debts to spouse	I.A., s.329	s.329
303	Final distribution	I.A., s.330	s.330
304	Final meeting	I.A., s.331	s.331
305	Saving for bankrupt's home	I.A., s.332	s.332
SUPPLEMENTAL			
306	Duties of bankrupt in relation to trustee	I.A., s.333	s.333
307	Stay of distribution in case of second bankruptcy	I.A., s.334	s.334
308	Adjustment between earlier and later bankruptcy estates	I.A., s.335	s.335

PART IX: CHAPTER V: EFFECT OF BANKRUPTCY ON CERTAIN RIGHTS, TRANSACTIONS, ETC.

Article	Title of Provision	Derivation	Corresponding Provision
RIGHTS OF OCCUPATION			
309	Rights of occupation, etc., of bankrupt's spouse	I.A., s.336	s.336
310	Rights of occupation of bankrupt	I.A., s.337	s.337
311	Payments in respect of premises occupied by bankrupt	I.A., s.338	s.338

Article of Insolvency (N.I.) Order 1989	Title of Provision	Derivation	Corresponding Provision of Insolvency Act 1986
ADJUSTMENT OF PRIOR TRANSACTIONS, ETC.			
312	Transactions at an undervalue	I.A., s.339	s.339
313	Preferences	I.A., s.340	s.340
314	"Relevant time" under articles 312, 313	I.A., s.341	s.341
315	Orders under articles 312, 313	I.A., s.342	s.342
316	Extortionate credit transactions	I.A., s.343	s.343
317	Avoidance of general assignment of book debts	I.A., s.344	s.344
318	Contracts to which bankrupt is a party	I.A., s.345	s.345
319	Apprenticeships, etc.	I.A., s.348	s.348
320	Unenforceability of liens on books, etc.	I.A., s.349	s.349

PART IX: CHAPTER VI: BANKRUPTCY OFFENCES

Article of Insolvency (N.I.) Order 1989	Title of Provision	Derivation	Corresponding Provision of Insolvency Act 1986
PRELIMINARY			
321	Scheme of this Chapter	I.A., s.350	s.350
322	Definitions for the purposes of this Chapter	I.A., s.351	s.351
323	Defence of innocent intention	I.A., s.352	s.352
WRONGDOING BY THE BANKRUPT BEFORE AND AFTER BANKRUPTCY			
324	Non-disclosure	I.A., s.353	s.353
325	Concealment of property	I.A., s.354	s.354
326	Concealment of books and papers; falsification	I.A., s.355	s.355
327	False statements	I.A., s.356	s.356
328	Fraudulent disposal of property	I.A., s.357	s.357
329	Absconding	I.A., s.358	s.358
330	Fraudulent dealing with property obtained on credit	I.A., s.359	s.359
331	Obtaining credit; engaging in business	I.A., s.360	s.360
332	Failure to keep proper accounts of business	I.A., s.361	s.361
333	Gambling	I.A., s.362	s.362

PART IX: CHAPTER VII: POWERS OF HIGH COURT IN BANKRUPTCY

Article of Insolvency (N.I.) Order 1989	Title of Provision	Derivation	Corresponding Provision of Insolvency Act 1986
334	General control of High Court	I.A., s.363	s.363
335	Power of arrest	I.A., s.364	s.364
336	Seizure of bankrupt's property	I.A., s.365	s.365
337	Inquiry into bankrupt's dealings and property	I.A., s.366	s.366
338	High Court's enforcement powers under article 337	I.A., s.367	s.367
339	Provision corresponding to article 337, where interim receiver appointed	I.A., s.368	s.368
340	Order for production of documents by Inland Revenue	I.A., s.369	s.369
341	Power to appoint special manager	I.A., s.370	s.370
342	Re-direction of bankrupt's letters, etc.	I.A., s.371	s.371

Article of Insolvency (N.I.) Order 1989	Title of Provision	Derivation	Corresponding Provision of Insolvency Act 1986

PART X: INDIVIDUAL INSOLVENCY: GENERAL PROVISIONS

343	Supplies of water, electricity, etc.	I.A., s.372	s.372
344	Time limits	I.A., s.376	s.376
345	Formal defects	I.A., s.377	s.377

PART XII: INSOLVENCY PRACTITIONERS AND THEIR QUALIFICATIONS

RESTRICTIONS ON UNQUALIFIED PERSONS ACTING AS LIQUIDATOR, TRUSTEE IN BANKRUPTCY, ETC.

348	Acting as insolvency practitioner without qualification	I.A., s.389	s.389

THE REQUISITE QUALIFICATION, AND THE MEANS OF ACHIEVING IT

349	Persons not qualified to act as insolvency practitioners	I.A., s.390	s.390
350	Recognised professional bodies	I.A., s.391	s.391
351	Authorisation by competent authority	I.A., s.392	s.392
352	Grant, refusal and withdrawal of authorisation	I.A., s.393	s.393
353	Notices	I.A., s.394	s.394
354	Right to make representations	I.A., s.395	s.395

PART XIII: PUBLIC ADMINISTRATION

OFFICIAL RECEIVERS

355	Appointment, etc., of Official Receivers	I.A., s.399(6) (part)	s.399
356	Functions and status of Official Receivers	I.A., s.400	s.400
357	Deputy Official Receivers	I.A., s.401 (1), (2)	s.401

INSOLVENCY ACCOUNT

358	Insolvency account	C.O., Art. 502(1), (2), (4), (5); I.A., 407(1)	ss.403–409

INSOLVENCY RULES

359	Insolvency Rules	C.O., Art. 613(1), (2) (part); I.A., ss.411, 412	ss.411, 412
360	Committee to review Rules under article 359	C.O., Art. 613(4), (5); I.A., s.413	s.413

FEES

361	Fees orders	C.O., Art. 613(6), (7); I.A., ss.414, 415	ss.414, 415

Article of Insolvency (N.I.) Order 1989	Title of Provision	Derivation	Corresponding Provision of Insolvency Act 1986
SPECIFICATION, INCREASE AND REDUCTION OF MONEY SUMS RELEVANT IN THE OPERATION OF THE ORDER			
362	Monetary limits	C.O., Art. 614(1) (part), (2); I.A., ss.416–418	ss.416–418
INSOLVENCY PRACTICE			
363	Regulations for purposes of Part XII	I.A., s.419	s.419
OTHER ORDER-MAKING POWERS			
364	Insolvent partnerships	I.A., s.420	s.420
365	Insolvent estates of deceased persons	I.A., s.421	s.421
366	Recognised banks, etc.	I.A., s.422	s.422
PART XIV: MISCELLANEOUS			
PROVISIONS AGAINST DEBT AVOIDANCE			
367	Transactions defrauding creditors	I.A., s.423	s.423
368	Those who may apply for an order under article 367	I.A., s.424	s.424
369	Provisions which may be made by order under article 367	I.A., s.425	s.425
DISQUALIFICATIONS, REVIEWS AND REPORTS			
370	Northern Ireland Assembly disqualification	I.A., s.427	s.427
371	Review, etc., by High Court of its orders	I.A. s.375(1)	s.375
372	Annual report	C.O., Art. 677	s.379
LEGAL PROCEEDINGS			
373	Prosecution and punishment of offences	C.O., Art. 678	s.430
374	Summary proceedings	C.O., Art. 679	s.431
375	Admissibility in evidence of statement of affairs, etc.	I.A., s.433	s.433
SUPPLEMENTAL			
376	Judicial notice of court documents	C.O., Art. 598	s.196
377	Exemption from stamp duty	C.O., Art. 591; I.A., ss.190, 378	ss.190, 378
378	Crown application	I.A., s.434	s.434
379	Transitional provisions and savings	I.A., s.437 (part)	s.437

Article of Insolvency (N.I.) Order 1989	Title of Provision	Derivation	Corresponding Provision of Insolvency Act 1986
380	Amendments of Industrial Relations (Northern Ireland) Order 1976	Insolvency Act 1985, s.218	
381	Other amendments	I.A., s.439 (1), (2) (part)	s.439
382	Repeals	I.A., s.438	s.438
SCHEDULES			
Schedule 3	Powers of trustee in bankruptcy	I.A., Sch. 5	Sch.5
Schedule 4	The categories of preferential debt	C.O., Sch. 18; I.A., Sch. 6	Sch.6
Schedule 6	Provisions capable of inclusion in individual insolvency rules	I.A., Sch. 9	Sch.9
Schedule 7	Punishment of offences under this Order	C.O., Sch. 23; I.A., Sch. 10	Sch.10
Schedule 8	Transitional provisions and savings	I.A., Sch. 11	Sch.11

APPENDIX IX

Inland Revenue Modification Sheet

(If any of the following modifications are not accepted then the Revenue vote must be taken as a rejection.)

1. All outstanding accounts, tax returns, and annual P35's—S/C35's (to the date of the meeting) and any other information or explanations required by the Inspector of Taxes must be provided within 3 months of the approval date so that any estimated liabilities can be adjusted for the benefit of other creditors and to enable the Revenue to lodge a final claim for the actual liability. If, within 6 months of the approval date the debtor has not co-operated in this respect the Supervisor will accept all estimated assessments from the Revenue for dividend purposes.
2. The Revenue's final claim in the arrangement will include tax assessed to April 5 following the date of the meeting and any PAYE/NIC liability to the relevant date.

   Post VA liability shall be paid in full IMMEDIATELY this becomes due and the Crown reserves the right to commence BY proceedings in respect of any post VA liability which remains unpaid.
3. If, during the currency of the arrangement any creditor obtains a bankruptcy order against the debtor the voluntary arrangement will be deemed to have failed and the Supervisor will IMMEDIATELY issue a certificate of non-compliance.
4. The Supervisor shall petition for a bankruptcy order IMMEDIATELY the debtor fails to comply with his obligations under the voluntary arrangement or fails to co-operate with the Supervisor.

   The Supervisor shall set aside sufficient funds for this purpose and such funds shall rank ahead of the Supervisors remuneration.
5. If any voluntary contribution falls 60 days in arrear or falls below the amount specified in the proposals accepted by creditors, this shall be taken as a failure of the arrangement and the Supervisor will petition for bankruptcy.
6. The Supervisor is to conduct a full review every 6 months of the debtors income/expenditure and obtain an increase in voluntary contributions of not less than 50 per cent of any rise in the debtors net income after provision for tax and NIC.
7. Full details of debtors income/expenditure is to be made available to the Inland Revenue, and any other creditor who may seek it, with the Supervisors annual report.
8. All claims will rank, in their respective classes, for dividend from the first dividend date after they have been lodged with and admitted by the Supervisor.
9. Where the Inland Revenue has not notified a final claim under the arrangement prior to payment of a dividend, the Supervisor is to calculate the dividend by reference to the Inland Revenue claim for voting purposes.
10. The Supervisor will secure creditors' interests in the matrimonial home, and any other property in which the debtor has a beneficial interest, by registering a caution with the Land Registry.
11. Should Supervisors fees exceed Official Receivers scale rates in bankruptcy, creditors approval must be sought before fees are drawn.
12. Should it become necessary, during the term of the arrangement to call a further creditors meeting then any resolutions passed must have a 75 per cent majority, in value, of creditors voting at the meeting.

13. Where creditors claims are met in full, statutory interest at 8 per cent shall be paid from the date the voluntary arrangement is approved, or any earlier a bankruptcy/winding up order to the date of payment so far as available funds will allow.
14. If, in order to achieve 100p in the £ to all creditors, the arrangement needs to be extended beyond 3 years then a meeting of creditors will be called to determine the terms and further duration of the arrangement, BUT full statutory interest will be chargeable from the original relevant date.
15. Any power of attorney or trust shall cease to be valid on the making of a bankruptcy/winding up order and the VA will be deemed to have failed.
16. Associated creditors claims shall be treated as deferred and only rank for dividend once unsecured claims have been satisfied.

APPENDIX X

Sections 175 and 328: Priority of expenses and debts

23. Sections 175 and 328(1) to (3) and (6) are modified so as to read as follows:

"Priority of expenses

175.—(1) The provisions of this section shall apply in a case where article 8 of the Insolvent Partnerships Order 1994 applies, as regards priority of expenses incurred by a responsible insolvency practitioner of an insolvent partnership, and of any insolvent member of that partnership against whom an insolvency order has been made.

(2) The joint estate of the partnership shall be applicable in the first instance in payment of the joint expenses and the separate estate of each insolvent member shall be applicable in the first instance in payment of the separate expenses relating to that member.

(3) Where the joint estate is insufficient for the payment in full of the joint expenses, the unpaid balance shall be apportioned equally between the separate estates of the insolvent members against whom insolvency orders have been made and shall form part of the expenses to be paid out of those estates.

(4) Where any separate estate of an insolvent member is insufficient for the payment in full of the separate expenses to be paid out of that estate, the unpaid balance shall form part of the expenses to be paid out of the joint estate.

(5) Where after the transfer of any unpaid balance in accordance with subsection (3) or (if any estate is insufficient for the payment in full of the expenses to be paid out of that estate the balance then remaining unpaid shall be apportioned equally between the other estates.

(6) Where after an apportionment under subsection (5) one or more estates are insufficient for the payment in full of the expenses to be paid out of those estates, the total of the unpaid balances of the expenses to be paid out of those estates shall continue to be apportioned equally between the other estates until provision is made for the payment in full of the expenses, there is no estate available for the payment of the balance finally remaining unpaid, in which case it abates in equal proportions between all the estates.

(7) Without prejudice to subsections (3) to (6) above, the responsible insolvency practitioner may, with the sanction of any creditors' committee established under section 141 with the leave of the court obtained on application—

(a) pay out of the joint estate as part of the expenses to be paid out of that estate as expenses incurred for any separate estate of an insolvent member; or

(b) pay out of any separate estate of an insolvent member any part of the expenses incurred for the joint estate which affects that separate estate.

Priority of debts in joint estate

175A.—(1) The provisions of this section and the next (which are subject to the provisions of section 9 of the Partnership Act 1890 as respects the liability of the estate of a deceased member) shall apply as regards priority of debts in a case where article 8 of the Insolvent Partnerships Order 1994 applies.

(2) After payment of expenses in accordance with section 175 and subject to section 175C(2), the joint debts of the partnership shall be paid out of its joint estate in the following order of priority—

(a) the preferential debts;
(b) the debts which are neither preferential debts nor postponed debts;
(c) interest under section 189 on the joint debts (other than postponed debts);
(d) the postponed debts;
(e) interest under section 189 on the postponed debts.

(3) The responsible insolvency practitioner shall adjust the rights among themselves of the members of the partnership as contributories and shall distribute any surplus to the members or, where applicable, to the separate estates of the members, according to their respective rights and interests in it.

(4) The debts referred to in each of paragraphs (a) and (b) of subsection (2) rank equally between themselves, and in each case if the joint estate is insufficient for meeting them, they abate in equal proportions between themselves.

(5) Where the joint estate is not sufficient for the payment of the joint debts in accordance with paragraphs (a) and (b) of subsection (2), the responsible insolvency practitioner shall aggregate the value of those debts to the extent that they have not been satisfied or are not capable of being satisfied, and that aggregate amount shall be a claim against the separate estate of each member of the partnership against whom an insolvency order has been made which—
(a) shall be a debt provable by the responsible insolvency practitioner in each such estate, and
(b) shall rank equally with the debts of the member referred to in section 175B(1)(b) below.

(6) Where the joint estate is sufficient for the payment of the joint debts in accordance with paragraphs (a) and (b) of subsection (2) but not for the payment of interest under paragraph (c) of that subsection, the responsible insolvency practitioner shall aggregate the value of that interest to the extent that it has not been satisfied or is not capable of being satisfied, and that aggregate amount shall be a claim against the separate estate of each member of the partnership against whom an insolvency order has been made which—
(a) shall be a debt provable by the responsible insolvency practitioner in each such estate, and
(b) shall rank equally with the interest on the separate debts referred to in section 175B(1)(c) below.

(7) Where the joint estate is not sufficient for the payment of the postponed joint debts in accordance with paragraph (d) of subsection (2), the responsible insolvency practitioner shall aggregate the value of those debts to the extent that they have not been satisfied or are not capable of being satisfied, and that aggregate amount shall be a claim against the separate estate of each member of the partnership against whom an insolvency order has been made which—
(a) shall be a debt provable by the responsible insolvency practitioner in each such estate, and
(b) shall rank equally with the postponed debts of the member referred to in section 175B(1)(d) below.

(8) Where the joint estate is sufficient for the payment of the postponed joint debts in accordance with paragraph (d) of subsection (2) but not for the payment of interest under paragraph (e) of that subsection, the responsible insolvency practitioner shall aggregate the value of that interest to the extent that it has not been satisfied or is not capable of being satisfied, and that aggregate amount shall be a claim against the separate estate of each member of the partnership against whom an insolvency order has been made which—
(a) shall be a debt provable by the responsible insolvency practitioner in each such estate, and

(b) shall rank equally with the interest on the postponed debts referred to in section 175B(1)(e) below.

(9) Where the responsible insolvency practitioner receives any distribution from the separate estate of a member in respect of a debt referred to in paragraph (a) of subsection (5), (6), (7) or (8) above, that distribution shall become part of the joint estate and shall be distributed in accordance with the order of priority set out in subsection (2) above.

Priority of debts in separate estate

175B.—(1) The separate estate of each member of the partnership against whom an insolvency order has been made shall be applicable, after payment of expenses in accordance with section 175 and subject to section 175C(2) below, in payment of the separate debts of that member in the following order of priority—

(a) the preferential debts;

(b) the debts which are neither preferential debts nor postponed debts (including any debt referred to in section 175A(5)(a));

(c) interest under section 189 on the separate debts and under section 175A(6);

(d) the postponed debts of the member (including any debt referred to in section 175A(7)(a));

(e) interest under section 189 on the postponed debts of the member and under section 175A(8).

(2) The debts referred to in each of paragraphs (a) and (b) of subsection (1) rank equally between themselves, and in each case if the separate estate is insufficient for meeting them, they abate in equal proportions between themselves.

(3) Where the responsible insolvency practitioner receives any distribution from the joint estate or from the separate estate of another member of the partnership against whom an insolvency order has been made, that distribution shall become part of the separate estate and shall be distributed in accordance with the order of priority set out in subsection (1) of this section.

Provisions generally applicable in distribution of joint and separate estates

175C.—(1) Distinct accounts shall be kept of the joint estate of the partnership and of the separate estate of each member of that partnership against whom an insolvency order is made.

(2) No member of the partnership shall prove for a joint or separate debt in competition with the joint creditors, unless the debt has arisen—

(a) as a result of fraud, or

(b) in the ordinary course of a business carried on separately from the partnership business.

(3) For the purpose of establishing the value of any debt referred to in section 175A(5)(a) or (7)(a), that value may be estimated by the responsible insolvency practitioner in accordance with section 322 or (as the case may be) in accordance with the rules.

(4) Interest under section 189 on preferential debts ranks equally with interest on debts which are neither preferential debts nor postponed debts.

(5) Sections 175A and 175B are without prejudice to any provision of this Act or of any other enactment concerning the ranking between themselves of postponed debts and interest thereon, but in the absence of any such provision postponed debts and interest thereon rank equally between themselves.

(6) If any two or more members of an insolvent partnership constitute a separate partnership, the creditors of such separate partnership shall be deemed to be a separate set of creditors and subject to the same statutory provisions as the separate creditors of any member of the insolvent partnership.

(7) Where any surplus remains after the administration of the estate of a separate partnership, the surplus shall be distributed to the members or, where applicable, to the separate estates of the members of that partnership according to their respective rights and interests in it.

(8) Neither the official receiver, the Secretary of State nor a responsible insolvency practitioner shall be entitled to remuneration or fees under the Insolvency Rules 1986, the Insolvency Regulations 1986 or the Insolvency Fees Order 1986 for his services in connection with—

(a) the transfer of a surplus from the joint estate to a separate estate under section 175A(3),

(b) a distribution from a separate estate to the joint estate in respect of a claim referred to in section 175A(5), (6), (7) or (8), or

(c) a distribution from the estate of a separate partnership to the separate estates of the members of that partnership under subsection (7) above.".

Section 328: Priority of expenses and debts

21. Section 328 is modified so as to read as follows:

"Priority of expenses

328.—(1) The provisions of this section shall apply in a case where article 11 of the Insolvent Partnerships Order 1994 applies, as regards priority of expenses incurred by a person acting as a trustee of the estates of the members of an insolvent partnership and as trustee of that partnership.

(2) The joint estate of the partnership shall be applicable in the first instance in payment of the joint expenses and the separate estate of each insolvent member shall be applicable in the first instance in payment of the separate expenses relating to that member.

(3) Where the joint estate is insufficient for the payment in full of the joint expenses, the unpaid balance shall be apportioned equally between the separate estates of the insolvent members against whom insolvency orders have been made and shall form part of the expenses to be paid out of those estates.

(4) Where any separate estate of an insolvent member is insufficient for the payment in full of the separate expenses to be paid out of that estate, the unpaid balance shall form part of the expenses to be paid out of the joint estate.

(5) Where after the transfer of any unpaid balance in accordance with subsection (3) or (4) any estate is insufficient for the payment in full of the expenses to be paid out of that estate, the balance then remaining unpaid shall be apportioned equally between the other estates.

(6) Where after an apportionment under subsection (5) one or more estates are insufficient for the payment in full of the expenses to be paid out of those estates, the total of the unpaid balances of the expenses to be paid out of those estates shall continue to be apportioned equally between the other estates until provision is made for the payment in full of the expenses or there is no estate available for the payment of the balance finally remaining unpaid, in which case it abates in equal proportions between all the estates.

(7) Without prejudice to subsections (3) to (6) above, the trustee may, with the sanction of any creditors' committee established under section 301 or with the leave of the court obtained on application—

(a) pay out of the joint estate as part of the expenses to be paid out of that estate any expenses incurred for any separate estate of an insolvent member; or

(b) pay out of any separate estate of an insolvent member any part of the expenses incurred for the joint estate which affects that separate estate.

Priority of debts in joint estate

328A.—(1) The provisions of this section and the next (which are subject to the provisions of section 9 of the Partnership Act 1890 as respects the liability of the estate of a deceased member) shall apply as regards priority of debts in a case where article 11 of the Insolvent Partnerships Order 1994 applies.

(2) After payment of expenses in accordance with section 328 and subject to section 328C(2), the joint debts of the partnership shall be paid out of its joint estate in the following order of priority—

(a) the preferential debts;
(b) the debts which are neither preferential debts nor postponed debts;
(c) interest under section 328D on the joint debts (other than postponed debts);
(d) the postponed debts;
(e) interest under section 328D on the postponed debts.

(3) The responsible insolvency practitioner shall adjust the rights among themselves of the members of the partnership as contributories and shall distribute any surplus to the members or, where applicable, to the separate estates of the members, according to their respective rights and interests in it.

(4) The debts referred to in each of paragraphs (a) and (b) of subsection (2) rank equally between themselves, and in each case if the joint estate is insufficient for meeting them, they abate in equal proportions between themselves.

(5) Where the joint estate is not sufficient for the payment of the joint debts in accordance with paragraphs (a) and (b) of subsection (2), the responsible insolvency practitioner shall aggregate the value of those debts to the extent that they have not been satisifed or are not capable of being satisfied, and that aggregate amount shall be a claim against the separate estate of each member of the partnership against whom an insolvency order has been made which—

(a) shall be a debt provable by the responsible insolvency practitioner in each such estate, and
(b) shall rank equally with the debts of the member referred to in section 328B(1)(b) below.

(6) Where the joint estate is sufficient for the payment of the joint debts in accordance with paragraphs (a) and (b) of subsection (2) but not for the payment of interest under paragraph (c) of that subsection, the responsible insolvency practitioner shall aggregate the value of that interest to the extent that it has not been satisfied or is not capable of being satisfied, and that aggregate amount shall be a claim against the separate estate of each member of the partnership against whom an insolvency order has been made which—

(a) shall be a debt provable by the responsible insolvency practitioner in each such estate, and
(b) shall rank equally with the interest on the separate debts referred to in section 328B(1)(c) below.

(7) Where the joint estate is not sufficient for the payment of the postponed joint debts in accordance with paragraph (d) of subsection (2), the responsible insolvency practitioner shall aggregate the value of those debts to the extent that they have not been satisfied or are not capable of being satisfied and that aggregate amount shall be a claim against the separate estate of each member of the partnership against whom an insolvency order has been made which—

(a) shall be a debt provable by the responsible insolvency practitioner in each such estate, and

(b) shall rank equally with the postponed debts of the member referred to in section 328B(1)(d) below.

(8) Where the joint estate is sufficient for the payment of the postponed joint debts in accordance with paragraph (d) of subsection (2) but not for the payment of interest under paragraph (e) of that subsection, the responsible insolvency practitioner shall aggregate the value of that interest to the extent that it has not been satisfied or is not capable of being satisfied, and that aggregate amount shall be a claim against the separate estate of each member of the partnership against whom an insolvency order has been made which—

(a) shall be a debt provable by the responsible insolvency practitioner in each such estate, and

(b) shall rank equally with the interest on the postponed debts referred to in section 328B(1)(e) below.

(9) Where the responsible insolvency practitioner receives any distribution from the separate estate of a member in respect of a debt referred to in paragraph (a) of subsection (5), (6), (7) or (8) above, that distribution shall become part of the joint estate and shall be distributed in accordance with the order of priority set out in subsection (2) above.

Priority of debts in separate estate

328B.—(1) The separate estate of each member of the partnership against whom an insolvency order has been made shall be applicable, after payment of expenses in accordance with section 328 and subject to section 328C(2) below, in payment of the separate debts of that member in the following order of priority—

(a) the preferential debts;

(b) the debts which are neither preferential debts nor postponed debts (including any debt referred to in section 328A(5)(a));

(c) interest under section 328D on the separate debts and under section 328A(6);

(d) the postponed debts of the member (including any debt referred to in section 328A(7)(a));

(e) interest under section 328D on the postponed debts of the member and under section 328A(8).

(2) The debts referred to in each of paragraphs (a) and (b) of subsection (1) rank equally between themselves, and in each case if the separate estate is insufficient for meeting them, they abate in equal proportions between themselves.

(3) Where the responsible insolvency practitioner receives any distribution from the joint estate or from the separate estate of another member of the partnership against whom an insolvency order has been made, that distribution shall become part of the separate estate and shall be distributed in accordance with the order of priority set out in subsection (1) of this section.

Provisions generally applicable in distribution of joint and separate estates

328C.—(1) Distinct accounts shall be kept of the joint estate of the partnership and of the separate estate of each member of that partnership against whom an insolvency order is made.

(2) No member of the partnership shall prove for a joint or separate debt in competition with the joint creditors, unless the debt has arisen—

(a) as a result of fraud, or

(b) in the ordinary course of a business carried on separately from the partnership business.

(3) For the purpose of establishing the value of any debt referred to in section 328A(5)(a) or (7)(a), that value may be estimated by

the responsible insolvency practitioner in accordance with section 322.

(4) Interest under section 328D on preferential debts ranks equally with interest on debts which are neither preferential debts nor postponed debts.

(5) Sections 328A and 328B are without prejudice to any provision of this Act or of any other enactment concerning the ranking between themselves of postponed debts and interest thereon, but in the absence of any such provision postponed debts and interest thereon rank equally between themselves.

(6) If any two or more members of an insolvent partnership constitute a separate partnership, the creditors of such separate partnership shall be deemed to be a separate set of creditors and subject to the same statutory provisions as the separate creditors of any member of the insolvent partnership.

(7) Where any surplus remains after the administration of the estate of a separate partnership, the surplus shall be distributed to the members or, where applicable, to the separate estates of the member of that partnership according to their respective rights and interests in it.

(8) Neither the official receiver, the Secretary of State nor a responsible insolvency practitioner shall be entitled to remuneration or fees under the Insolvency Rules 1986, the Insolvency Regulations 1986 or the Insolvency Fees Order 1986 for his services in connection with—

(a) the transfer of a surplus from the joint estate to a separate estate under section 328A(3),

(b) a distribution from a separate estate to the joint estate in respect of a claim referred to in section 328A(5), (6), (7) or (8), or

(c) a distribution from the estate of a separate partnership to the separate estates of the members of that partnership under subsection (7) above.

Interest on debts

328D.—(1) In the bankruptcy of each of the members of an insolvent partnership and in the winding up of that partnership's business and administration of its property, interest is payable in accordance with this section, in the order of priority laid down by sections 328A and 328B, on any debt proved in the bankruptcy including so much of any such debt as represents interest on the remainder.

(2) Interest under this section is payable on the debts in question in respect of the periods during which they have been outstanding since the relevant order was made by virtue of article 11 of the Insolvent Partnerships Order 1994.

(3) The rate of interest payable under this section in respect of any debt ("the official rate" for the purposes of any provision of this Act in which that expression is used) is whichever is the greater of—

(a) the rate specified in section 17 of the Judgments Act 1838 on the day on which the relevant order was made, and

(b) the rate applicable to that debt apart from the bankruptcy or winding up.".

INDEX